ALL·IN·ONE

LPI® Linux Essentials
Certification

EXAM GUIDE

ALL·IN·ONE

LPI® Linux Essentials Certification

Certification

EXAM GUIDE

Robb H. Tracy

New York • Chicago • San Francisco • Lisbon
London • Madrid • Mexico City • Milan • New Delhi
San Juan • Seoul • Singapore • Sydney • Toronto

Cataloging-in-Publication Data is on file with the Library of Congress

McGraw-Hill books are available at special quantity discounts to use as premiums and sales promotions, or for use in corporate training programs. To contact a representative, please e-mail us at bulksales@mcgraw-hill.com.

LPI® Linux Essentials Certification All-in-One Exam Guide

1 2 3 4 5 6 7 8 9 0   DOC DOC   1 0 9 8 7 6 5 4 3

ISBN: Book p/n 978-0-07-181098-2 and CD p/n 978-0-07-181099-9
of set 978-0-07-181101-9

MHID: Book p/n 0-07-181098-6 and CD p/n 0-07-181099-4
of set 0-07-181101-X

Sponsoring Editor *Tim Green*	**Technical Editor** *Elizabeth Zinkann*	**Production Supervisor** *Jean Bodeaux*
Editorial Supervisor *Patty Mon*	**Copy Editor** *Sally Engelfried*	**Composition** *Cenveo® Publisher Services*
Project Editor *Rachel Gunn*	**Proofreader** *Nancy Bell*	**Cover Designer** *Jeff Weeks*
Acquisitions Coordinator *Stephanie Evans*	**Indexer** *Ted Laux*	

This book is dedicated to all the individuals who have made a difference in my life. To my Dad, for instilling in me a love of teaching and of all things technical. To my Mom, for teaching me the value of hard work and commitment. To my mentor, Dennis Simmons, for teaching me to strive for excellence in all I do. To my wife and best friend, for supporting and loving me through the process of writing this book.

—Robb H. Tracy

ABOUT THE AUTHOR

Robb H. Tracy (CNA, CNE, CNI, A+, Network+, Linux+) has been a professional technology instructor and courseware developer since 1996. He has designed and implemented technical training products and curricula for major hardware and software vendors including Novell, Micron Technology, TestOut, Messaging Architects, Caselle, MoveNetworks, Makau, Cymphonix, Motorola Solutions, and NextPage. Robb previously served on CompTIA's Network+ Advisory Committee where he helped define the objectives that comprise the CompTIA Network+ certification. He is a cofounder of Nebo Technical Institute, Inc., a leading provider of information technology training and consulting. Robb is the author of *Novell Certified Linux Engineer (Novell CLE) Study Guide* (Novell Press, 2005), *Novell Certified Linux Engineer 9 (CLE 9) Study Guide* (Novell Press, 2006), *Linux+ Certification Study Guide* (Certification Press, 2008), *LPIC-1/CompTIA Linux+ Certification All-in-One Exam Guide* (McGraw-Hill Media, 2011), and *CompTIA Network+ Certification Practice Exams* (McGraw-Hill Media, 2012). Robb was also a contributing author to *SUSE Linux 10 Unleashed* (Sams Publishing, 2006).

About the Technical Editor

Elizabeth Zinkann is a logical Linux catalyst, a freelance technical editor, and an independent computer consultant. She was a contributing editor and review columnist for *Sys Admin* magazine for ten years. As an editor, some of her projects have included *RHCSA™/RHCE® Red Hat® Linux Certification Study Guide, Sixth Edition*; *Mastering Fedora Core Linux 5*; *LPIC-1 in Depth*; *Linux Patch Management*; and *Linux All-in-One Desk Reference for Dummies, Fourth Edition*. In a former life, she also programmed communications features, including ISDN at AT&T Network Systems.

About LearnKey

LearnKey provides self-paced learning content and multimedia delivery solutions to enhance personal skills and business productivity. LearnKey claims the largest library of rich streaming-media training content that engages learners in dynamic media-rich instruction complete with video clips, audio, full motion graphics, and animated illustrations. LearnKey can be found on the Web at www.LearnKey.com.

CONTENTS AT A GLANCE

CONTENTS

ACKNOWLEDGMENTS

The title page of this book lists Robb H. Tracy as its author. However, this attribution is deceiving. By no means was this a one-person job. Behind every book is a team of individuals who rarely get the credit they deserve. They are the unsung heroes who make sure the job gets done.

First, I would also like to acknowledge the efforts of the production team behind this book. These folks were the glue that kept everything together. Thanks to Timothy Green for giving me the opportunity to write this book. I appreciate your confidence in me! Thanks to Stephanie Evans for managing the development process. No matter what the time of day, Steph was always there with the information I needed. Thanks, Steph! Thanks also to Rachel Gunn for helping me through the final review process. Her experienced eyes are the reason this title looks good.

Finally, a huge thank you to Elizabeth Zinkann. Elizabeth reviewed each and every word and exercise step in this book for technical accuracy. Her efforts kept me honest and were absolutely invaluable, dramatically increasing the overall quality of this title. Elizabeth spent many late nights testing the lab exercises in this book, ensuring that you have a successful experience. Thanks, Elizabeth!

INTRODUCTION

We first need to introduce you to the nuts and bolts of this book and the Linux Essentials program. Let's take a look at the following:

- Who this book is for
- How this book is organized
- Special features of the All-in-One Certification series
- The Linux Essentials exam
- Tips for succeeding on the Linux Essentials exam

Who This Book Is For

Before you start this book, you need to be aware that I have two primary goals in mind as I write:

- To help you prepare for and pass the Linux Essentials exam offered by the Linux Professional Institute (LPI).
- To provide you with the extra skills and knowledge you need to be successful on the job.

Essentially, when we're done here I want you to be able to do more than just recite facts. I want you to be able to walk the walk and talk the talk. I want you to be able to actually do the job once hired.

To accomplish this, we're going to focus heavily on the core Linux knowledge and skills in this book required by the Linux Essentials exam. You should already have a basic level of familiarity with computers and how they work, including:

- Powering a computer system on and logging in
- Using a mouse and keyboard
- Running applications
- Completing basic management tasks such as sending print jobs to printers, saving files, copying and pasting files, and so on
- Accessing network resources such as shared directories, network printers, and web sites
- Configuring basic network settings such as IP address, subnet mask, default router address, and DNS server address
- Logging out and powering the system down

If you have this background, you're ready to roll!

How This Book Is Organized

I love LPI certification programs. They go the extra mile to make sure their programs truly reflect current trends in the information technology industry, and Linux Essentials is no exception. LPI has published objectives that list the skills and knowledge that a person with a Linux Essentials certificate should have.

These objectives, as currently published, are organized by topic. They aren't organized into a logical instructional flow. As you read through this book, you'll quickly notice that I don't address the Linux Essentials objectives in the same order as they are published by LPI. All of the objectives are covered; however, I've reorganized them such that we start with the most basic Linux concepts first. Then, as we progress through the course, we'll address increasingly more advanced objectives, building upon the skills and knowledge covered in preceding chapters.

Special Features of the All-in-One Certification Series

To make our exam guides more useful and a pleasure to read, we have designed the All-in-One Certification series to include several conventions.

Icons

To alert you to an important bit of advice, a shortcut, or a pitfall, you'll occasionally see Notes, Tips, Cautions, and Exam Tips peppered throughout the text.

NOTE Notes offer nuggets of especially helpful stuff, background explanations, and information, and define terms occasionally.

TIP Tips provide suggestions and nuances to help you learn to finesse your job. Take a tip from us and read the Tips carefully.

CAUTION When you see a Caution, pay special attention. Cautions appear when you have to make a crucial choice or when you are about to undertake something that may have ramifications you might not immediately anticipate. Read them now so you don't have regrets later.

EXAM TIP Exam Tips give you special advice or provide information specifically related to preparing for the exam itself.

End-of-Chapter Reviews and Chapter Tests

An important part of this book comes at the end of each chapter where you will find a brief review of the high points, along with a series of questions followed by the answers to those questions. Each question is in multiple-choice format. The answers provided also include a small discussion explaining why the correct answer is the correct answer.

The questions are provided as a study aid to you, the reader and prospective Linux Essentials exam taker. We obviously can't guarantee that if you answer all of the questions correctly you will absolutely pass the exam. Instead, what we can guarantee is that the questions will provide you with an idea about how ready you are for the exam.

The CD-ROM

LPI® Linux Essentials Certification All-in-One Exam Guide provides you with a CD-ROM containing even more test questions and their answers to help you prepare for the certification exam. Read more about the companion CD-ROM in the About the CD appendix.

The Linux Essentials Exam

Now that you understand how this book is organized, it's time for you to become familiar with the Linux Essentials program and its associated exam. Let's review the following:

- About the Linux Essentials program
- Taking the Linux Essentials exam
- Exam makeup

About the Linux Essentials Program

Linux Essentials is an excellent program! It is a vendor-neutral program designed and administered by the Linux Professional Institute. It's the first Linux certificate program designed especially for the academic sector, specifically for students and other new Linux users.

To create the Linux Essentials program, LPI partnered with instructors and Linux experts from around the world. The goal of the program is to introduce younger people to the Linux operating system and provide them with the skills they need to fill responsible roles in modern IT environments.

Linux Essentials is considered to be *vendor-neutral* because the program isn't based on one particular vendor's hardware or software. This is somewhat unique in the information technology industry. Many IT certification programs are centered on one particular vendor's hardware or software, such as Microsoft's Certified System Engineer (MCSE) certification, Novell's Certified Linux Engineer (CLE) certification, or Red Hat's Certified Engineer (RHCE) certification. The Linux Essentials program, on the other hand, is designed to verify your knowledge and skills with the Linux operating system in general, not on any one particular distribution.

To verify your Linux knowledge, LPI requires you to take the Linux Essentials exam to earn your Certificate of Achievement. According to the LPI web site (https://www .lpi.org/linux-certifications/introductory-programs/linux-essentials), to pass your Linux Essentials exam, you must be able to demonstrate that you:

- Understand the basic concepts of processes, programs, and the components of an operating system
- Have a working knowledge of computer hardware
- Understand open source applications in the workplace as they relate to closed source equivalents
- Understand how to navigate the Linux desktop and know where to go for help
- Can work from the command line and can manage files
- Can use a basic command line editor

LPI has published a set of more detailed objectives for the Linux Essentials exam, which we will explore in more detail later in this introduction. You can also view the objectives on the LPI web site using the URL listed previously. The key thing to remember is that all of the items on the exam are based on these objectives. If you're going get your Linux Essentials Certificate of Achievement, then you have to be able to do the tasks specified in these objectives. As you go through this book, you'll see that the complete list of Linux Essentials objectives is quite extensive.

Taking the Linux Essentials Exam

The Linux Essentials exam is a timed exam delivered electronically on a computer at testing centers around the world. Check the LPI web site for the most up to date list of participating testing centers as well as information about how to register for and take the exam.

The exam is composed of 40 questions, and you will have 60 minutes to answer them. The exam interface is fairly straightforward. Each item is displayed one at a time on the screen. You are presented with a question along with a series of responses. You mark the appropriate response and then go to the next question.

The exam is composed primarily of multiple-choice items. This testing format presents you with a question and asks you to mark the correct answer from a list of choices. Most of the multiple-choice questions require only one answer; however, some will require you to select multiple correct responses from the list displayed. If this is the case, the test question will end with the text "(Choose *x*.)," where *x* is the number of responses you should mark.

After you complete your exam, the computer will immediately evaluate it and your score will be printed out. Hopefully, you will pass your exam on the first try. However, if you don't, your score printout will list the objectives where you missed questions. You can use this information to review and prepare yourself to retake the exam.

Be aware that the testing center where you take your exam will need to verify your identity before they can sign you up, so be prepared to provide proof of who you are.

The test provider should send you a confirmation e-mail listing the date, time, and location of your exam.

On the day of the test, be sure you allow adequate travel time. You never know when you will run into a traffic jam or experience other difficulties. I had this happen to me recently, in fact. I was scheduled to take an IT certification exam early in the morning at a testing center 40 miles away. It was a very cold January morning with the temperature well below zero. As I began to drive, I found that my car was nearly out of gas (likely the fault of my teenage children), so I pulled into a gas station to fill up. Unfortunately, due to the extremely cold temperatures, the gas filler door on my car was frozen shut! Needless to say, I was quite late for my exam. Fortunately, the testing center wasn't busy that day and they were able to accommodate me.

In addition, you should try to show up early enough to find a parking spot and walk to the testing center. If you're taking your exam at a community college, for example, you may find that you have to walk a very long distance to get from the parking lot to the building where the exam is delivered. The last thing you need right before your exam is to feel rushed and stressed!

When you check in at the testing center, you will probably be required to show two forms of identification, one of which must have your photo on it. Consider taking two of the following with you:

- Driver's license
- Social Security card
- Credit card
- Student ID card
- Military ID card
- State-issued ID card

Be warned that, when you check in, you must surrender your phone, iPod, tablet, laptop, or any other electronic devices to the test proctor. Some testing centers may provide you with a locker to store your personal items, but others won't. You're not allowed to take any reference materials into the exam room, including blank paper. Most testing centers will provide you with note-taking materials that must remain in the room where the test is being administered. Some testing centers will provide you with paper and a pencil; others may provide a small whiteboard slate with an erasable pen.

Exam Makeup

The Linux Essentials exam is divided up into several topic areas, which are shown in Table 1. Each topic is assigned a weight value between 1 and 10, which is used to help you gauge the relative importance of the topic and how heavily tested it will be on the exam. Essentially, the higher the weight, the more items related to that topic you will probably see on the exam.

As you can see in the table, some topics are tested more heavily than others. When studying, be sure to pay special attention to those topics with the highest percentage of

Topic	Weight
Topic 1: The Linux community and a career in open source	7
Topic 2: Finding your way on a Linux system	8
Topic 3: The power of the command line	10
Topic 4: The Linux operating system	8
Topic 5: Security and file permissions	7

Table 1   Linux Essentials Exam Topics

exam questions. In particular, I strongly recommend that you be very familiar with how to use command-line tools to manage a Linux system.

It's important to note here that the Linux Essentials exam is a great stepping stone to more advanced Linux certifications, such as the LPIC-1/CompTIA Linux+ certification, which is jointly administered by LPI and the Computing Technology Industry Association, affectionately known as CompTIA. In fact, LPI recommends that you complete Linux Essentials as a prerequisite before attempting the LPIC-1/CompTIA Linux+ certification.

Tips for Succeeding on the Linux Essentials Exam

I'll never forget the first time I took an IT certification exam back in the early 1990s. I was so nervous that I almost couldn't function. Fortunately, the exam went very well and I passed it. Over the last decade, I've helped a lot of folks prepare themselves for a number of certification exams. I've even written industry certification exams myself for companies such as Novell. As a result, I've learned a number of things that you can do to increase the likelihood that you will pass your exam. We'll discuss the following here:

- Preparing for the exam
- Taking the exam

Preparing for the Exam

The most important thing you can do to prepare for your Linux Essentials exam is to study thoroughly. No tip, trick, or strategy can compensate for a lack of study. The goal is to move the information you need to pass the exam into your long-term memory. Following are some study tips that can help you prepare for your exam.

One to Two Months Before Your Exam

- **Schedule your Linux Essentials exam**   Ideally, you should schedule it to take place about 30–60 days after you begin this book. If you don't give yourself a deadline, you probably will never "get around" to studying for and taking the exam.

- **Pace yourself**   Don't try to cram for the exam the night before. This is a very common mistake made by many students (I did it myself in college). Cramming rarely works because your short-term memory can only hold a limited amount of information. All that stuff you're trying to cram into your short-term memory gets lost. Instead, successful test-takers spend a good deal of time loading information into their long-term memory. You can do this by setting a goal to read a certain number of pages or chapters each day and sticking to it.

- **Take notes**   As you read each chapter, write down important information that stands out to you. Writing it down helps reinforce the information, moving it from short-term memory into long-term memory in your brain. It also provides you with a valuable review resource.

- **Do the lab exercises, even the simple ones**   Doing the lab exercises helps you learn the practical implementation of the conceptual skills and knowledge presented in each chapter.

- **Tackle the practice questions for each chapter**   After you read a chapter, get a blank piece of paper and run through the questions, recording your responses on the paper. (Don't write in the book! You'll want it to be pristine for later study sessions.) Check your answers and review the topics you missed.

- **Review the Chapter Review and Accelerated Review at the end of each chapter**.

Two to Three Days Before Your Exam

- Review your notes.

- Review the practice questions at the end of each chapter. Review any topics that you are still struggling with.

- Repeat the lab exercises for each chapter. This time, however, try to complete the exercises without looking at the steps in the book.

The Night Before Your Exam

- Relax! Being well rested is a key to performing well on your exam. Don't get so worked up and nervous that you can't sleep the night before your exam. Get to bed at a reasonable hour.

- Review your notes.

- Review the Chapter Review and Accelerated Review again for each chapter. Repetition is the key to retention!

The Morning of Your Exam

- Eat a good breakfast. Your brain requires a tremendous amount of calories to operate. Give it what it needs!

- Review your notes.

- Review the Chapter Review and Accelerated Review once again for each chapter. Did I mention that repetition is the key to retention?

- Run through your practice questions one more time for each chapter.

- Allow yourself plenty of time to get to the testing center. Don't get stressed out by being late.

What you're trying to do is upload the information you need to pass your tests into your long-term memory through repetition and practice. Then, shortly before the exam, you're exercising the brain by retrieving that stored information and bringing it to the forefront of your thoughts (kind of like loading data from a hard drive into system RAM) so that it is ready and available when you take the test.

 EXAM TIP From my observations, LPI certification candidates who study their shell commands and associated options (especially some of the more obscure ones) are the candidates who pass. LPI exams have a reputation for being nitpicky on command line utility options. In fact, some candidates have criticized these exams for focusing too much on vague or obscure command options that aren't used very often. I've tried to cover the command options that I think you'll be tested on in this book. However, I obviously don't have access to the exam banks, so I can't guarantee that all of the command options that you'll see on the exam will covered in this book. Addressing all of the options for all of the commands isn't realistic, as it would easily double the page count of this book (and put you to sleep). I strongly recommend that you review the man pages for all of the commands I've covered in this book and review their various options.

Taking the Exam

As I mentioned earlier, I've written a number of industry certification exams in addition to developing training materials for them. Because I've done this, I have some insights as to what goes on inside the devious minds of exam developers. I'm going to share some tips and tricks that you should be aware of when you take your exam:

- *Carefully read the text of each question (called the stem)*   Some of the information in the stem is superfluous and intended to distract you. However, the question stem usually contains one or two critical pieces of information that influence the correct answer. If your testing center provides you with writing materials (and they should), I suggest you quickly jot down the key points from the stem.

- *Carefully read each response*   Don't just skim them. Exam authors deliberately include responses that are *almost* correct, but not quite (we call them *red herrings*). The intent is to distract you from the real answer. I know it sounds sneaky, but the intent is to make the exam such that you can't divine the correct answer without really knowing your stuff.

- *Eliminate responses that are obviously wrong*   Each item will have one or more responses that are blatantly wrong. (Usually, it's because the exam author couldn't think of anything better to include as a response.) Eliminate these answers and focus only on the responses that could be correct.

- *Make your best choice and move on*   My experience has been that your first impression is usually the correct one. If you agonize over the answers, you can overthink the question and end up picking the wrong response. You also waste valuable time. After carefully reading the question and each response, go with your intuition and then go on to the next item.

- *If you get stuck on a particularly difficult item, don't waste a lot of time trying to figure out the right answer*   You can skip the item and come back to it later. Many students get obsessed with finding the right answer to a particularly difficult question and end up with insufficient time to answer the rest of the items on the exam. Remember, you only have about a minute and a half to complete each question. Answer the questions that you can and then come back to the difficult questions that will require more time.

After you finish your exam, your results will be automatically printed out for you. The report will be embossed by your test proctor to certify the results. Don't lose this report; it's the only hard copy you will receive!

The report will display your performance on each section of the exam. The Linux Essentials exam is pass/fail. If your score exceeds the cut score LPI has set for the exam, you pass!

If you didn't pass, you can use the information on your report to identify the areas where you need to study. You can retake the exam immediately, if you wish. However, there are two things you need to keep in mind before you do this:

- You have to pay full price for the retake.

- The retake exam probably won't be the same as the first. LPI publishes multiple forms of their exams.

If you fail, I suggest that you step back, take a deep breath, go home, and study up on the items you missed. Then schedule your retake within a day or two. If you wait any longer than that, your mind will probably go "cold" and you may need to go through the entire preparation process again from scratch.

Topic	Subtopic	Chapter
Topic 1: The Linux community and a career in open source	1.1 Linux evolution and popular operating systems	
	Key knowledge areas: • Open source philosophy • Distributions • Embedded systems	Chapter 4: Open Source Software Chapter 1: An Introduction to Linux

Topic	Subtopic	Chapter
	The following is a partial list of the used files, terms, and utilities: • Android • Debian • CentOS	Chapter 1: An Introduction to Linux
	1.2 Major open source applications	Chapter 4: Open Source Software
	Key knowledge areas: • Desktop applications • Server applications • Mobile applications • Development languages • Package management tools and repositories	Chapter 4: Open Source Software
	The following is a partial list of the used files, terms, and utilities: • OpenOffice.org, LibreOffice, Thunderbird, Firefox • Blender, Gimp, Audacity, ImageMagick • Apache, MySQL, PostgreSQL • NFS, Samba, OpenLDAP, Postfix, DNS, DHCP • C, Perl, shell, Python, PHP	Chapter 4: Open Source Software
	1.3 Understanding open source software and licensing	Chapter 4: Open Source Software
	Key knowledge areas: • Licensing • Free Software Foundation (FSF), Open Source Initiative (OSI)	Chapter 4: Open Source Software
	The following is a partial list of the used files, terms, and utilities: • GPL, BSD, Creative Commons • Free software, open source software, FOSS, FLOSS • Open Source business models	Chapter 1: An Introduction to Linux Chapter 4: Open Source Software
	1.4 ICT skills and working in Linux	
	Key knowledge areas: • Desktop skills • Getting to the command line • Industry uses of Linux, cloud computing, and virtualization	Chapter 4: Open Source Software Chapter 5: Command Line Basics Chapter 1: An Introduction to Linux
	The following is a partial list of the used files, terms, and utilities: • Using a browser, privacy concerns, configuration options, searching the Web and saving content • Terminal and console • Password issues • Privacy issues and tools • Use of common open source applications in presentations and projects	Chapter 4: Open Source Software Chapter 5: Command Line Basics

Topic	Subtopic	Chapter
Topic 2: Finding your way on a Linux system	**2.1 Command line basics**	
	Key knowledge areas: • Basic shell • Formatting commands • Working with options • Variables • Globbing • Quoting	Chapter 5: Command Line Basics
	The following is a partial list of the used files, terms, and utilities: • echo • history • PATH env variable • which	Chapter 5: Command Line Basics
	Nice to know: • Substitutions • ||, && and ; control operators	Chapter 5: Command Line Basics Chapter 12: Creating Scripts
	2.2 Using the command line to get help	
	Key knowledge areas: • Man • Info	Chapter 5: Command Line Basics
	The following is a partial list of the used files, terms, and utilities: • man • info • Man pages • /usr/share/doc • locate	Chapter 5: Command Line Basics
	Nice to know: • apropos, whatis, whereis	Chapter 5: Command Line Basics Chapter 6: Working with Files and Directories
	2.3 Using directories and listing files	
	Key knowledge areas: • Files, directories • Hidden files and directories • Home • Absolute and relative paths	Chapter 6: Working with Files and Directories
	The following is a partial list of the used files, terms, and utilities: • Common options for ls • Recursive listings • cd • . and .. • home and ~	Chapter 6: Working with Files and Directories

Topic	Subtopic	Chapter
	2.4 Creating, moving, and deleting files	
	Key knowledge areas • Files and directories • Case sensitivity • Simple globbing and quoting	Chapter 6: Working with Files and Directories
	The following is a partial list of the used files, terms, and utilities: • mv, cp, rm, touch • mkdir, rmdir	Chapter 6: Working with Files and Directories
Topic 3: The power of the command line	**3.1 Archiving files on the command line**	
	Key knowledge areas: • Files, directories • Archives, compression	Chapter 6: Working with Files and Directories Chapter 10: Archiving Files
	The following is a partial list of the used files, terms, and utilities: • tar • Common tar options • gzip, bzip2 • zip, unzip	Chapter 10: Archiving Files
	Nice to know: • Extracting individual files from archives	Chapter 10: Archiving Files
	3.2 Searching and extracting data from files	
	Key knowledge areas: • Command line pipes • I/O redirection • Partial POSIX Regular Expressions (., [ ], *, ?)	Chapter 7: Extracting Data from Files
	The following is a partial list of the used files, terms, and utilities: • find • grep • less • head, tail • sort • cut • wc	Chapter 6: Working with Files and Directories Chapter 7: Extracting Data from Files Chapter 12: Creating Scripts
	Nice to know: • Partial POSIX Basic Regular Expressions ([^], ^, $) • Partial POSIX Extended Regular Expressions (+, ( ), |) • xargs	Chapter 7: Extracting Data from Files

Topic	Subtopic	Chapter
	3.3 Turning commands into a script	
	Key knowledge areas: • Basic text editing • Basic shell scripting	Chapter 5: Command Line Basics Chapter 12: Creating Scripts
	The following is a partial list of the used files, terms, and utilities: • /bin/sh • Variables • Arguments • for loops • echo • Exit status	Chapter 12: Creating Scripts
	Nice to know: • pico, nano, vi (only basics for creating scripts) • Bash • if, while, case statements • read and test, and [commands	Chapter 5: Command Line Basics Chapter 12: Creating Scripts
Topic 4: The Linux operating system	**4.1 Choosing an operating system**	
	Key knowledge areas • Windows, Mac, Linux differences • Distribution life cycle management	Chapter 1: An Introduction to Linux Chapter 4: Open Source Software
	The following is a partial list of the used files, terms, and utilities: • GUI versus command line, desktop configuration • Maintenance cycles, beta and stable	Chapter 4: Open Source Software
	4.2 Understanding computer hardware	
	Key knowledge areas: • Hardware	Chapter 3: PC Hardware
	The following is a partial list of the used files, terms, and utilities: • Hard drives and partitions, motherboards, processors, power supplies, optical drives, peripherals • Display types • Drivers	Chapter 3: PC Hardware
	4.3 Where data is stored	
	Key knowledge areas: • Kernel • Processes • syslog, klog, dmesg • /lib, /usr/lib, /etc, /var/log	Chapter 11: Managing Linux Processes and Log Files

Topic	Subtopic	Chapter
	The following is a partial list of the used files, terms, and utilities: • Programs, libraries, packages and package databases, system configuration • Processes and process tables, memory addresses, system messaging and logging • ps, top, free	Chapter 4: Open Source Software Chapter 11: Managing Linux Processes and Log Files
	4.4 Your computer on the network	
	Key knowledge areas • Internet, network, routers • Domain Name Service • Network configuration	Chapter 13: Connecting Linux to a Network
	The following is a partial list of the used files, terms, and utilities: • route • resolv.conf • IPv4, IPv6 • ifconfig • netstat • ping	Chapter 13: Connecting Linux to a Network
	Nice to know: • ssh • dig	Chapter 13: Connecting Linux to a Network
Topic 5: Security and file permissions	**5.1 Basic security and identifying user types**	
	Key knowledge areas • Root and standard users • System users	Chapter 8: Managing Users and Groups
	The following is a partial list of the used files, terms, and utilities: • /etc/passwd, /etc/group • id, who, w • sudo	Chapter 8: Managing Users and Groups
	Nice to know: • su	Chapter 8: Managing Users and Groups
	5.2 Creating users and groups	
	Key knowledge areas • User and group commands • User IDs	Chapter 8: Managing Users and Groups
	The following is a partial list of the used files, terms, and utilities: • /etc/passwd, /etc/shadow, /etc/group • id, last • useradd, groupadd • passwd	Chapter 8: Managing Users and Groups
	Nice to know: • usermod, userdel • groupmod, groupdel	Chapter 8: Managing Users and Groups

Topic	Subtopic	Chapter
	5.3 Managing file permissions and ownership	
	Key knowledge areas • File/directory permissions and owners	Chapter 9: Managing File Ownership and Permissions
	The following is a partial list of the used files, terms, and utilities: • ls –l • chmod, chown	Chapter 9: Managing File Ownership and Permissions
	Nice to know: • chgrp	Chapter 9: Managing File Ownership and Permissions
	5.4 Special directories and files	
	Key knowledge areas • System files, libraries • Symbolic links	Chapter 1: An Introduction to Linux Chapter 6: Working with Files and Directories
	The following is a partial list of the used files, terms, and utilities: • /etc, /var • /tmp, /var/tmp and Sticky Bit • ls –d • ln –s	Chapter 6: Working with Files and Directories Chapter 9: Managing File Ownership and Permissions
	Nice to know: • Hard links • Setuid/Setgid	Chapter 6: Working with Files and Directories Chapter 9: Managing File Ownership and Permissions

An Introduction to Linux

In this chapter, you will learn about

- The role of an operating system
- How Linux came to be
- The open source software philosophy
- Linux distributions
- Choosing an operating system
- Common Linux implementations

The introduction and adoption of Linux has been an interesting drama to observe. When Linux was first introduced back in the early 1990s, it largely went unnoticed. Professionals in the information technology industry were focused on the big operating systems of the day, including Microsoft Windows, Novell NetWare, Mac OS, and UNIX. At the time, Linux was considered experimental; something you would play with in the lab but never actually implement in production.

Since that time, however, things have changed dramatically. Linux has become a mainstay in the server room for many major organizations around the world. Using the wide variety of network services available for Linux, it can be configured to perform just about any networking role that competing server operating systems can perform.

In addition to the server room, Linux has started making inroads into the desktop market, in many cases replacing Microsoft Windows. Many Linux desktop applications are available (most of them free of charge) that allow end users to perform their day to day work, including word processing, database, spreadsheet, and presentation applications. In other words, Linux has evolved from an after-hours hobby for computer geeks to a major force for change in the information technology industry.

As such, there is a growing demand for network administrators who can implement, maintain, and support the Linux operating system. If you've had any experience with Linux, you know that it is very different than the operating systems most users are familiar with, such as Microsoft Windows. Migrating to Linux requires a degree of expertise. By the time you're done with this book, you will have the knowledge and skills required to make this happen.

The Role of an Operating System

First, you must understand the role Linux plays in a computer system. Linux is an *operating system*, not an application. All operating systems, including Linux, provide five key functions in a computer system:

- **Application platform**   An operating system provides a platform where applications can run, managing their access to the CPU and system memory.

- **Hardware moderator**   The operating system also serves as a mediator between running applications and the system hardware. Most applications are not written to directly address a computer's hardware. Instead, they include prewritten code that can be called from an application to access system hardware, such as memory, hard drives, and communication ports. This feature makes life much easier for programmers. Instead of having to write code for completing these tasks in each and every program, they can simply reuse this existing code provided by the operating system. The operating system also manages access to the system hardware. For example, two of its key jobs are to ensure that one application running on the system doesn't try to use memory already in use by another application and to ensure that applications don't use an inordinate amount of CPU time.

- **Data storage**   The operating system is also responsible for providing an efficient and reliable means for storing information. Usually this is done using some type of storage device, such as a hard disk drive, that has been formatted with a particular type of file system that organizes the information in an easily retrievable format.

- **Security**   The operating system is responsible for providing a degree of security for the data stored on it. The system administrator can create rules and grant rights that determine who can access what information. Some operating systems, such as Linux and later versions of Windows, do this job very well. Older operating systems, such as DOS or Windows 95/98/ME, provided little or no security.

- **Connectivity**   The operating system manages connectivity between computer systems using a variety of network media and interfaces, including Bluetooth, Ethernet, RS-232, 802.11*x* (WiFi) wireless, and even mobile broadband wireless.

Believe it or not, I occasionally encounter people who don't understand the role Linux plays in a computer system. They are under the mistaken impression that Linux is some kind of killer application they can run under Windows on their workstation.

This is usually because most users have grown up using Microsoft Windows on their computers. Their home computer came with Windows bundled on it; their computer at work probably runs Windows as well. Because of this, they perceive the operating system and the hardware of their computer as being married together in an inseparable union. You may have heard someone refer to his or her computer as a "Windows computer."

Actually, the computer hardware and the operating system are independent of each other. That's because the modern PC is modular in nature. The Windows operating system can be easily removed, and any compatible operating system can be installed in its place, including Linux.

 TIP You can resize the existing partitions on the hard disk and install Linux in the resulting free space, creating a dual-boot Windows/Linux system.

The Linux operating system is composed of the following components:

- **The Linux kernel** This is the heart of Linux (hence its name). The kernel is the actual operating system itself. It's the component that fulfills the key operating system duties just listed.

- **Libraries** Prewritten code elements that application programmers can use in their programs. As discussed earlier, this can be a huge time saver. Imagine if you were a programmer and had to include code in your applications that would allow it to work with every type of hard disk drive interface currently on the market. What a task! With libraries, it doesn't matter to the programmer whether a SCSI, IDE, or SATA hard drive is installed in the system. The programmer simply calls the appropriate library and tells the operating system that data is to be written or read from the drive. The operating system takes care of the rest.

- **Utilities** Linux includes a wide variety of utilities that you can use to complete operating system management tasks, such as maintaining the file system, editing text files, managing running processes, and installing new software packages.

- **User Interface** Of course, the end user needs some means of interacting with the operating system. Linux includes both a command-line interface (CLI) and an optional graphical user interface (GUI). We'll explore both of these interfaces later in this book.

How Linux Came to Be

Linux is somewhat of an anomaly in the software development industry. Most software products, whether they are applications or operating systems, are developed as a part of a well-organized design and development effort. I've worked for many years in the software development industry, and I've seen how it works first hand. Here's what happens in most companies:

1. The organization identifies a customer need.
2. A design team is put together, usually composed of programmers, project managers, and marketers.
3. The design team hashes out a product requirements document (PRD) that specifies exactly what the product will do.
4. The tasks identified in the PRD are assigned to teams of programmers who write their assigned code elements.

5. When complete, the code is checked in and the product is run through a series of testing cycles.

6. When the product has its bugs worked out (or at least most of them), the finished product is shipped to the customer.

7. The customer uses the product for a period of time and usually identifies bugs that were missed during the initial testing. In addition, they usually identify new features and functionality that they would like to see added.

8. The software company receives feedback from the customers and the cycle begins all over again.

This is how most commercial software products are developed. Interestingly, Linux didn't conform to this cycle when it was originally developed. Instead, a graduate student at the University of Helsinki in Finland named Linus Torvalds developed the Linux kernel. In the early 1990s, Torvalds became interested in a minimal freeware operating system called *Minix*. Dr. Andrew S. Tanenbaum, a university professor who taught computer programming in the Netherlands, developed Minux as a clone of the commercial UNIX operating system. At the time, there were three main operating systems that were generally available:

- DOS
- Mac OS
- UNIX

Windows was also on the horizon at the time. However, back then it was simply a graphical shell that ran on top of DOS and wasn't a true operating system yet. Each of these operating systems was commercially developed. As such, the source code for each product was carefully protected by patents and copyrights. Most operating systems have a section in their end-user license agreement (EULA) that prevents users from reverse-compiling the operating system to access the source code.

 NOTE There are applications available that can reverse-compile a binary program file. This process re-creates the program's source as a text file. The source code generated isn't an exact duplicate of the original source code but an approximation that can be very close to the original source code.

At one point in time, the source code to the UNIX operating system had been made available to universities for educational purposes. However, in the late 1980s, this practice had been stopped, leaving Tanenbaum without an effective tool to teach his students about the inner workings of an operating system.

Undaunted, Tanenbaum decided to make his own operating system to use in class and developed a small clone of the UNIX kernel called Minix. His goal was to provide students with a real operating system and its accompanying source code. Tanenbaum even included the source code to Minix in his textbook, *Operating Systems: Design and Implementation* (Prentice Hall, 1987).

Inspired by Tanenbaum and Minix, Torvalds developed his own UNIX clone in 1991, which he dubbed *Linux*. This first version of Linux was very minimal in nature; it wasn't a full-blown operating system complete with applications and utilities. Instead, Linux version 0.02, released on October 5, 1991, consisted of only the Linux kernel and three basic utilities:

- **bash**   A command-line interface
- **update**   A utility for flushing file system buffers
- **gcc**   A C++ compiler

In an unprecedented move, Torvalds posted the source code for his Linux operating system on the Internet and made it freely available to anyone who wanted to download it. With that, the corporate software development model had been completely broken. Torvalds even took things one step further. He invited other programmers to modify his Linux source code and enhance it. Linux took on a life of its own and became a world-wide collaborative development project. No secrecy, no tightly guarded copyrights. Access to the Linux source code was open to anyone who wanted it.

This collaborative development project on Linux continued for several years. In 1994, Linux version 1.0 was ready for release. The results since have been nothing short of amazing.

GNU and Linux

So why did Torvalds "give away" Linux to anyone who wanted it? Why didn't he follow the standard corporate development model and try to make a mountain of money? To understand this, you need to be familiar with the *GNU's Not UNIX (GNU)* movement. In the early 1980s a programmer named Richard Stallman at the Massachusetts Institute of Technology proposed an alternative to the standard corporate software development model. He objected to the proprietary nature of the process and the product.

In 1983, Stallman launched the *GNU Project* centered on the idea that the source code for applications and operating systems should be freely distributable to anyone who wants it. He felt that the source code for programs should be free from all restrictions that prevent copying, modification, and redistribution. Stallman hoped that allowing programmers around the world to modify an application's source code would result in higher-quality software. Software developed under GNU is frequently referred to as *Free Software*. A variation on the free software concept is called open source software. Both free software and open source software will be discussed in more detail in Chapter 4.

The GNU Project slowly took hold. Many useful utilities, such as the GNU C Compiler (gcc) were developed under GNU. Torvalds was heavily influenced by the GNU Project and released the source code for his Linux operating system kernel to the world as a result.

Linux itself is licensed under the *GNU General Public License (GPL)*. The key point to remember about the GPL is that it requires that the source code remain freely available to anyone who wants it. As a result, you can download the Linux kernel's source code, modify it, recompile it, and run it. You can even create your own custom version, or distribution, of Linux.

Linux Distributions

The philosophy of GNU software leads us directly to a discussion of Linux distributions. The concept of a *distribution* can be confusing to many new to Linux. To help you navigate the myriad of Linux distributions currently available, we will discuss the following topics in this part of the chapter:

- What is a distribution?
- Commonly used distributions
- The life cycle of a Linux distribution

What Is a Distribution?

Perhaps the best way to think of a distribution is to compare Linux to ice cream. Ice cream comes in a variety of flavors; however, the basic formula for the ice cream itself is the same. Most ice cream is made from:

- Cream
- Milk
- Sugar
- Eggs

Companies that sell ice cream take this basic ice cream recipe and customize it by adding additional ingredients, such as chocolate, vanilla, fruit, cookies, nuts, and candy. By doing this, they create their own flavors of ice cream.

Linux distributions work in much the same way: the kernel source code is comparable to the basic recipe for ice cream. Because the Linux kernel source code, the core of the operating system around which everything else runs, is freely distributable, software vendors are free to download it.

Just as ice cream companies add additional ingredients to the basic ice cream recipe, software vendors can then modify and enhance the Linux source code and create a customized kernel. They can also add specialized tools, utilities, and applications to the operating system to enhance its usefulness. The result is a Linux distribution.

You may already be aware that there are many different Linux distributions available. This is yet another unique characteristic of Linux that differentiates it from other operating systems. Nearly every other operating system is developed and marketed by a single vendor. For example, the only vendor who develops and sells OS X is Apple, Inc. You can't go to Novell for their version of the Mac OS, nor can you go to Microsoft for their version of the Mac OS. Likewise, you can't get a copy of Windows from Apple or Sun.

Imagine what the world would be like if other operating systems were developed in the same manner as Linux. Suppose you wanted to purchase a copy of the latest version of Windows. If Windows were licensed under the GPL, you would visit your local computer store and find that there were many different Windows distributions available from a variety of different software vendors, only one of which would be Microsoft.

Each distribution would be slightly different from the others, although they would still be based on the same kernel. You would be able to browse through the different distributions and find the one that is best for you.

This scenario is very unlikely as far as Windows is concerned. With Linux, however, that's exactly what is available to you. Many different software developers have taken the basic Linux kernel and modified it to suit some particular purpose. They may have also bundled many powerful applications with it. Some distributions may be customized to provide high-end network services to remote end users. Others may be customized to provide excellent productivity applications on end users' desktops. Either way, the result is a customized Linux distribution.

Commonly Used Distributions

Today there are literally hundreds of different distributions available. Some are freely available, and some require you to pay a fee. Some of the more popular Linux distributions include:

- openSUSE Linux
- Ubuntu Linux
- Fedora Linux
- Red Hat Enterprise Linux
- Oracle Linux
- Knoppix
- Debian Linux
- Mandriva Linux
- Gentoo Linux
- Slackware Linux
- CentOS
- Scientific Linux

 NOTE A great table providing an overview and comparison of most Linux distributions is available at http://en.wikipedia.org/wiki/Comparison_of_Linux_ distributions. The http://distrowatch.com/ web site is also a great resource for information on all available Linux distributions.

So which distribution is best? That is a dangerous question. Pacifist system administrators and programmers can come to blows while debating it. That's because the distribution that works the best for you may not meet the needs of someone else. The key is to try out several distributions and pick the one you like.

Personally, I have grown to love SUSE Linux, and it has become my Linux distribution of choice. You can download a copy of this distribution from opensuse.org. I also really like Fedora from Red Hat and Ubuntu. You can download a copy of Fedora from fedora.redhat.com and a copy of Ubuntu from ubuntu.com. Security administrators tend to like Knoppix, which can be downloaded from knopper.net.

The Life Cycle of a Linux Distribution

Let's look at the life cycle of a typical Linux distribution. Understand that nothing lasts forever, including Linux distributions. Eventually newer, better versions of a Linux distribution will be released, making older versions obsolete. Essentially, a Linux distribution goes through the same life cycle as any other software:

- **Design** During this phase, the goal or purpose of the distribution is identified, features or functions are defined, and roles are assigned. Typically, this phase involves determining what didn't work so well in the previous version of the distribution and how the problems can be fixed. It also usually involves determining what new functionality needs to be added to the distribution.

- **Develop** The distribution is created according to the plans made during the design phase. The way this is carried out depends upon the development model employed. It may use a tightly controlled, cathedral-style development process, or it could be a wild free-for-all over the Internet using the bazaar-styled development process. Usually some form of testing and validation is employed to ensure the distribution is as bug-free as possible.

- **Deploy** The completed distribution is released and end users begin deploying it in a variety of environments.

- **Manage** The deployed distribution is managed on a day-to-day basis. Because it is used in such a diversity of environments, inevitably a host of bugs are discovered that eluded the developers in the develop phase. As a result, interim updates need to be released to fix these bugs. The frequency of update releases in Linux is typically much faster than in commercial operating systems and applications, usually every few months.

- **Retire** Distributions typically remain supported for a period of time, called the support life cycle. However, the length of the support life cycle will vary greatly from distribution to distribution. For example, Red Hat Linux currently provides a ten-year life cycle (although it can be extended to 13 years). By way of contrast, Debian only provides a three-year life cycle. Once the support life cycle ends, the distribution is obsolete and must be retired. When the distribution reaches this state, it should be removed from your production environment.

During this process, new versions of the given Linux distribution may be released before the end of the support life cycle of earlier versions. The developers don't typically wait for the retirement of a distribution before releasing a new one. Therefore, it's possible for multiple versions of a given Linux distribution to be supported at the same time; however, they will all be at different points in the support life cycle.

Choosing an Operating System

At this point we need to discuss how to go about choosing an operating system. You should carefully analyze the environment a system will be deployed into *before* you pick an operating system and start installing. As much as I love Linux, it isn't always the correct operating system for a given situation. If it is, you still need to carefully identify which distribution is most appropriate for the role the system will fulfill. If you don't, you'll be spending a lot of time fixing your mistakes later.

In this part of this chapter, we'll discuss how you go about selecting an operating system for a deployment. The following topics will be addressed:

- Conducting a needs assessment
- Selecting a distribution
- Verifying system requirements and hardware compatibility

Conducting a Needs Assessment

Before you select an operating system, choose your application software, or order your system hardware, the first and most important step in any deployment is to conduct a needs assessment. As important as a needs assessment is, it's usually skipped by most system administrators and, even when it is done, it's usually done poorly.

Case Study

When determining goals, be sure to talk to everyone involved. If you don't, you won't get a clear picture of what is expected, and you will probably fail to meet a particular goal. Let me give you an example. Several years ago, I was contracted by a financial organization to deploy a Linux server in their new main office and implement all of the wiring necessary to provide network connectivity to each employee's office. I spent a considerable amount of time interviewing one of the owners when I conducted the needs assessment. When I was done, I felt that I had a pretty solid understanding of what they wanted.

To make a long story short, I wired the office and then implemented the Linux server. I was feeling very good about the smoothness of the deployment. As I was packing up to leave, the owner walked into the server room and handed me a CD containing a popular server-based financial accounting software application. He told me that his staff needed to use this software to complete their day-to-day jobs. I cringed when I looked at the system requirements and discovered that it required a Windows server.

Where did I go wrong? I didn't take the time to talk to the employees in the office who would be using the new server. Talking to just one person wasn't enough. The owner didn't know this particular software package was needed when I initially interviewed him during the needs assessment. If he had, I could have accounted for this software in our plan and I could have gone home on time that night.

A needs assessment is the process of determining *why* the deployment is being undertaken, *what* outcomes are expected, and *when* it is expected to be complete. Completing a needs assessment will require you to remove your technician hat and put on your project manager hat.

In this role, you will need to meet with a variety of different individuals and gather data about the deployment. Yes, this means you will have to interface with carbon-based life forms (that is, people). You can do it! I have faith in you!

Your findings should be recorded in a word processing document that can be easily distributed and reviewed by others. When you're done, the needs assessment should contain the following information (at a minimum):

- **What are the goals of the deployment?** Find out why the new system is being requested. What problem will this installation fix? What will be the final result of the implementation? What organizational objectives will be met by the implementation? When you list the goals of the project, be sure to use language that is clear and measurable.

- **Who are the stakeholders in this project?** Identify all individuals who will be impacted by the deployment in any way. You should ask the following questions:
  - Who requested the new system?
  - Who will use the system after it's installed?
  - Who has the authority to approve funds for the system?
  - Who has authority to allocate your time to the project?
  - Who must give final approval to this project before it can begin?
  - Who will maintain and support the system after it is implemented?
  - Is the new system a fit with the client's current technology environment and strategic direction?
  - What is the learning curve associated with the project? Will it require user and administrator retraining? Who will pay for it if it does?

  These are absolutely critical questions that must be answered before you begin any project. You'd be surprised at how many end users try to circumvent established policies and get you to do something for them without the proper approvals. Don't make the mistake of assuming that a deployment has been approved and funded simply because someone asks you to work on it for them. (Trust me, it happens all the time.) If you identify all the stakeholders in the project, you can be sure that the deployment has been approved and that the necessary funds have been allocated.

- **When is the system needed?** Before you can create a schedule, you need to know when your stakeholders expect everything to be complete.

By gathering this data in your needs assessment, you can define one of the most critical components in your installation plan: the project *scope*. The project scope defines exactly *what* to do, *when* to do it, and *who* will do it. You will also have identified the requirements and goals that must be met in the project. This information will let you intelligently decide whether Linux is the most appropriate operating system or whether an operating system from some other unmentionable company is a better fit.

Selecting a Distribution

If your needs analysis dictates that Linux is the best choice of operating systems to deploy, then the next step is to decide which Linux distribution will best meet the goals of the implementation.

Which one is best depends on your preferences and what you want the system to do. Here are some questions you can use as guidelines to help you select the right distribution.

Will the system function as a workstation or a server? One of the cool things about Linux is the fact that you can implement just about any distribution as either a workstation or a server. This is unique among operating systems. Most other operating systems, such as Windows Server 2012 or Windows 8, are designed to function either as a server or as a workstation, but not both. Most Linux distributions, on the other hand, can be used in either role.

However, be aware that there are some Linux distributions available that are specifically designed and optimized to function as servers while others are designed to work best as workstations. For example, Red Hat provides the Red Hat Enterprise Server distribution, which is designed for providing network services for medium to very large organizations with heavy server utilization. Red Hat also provides the Red Hat Enterprise Desktop distribution, which is designed specifically for use in desktop systems.

Likewise, Novell offers the SUSE Linux Enterprise Server distribution, which is designed for use in high-end server systems in very large organizations. It also offers the SUSE Linux Enterprise Desktop distribution, which is designed for use by end users on their desktop workstations.

Does the distribution offer support? Some vendors offer technical support for their Linux distributions, while others offer limited support or no support at all. If the system will be used in a corporate environment, you should implement a well-supported distribution. If a problem occurs at some point after the system has been installed, you need to be able to resolve the issue and get the system back into production as fast as possible. You're not going to have time to scour the Internet trying to find a solution; you need to be able to call someone and get an answer immediately.

Be aware that, while the distribution itself may be free or nearly free, you will be required to pay for technical support. The price charged for support varies from vendor to vendor, so it pays to shop around.

Before we go any further, you should know that several vendors offer multiple Linux distributions, and this is causing a significant amount of confusion in the industry right now. Typically, you will find that one version is free while the other requires a fee, and folks wonder what the difference is between them. For example, you can purchase a copy of Red Hat Enterprise Linux Desktop or you can download a copy of Fedora for free.

One of the key differences is support. If you purchase a copy of Red Hat Enterprise Linux Desktop, you are entitled to tech support from Red Hat. The more you pay, the better the level of support you receive.

The same holds true with SUSE Linux. You can either purchase a copy of SUSE Linux Enterprise from Novell or download a free copy of openSUSE from www.opensuse.org. Once again, the difference is the level of support. If you purchase a copy, you have access to tech support. If you download a free copy, you must support yourself using web sites, forums, and newsgroups.

If you are planning to deploy the computer in a lab environment where you will geek out with the operating system to see what it can do, then a free version would probably be the most appropriate. However, I strongly recommend that you purchase a supported version of Linux if you're going to deploy it in a production environment.

Will the applications you need run on the distribution?   Before selecting a specific distribution, you should evaluate the software you want to run and verify that it is supported by the operating system.

Verifying System Requirements and Hardware Compatibility

In addition to the considerations discussed in the previous two sections, you should also verify that the distribution you want to use runs on your system hardware. As a techie, you probably love ordering hardware. It's even more fun if your employer is paying the bill! Because of this, you may be strongly tempted to start browsing vendor web sites to order your new systems before your Linux deployment planning is complete.

Resist this urge at all costs! Before you download or purchase your Linux distribution, you need to make sure it will actually run on your hardware. Many system administrators I work with ignore this process. In fact, I'll admit to having done this myself. It's a poor practice, and if you follow it you're pretty much guaranteed to have a "duh" moment at some point. You run the risk of ending up with hardware that isn't compatible with your operating system. When this happens, your project schedule will be put at risk and lots of people will be unhappy with you. It can take a considerable amount of time to return and reorder hardware. If this happens, you'll get to spend quality time in your supervisor's office explaining why the deployment is behind schedule.

There are two things you can do to keep this from happening:

- Check hardware compatibility
- Verify system requirements

Checking Hardware Compatibility

Back in the early days of Linux, hardware compatibility was problematic, especially if you were trying to install Linux on a notebook or other system with a lot of proprietary hardware. There just weren't enough developers writing Linux drivers. If you were installing Linux on a generic system using common hardware components, you could usually get Linux installed and working correctly. However, if your system used nontypical or proprietary hardware, such as a high-end video board, then you may or may not have been able to get Linux running correctly.

Back then, most hardware vendors didn't provide Linux device drivers for their devices. They didn't perceive Linux as a widely used operating system and didn't want to devote time and money to developing device drivers for it. Instead, you had to rely on the good will of a developer somewhere in the world to write a driver for your particular piece of hardware. If a driver didn't exist for your device, you were out of luck.

Today, this is less of an issue. It's been a long time since I've had to scour the Internet trying to find a Linux driver. Most vendors now offer a Linux version of the drivers for their hardware. In addition, most of the drivers for common PC hardware are now included with the various Linux distributions.

To be safe, however, it is still a very good idea to check your distribution's web site and verify that your system hardware is listed on the distribution's hardware compatibility list (HCL). Even though hardware support for Linux has become much better in the last decade, there are still some devices that aren't supported. You can use your distribution's HCL to verify that your system's devices are.

HCLs are usually available in two locations. Most distributions include a list of supported hardware in a text file on the installation media. However, I rarely use this version of the HCL because it probably hasn't been updated lately.

Instead, I prefer using the HCL that's maintained on most distribution web sites. This version of the HCL usually contains the most current data on supported hardware. For example, if you choose to install the openSUSE distribution on your system, you can use a web browser to access its HCL at http://en.opensuse.org/Hardware. Once there, you can search for your particular system hardware and see if it is supported. In Figure 1-1, the openSUSE HCL for video boards is displayed.

Figure 1-1 Using the openSUSE HCL

If you choose to use a Red Hat distribution, you can likewise check the HCL on Red Hat's web site (http://hardware.redhat.com) to verify that your system hardware is supported. This site is shown in Figure 1-2.

Most distributions include some kind of HCL on their web site, but not all. Some distribution vendors simply don't have the time or resources to conduct extensive hardware testing to verify the myriad of PC devices available on the market.

 NOTE Driver availability is one of the reasons I prefer to stick with big-name, well-supported Linux distributions when deploying in a production environment. I'm comfortable experimenting with a poorly supported distribution at home or in a lab environment at work. If something goes wrong, nothing is lost in this situation. However, one of my key roles as a Linux system administrator in a production environment is to protect data and to ensure systems run at maximum efficiency. In this situation I need to know that my hardware is supported. I can't afford to mess around scouring the Internet trying to find a driver, nor do I want to waste time troubleshooting a system that functions erratically.

Verifying System Requirements

In addition to checking the HCL, you also need to check your distribution's system requirements. Back in the early days of Linux, we didn't worry much about system requirements for the various distributions because the early Linux distributions ran on ridiculously minimal hardware. They didn't require much memory, disk space, or processing power.

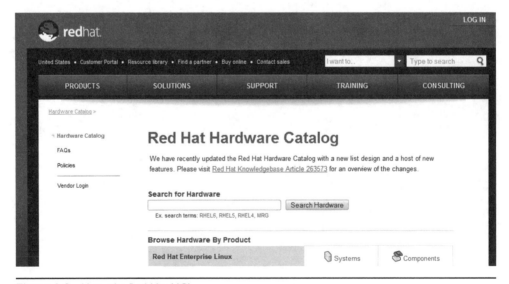

Figure 1-2 Using the Red Hat HCL

However, as Linux has matured over the years, most distributions are now begin-ning to require much more robust system hardware to provide an acceptable degree of performance. How do you know what the system requirements are? Once again, check your distribution vendor's web site.

A key aspect of your system requirements is your PC's CPU architecture. When downloading your Linux distribution, be sure you select the correct architecture for your system's CPU. For years, we didn't worry much about this issue because we really only worked with a single architecture: Intel's 32-bit x86 architecture. Although most early distributions were available for the x86 and the Alpha CPU architectures, the average system administrator didn't have many Alpha machines. Nearly every system we worked with ran on some variation of the x86 architecture.

Today, however, there are many more hardware options available to us. We still have the venerable x86 and Alpha architectures, but we also have the newer 64-bit x86 architecture. In addition, Intel produces the IA-64 architecture used by their Itanium CPUs. Each of these architectures requires a different version of Linux. In fact, many Linux distributions have even been ported to run on the Power PC (PPC) architecture from Apple Computer. Other distributions are available for the iSeries, pSeries, and RS/6000 servers from IBM.

The important point is to be sure that you select the appropriate architecture for your distribution. For example, if you selected Ubuntu as your distribution and accessed the distribution's download page on the Internet, you would see the options displayed in Figure 1-3.

Regardless of which distribution you choose, make sure you download the correct version for your system's architecture. For example, if you are going to install Linux on 32-bit CPU, then you need the x86 (32-bit) version of your distribution. If your hard-ware uses 64-bit CPU, then you need x86-64 (64-bit) version of the distribution. If you pick the wrong one, most Linux installers will generate an error and you won't be able to complete the installation.

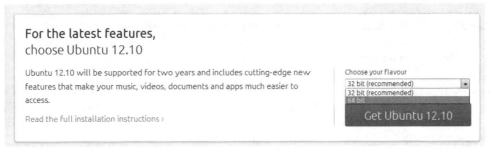

Download Ubuntu for your desktop

You can choose between two options when you download Ubuntu for a desktop PC. Ubuntu 12.10 gives you all the latest features, while Ubuntu 12.04.1 LTS comes with extended support.

For the latest features,
choose Ubuntu 12.10

Ubuntu 12.10 will be supported for two years and includes cutting-edge new features that make your music, videos, documents and apps much easier to access.

Read the full installation instructions ›

Choose your flavour

32 bit (recommended)
32 bit (recommended)
64 bit

Get Ubuntu 12.10

Figure 1-3   Ubuntu architectures

Common Linux Implementations

Because Linux is distributed under the GPL, software vendors have been able to tweak and customize the operating system to operate in a variety of roles. While the number of these roles is virtually limitless, you should be familiar with the following roles:

- Using Linux on the desktop
- Using Linux on the server
- Embedding Linux in firmware
- Using Linux for virtualization
- Using Linux with cloud computing

Linux on the Desktop

Linux can be optimized to function extremely well as a desktop system. However, Linux has been somewhat slow to make inroads into this market. There are two important reasons for this.

First, historically there has been a lack of desktop productivity applications available for Linux. Users need word processing, spreadsheet, and presentation software on their desktops to do their day-to-day work. Until recently, productivity applications haven't been readily available for Linux users. However, the release of the OpenOffice .org productivity suite has rectified this situation and made Linux a viable option for the desktop.

The second (and most vexing) issue is the fact that the average end user tends to find Linux intimidating. For "techies" like you and me, this isn't a problem. We're comfortable with new applications and operating systems. We can learn them quickly and use them effectively. Unfortunately, the average end user in most organizations probably first learned how to use a computer using a version of Windows. As a result, that's what they are most comfortable with, and they tend to be resistant to learning a new operating system. The key to making Linux viable on the desktop is to

- Provide users with the applications they need to get their work done.
- Make the user interface easy and intuitive such that a migration from Windows to Linux is as painless as possible.

 TIP Because Linux can be intimidating to the average end user, you should consider implementing an extensive training program as an integral part of your overall deployment plan.

Many vendors have been working on desktop-oriented Linux distributions that seek to do just this. They've optimized Linux to run efficiently and fast as a desktop system. They've also bundled application suites such as OpenOffice.org with their distributions. Additionally, they've optimized their Linux window managers to provide the end user with an easy-to-use graphical interface. Some of the more popular desktop Linux distributions include the following:

- Ubuntu Desktop Edition
- openSUSE
- Fedora Desktop Edition

One of the key advantages of using Linux on the desktop is the fact that Linux systems are much more immune than other operating systems to most of the viruses circulating today. If you've ever been responsible for managing a computer network, you know what a daunting task virus protection can be. Using Windows-based e-mail clients and browsers exposes your network to a wide variety of virus, worm, and spyware threats. You probably spend a lot of time and money deploying antivirus software to keep your network systems from becoming infected.

However, most viruses, worms, and spyware apps won't run on Linux. Linux virus protection software is available; however, it is actually targeted at Windows viruses and meant to run once instead of daily. By deploying Linux on the desktop, you can conserve valuable time and money by eliminating the need for antivirus software.

Linux on the Server

Linux works great as a server. In fact, Linux is experiencing widespread acceptance in the server room, much more so than on the desktop. That's because Linux can assume a variety of server roles, including the following:

- **File server**   Using the Network File System (NFS) or Samba services, Linux can be configured to provide network storage of users' files. NFS works great for Linux or UNIX client systems, but it doesn't work as well for Windows clients. Samba is a better choice for Windows client systems. Using Samba, your Linux server can even be configured to function as a Windows domain controller.

- **Print server**   Using the Common UNIX Printing System (CUPS) and Samba services together, Linux can be configured to provide shared printing for network users.

- **Database server**   Linux can be configured as a powerful database server. There are a variety of database services available for Linux, including MySQL, MariaDB, NoSQL, and PostgreSQL.

- **Web server**   Linux has been widely deployed as a Web server. In fact, the most popular Web service currently used on Linux is the Apache Web server.

- **E-mail server**   There are a variety of e-mail services available for Linux that can turn your system into an enterprise-class mail server.

The widespread popularity of Linux as a server is due to a number of reasons. First of all, Linux is extremely stable. Simply put, a Linux server rarely crashes. It just keeps running and running. Other server operating systems have had a notorious reputation for crashing on a regular basis.

Second, Linux servers are very fast. Many benchmark tests have been run pitting Linux servers against other server operating systems. Each time, Linux servers have performed as well as, if not much better than, comparable operating systems running similar services under a similar workload.

Third, Linux servers tend to be less expensive to own. Most server operating systems charge expensive per-seat licensing fees, making them very expensive to deploy in large organizations. Most Linux distributions do not. In fact, depending upon the distribution you choose, you may only need to pay for your server hardware, your support contract, and staff to manage the system.

Although you can configure almost any Linux distribution to provide network services, you should use a distribution specifically optimized to function as a server if you are going to deploy a Linux server in a large organization. Red Hat offers the Red Hat Enterprise Linux Server distribution, which has a proven track record as enterprise-class server. Likewise, you can also use the SUSE Linux Enterprise Server (SLES) distribution, which is also optimized for the server role.

Embedded Linux

In addition to running on standard desktop and server PC hardware, Linux can also be embedded in the firmware of mobile devices. The Android operating system that is very widely deployed on phones and tablets today is really a modified Linux distribution that is designed to be embedded within the hardware of the device itself.

Virtualization

Virtualization is an aspect of information technology that is gaining a great deal of momentum in the industry. To understand how virtualization works, you first need to understand how operating systems are traditionally deployed on computer hardware.

In the traditional model, one operating system was installed on one hardware device. For example, if you were installing a new system, you would go out and purchase your system hardware and then install the Linux operating system on that hardware. The relationship between the operating system and the hardware in this type of deployment is shown in Figure 1-4.

Figure 1-4
Traditional
installation

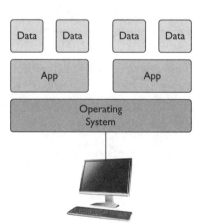

In this scenario, the operating system has full reign over all the resources in the server hardware, including:

- RAM
- Processor time
- Storage devices
- Network interfaces

Now, this is how we have typically installed operating systems in the past. However, this deployment model is very inefficient. Generally speaking, the operating system doesn't fully utilize all of these resources all of the time, especially on server systems. In fact, much of the time your computing resources are woefully underutilized. This means computing capacity is available but remains unused and is therefore wasted.

For example, suppose you have three servers, each installed on their own physical hardware. The CPU utilization on each system usually hovers around 8–9 percent with occasional spikes up to 50 percent. The system RAM, storage, and network devices are utilized in the same manner. You don't actually need this much processing power in this scenario. About 90 percent of each server's capacity goes unused most of the time.

Virtualization offers an alternative deployment model. Virtualization pools multiple operating system instances onto the same physical hardware and allows them to run concurrently. To do this, virtualization uses a mediator called a *hypervisor* to manage access to system resources.

Each operating system instance is installed into a *virtual machine* instead of onto physical hardware. Each virtual machine is allocated CPU time, an area of RAM to work in, a storage device, and its own virtual network interface. Each virtual machine appears and functions just like a physical host. The relationship between the virtual machines, hypervisor, and physical hardware is depicted in Figure 1-5.

Figure 1-5
Hypervisor
installation

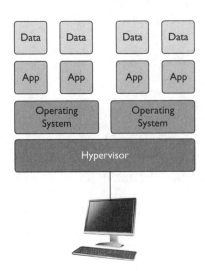

One of the key benefits of virtualization is the fact that it uses system resources more efficiently. The available computing capacity of the system hardware is allocated among all of the virtual machines running on the system.

Another benefit of virtualization is the fact that it allows multiple platforms to run at the same time on the same hardware, including Windows and Linux. This is a huge benefit for software developers and testers, making it much easier to test how an application in development performs on different platforms.

Virtualization also allows you to implement thin clients in your organization. In this configuration, you run multiple desktops on the same virtualization server. All of your end-user desktops are provided as virtual machines on the server. This can save a ton of cash because it allows you to deploy very minimal, low-end workstations for your users. The wimpy workstations are simply used to display (using a network connection) the desktop environment running as a virtual machine on the server.

Several high-performance virtualization platforms are available for Linux, including

- Xen (open source)
- VMware ESX and ESXi (proprietary)

When you install one of these systems, you turn your Linux system into a hypervisor that can run virtual machines.

Virtualization is a key component of *cloud computing*. With cloud computing, the hardware, software, and/or network resources that we historically implemented locally on-site are moved off-site and delivered to you over a network connection. Many cloud-computing providers even offer their services through the Internet. For example, let's suppose you need to deploy an additional Linux server in your organization. Traditionally, you would purchase new hardware, pick a distribution, install it, and configure it to work in your network. With cloud computing, on the other hand, a provider on the Internet could deploy a new Linux virtual machine on a hypervisor at their site. You could then pay a fee to access this virtual server through your organization's network connection. The provider assumes all the cost of implementing, maintaining, and protecting the server. This model is referred to Infrastructure as a Service (IaaS).

In addition to IaaS, there are several other cloud computing models:

- **Software as a Service (SaaS)**   Provides access to software and data through the cloud.

- **Network as a Service (NaaS)**   Provides network connectivity through the cloud.

- **Storage as a Service (STaaS)**   Provides access to storage devices through the cloud.

- **Desktop as a service (DaaS)**   Provides access to desktop operating systems through the cloud.

- **Platform as a Service (PaaS)**   Provides access to a full solution suite to accomplish a computing task, including networking, infrastructure, storage, and software.

In fact, you can use Linux and virtualization to create your own private cloud, offering on-demand computing resources through a network connection to other users in your organization.

Chapter Review

In this chapter, you were introduced to the Linux operating system. We first discussed what an operating system is and the components that compose the Linux operating system. We emphasized the fact that modern computer systems and operating systems are modular. You can install Linux on any compatible computer.

We then spent some time reviewing the historical development of Linux. We went over the typical corporate software development model and related how Linux was developed outside this norm. We talked about GNU and the GPL and the fact that Linux is developed under the GPL, allowing anyone free access to the source code. We then discussed the open source software movement and identified how it is related to GNU. We related that open source offers free software whose source code must remain publicly available.

Next, we discussed the importance of creating a plan before implementing new computer systems. The first component in this plan is to conduct a needs assessment. When conducting a needs assessment, you should first determine the goals of the project and identify who the stakeholders are. You should get approval from all concerned parties before actually starting the project. You should use the information gathered in the needs assessment to develop the project scope, which states exactly what will be done in the project. The project scope comprises the project schedule, the resources assigned to the project, and the range of tasks to be completed. It also identifies which operating system would best meet the goals of the project.

If you elect to use Linux, the next task is to select a Linux distribution to install. I emphasized that you must evaluate the role of the system to determine the best distribution. If the system is going to provide network services to client systems, then a Linux distribution optimized to function as a server would be the best choice. If the system is going to be used as a desktop system, then a distribution optimized to function as a workstation would be the best choice. I also emphasized the importance of technical support. An unsupported distribution may be a fine choice for an experimental lab system, but a supported distribution is a better choice for systems that will be used in a production environment.

The next task is to verify that your hardware is compatible with your chosen Linux distribution. I pointed out that most distributions include some type of hardware compatibility list. You should check your hardware against this list. You should also verify that your hardware meets your distribution's minimum system requirements. I emphasized that you must download the correct version of the distribution for your CPU's architecture.

We ended this chapter by reviewing how Linux distributions are created and listed several of the more popular distributions. We also discussed the different roles that Linux can play in a typical organization, including servers, desktops, and hypervisors.

Accelerated Review

- Linux is an operating system.
- Operating systems provide four key functions:
  - Application platform
  - Hardware moderator
  - Data storage
  - Security
- Linux is composed of the following components:
  - Kernel
  - Libraries
  - Utilities
  - User interfaces
- Linus Torvalds first developed Linux in the early 1990s.
- Linux is licensed under the GPL.
- Anyone can download and modify the Linux kernel source code.
- Properly planning and documenting a Linux deployment will save time and money in the long run.
- The first task in a Linux deployment is conducting a needs assessment.
- You should ask the following questions in your needs assessment:
  - What are the goals of the project?
  - Who are the stakeholders?
  - What is the scope of the project?
- The project scope defines who will do what and when.
- Different software companies develop unique Linux flavors called distributions.
- Your plan should specify which distribution you are going to use.
- You should determine the role of the system before selecting a distribution.
- Systems used in a production environment should provide technical support.
- You should verify that your software applications will run on your selected distribution before deploying it.
- You should check your distribution's HCL to determine if your hardware is compatible.
- You should verify that your hardware meets your distribution's minimum system requirements.
- You need to determine your CPU's architecture before downloading a distribution.
- Linux can function as a server, desktop, or hypervisor in a computer network.

Questions

1. Your company recently purchased 12 new computer systems. The computers have Intel Core i3 dual-core 3.4 GHz CPUs and 1TB hard drives. Your deployment plan calls for Linux to be installed on them, but the department manager who requested the computers is concerned that this can't be done because they already have Windows 7 preinstalled. Can this be done?

   A. Yes, but you must install a new hard drive for Linux.

   B. No, the hardware is probably optimized for Windows and won't support Linux.

   C. No, modern motherboards are hard-coded to recognize your Windows Certificate of Authority. If it doesn't find it, the system won't boot.

   D. Yes, you can erase the hard drive and install Linux.

2. Which of the following represents the actual operating system component within a Linux system?

   A. Libraries

   B. Kernel

   C. Desktop environment

   D. bash shell functions

3. Which of the following provides prewritten code elements that programmers can call when writing Linux programs?

   A. The kernel

   B. Kernel modules

   C. Libraries

   D. bash shell profiles

4. What was the name of the UNIX clone written by Andrew Tanenbaum?

   A. CPM

   B. DR-DOS

   C. Linux

   D. Minix

   E. Solaris

5. What did Linus Torvalds do with the source code for Linux?

   A. He sold it to IBM.

   B. He gave it to Microsoft for free.

   C. He developed Minix.

   D. He patented and copyrighted it.

   E. He posted it on the Internet for anyone who wanted a copy.

6. Who initiated the GNU Project?

   A. Richard Stallman

   B. Andrew Tanenbaum

   C. Linus Torvalds

   D. Richard Berkley

7. You are a computer programmer. Your supervisor wants you to download
   the source code for the latest Linux kernel and modify it to support a
   custom application your company is developing for use in-house. Can
   you do this?

   A. No, the source code for Linux is no longer available on the Internet.

   B. No, the copyright on the source code won't permit it.

   C. Yes, but you must pay a royalty to the GNU Project.

   D. Yes, you can create a new Linux flavor and even redistribute it as long as the
   source code remains freely available.

8. You have been tasked with setting up an e-mail server for your organization
   of 150 people. You're considering using a Linux system to do this. Is this
   possible?

   A. Yes, Linux can be configured to provide e-mail services.

   B. No, while Linux can be configured to provide e-mail services, it's not recommended for more than 25 users.

   C. Yes, but you'll have to purchase special e-mail software that's compatible
   with Linux.

   D. No currently available commercial groupware software suite has been
   ported to run on Linux.

9. Which Linux services can be used to configure shared network printing on a
   Linux server for both Linux and Windows client workstations? (Choose two.)

   A. MySQL

   B. NFS

   C. CUPS

   D. Samba

   E. NIS

   F. OpenPrint

10. Which services can be used to configure shared file storage on a Linux server for network users using Windows workstations? (Choose two.)

    A. MySQL

    B. NFS

    C. PostgreSQL

    D. Samba

    E. NIS

    F. FileManager

11. When conducting a needs assessment, what questions should you ask? (Choose two.)

    A. What problem will this installation fix?

    B. Which distribution should I use?

    C. Where can I get the best price on a new server?

    D. Who is requesting the new systems?

12. Which of the following is a properly stated goal in a needs assessment?

    A. Jan's boss wants a new server, so we're going to install it.

    B. We're going to install Linux on everyone's desktop.

    C. We need a new Linux server.

    D. The new Linux system will be configured as a hypervisor for virtualization to increase the software development team's productivity by an anticipated 20 percent.

13. Suppose Sarah from Sales approaches you and asks for a new Linux server for her team. Who else should you talk to as a part of your needs assessment? (Choose two.)

    A. Sarah's boss

    B. Sarah's reports

    C. The Marketing team's supervisor

    D. Your hardware vendor

14. You're responsible for implementing five new Linux servers in your organization's Accounting department. The Accounting supervisor has asked that four additional servers be added to the project. Due to time constraints, he won't allow you to adjust the original schedule. Which of the following is the most appropriate response?

    A. Ignore the request.

    B. Inform the supervisor that additional resources will have to be added to the project.

    C. Resign in protest.

    D. Cheerfully agree to the request and then miss the deadline.

15. You're installing a new Linux server that will be used to host mission-critical database applications. This server will be heavily utilized by a large number of users every day. Which distributions would be the best choice for this deployment? (Choose two.)

    A. Red Hat Enterprise Linux Server

    B. Red Hat Enterprise Linux Desktop

    C. SUSE Linux Enterprise Server

    D. SUSE Linux Enterprise Desktop

16. You're planning to install Linux on a Frankenstein system that you've built out of spare parts. Several components in the system aren't listed on your distribution's HCL. This system will be used by your team's administrative assistant to manage employee schedules, send and receive e-mail, and track employee hours. What should you do?

    A. Install the distribution and hope for the best.

    B. Install the distribution and then install the latest product updates.

    C. Replace the incompatible parts with supported hardware.

    D. Spend three days scouring the Internet looking for drivers.

17. You're planning to install Fedora on a system that uses a Pentium 4 hyper-threading CPU. Which distribution architecture should you download?

    A. IA-64

    B. x86-Celeron

    C. x86-64

    D. x86

    E. PPC

18. You're planning to install Fedora on a system that uses a 64-bit quad-core CPU. Which distribution architecture should you download?

    A. IA-64

    B. x86-64

    C. x86

    D. PPC

Answers

1. **D.** Hardware and operating systems are modular. As long as the hardware is supported, you can install any operating system designed for your specific CPU architecture. Be aware, however, that some Windows 8 systems may have the SecureBoot feature enabled, which prevents the BIOS from loading any operating system not digitally signed by Microsoft. You will need to turn this feature off before you can install Linux on this type of system.

2. **B.** The Linux kernel is the component that handles operating system functions.

3. **C.** Libraries contain prewritten code that programmers can reuse in their applications.

4. **D.** Andrew Tanenbaum wrote the Minix operating system when universities were no longer allowed access to the UNIX source code.

5. **E.** Linus Torvalds posted the source code for his Linux kernel on the Internet and invited other programmers to modify and enhance it.

6. **A.** Richard Stallman championed the freely distributable source code concept behind GNU.

7. **D.** Under the GPL, you are free to download the Linux source code and modify it.

8. **A.** A variety of powerful e-mail packages are available for Linux that make it highly suitable for large organizations.

9. **C, D.** The CUPS service provides network printing to other Linux systems. When combined with Samba, network printing can be extended to Windows systems (as well as any other operating system that supports Samba, including Linux and Mac OS X).

10. **D.** The Samba service can be used to support Samba-compatible clients, including Windows, Mac OS X, and Linux systems.

11. **A, D.** You should determine why the new systems are needed and who will be using them.

12. **D.** This response clearly states the goal of the project and is measurable.

13. **A, B.** Sarah's boss and her direct reports are key stakeholders in the project.

14. **B.** The best response to this situation is to have a frank discussion with the stakeholder and point out the consequences of the decision. Either the scale will have to be reduced or more resources must be added to the project to complete it in the same time frame.

15. **A, C.** These distributions are designed for high-demand network servers.

16. **C.** The best approach is to use supported hardware.

17. **D.** The Pentium 4 hyperthreading CPU uses the Intel x86 architecture.

18. **B.** The 64-bit AMD CPU uses a 64-bit x86 architecture.

Getting Around in Linux

In this chapter, you will learn about
- Booting the system and logging in
- Using the Linux graphical desktop environment
- Using the Linux command line environment

In many organizations, all you have to do is say the word "Linux" and users start to shake with fear. They have heard so many horror stories about how hard Linux is to use that they frequently don't even want to try it. This "Linux is hard to use" reputation may have been deserved back in the old days when nearly everything was done at the command line. However, this operating system has come a very long way in the last decade. In fact, I believe a modern Linux distribution is just as easy to use as a Windows or Mac system.

In this chapter, we're going to spend some time learning the basics of how to get around in a Linux system. By the time we are done, I think you'll agree that Linux is actually quite easy to use. Be careful: you may even find that you like it better than your Windows system!

Booting the System and Logging In

Let's begin with some nuts-and-bolts basics of using a Linux system. In order to really learn about Linux, you first need to be able to boot the system and log in as a Linux user. We'll look at the following:

- Booting the system
- Logging in
- Keeping information secure
- Shutting down the system

Booting the System

The process of booting a Linux system is the same as that for other operating systems. Simply press the power button on your system and wait while the system boots and the operating system loads. Depending upon your distribution and how it is configured, you may see a graphical boot menu displayed that allows you to select an operating system to boot, as shown in Figure 2-1.

The boot menu shown in Figure 2-1 has three options you can choose from:

- **Desktop**   Loads the full Linux operating system.
- **Failsafe**   Loads Linux with a minimal set of drivers and services. In many ways, this option is very similar to Safe Mode on a Windows system. It can be useful in situations where a misbehaving driver or service is causing the system to not start correctly by allowing you to get a basic system up and running so you can fix whatever is causing the issue.
- **Floppy**   Allows you to boot an operating system from a floppy diskette (if you still have one somewhere, gathering dust).

 TIP   The Boot Options field at the bottom of the screen shown in Figure 2-1 can be used to send custom parameters and options to the Linux kernel to modify the way it boots, but that's way beyond the scope of this chapter.

Other distributions may have more or fewer menu options displayed in the boot menu. On a dual-boot system, you can even launch other operating systems, such as Microsoft Windows, from the boot menu.

Figure 2-1   The boot menu

NOTE The boot menu is managed by the GRUB or GRUB2 bootloader on most Linux distributions. Older Linux distributions used the LILO bootloader to manage the boot menu. You can customize the boot menu by editing the /etc/grub.conf file or the /boot/grub/grub.conf file, depending upon your distribution. You can load these files in a text editor and make various changes, such as the default menu item and how long the bootloader will wait for you to make a selection before automatically selecting the default menu item for you.

Logging In

Once you select the operating system to boot, the system will start up. When it's finished, you will need to authenticate before you can use the system. Authentication is the process of providing credentials to the system. If the security subsystem in Linux determines that the credentials you supplied are valid, then you are granted access to the system and allowed to use whatever resources you have permission to use.

The way you authenticate to the system depends on how the system is configured. Most desktop Linux distributions are configured to boot into a graphical environment (called runlevel 5). For these types of systems, you should see a login screen that is similar to that shown in Figure 2-2.

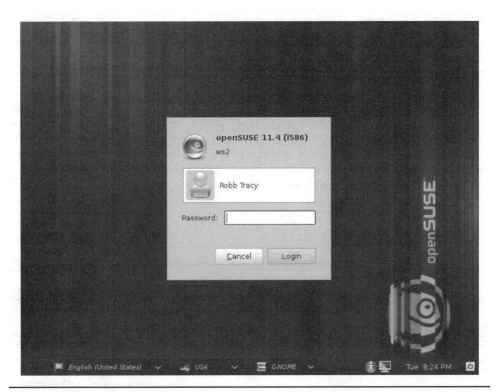

Figure 2-2 A sample graphical login screen

To authenticate in a graphical environment, select the user you wish to log in as, supply the appropriate password, and then click Login.

However, some Linux systems, particularly server systems, may be configured to boot into a text-based environment. The login screen for these systems is quite different, as shown in Figure 2-3.

To log in, enter your username at the login: prompt, and then enter the appropriate password at the Password: prompt.

Regardless of which type of environment your system is configured to use, you authenticate to the system using the Linux user accounts stored in the /etc/passwd file. After logging in, either a text-based command line environment or a graphical environment will be displayed, depending upon how your system is configured.

 TIP The type of environment loaded is controlled by the initdefault parameter in the /etc/inittab file. When set to runlevel 3, the system boots into a text-based environment by default. When set to runlevel 5, the system boots into a graphical environment by default. You can change runlevels on the fly while the system is running by entering init *runlevel_number* at the shell prompt as your root user. For example, to change to a text-based environment from a graphical environment, you enter **init 3** at the shell prompt.

Keeping Information Secure

In today's computing world, you should keep security foremost in your mind. Two decades ago, security was a nonissue. We just didn't worry about it. We were more concerned with what we could make computers do than we were with preventing unauthorized access.

That has all changed in recent years. Security breaches cost the industry millions of dollars each year. Therefore, you should take steps to keep your systems as secure as possible. For example, you should be sure to use strong passwords for your Linux user accounts. A strong password has 8 or more characters, is not found in the dictionary, uses numbers and/or symbols as well as letters, and uses upper- and lowercase characters. Here are some examples of strong passwords:

- *)(*S88v
- Il0ve23atIc3Cr3am
- &@W8842ss

```
ws2 login: rtracy
Password:
Last login: Tue Jan 15 20:26:36 MST 2013 from console on :0
Have a lot of fun...
rtracy@ws2:~>
```

Figure 2-3   Logging into a text-based Linux environment

In addition, you should protect the privacy of information after authenticating to the system. There are several key measures you should consider. Some of them are high-tech, but many are rather low-tech:

- Many system administrators configure their Linux systems to use a screensaver password. In this configuration, you must re-authenticate to the system before you can start using the system again after the screen saver shuts off.

- When you are done using the system, be sure to log off. Don't leave your system logged in and unattended. In a text-based environment, enter **logout** at the command line. In a graphical environment, select the logout option from the start menu.

- You should not write down your passwords on sticky notes and stick them to your desk, monitor, or keyboard (a very common practice). You should also not throw these sticky notes in the garbage.

- Become educated as to how to handle social engineering strategies. For example, if someone calls claiming to be a bigwig in your company and demands that you give him your password, you should forward the call to your Help Desk rather than comply with the request. Chances are you will hear a click on the other end of the line.

- Keep your systems in a secured area. No one should be able to access your systems unless they have been properly identified.

- If privacy is a very serious matter for your organization (which is the case for nearly all organizations), you may want to consider physically securing your systems with a cable lock.

- Use screen filters. Screen filters dramatically reduce the viewing angle of the monitor display, preventing prying eyes from seeing what is on the screen.

Shutting Down the System

As with any other operating system, you need to shut down a Linux system properly. This ensures that any pending disk write operations will be committed to disk before powering the system off.

 CAUTION   If you power off a Linux system unexpectedly, you may introduce corruption and inconsistencies into your file system. Always use the proper shutdown procedure. In addition, I strongly recommend that you implement an uninterruptible power supply (UPS) with your systems. They are expensive, but they will save your bacon if the power goes off. Trust me, I know. I lost an unprotected server once due to a power outage, and I had to stay up all night restoring it from backup tapes. Never again!

There are many ways to shut down a Linux system. Most graphical desktop environments include an option you can click to shut the system down with your mouse, just like Windows and Mac systems. You can also use several commands at the command line to properly shut down a Linux system, including the following:

- **init 0** Switches the system to runlevel 0, which halts the system.
- **init 6** Switches the system to runlevel 6, which reboots the system.
- **halt** Shuts down the system.
- **reboot** Reboots the system.

In addition to these commands, you can use the **shutdown** command to either shut down or reboot the system. It has several key advantages over the preceding commands:

- You can specify that the system be shut down after a specified period of time. This gives your users time to save their work and log out before the system goes down. It also allows you to shut down the system at a specified time even if you're not there to do it.
- It allows you to send a message to all logged-in users warning them that a shutdown is pending.
- It does not allow other users to log in from the time you enter the command until the pending shutdown starts.

The syntax for using shutdown is shutdown +*m* –h|–r *message*. The +*m* option specifies the amount of time (in minutes) before shutting down the system. You can also use the now option instead of +*m* to specify that the system go down immediately. If you need the system to go down at a specific time, you can replace +*m* with the time (entered as *hh:mm*) when the shutdown should occur. The –h option specifies that the system be halted, while the –r option specifies that the system be rebooted. Some examples of using shutdown are shown here:

```
shutdown +10 -h Please save your work and log out.
```

When you enter this command, all other logged-in users see the following message:

```
tux@ws2:~/Desktop>
Broadcast message from root@ws2 (pts/3) (Thu Feb 17 10:29:59 2011):

Please save your work and log out.
The system is going DOWN for system halt in 10 minutes!
```

If you've scheduled a shutdown using the shutdown command and later need to cancel that shutdown, enter **shutdown –c** at the shell prompt.

Using the Linux Graphical Desktop Environment

Let's change our focus now and discuss how to use Linux in graphical mode. Most Linux system administrators primarily manage Linux from the shell prompt, and you'll spend a significant amount of time learning how to do this in Chapter 5. However, you can also implement a powerful graphical user interface (GUI) on your Linux system. This is a good thing, because most end users are much more comfortable with a GUI than they are with a command-line interface (CLI).

In this part of the chapter, we'll look at the following:

- The Linux graphical user interface
- Graphical desktop components
- Graphical environment configuration settings
- Common Linux applications

The Linux Graphical User Interface

Because of the dominance of Microsoft Windows and the Mac OS in the home computer market, most end users have never even used a command-line interface. To make life easier for them, you can implement a GUI on Linux using a window manager and a desktop environment (such as GNOME or KDE). With a GUI in place, your users can interact with the Linux kernel using a mouse instead of just the keyboard. The GNOME desktop environment is shown in Figure 2-4.

The GUI on a Linux system is created using the X Window System software.

Figure 2-4 The GNOME desktop environment

NOTE Many times you will hear the X Window System referred to as "X Windows," "X11," or just "X."

The X Window System provides the base system for the graphical interface on Linux. It allows programmers to run applications in windows. It also allows users to move windows around on the screen as well as click items with the mouse. Essentially, you can implement a graphical user interface on your Linux system that works in a manner very similar to Microsoft Windows or the Mac OS. In fact, you will find many of the desktop components that you are already familiar with in the Linux GUI. For example, there are Computer, Home directory, and Trash icons, as shown in Figure 2-5.

Whenever you delete a file from within the desktop environment, it is moved to the Trash. You can empty the Trash by right-clicking it and selecting Empty Trash. You can also restore deleted files by doing the following:

1. Click the Trash icon.

2. Click the file or directory you want to restore.

3. Click Restore Selected Items, as shown in Figure 2-6.

You can browse other computers on the network by selecting Browse Network; a screen similar to the one shown in Figure 2-7 will be displayed.

In addition, the desktop has a startup menu with icons that can be used to launch applications. As you see in Figure 2-8, you can launch the Firefox web browser, start a file browser, or run LibreOffice applications by selecting the appropriate menu item.

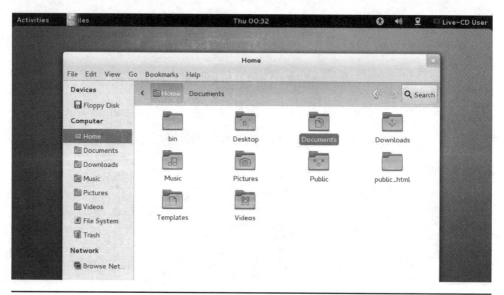

Figure 2-5 Computer, Home directory, and Trash icons on the GNOME desktop

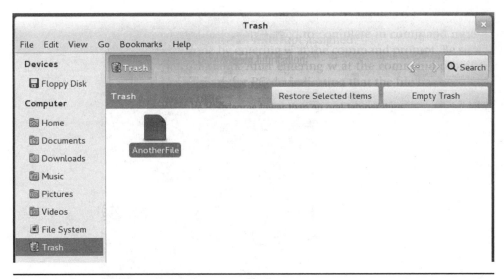

Figure 2-6   Restoring deleted files

The Linux GUI also includes a taskbar across the top or bottom of the desktop, just as a Windows system does. On the far right side of the taskbar are system applets that allow you to control such things as the audio volume level, network settings, and display settings. The system clock is also displayed. This is shown in Figure 2-9.

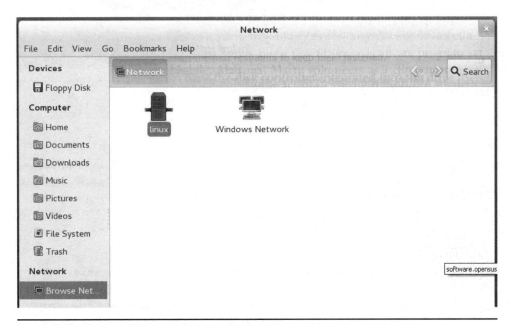

Figure 2-7   Browsing the network

Figure 2-8
Application short-
cuts in GNOME

Figure 2-9   The GNOME taskbar

Graphical Desktop Components

One of the great things about the Linux GUI is that it is very modular: it's composed of
several different pieces that work together to create the graphical interface. Because the
GUI is modular, you can mix and match different components together to customize
the way it works. This provides a degree of flexibility that just isn't available with other
operating systems. The Linux GUI is composed of the following components:

- **X server**   The heart of the Linux GUI. The X server software is the component
  that draws windows graphically on the display screen. It's also responsible for
  managing your mouse and your keyboard. We call it a *server* because it is capable
  of displaying output not only on the local monitor, but also on any other system
  on the network that is running X server software. The host to which the X server
  software sends its output is controlled by the DISPLAY environment variable.

Over the years, two different X server software packages have been implemented on Linux systems:

- **X.org-X11**   The most commonly implemented X server system and is the default X server used by most modern Linux distributions.

- **XFree86**   Until about 2004, this was the default version of X server used by most Linux distributions. It works in pretty much the same manner as X.org. In fact, the development of X.org was based on XFree86. Unfortunately, there were licensing issues associated with XFree86 that drove the Linux community to X.org as an alternative X server.

- **Window manager**   While X server creates windows within the GUI environment, the window manager's job is to customize how the windows look and behave. A wide variety of window managers are currently available for Linux. Each one offers a different look and feel for your GUI environment. Some of the more popular window managers include the following:

  - enlightenment
  - fvwm
  - kwin
  - sawfish
  - twm
  - wmaker

  Which is best? It all depends on what you like. Some window managers are complex and full-featured, such as enlightenment, kwin, and sawfish. Of these, the enlightenment and sawfish window managers are commonly used with the GNOME desktop environment, while the kwin window manager is commonly used with the KDE desktop environment.

  Other window managers are very basic or even minimalistic in nature. These include the f virtual window manager (fvwm), the tab window manager (twm), and the window maker (wmaker) window manager. Depending on your users' preferences, I suggest that you deploy a more full-featured window manager on your system, such as enlightenment, sawfish, or kwin. These window managers create a look and feel that is very similar to Microsoft Windows and the Mac OS, making it easy for your users to transition over to Linux.

- **Desktop environment**   Leverages the look and feel created by the window manager and adds a series of tools and utilities that make the GUI truly useful. Basically, it ties all of your GUI components together into a cohesive environment. The desktop environment is optional but highly recommended. As with X server and window managers, the desktop environment is modular. You can try out the available environments and choose the one you like best. Two desktop environments are predominantly used with Linux systems today:

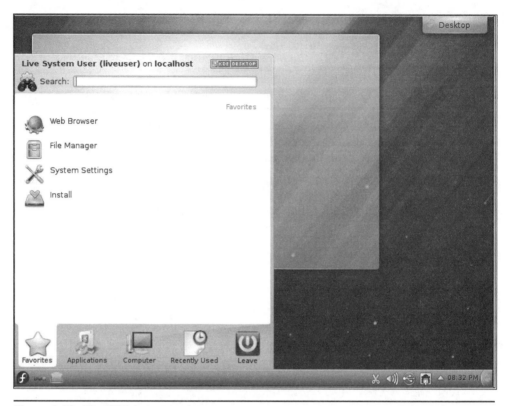

Figure 2-10 The KDE desktop environment

- **KDE** An excellent desktop environment that provides functionality very similar to Microsoft Windows. KDE is the default environment on many distributions. An example of the KDE desktop running on a Fedora system is shown in Figure 2-10.

- **GNOME** Another excellent desktop environment, GNOME also provides a look and feel that is reminiscent of Microsoft Windows. GNOME is the default environment used on distributions such as OpenSUSE. An example of the GNOME desktop running on an OpenSUSEsystem is shown in Figure 2-11.

These three components—the X server software, the window manager, and the desktop environment—all work hand in hand to create the GUI environment on a Linux system. You can mix and match between these three different components to customize the system to match your particular tastes and preferences.

Graphical Environment Configuration Settings

Next, let's look at how to configure the graphical environment on a Linux system. Because the X server works directly with your video board and monitor, configuring it is the most critical of all your GUI management tasks. It's imperative that you use the

Figure 2-11   The GNOME desktop environment

correct settings in your configuration. If you proceed incorrectly, you could potentially damage your monitor.

I know this because it happened to me once. I configured my system to use a sync rate that was too fast for an older CRT monitor I was using. It worked okay for a couple of weeks. However, one evening my monitor started hissing, sparking, and smoking. I pushed it too fast for too long and burned it up. Always check your video board and monitor documentation to obtain the correct specs!

Before you begin, you should pull out your video board and monitor documentation and identify the following information:

- Who's the manufacturer of the video board?
- What model number is the video board?
- How much memory is installed on the video board?
- What chipset is installed on the board?
- If you're using an older CRT monitor, what's the maximum horizontal and vertical sync rate supported by your monitor?
- If you're using an LCD or LED monitor, what is its native resolution?
  - With this information in hand, you need to check the HCL for your distribution and make sure your video board and monitor are supported. Trust me, having this information in hand before you begin will save you a lot of trouble. Be warned, however, that you will often find that newer video boards are not listed in the HCL. Does this mean it's not supported and won't work? Maybe, maybe not. Here's what you can do:
  - See if an older driver will support your newer video board until a newer driver is released. Most X server implementations will include a set of generic

drivers that support most video boards at some level. It won't look great, but you can at least get your system up and running.

- Check the video board manufacturer's web site and see if they have released a driver for their board that isn't included with your X server implementation.

Once you have gathered this information, you're ready to start configuring your X server. Just like everything else Linux, your X configuration is stored in a text file in the /etc directory.

 NOTE A good Linux axiom to remember: "Everything in Linux is a file." All of your system and service configurations are stored in files. You even access hardware devices through a file.

If you're using X.org, your configuration settings are saved in /etc/X11/xorg.conf. If you're using XFree86, your configuration settings are saved in /etc/X11/XF86Config.

As with most Linux services, your X server configuration file can be modified with a simple text editor. However, I strongly suggest that you *do not* do this unless absolutely necessary. This configuration file is complex, and a simple mistake can damage your hardware. You should instead use the configuration utility that came with your distribution to configure your graphical environment settings. For example, on OpenSUSE systems, you can use the Monitor Preferences applet, shown in Figure 2-12.

This applet allows you to configure your screen resolution and refresh rate. On some distributions, you can also run the sax2 command from the shell prompt. This provides you with a very handy interface that you can use to configure just about every aspect of

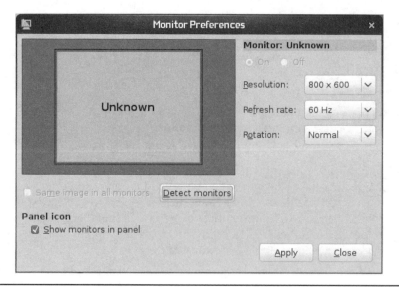

Figure 2-12 The Monitor Preference applet

your video subsystem. If you run SaX2 from within a graphical environment, the interface shown in Figure 2-13 is displayed.

You can use the SaX2 utility to configure your system's video adapter, monitor, resolution, and color depth. One of the things I like about SaX2 is that you can run it from a text-only environment (such as when your video settings are so messed up that you have to boot into runlevel 3 just to get the system running). If SaX2 can't get your graphical environment running due to a misconfiguration, it will load its own generic X server, probe your video subsystem, and automatically generate a proposed set of settings.

Other distributions, such as Fedora, use other utilities to commands to configure the X server system. Here is a sampling of utilities:

- **system-config-display**   Runs the Display Settings utility, which allows you to configure your video board, monitor type, resolution, and color depth.

- **system-config-keyboard**   Runs the Keyboard utility, which allows you to select your keyboard layout.

- **system-config-mouse**   Runs the Mouse utility, which allows you to configure your mouse.

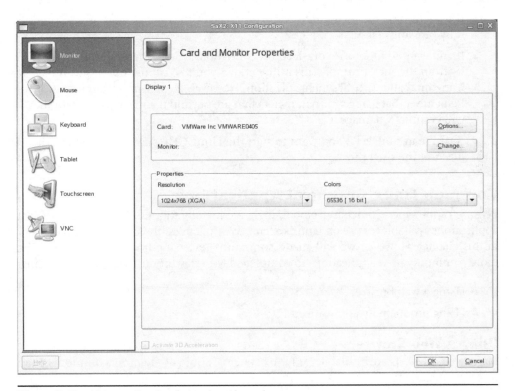

Figure 2-13   Using sax2 to configure the video subsystem

If your distribution still uses the XFree86 X server, you can use the following utilities to accomplish the same tasks:

- **XFree-86 –configure**   Detects your hardware and creates a file named /etc/X11/ XF86Config.new that you can rename to XF86Config.
- **xf86config**   A text-based X server configuration utility.
- **xf86cfg**   A graphical X server configuration utility.

After making any changes to your X server configuration, keep the following in mind:

- The configuration utility will prompt you to test the new settings to make sure they work. You should always do this. It will save a ton of time if you've made a mistake somewhere in the configuration.
- After testing the configuration, you must restart your X server to apply the changes. The easiest way to do this is to simply log out and then log back in. Rebooting the system will also accomplish the same task. You can also restart the desktop environment by switching to your init directory and restarting the desktop manager with its init script (such as xdm).
- If something is misconfigured and your X server software gets hung, you can kill it by pressing CTRL-ALT-BACKSPACE.
- If you want to fine-tune your X server configuration, run the xvidtune utility from the shell prompt. This utility allows you to customize your monitor's horizontal and vertical synchronization. However, do so with extreme caution. Remember that using sync parameters that are beyond the monitor's capabilities will eventually damage it.
- If you're in runlevel 3 and want to start the Linux GUI, simply enter **startx** or just **X** at the shell prompt.

Common Linux Graphical Applications

Because of the Open Source movement, there are literally thousands of free or low-cost applications available for use on Linux systems. We can't possibly cover a fraction of them in this chapter. However, we will spend some time reviewing how to use some of the more commonly used applications to complete day-to-day productivity tasks, including:

- Using a web browser
- Using productivity applications

Using a Web Browser

Many web browsers are available for Linux systems. Some of the more commonly used browsers include the following:

- **Firefox**   Probably the most popular web browser and frequently the default browser used by many Linux distributions.

- **Konqueror**   The default KDE web browser, very widely used on Linux systems. Konqueror includes web browsing, file management, and document viewing functionality.

- **Chromium**   The Linux version of the Google Chrome web browser.

- **Opera**   Another popular Linux web browser.

- **Epiphany**   A minimalistic browser that provides basic Web browsing functionality.

To launch a web browser, click its shortcut on your system's startup menu in the graphical environment. Once the browser starts, enter the URL you want to visit in the browser's location or URL field. An example of using the Firefox browser to access www.google.com is shown in Figure 2-14.

Figure 2-14   Using Firefox

When using a browser such as Firefox to access Web sites in the wilds of the Internet, you need to pay special attention to security and privacy issues. Some of the most important issues include the following:

- **Disable pop-ups** Pop-ups are bad because they can covertly install malware on your computer or redirect you to a dubious web site if you click the links contained in the pop-up. (Pop-ups are also very annoying.) Be aware, however, that some legitimate sites and web applications require pop-ups. Enable pop-ups only for legitimate sites that absolutely need them. In Firefox, you can disable pop-ups by selecting Edit | Preferences | Content and marking Block Popup Windows.

- **Enable automatic updates on your system** Most Linux distributions provide an update mechanism that you can use to keep your system up to date.

- **Stay abreast of current security trends** A good way to do this is to subscribe to security alerts that are offered by most antimalware software vendors. These alerts can let you know what to look for to identify exploits and infections.

- **Educate yourself about good security practices** I mentioned a few of these practices earlier in this chapter, such as using strong passwords. You should also:

  - **Distrust anything coming from the web** Don't click something just because the site says you must do so.

  - **View all e-mail with suspicion** No reputable company will send an e-mail asking for personal information.

- Be on the look-out for browser-based threats, such as:

  - **Redirection to rogue web sites** Designed to look like commonly used legitimate sites, the goal of these sites is to trick you into supplying personal information. Check URLs to verify that they aren't redirecting you somewhere you don't want to go.

  - **Pharming attacks** These redirect one web site's traffic to a different, bogus web site that is loaded with exploits. These attacks are conducted either by changing the hosts file on your local computer or by manipulating a vulnerability in DNS software to "poison" the server. This exploit can also be carried out by reconfiguring DHCP servers to send the wrong DNS server address to clients. Any of these exploits changes the name resolution mechanism such that legitimate hostnames are resolved to malicious IP addresses.

- **Watch out for rogue antivirus exploits** This exploit is becoming more and more common. Malicious web sites display a message indicating your computer is infected with malware. To clean it off, you must click a link on the site. At best, you pay for junk antimalware software you don't need. At worst, you unknowingly download a truckload of nasty malware.

- **Carefully manage your browser cookies** Cookies are small files that are sent by the web server to the web browser and are stored on the client system. They are primarily used to allow the web server to keep track of the individual user across multiple sessions. A good example is an e-commerce shopping cart: when you add an item to your cart, it is typically saved in a cookie. By default, cookies can only be retrieved by the server that set them. However, some exploits can steal cookies from your system. The goal is to grab information that could be used to allow the attacker to hijack a session and impersonate you. For example, if an attacker can steal a cookie from an e-commerce web site, they could gain unauthorized access to your account on that site and use it to purchase stuff for themselves at your expense.

- **Carefully guard your browser history and the browser cache** As you visit web sites, the browser saves these web pages in its cache and browser history. If an attacker gains access to the cache or browser history, personal information can be gleaned that can be used in other exploits. For example, if the attacker can learn which financial web sites you use, they'll know what cookies to look for.

Using Productivity Applications

In addition to web browsers, there are also many different productivity applications available for Linux; one of the most popular is Apache OpenOffice (or its derivative, LibreOffice). Both are full productivity suites designed to provide the same functionality provided by Microsoft Office, as shown in Figure 2-15.

Figure 2-15 Using LibreOffice

Both of these suites includes the following applications:

- **Base**   A powerful database application, comparable to Microsoft Access. You can use this application to create a database that manages large quantities of information.

- **Calc**   A full-function spreadsheet application, comparable to Microsoft Excel. You can create a new spreadsheet by launching it and then selecting File | New | Spreadsheet.

- **Impress**   A very useful presentation application, comparable to Microsoft PowerPoint. You can create a new presentation by launching Impress and then selecting File | New | Presentation.

- **Writer**   A full-function word processor, comparable to Microsoft Word. You can create a new document by launching Writer and then selecting File | New | Document. An example of a Writer document is shown in Figure 2-16.

A full discussion of how to use all of the features and functions of OpenOffice/LibreOffice is beyond the scope of this book. There are a host of tutorials and examples available on the Internet to help you learn how to use these applications.

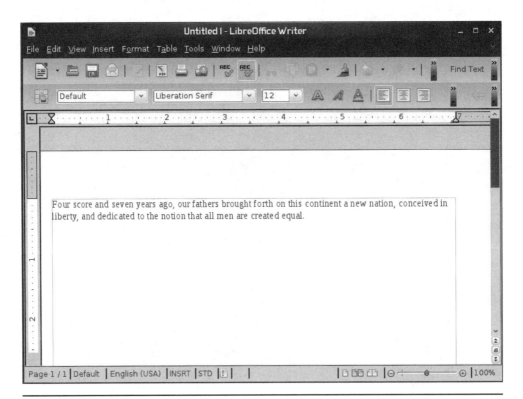

Figure 2-16   Using Writer to edit a document

Using the Linux Command Line Environment

At this point, we need to shift gears and discuss the command-line interface (CLI) in Linux. I will only briefly introduce you to the CLI in this chapter. We will spend all of Chapter 5 of this book learning how to use the CLI in depth.

When using the command-line interface, you interact with the operating system by entering commands at a shell prompt using your keyboard. An example of the Linux CLI is shown in Figure 2-17.

As mentioned earlier in this chapter, you can switch your system into runlevel 3, which is a completely text-based computing environment. In this configuration, the only way you can interact with the Linux operating system is through the command-line environment. You can also run terminal sessions within the Linux GUI by running a terminal program such as Konsole or GNOME Terminal. When you do, you should see a window displayed similar to that shown in Figure 2-17.

Running a program or command from the command-line environment is relatively easy. You simply type the command, script filename, or program filename at the shell prompt and press ENTER. However, there are some unique features to the Linux CLI environment that you should keep in mind. Key among these is that Linux commands, filenames, and directory names are case-sensitive. If the executable file you are going to run is named update.sh, then you must enter **update.sh** at the shell prompt. Entering Update.sh, UPDATE.SH, or Update.SH won't work. The shell sees each of those names as completely different files.

This rule applies to directory names as well. For example, if you're need to access the /var/log directory, then you must enter the directory using the exact case; for example, /Var/LOG points to a completely different place in the file system.

Figure 2-17   Using the CLI

Chapter Review

In this chapter, you learned how to get around in Linux. We first discussed how to boot the system. We looked at the GRUB boot menu that is usually displayed by default on most distributions that allows you to select which operating system you want to boot. The boot menu is managed by the GRUB or GRUB2 bootloader on most Linux distributions.

We then discussed the process for authenticating to the system. We reviewed how to log in from within the graphical user environment as well as from the text-based environment, and we discussed the importance of using strong passwords to protect the system.

We also emphasized the importance of protecting private information on the system. We also reviewed how to properly shut down a Linux system.

We then discussed how to configure the graphical user environment on your Linux system. We pointed out that the Linux graphical environment is composed of the following components:

- X server
- Window manager
- Desktop environment

Each of these components is modular. You can choose from a variety of packages to customize your graphical environment to suit your tastes.

We next looked at the process of configuring your graphical environment and noted that it's imperative to use the correct settings in your configuration. If you don't, you could potentially damage your monitor.

Just like everything else Linux, your X configuration is stored in a text file in the /etc directory. If you're using X.org, your configuration settings are saved in /etc/X11/xorg.conf. If you're using XFree86, your configuration settings are saved in /etc/X11/XF86Config.

We pointed out that you should avoid directly editing your X server configuration file. Instead, you should use a configuration utility to avoid mistakes that could potentially damage your hardware. Depending on your distribution, you can use one of the following utilities:

- YaST
- SaX2
- system-config-display
- system-config-keyboard
- system-config-mouse
- Xorg –configure
- XFree-86 –configure
- xf86config or xf86cfg
- xvidtune

We then shifted gears and reviewed some common Linux applications that are used within the graphical environment. Some of the more commonly used web browsers include the following:

- Firefox
- Konqueror
- Chromium
- Opera
- Epiphany

We discussed privacy and security issues you should be aware of when using a web browser on a Linux system and reviewed actions you should take to help ensure your security:

- Disable pop-ups.
- Enable automatic updates on your system.
- Stay abreast of current security trends.
- Educate yourself about good security practices.
- Be on the look-out for browser-based threats, such as:
  - Redirection to rogue web sites
  - Pharming attacks
- Watch out for rogue antivirus exploits.
- Carefully manage your browser cookies.
- Carefully guard your browser history and the browser cache.

We also reviewed how to create documents within the graphical environment on a Linux system. There are many different productivity applications available, but some of the more popular include OpenOffice.org and LibreOffice. Both are full productivity suites designed to provide the same functionality as Microsoft Office. Both of these suites include the following applications:

- Base
- Calc
- Impress
- Writer

We ended this chapter by introducing you to the command-line interface used with Linux. In the command-line interface, you interact with the operating system by entering commands at a shell prompt using your keyboard. To run a program or command from the command line, type the command, script filename, or program filename at the shell prompt and press ENTER. When working at the command line, keep in mind that Linux commands, filenames, and directory names are case-sensitive.

Accelerated Review

- The GRUB boot menu is usually displayed by default on most distributions.
- You use the boot menu to select which operating system you want to boot.
- You can customize the behavior and appearance of the boot menu by editing the /etc/grub.conf file or the /boot/grub/grub.conf file.
- You must authenticate before you can start using a Linux system.

- Authentication is the process of providing credentials to the system.
- You can log into a Linux system from either the graphical user interface or from the command-line environment.
- To log in, enter your username and then enter the appropriate password.
- Linux user accounts are typically stored in the /etc/passwd file.
- You should use strong passwords that:
  - Have eight or more characters
  - Include numbers and/or symbols as well as letters
  - Include upper- and lowercase characters.
- You should protect private information on a Linux system by doing the following:
  - Use screensaver passwords.
  - Don't allow users to write passwords down.
  - Train users how to handle social engineering exploits.
  - Keeps systems in a secure area.
  - Lock down sensitive systems with cable locks.
  - Use screen filters.
- You should properly shut down a Linux system using one of the following commands:
  - init 0
  - init 6
  - halt
  - reboot
  - shutdown
- The Linux graphical environment is composed of the following components:
  - X server
  - Window manager
  - Desktop environment
- Two different X server software packages have been implemented on Linux systems:
  - X.org-X11
  - XFree86
- Some of the more popular window managers include the following:
  - enlightenment
  - fvwm
  - kwin

- sawfish
- twm
- wmaker
- Two desktop environments are predominantly used with Linux systems today:
  - KDE
  - GNOME
- Before implementing a video board/monitor combination with Linux, you need to check the HCL for your distribution and make sure your video board and monitor are supported.
- Your X configuration is stored in a text file in the /etc directory:
  - XFree86: /etc/X11/XF86Config
  - X.org: /etc/X11/xorg.conf
- You should use a configuration utility to configure your X server software and avoid mistakes that could potentially damage your hardware.
- You can use one of the following utilities to configure your X server software:
  - YaST
  - SaX2
  - system-config-display
  - system-config-keyboard
  - system-config-mouse
  - xorgconfig or xorgcfg
  - Xorg–configure
  - XFree-86–configure
  - xf86config or xf86cfg
  - xvidtune
- Some of the more commonly used Linux web browsers include the following:
  - Firefox
  - Konqueror
  - Chromium
  - Opera
  - Epiphany
- Be aware of privacy and security issues when using a web browser on a Linux system:
  - Disable pop-ups.
  - Enable automatic updates on your system.

- Stay abreast of current security trends.
- Educate yourself about good security practices.
- Be on the look-out for browser-based threats, such as:
  - Redirection to rogue web sites
  - Pharming attacks
- Watch out for rogue antivirus exploits.
- Carefully manage your browser cookies.
- Carefully guard your browser history and the browser cache.
- Some of the more popular productivity applications on Linux include OpenOffice.org and LibreOffice.
- OpenOffice.org and LibreOffice are full productivity suites designed to provide the same functionality provided by Microsoft Office.
- The OpenOffice.org and LibreOffice suites include the following applications:
  - Base
  - Calc
  - Impress
  - Writer
- When using the command-line interface, you interact with the operating system by entering commands at a shell prompt using your keyboard.
- To run a program or command from the command line, type the command, script filename, or program filename at the shell prompt and press ENTER.
- Linux commands, filenames, and directory names are case-sensitive.

Questions

1. Which files are used to configure the boot menu displayed by GRUB bootloader? (Choose two.)

   A. /etc/menu.lst

   B. /etc/grub.conf

   C. /boot/grub/grub.conf

   D. /boot/grub/menu.lst

2. Which command can be used to switch runlevels while the system is running?

   A. runlevel

   B. chrun

   C. mode

   D. init

3. Which of the following is an example of a strong password?

   A. skippy

   B. DogB3rt#

   C. N0v3ll

   D. mydogisthebest

4. Which commands will shut down and restart a Linux system? (Choose two.)

   A. init 0

   B. init 6

   C. halt

   D. reboot

5. Which of the following draws graphical windows on the display?

   A. KDE

   B. fvwm

   C. sawfish

   D. X.org

6. Your Linux system uses X.org as its X server. Which configuration file is used to configure this service?

   A. /etc/X11/XF86Config

   B. /etc/X11/x11.conf

   C. /etc/X11/XFree86.conf

   D. /etc/X11/xorg.conf

7. Which utility could you use on a Fedora Linux system to configure the X server?

   A. system-config-display

   B. xf86config

   C. YaST

   D. xf86cfg

8. You just clicked a link in a web advertisement for a banking web site. However, when you hover over links in the page, the domain name in the URLs doesn't match the bank's domain name. What kind of attack has occurred?

   A. None, the site is functioning as it should.

   B. Rogue antivirus.

   C. Stolen cookie.

   D. Web site redirection.

9. An attacker reconfigures an ISP's DHCP server to give out the wrong DNS server address, allowing her to redirect web requests to her own bogus web site. Which type of attack has occurred here?

    A. DHCP server poisoning

    B. Pharming

    C. Rogue antivirus

    D. Phishing

10. You need to create a slide show for a presentation to a potential client. Which application could you use to do this on your Linux system?

    A. PowerPoint

    B. Writer

    C. Impress

    D. Base

11. You need to view the contents of the /var/log directory on your Linux system, so you open a shell prompt and enter **ls /Var/Log**. An error is displayed indicating the directory doesn't exist. Why did this happen?

    A. You should have entered **ls /var/log**.

    B. You should have used the dir command instead of ls.

    C. You should have entered **LS /VAR/LOG**.

    D. You didn't do anything wrong. There's a bug in the software.

Answers

1. **B, D.** The /boot/grub/menu.lst and the /etc/grub.conf files are typically used to configure GRUB.

2. **D.** The init command can be used to switch runlevels while the system is running.

3. **B.** The DogB3rt# password is a strong password because it is eight characters long, uses upper- and lowercase letters, and uses numbers and symbols.

4. **B, D.** The init 6 and reboot commands can be used to restart a Linux system.

5. **D.** The X.org X server graphically draws windows on the display.

6. **D.** X.org uses the /etc/X11/xorg.conf configuration file.

7. **A.** The system-config-display utility can be used to configure X on a Fedora system.

8. **D.** A web site redirection attack has occurred, as indicated by the fact that the URLs on the site do not contain the correct domain name.

9. **B.** A pharming attack has occurred. The DNS server in this scenario is sending web clients to a malicious web site.

10. **C.** You can use Impress within OpenOffice or LibreOffice to create presentations.

11. **A.** Linux commands, directory names, and filenames are case sensitive. Therefore, you should have entered ls /var/log.

PC Hardware

In this chapter you will learn about:

- PC Hardware Components
- PC Peripherals
- Device Drivers

In order for you to work effectively with Linux systems, you need to have a solid understanding of PC hardware. While you don't have to have to be a PC guru, you do need to know how to complete tasks such as installing an expansion board in an expansion slot, configuring system memory, managing system storage devices, and managing peripheral devices.

You might be wondering why you need PC hardware knowledge to work effectively with Linux systems. This is because Linux expects a lot more from both the user and the system administrator. Other operating systems hide a lot of their functionality behind the scenes. Their philosophy can be summed up as, "Don't ask how it works; you don't need to know."

Linux, on the other hand, expects you to ask how the nuts and bolts of the system work. It was designed by geeks for geeks. As such, Linux provides you with an extensive set of tools to customize and configure the system. In essence, Linux provides you with the tools and the parts; it's up to you to put it all together to function the way you want.

Because Linux operates on this philosophy, it assumes that you, as the end user, understand how the underlying system works, including the hardware itself. Therefore, in this chapter, you'll learn how the hardware in a typical PC system works.

Let's begin by discussing the components found in a personal computer.

PC Hardware Components

Within a typical PC computer system, there are several key components that work together to process data:

- Power supplies
- Motherboards
- CPUs
- Memory

- Expansion slots
- Video adapters
- Expansion boards
- Storage devices
- Input/output devices

Power Supplies

One of the most important components in any PC system (and probably the most overlooked) is the power supply. This is because the various components inside a PC perform their various functions using direct current (DC). However, the wall outlet that you plug the PC system into uses alternating current (AC). For the system to run, the AC current from the wall must be converted into DC current that the system components can use.

That's the job of the power supply. It converts 110-volt AC current from your wall outlet into DC current. Without a good power supply, nothing else in the system works. The power supply in a PC system is kind of like the battery and tires on your car. Batteries and tires aren't glamorous. In fact, they are downright boring. However, nothing will stop your car faster than a bad battery or a bad tire. The same principle holds with power supplies. A bad power supply results in a dead system.

A typical power supply is shown in Figure 3-1.

Figure 3-1 A PC power supply

In Figure 3-1, you can see that there is a black socket into which you plug a standard electrical cord that plugs into a wall outlet. This is the AC side of the power supply. The back of the power supply has a series of wires and plugs that carry DC current to the various components in the PC system.

 TIP Never open a power supply to work on it. You will be exposed to 110-volt AC wall current that could kill you!

The various components inside your PC need different voltage levels of DC current. In most modern systems, the power supply provides three different voltages:

- 3.3 volts
- 5 volts
- 12 volts

However, not all power supplies are created equal. Power supplies are manufactured to provide a variety of wattages, ranging from 200 watts on the low end to 600 or more watts on the high end. Simply put, the more wattage a power supply offers, the more components inside the PC it can deliver power to at the same time.

 TIP The power supply has one special wire that plugs into your motherboard called the POWER_GOOD wire. If, at any time, the power supply fails to supply the appropriate level of voltage on this wire, the motherboard will immediately shut off.

Power supplies have one other key job: they are responsible for helping to cool the system. Notice in Figure 3-1 that the power supply includes a built-in fan. This fan is responsible for cooling all of the components running inside the system. This is a very important job. A PC system generates a great deal of heat. Without some way to dissipate all that heat, the components within the computer would quickly degrade and eventually fail. As you can see, the power supply is a very important part of the PC!

Motherboards

The motherboard is really the heart of the PC system. Its job is to create electrical pathways that connect everything together. A typical motherboard is shown in Figure 3-2.

The motherboard connects the CPU with the system RAM. It also connects the CPU and the RAM with the expansion slots and provides connectors that allow you to connect peripheral devices (such as keyboards, mice, printers, and external storage devices).

In additional to these tasks, the motherboard also contains an important chip called the BIOS. The BIOS contains a series of very small programs that allow the system to function. For example, have you ever wondered how the system knows what letter you've pressed on the keyboard? The BIOS provides the software that allows the keyboard to send data to the CPU.

Figure 3-2 A typical PC motherboard

The BIOS has many parameters you can configure by accessing the CMOS Setup program. When you boot most PC systems, you will see a message stating something to the effect of "Press F1 to Enter Setup."

 TIP The actual keystroke used to access the CMOS Setup program varies from system to system. Some commonly used keystrokes are F1, F2, and DEL.

When you press the key indicated, the CMOS Setup program (one of the small programs that resides within the BIOS) is run, allowing you to configure various system parameters. A typical CMOS setup program is shown in Figure 3-3.

You can use the CMOS setup program to configure system parameters such as:

- The system date and time
- The type of floppy drive installed in the system (if the system still uses one)

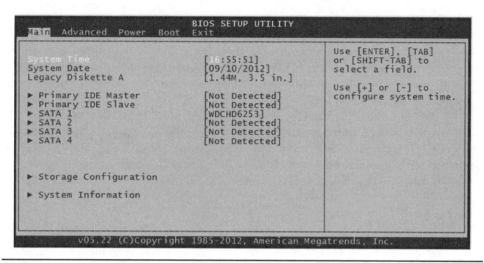

```
                         BIOS SETUP UTILITY
 Main   Advanced  Power   Boot   Exit

  System Time                [16:55:51]          Use [ENTER], [TAB]
  System Date                [09/10/2012]        or [SHIFT-TAB] to
  Legacy Diskette A          [1.44M, 3.5 in.]    select a field.

  ▶ Primary IDE Master       [Not Detected]      Use [+] or [-] to
  ▶ Primary IDE Slave        [Not Detected]      configure system time.
  ▶ SATA 1                   [WDCHD6253]
  ▶ SATA 2                   [Not Detected]
  ▶ SATA 3                   [Not Detected]
  ▶ SATA 4                   [Not Detected]


  ▶ Storage Configuration

  ▶ System Information



        v05.22 (C)Copyright 1985-2012, American Megatrends, Inc.
```

Figure 3-3 The CMOS setup program

- The type of hard drive(s) installed in the system
- Power management features of the motherboard
- The order of boot devices in the system

The motherboard also includes a socket into which you can insert the system CPU.

CPUs

If the motherboard is the heart of a PC, then the central processing unit (CPU) is the brains of the system. The motherboard itself doesn't have any intelligence; it simply provides the pathways necessary for data to get from one part of the system to another. The intelligent part of the PC is the CPU.

TIP You may hear the CPU referred to by a variety of names, including logic chip, processor, or microprocessor.

The CPU is an integrated circuit built on a slice of silicon. A typical CPU is shown in Figure 3-4.

Figure 3-4
The CPU

Have you ever wondered how a PC can calculate a spreadsheet or render a 3-D game on the screen? It's all done with electricity. The CPU contains millions of transistors connected by hairline traces of aluminum. These transistors work together to store and manipulate data. By manipulating the electrical charges in these transistors, the CPU can perform arithmetic and logical operations. To do this, each CPU has sets of instructions designed into the processor itself.

Over the years, the CPUs used by computers have evolved from relatively slow CPUs in the original IBM PC to the speed demons we use today. Two primary manufacturers produce CPUs today: Intel and Advanced Micro Devices (AMD). The main families of CPUs that are currently produced by Intel include the following:

- Pentium 4
- Core 2
- Pentium Dual Core
- Celeron
- Celeron M
- Core i3 (1st and 2nd Generation)
- Core i5 (1st and 2nd Generation)
- Core i7 (1st and 2nd Generation)
- Xeon (1st and 2nd Generation)

 NOTE Celeron CPUs are scaled-down versions of the Intel Pentium CPU. When the first Pentiums came out, they were priced beyond the reach of many home users. To capture this market, Intel took the standard Pentium CPU and reduced the amount of Level 2 cache installed, reducing production costs and making them more affordable. Celeron CPUs typically have reduced performance compared to a standard Pentium CPU of the same clock speed. In addition, 1st Generation Intel processors are built on the Nehalem architecture while 2nd Generation Intel processors are built on the Sandy Bridge architecture.

CPUs produced by AMD include the following:

- Opteron
- Phenom FX
- Phenom X4
- Phenom X3
- Athlon 6-series
- Athlon 4-series
- Athlon X2
- Sempron

- Phenom II
- Athlon II
- Turion II

When working with CPUs, there are a variety of factors you need to be aware of:

- **Socket**   Motherboards provide a socket that the CPU fits into. Different CPUs have different physical dimensions and must, therefore, use different types of sockets to connect to the motherboard. A variety of socket sizes and shapes have been used over the years, including the following:

  - LGA 775
  - Socket M
  - Socket 441
  - Socket AM2/AM2+/AM3/AM3+
  - LGA 1366
  - LGA 1156

A motherboard connector for an AMD CPU is shown in Figure 3-5.

Figure 3-5   An AMD CPU socket

- **Speed**   All motherboards use a clock, but this clock isn't the system clock you're probably familiar with. Instead, the motherboard clock is an oscillator that generates a certain number of electrical pulses every second. These pulses set the tempo for the CPU and are measured in megahertz (MHz) or millions of pulses per second. The number of pulses per second is determined by a quartz crystal and is referred to as the clock speed.

  Older CPUs ran at the speed of the motherboard clock. However, newer CPUs use a function called a multiplier to run at a clock speed that is a multiple of the motherboard clock speed.

- **Cache**   In addition to speed, you also need to be concerned with cache. Most CPUs have their own memory built into the CPU itself called cache RAM. This isn't the same memory as your system RAM. Instead, cache is made of static RAM, which is much faster than regular system RAM. The CPU can store frequently needed data in its cache, which dramatically increases system performance. There are three types of cache you should be aware of:

  - **Level 1 (L1)**   L1 cache is a small SRAM chip built into the CPU. The CPU loads upcoming program code into the L1 cache. Instead of stopping and waiting for a time-consuming task to be completed, such as writing data to disk, the CPU can keep processing code from the L1 cache. The L1 cache is typically very small and very fast.

  - **Level 2 (L2)**   Adding L1 cache to the CPU dramatically increases its performance, so why not add even more? Most modern systems have additional SRAM cache incorporated into a chip on the motherboard to further increase performance. Some processors include the L2 cache directly in the CPU package itself, just like L1 cache. The L2 cache is usually larger than the L1 cache but slightly slower.

  - **Level 3 (L3)**   Many systems include even more cache memory on the motherboard called L3 cache. The L3 cache is usually much larger than L1 and L2 but considerably slower.

    The more cache a CPU has, the faster it runs, even if the clock speed isn't increased. In fact, many high-end CPUs designed for servers (such as Intel's Xeon CPU) incorporate huge amounts of cache.

    If the needed information isn't found in a given level of cache, the CPU looks to the next level of cache to find it. For example, if the information isn't present in the L1 cache, the CPU checks the L2 cache. If it isn't there, then the CPU will check the L3 cache.

The important point to understand is that to install a CPU in a motherboard, you must ensure that it uses the correct socket and the correct speed. If it doesn't, it won't work. (It may even start to smoke!)

System Memory

If you've worked with computers, you're probably already familiar with the concept of Random Access Memory (RAM). No matter how much RAM we install in any PC system, it never seems to be enough. Let's spend some time discussing what RAM is and how it works.

RAM is the place in a computer where programs and data currently in use on the system are stored. RAM is very fast. Information in RAM can be accessed very quickly because the CPU can directly access data in any memory location at any time. This makes it an ideal storage device for data that needs to be manipulated by the CPU.

For example, suppose you need to create a word processing document. The first thing you do is open your word-processing application. When you do, the program code for the application is loaded from your hard disk drive into RAM. When you open a word processing file in the application, the data you are working on is also loaded into RAM.

This brings up a very important point that you are probably already painfully aware of: RAM is nonpersistent. The programs and data in RAM stay there only as long as your computer is running. This is because system RAM is made up of a type of memory called Dynamic RAM (DRAM), which must be constantly refreshed every few milliseconds with electrical current. If this doesn't happen, the programs and data in RAM disappear! When you shut down your computer system, your system RAM is no longer refreshed and, hence, all the data is gone. That's why you always (at least, I hope so!) save your files to the hard drive before shutting down. When you power the system back on again, the programs and data you were working on must be reloaded into RAM again from persistent storage on the hard drive.

DRAM stores data one bit at a time in a storage cell. Each storage cell is composed of a capacitor and a transistor. The transistor regulates current or voltage flow and acts as a switch or gate for electronic signals. The capacitor stores an electrical charge. The absence or presence of a charge in the capacitor can be used by the system to represent binary data (a 0 or a 1). These capacitors lose their charge rather quickly and must be constantly recharged (or refreshed) every few milliseconds.

DRAM, in modern PCs, is implemented as a series of DRAM chips soldered to an interface board called a memory module. A typical memory module is shown in Figure 3-6.

Figure 3-6   A memory module

There are several types of memory commonly used in PC systems, all of which can be categorized by the RAM technology and the package type used.

RAM Technologies

Over the years, memory sticks have been manufactured using a variety of technologies. Some of the more common technologies include the following:

- **Synchronous Dynamic RAM (SDRAM)**   SDRAM was introduced in late 1996 as an entirely new type of memory module designed to accommodate faster CPUs and motherboards. SDRAM implements a clock on each memory module that it uses to synchronize the memory module with the motherboard clock and the CPU. The important point to remember when working with SDRAM is that you must use memory modules whose clock speed is exactly the same as the clock speed of the motherboard. For example:

  - 66 MHz bus requires PC66 SDRAM

  - 100 MHz bus requires PC100 SDRAM

  - 133 MHz bus requires PC133 SDRAM

- **Double-Data Rate Synchronous DRAM (DDR-SDRAM)**   DDR-SDRAM is similar to SDRAM; however, it runs two processes for every clock cycle. This effectively doubles your memory throughput. Like SDRAM, you must use the correct clock speed on your memory module for the motherboard clock and CPU you're using in the system. The following are common speed designations:

  - PC-1600: 100 MHz

  - PC-2100: 133 MHz

  - PC-2700: 166 MHz

  - PC-3200: 200 MHz

- **DDR2-SDRAM**   DDR2-SDRAM is an improved version of DDR-SDRAM. The key advantage of DDR2-SDRAM is that its supports higher clock speeds used in more modern motherboards. As with all other types of SDRAM, you must use the correct speed module for your particular motherboard. The following are DDR2-SDRAM speed designations:

  - PC2-4200: 266 MHz

  - PC2-5300: 333 MHz

  - PC2-6400: 400 MHz

- **DDR3-SDRAM**   DDR3-SDRAM is an improved version of DDR2-SDRAM. It transfers data at twice the rate of DDR2 memory. It also uses significantly less power than DDR2 memory. The following are DDR3-SDRAM speed designations:

  - PC3-6400: 800 MHz

  - PC3-8500: 1066 MHz

  - PC3-10600: 1333 MHz

You also need to be aware of the multichannel memory architecture used by most motherboards today. Multichannel memory increases data throughput by using multiple communication channels. It does this by treating multiple memory modules installed in the motherboard as if they were one big memory module. Because multiple data paths are used, data can be transferred in and out of RAM at a much faster rate than single-channel memory.

Two multichannel memory architectures are commonly used:

- **Dual channel**   Dual channel memory uses two 64-bit communication channels simultaneously. To enable dual channel memory, you must install two or four memory modules at a time in the motherboard, and they must be installed in the correct memory slots. Most motherboards have color-coded memory slots to help you identify which slots need to be populated to enable dual-channel functionality.

- **Triple channel**   Triple channel memory works in much the same manner as dual channel except that it uses three 64-bit communication channels at a time instead of two. Accordingly, memory modules must be installed three or six at a time in the correct slots in the motherboard. Again, most motherboards have color-coded memory slots to help you identify which slots need to be populated to enable triple-channel functionality.

Memory Module Packages

Memory modules have been manufactured in a variety of different packages over the years. Some of the more common types include the following:

- **168-Pin DIMMs**   DIMM stands for Dual Inline Memory Module. DIMMs are used with SDRAM. It uses two sets of memory chips, one on each side of the module, 64 bits (8 bytes) wide. Because most of the motherboards that use DIMMs use a 64-bit data bus, you usually don't have to worry about banking issues. You can install one DIMM at a time in most systems.

- **184-Pin DIMM**   A 184-pin DIMM is very similar to a 168-pin DIMM. The key differences are the number of pins and that 184-pin DIMMs are used with DDR-SDRAM.

- **240-Pin DIMM**   240-pin DIMMs are used with DDR2-SDRAM and DDR3-SDRAM.

 NOTE   Even though DDR2 and DDR3 modules both use a 240-pin package, they are electrically incompatible and therefore not interchangeable.

Expansion Slots

One of the most revolutionary ideas introduced by the IBM PC was that it was a modular computer system. Early computer systems built in the 1950s and 1960s were custom manufactured for a specific purpose. These computers were very expensive and not very flexible. You couldn't add or remove parts to modify or upgrade the functionality of the system.

IBM changed all that when they designed the original IBM PC to be modular. For the first time, you could purchase a basic PC system and then install additional components to add the functionality you needed.

To make this possible, IBM designed their original PC motherboards with an extension to the data bus called the expansion (or I/O) bus. The expansion bus allowed you to install expansion boards in expansion slots and have these devices be able to communicate with other critical system components, including the system memory, the CPU, and other expansion boards. Today, all PC motherboards use an expansion bus. In fact, most include several different types of expansion buses.

Over the years, a variety of different types of expansion buses have been implemented in personal computer systems. We'll discuss the following:

- The PCI bus
- The PCI Express bus
- Working with system resources

The PCI Bus

In the mid-1990s, a new type of expansion bus was introduced for personal computers that far outclassed older expansion buses used in early PCs: the Peripheral Component Interconnect (PCI) bus. PCI was designed and developed by an industry group called PCI-SIG. Most of the motherboards you will work with for the foreseeable future will have a PCI bus implemented. Typical PCI expansion slots are shown in Figure 3-7.

A PCI expansion board is shown in Figure 3-8.

The PCI bus offers some distinct advantages over the older buses it replaced that make it indispensable to us today. First of all, the PCI bus is relatively fast: it's 32 bits wide and runs at 33 MHz. This allows it to transfer data at a rate around 66 MBps. Some versions of PCI, used primarily in servers, are 64-bits wide and can run at 66 MHz.

In addition, PCI implements a new bus that resides between the data bus and the I/O bus on your motherboard. This new bus is called the local bus or the mezzanine bus. To do this, PCI uses a new type of chipset on the motherboard that is composed of two parts:

- **Northbridge** The Northbridge chip controls and manages the PCI expansion bus. Its job is to manage the devices installed in your PCI expansion slots and connect them to the CPU, the system memory, and other PCI expansion cards.

- **Southbridge** The Southbridge chip, sometimes referred to as the PCI bridge, acts as an intermediary between the PCI bus and other expansion buses on the motherboard. The Southbridge allows the PCI bus to function independently of the CPU and to co-exist with other expansion buses.

These features are all pretty cool. However, the best thing about the PCI bus is that PCI cards are self-configuring. You can simply plug a PCI board into an expansion slot and let the motherboard BIOS, the operating system, and the board itself negotiate and assign an interrupt, a port address range, and a DMA channel.

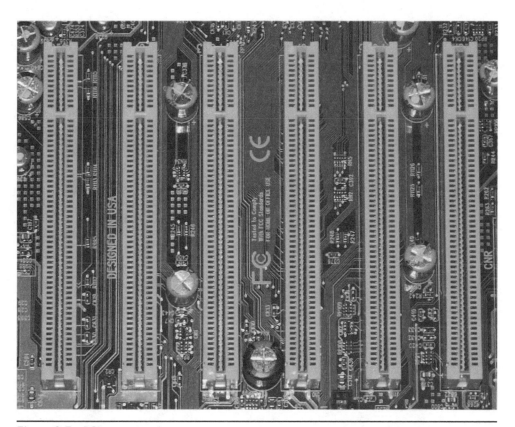

Figure 3-7 PCI expansion slots

NOTE   Not only can a PCI expansion board configure itself, but also multiple boards can share interrupts. We'll discuss this in more detail later in this chapter.

The PCI Express Bus

PCI Express (PCIe) is an updated version of the PCI bus that can transfer a lot of data very, very quickly. Most modern motherboards include both PCI and PCIe buses. PCIe is frequently used for high-throughput devices such as video boards.

A key difference between PCI and PCIe is that PCIe devices don't have to contend with each other to share the bandwidth available on the bus in the manner that PCI devices do. Instead, PCIe devices each have dedicated communication channels called transport lanes for data transmission and reception. The speed of each transport lane depends upon the PCIe version:

- PCIe version 1: 250 MBps
- PCIe version 2: 500 MBps

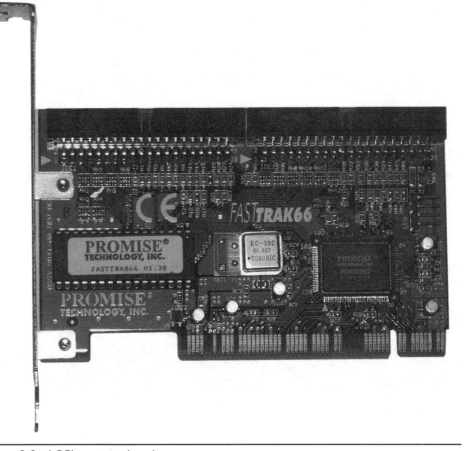

Figure 3-8 A PCI expansion board

- PCIe version 3: 1 GBps
- PCIe version 4: 2 GBps

Other key aspects of the PCIe bus that you should remember include:

- Some PCIe devices can be configured to use multiple transmission lanes, dramatically increasing the speed of the communication channel.
- Both PCIe and PCI buses can coexist in the same system. In fact, most modern motherboards include both PCIe and PCI expansion buses.
- PCIe buses are most commonly used for video cards in modern computer systems, although nearly any other device can be designed for a PCIe slot.

A PCI Express slot is shown in Figure 3-9.
A PCI Express video board is shown in Figure 3-10.

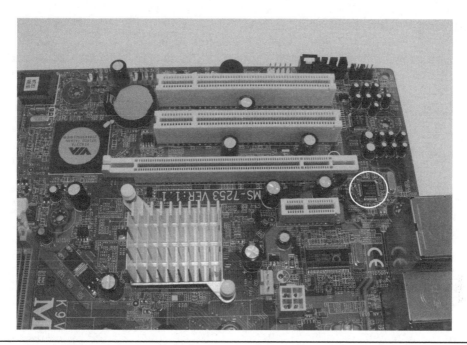

Figure 3-9 A PCI Express slot

Figure 3-10 A PCI Express expansion board

Working with System Resources

As we've discussed the various types of expansion buses, we've frequently mentioned the term *system resources*. Every device in a PC system has to be configured with a set of system resources that tell the device what communication channels and addresses it can use. To effectively manage a Linux system, you must have a solid understanding of what these system resources are and how they work. In this part of this chapter, we'll discuss the following:

- Interrupt request channels
- Input/output ports
- DMA channels
- Plug-n-play

Interrupt Request Channels   The first system resources you need to be familiar with are interrupt request channels, also referred to as "IRQs" or just "interrupts."

When a device is installed in a PC system, it needs some means of letting the CPU know when it needs attention. Many devices in your PC need lots of CPU time; other devices only need the CPU on occasion. With interrupts, the busy devices get the attention they need without wasting time on devices that don't need as much.

The CPU in your system has a wire on it called the interrupt (INT) wire. If current is applied to this wire, the CPU will stop what it is doing and service the device that placed current on the wire. If no current is present on the wire, the CPU will continue working on whatever processing task has been assigned to it.

The interrupt system in a PC is very similar to a typical classroom. In a classroom setting, the instructor usually presents the material she has prepared to the students. If a student has a question, he can raise his hand and interrupt the instructor's presentation. After the question is answered, the instructor resumes the presentation.

PC interrupts work in much the same manner. Like the instructor, the CPU goes about its business until it is interrupted. Once interrupted, the CPU diverts its attention to the device that raised the interrupt. When the device's request has been satisfied, the CPU goes back to what it was doing before.

The advantage to using interrupts is that the CPU only services system devices when they need it. It doesn't waste processing time on devices that are idle.

However, the scenario we've just discussed presents a problem. In a typical classroom, there are many students, not just one. Likewise, a PC system has many different devices that all need to get the CPU's attention from time to time. To allow many different devices to use that same INT wire, the system uses a programmable interrupt controller (PIC) chip.

The PIC chip has nine leads. One is connected to the INT wire on the CPU. The other eight are connected to interrupt wires in the motherboard's expansion slots. When a device in an expansion slot needs attention, it applies current to its interrupt wire. The PIC is alerted by this event and applies current to the CPU's INT wire. The CPU acknowledges the interrupt and the PIC tells the CPU which interrupt number was activated. The CPU can then service the device.

Early PCs had only 8 interrupts and a single PIC. However, modern PCs have 16 (or more) interrupts. To get the extra interrupts, multiple PIC chips are cascaded together. That is, the wire that would normally be connected to the CPU INT wire on one PIC is connected instead to the second interrupt wire on the first PIC chip (whose INT wire is connected to the CPU). The second interrupt wire on the second PIC, which should be numbered INT 9, is actually wired to INT 2 in the expansion slots. If you've ever heard someone say that INT 2 and INT 9 are the same interrupt, now you know why.

When working with interrupts, there are some important facts that you should keep in mind:

- Every device in the PC must be assigned an interrupt.

- Multiple PCI devices can share interrupts, but devices that use older expansion buses cannot.

- Because INT 2 and INT 9 are actually the same wire on the PIC chips, you assign either one to a device in the system, but you can't assign both at the same time.

- Some system devices have interrupts assigned to them by default. Some of these can be changed or disabled; some cannot:
  - IRQ 0   System timer
  - IRQ 1   Keyboard
  - IRQ 3   COM 2
  - IRQ 4   COM 1
  - IRQ 5   LPT 2
  - IRQ 6   Floppy drive
  - IRQ 7   LPT 1

- Interrupts 0, 1, and 8 are hard-wired. Under no circumstances can you use these interrupts for any other device in the system.

- If a device with a default interrupt assignment isn't installed in the system or is disabled, you can use its interrupt for another device.

Input/Output Addresses   Input/output (I/O) addresses go by a variety of names in a PC system, including I/O ports, port addresses, or simply ports.

I/O addresses allow communications between the devices in the PC and the operating system. I/O addresses are very similar to mailboxes. To send a letter to someone, you must know his or her mailing address. You write the address on the letter and the mail carrier delivers it to the box with that address. Likewise, the person you wrote to can respond to your letter and leave it in the mailbox for the mail carrier to pick up.

I/O addresses work in much the same manner. They serve as mailboxes for the devices installed in the system. Data can be left for a device in its I/O address. Data from the device can be left in the I/O address for the operating system to pick up.

I/O addresses are written in hexadecimal notation. The decimal numbering system that we use in our everyday work is a base-10 numbering system. When we count, we start at 0 and proceed to 9, and then we start over again at 10. Alternatively, hexadecimal is a base-16 numbering system. Like decimal numbers, hexadecimal starts at 0 and proceeds to 9. However, instead of starting over, hexadecimal continues on with six additional numbers represented by the letters A through F. Therefore, if you were to count in hex, you would say:

0, 1, 2, 3, 4, 5, 6, 7, 8, 9, A, B, C, D, E, F

Because hex and decimal numbers can sometimes be easily mistaken, we usually put a "0x" in front of or an "h" at the end of any hex number.

When working with I/O addresses, there are a number of important facts to keep in mind:

- All devices must have an I/O address assigned.

- Most devices will use a range of I/O addresses.

- Devices must use unique I/O ports.

A PC has 65,535 port addresses available for devices to use. The default I/O port assignments are as follows:

- **0000h** DMA controller
- **0020h** PIC 1
- **0030h** PIC 2
- **0040h** System timer
- **0060h** Keyboard
- **0070h** CMOS clock
- **00C0h** DMA controller
- **00F0h** Math coprocessor
- **0170h** Secondary IDE hard disk controller
- **01F0h** Primary IDE hard disk controller
- **0200h** Joystick
- **0278h** LPT2
- **02E8h** COM4
- **02F8h** COM2
- **0378h** LPT1
- **03E8h** COM3
- **03F0h** Floppy disk drive controller
- **03F8h** COM1

Direct Memory Access Channels   In addition to interrupts and I/O addresses, some devices also require that you configure it with a Direct Memory Access (DMA) channel. DMA channels are used by high-throughput devices to communicate directly with RAM without involving the CPU. Bypassing the CPU can dramatically increase the device's data transfer rate.

Not all devices need DMA. Other devices, however, would be severely handicapped if they couldn't use DMA. These devices include

- Soundboards
- Floppy diskette drives
- Hard disk drives

DMA is implemented on the motherboard using the DMA controller chip (DCC). The DCC is very similar to the PIC chip we discussed earlier. The DCC has four leads that connect it to the memory controller chip (MCC) and the expansion bus slots. Each of these leads is referred to as a DMA channel. Data from an expansion slot is routed through the DCC to the MCC, allowing direct access to the system memory.

When working with DMA, you should keep the following points in mind:

- No two devices can use the same channel.
- Modern systems use two cascaded DMA controllers to get eight DMA channels. Just as interrupt 2 and 9 are really the same interrupt due to cascading, DMA channels 0 and 4 are actually the same DMA channel.

Plug-n-Play   In the old days, we had to manually configure the system resources used by an expansion board in an expansion slot. Most early expansion boards had a series of jumpers or DIP switches that were used to configure the board's interrupt, I/O address, and DMA channel. This doesn't sound too difficult in theory, but in practice it could be very difficult.

The problem lay with the fact that most expansion boards, to cut manufacturing costs, couldn't be configured to any of the 16 interrupts or 65 thousand port addresses available on the system. Instead, most boards offered the choice of two or three interrupts and I/O address ranges. Unfortunately, most board manufacturers chose the exact same interrupts and I/O address ranges. As a result, you could easily run out of resources. For example, you could have had interrupts 2 and 3 available in your system, but the board you wanted to install could only be configured to use interrupts 4, 5, or 7. To implement the board, you would have to manually reconfigure other devices in the system in an attempt to free up an interrupt it could use.

In the mid-1990s, manually configured boards began to be replaced by software-configured boards. With these boards, you first installed it in an available expansion slot. Then you ran a program from a floppy diskette that came with the board and used it to specify what system resources it would use. This was better, but we still had to deal with a shortage of resources.

This was all fixed when the plug-n-play (PnP) standard was introduced in the late 1990s. PnP is great! In fact, it's still in use today. The PnP standard is designed to automatically configure the system resources used by your expansion boards for you every time you boot the system. All you have to do is install the board in an available slot and turn the system on. No jumpers, no DIP switches, no misplaced configuration diskettes.

A PnP system requires three components to be present in your system:

- A PnP-compatible BIOS
- A PnP-compatible device
- A PnP-compatible operating system

PnP is used for all modern expansion boards. When the system is powered on, the PnP BIOS negotiates with the PnP expansion board to determine what interrupt, I/O addresses, and DMA channels it will use. If necessary, the operating system can also add its input about what resources it thinks should be assigned.

Storage Devices

Recall our earlier discussion of system RAM. Do you remember the key drawback to DRAM? It has to be constantly refreshed with electricity every few milliseconds. If the system fails to do this, then the data and programs stored in RAM are forever lost. The DRAM we use for system memory is really fast, but it isn't persistent. To make a PC system truly usable, we need some kind of long-term, persistent storage medium that will retain data even if the power to the system is shut off.

In this topic, we're going to review several storage devices that can do just that. We'll cover the following:

- Hard disk drives
- Optical drives
- Flash memory drives

Hard Disk Drives

Hard disk drives are the primary type of persistent storage used in PC systems. They are fast, can store huge amounts of data, and are very reliable. Hard disk drives read and write magnetic information to and from spinning aluminum disks called platters. These are shown in Figure 3-11.

Most hard disk drives use multiple platters. The platters are coated with a magnetic surface material that allows the hard disk drive heads to read and write magnetic information to and from the drive.

CAUTION Don't open a hard disk drive as shown in Figure 3-11. Hard drives are sealed units that contain exceptionally pure air. If you open the drive, you allow dust into the system that can scratch the surface of the platters, rendering them useless.

Figure 3-11   Hard disk drive platters

Each platter has two heads. One reads the top side of the platter; the other reads the bottom side. The heads themselves don't actually touch the surface of the platters. As the platters spin, a thin cushion of air is created on their surface. The heads rest on this cushion of air.

Hard disk platters spin very fast. A low-end drive spins at about 5400 RPMs, but most workstation hard drives spin at 7200 RPMs. High-end server drives spin at 10,000 RPMs or faster. The faster the platters spin, the faster the drive can read or write data.

Every hard disk drive has several parameters that are collectively called the drive's geometry. These parameters are used by your system BIOS to determine how the drive is to be accessed and where data can be stored. The parameters that compose the drive geometry include the following:

- **Heads**   The number of read/write heads in the drive.

- **Cylinders**   The concentric parallel tracks on all sides of all platters in the hard disk drive. Imagine a hollow cylinder that penetrates down through all of the platters in a hard drive. Depending on how wide the cylinder is you can fit a certain number of progressively wider cylinders, beginning in the center of the platters and working your way outward to the edge, within the drive platters.

- **Sectors Per Track**   In addition to creating imaginary cylinders in the drive, you can also slice each platter up into imaginary pie-shaped wedges. Sectors per track refers to the number of wedges the platters have been divided into.

Many times, you will hear the drive geometry parameters referred to as CHS (cylinders, heads, and sectors per track). Back in the old days, we had to manually configure these parameters in the CMOS setup program whenever we added a new drive to the system. Today, this isn't as much of an issue. Your BIOS still needs to know these parameters to be able to address the disk. However, most CMOS setup programs come configured by default to query the hard drive each time the system boots and automatically update the BIOS with the drive's geometry.

Currently, there are two choices of hard disk drive families that you can use in PC systems: Parallel ATA (PATA) and Serial ATA (SATA).

PATA Hard Disk Drives For many years, PATA hard disk drives were the most widely used type of hard disk drive and were commonly implemented in desktop computer systems. They were inexpensive, could store a lot of data, and were relatively fast, making them ideal for most systems.

NOTE There have been many different versions of PATA hard drives used over the years. The original drives were called IDE. Later drives were called Enhanced IDE (EIDE). The current generation of IDE drives is also called PATA. Everyone refers to all of these drives as "IDE" or "PATA."

PATA drives implement the hard disk drive controller hardware on the drive itself instead of from a separate expansion board. A single controller on one drive can control a total of two different PATA devices.

Many desktop motherboards available today include two separate PATA channels called the Primary and the Secondary channels. Because one controller can manage two devices, you can install a maximum of two PATA drives on each channel. Each channel is configured using a 40-pin, 80-wire ribbon cable that connects each device to the motherboard.

CAUTION Older IDE drives used a 40-pin, 40-wire connector. Be sure you don't use one of these older cables in a newer ATA system.

PATA devices on the same channel operate in a master/slave relationship. If a PATA hard drive is set to be a master drive on the PATA channel, then its integrated drive controller is enabled and will take control of all PATA devices on the channel. If a PATA drive is set to be a slave, its controller is disabled and must be controlled by a controller on a different drive on the channel. The master/slave relationship is usually established by setting or removing a jumper from a set of pins on the drive itself.

Each PATA channel in a system can have one master and one (optional) slave drive. You can't configure two masters on the same channel, nor can you configure two slaves. It is acceptable, however, to implement a single master drive on the Primary PATA channel in the system and a second master drive on the Secondary PATA channel.

CAUTION The number one mistake made by PC technicians when working with IDE drives is forgetting to set the master/slave relationship correctly.

The last generation of PATA drives was available in four different versions:

- ATA 33 (33 MBps)
- ATA 66 (66 MBps)
- ATA 100 (100 MBps)
- ATA 133 (133 MBps)

Serial ATA Hard Drives Serial ATA (SATA) has become the default storage device interface in most desktop PC systems. SATA drives are much faster than the fastest PATA drives. In addition, SATA drives are not subject to the master/slave configuration rules that PATA drives are. Instead, each SATA drive in your system has its own dedicated hard disk channel that greatly enhances speed and throughput.

SATA is designed to replace PATA technology. Unlike PATA, which uses a parallel architecture, SATA uses a serial bus architecture that allows it to overcome the electrical constraints that limit the speed of PATA system.

The SATA bus uses two channels. The first serial channel transmits data serially, bit by bit. The second serial channel returns receipt acknowledgments to the transmitter, ensuring the data was received correctly.

In addition to dramatic speed enhancements, the SATA bus also allows you to use much longer data cables. SATA cables can be up to 1 meter in length, while PATA cables can only be 18 inches long. SATA devices use a 7-pin connector and a 7/8" wide 15-pin single row power connector.

Another key difference between PATA and SATA is that the SATA data bus uses a point-to-point connection topology, meaning that each device has its own cable and dedicated communication channel. Each channel is independent of all other SATA channels, so devices don't have to share the bandwidth of the SATA bus, eliminating contention between drives. Because of this, SATA devices don't require master/slave configuration as PATA devices do, making installation much easier.

SATA can transfer data at three rates, depending upon the version of SATA in use:

- SATA 1.0 (150 MBps)
- SATA 2.0 (300 MBps)
- SATA 30 (600 MBps)

As you can see, SATA devices are quite different from PATA devices and are not compatible with each other. SATA devices must be connected to the SATA bus, while PATA devices must be attached to the PATA bus, although both buses can coexist in the same system.

SCSI Hard Drives

SCSI stands for Small Computer System Interface. However, in the industry, we just call it "skuzzy." SCSI is a general-purpose interface that can be used to connect a variety of different types of devices to a PC system, including

- Hard disk drives
- CD/DVD drives
- Tape drives
- Scanners
- RAID arrays
- Printers

SCSI is very powerful and very flexible. However, you probably won't encounter many SCSI hard drives in desktop PC systems because SCSI hard disk drives are usually quite a bit more expensive than comparable SATA drives. As a result, SCSI hard disk implementations are usually reserved for high-end server systems.

SCSI implements a communications chain that connects a series of devices together. The SCSI chain runs cabling from device to device to device. These devices can be implemented inside the computer system and connected together using a ribbon cable, or they can be implemented externally using cables. Either way, the SCSI controller controls all devices in the chain. The SCSI controller is usually implemented as an expansion board in an expansion slot in the motherboard, and it usually has two connectors:

- **Internal**   Connects internal SCSI devices with a SCSI ribbon cable.
- **External**   Connects external SCSI devices to the controller.

Older SCSI controllers supported up to eight devices (including the SCSI controller itself) in the SCSI chain. Newer SCSI controllers support up to 16 devices (again, including the SCSI controller). The controller determines what data should be sent to which device in the chain using the SCSI ID. Each device in the SCSI chain must have a unique ID number between 0 and 7 (or between 0 and 15 on newer controllers).

Whenever I teach a class that covers SCSI, I always emphasize that the SCSI ID assigned to a device has nothing to do whatsoever with its physical location in the SCSI chain. It's simply a logical number we assign. However, the SCSI ID does perform a crucial function: it defines the priority of the device in the SCSI chain. The higher the SCSI ID assigned to a device, the higher its priority. By default, SCSI controllers are assigned a high-priority SCSI ID of 7. SCSI hard disk drives are usually assigned a lower priority ID of 0 or 1. CD/DVD drives are also usually assigned a lower priority SCSIID of 4 or 5.

However, the device ID is also used to determine the boot order, and it works in the opposite fashion. The lower the ID number, the higher the device is in the boot order. For example, if you have a SCSI hard drive with an ID of 0 connected to a SCSI controller and a second hard drive on the same bus assigned an ID of 1, your BIOS will try to boot from the device with an ID of 0 first.

Each SCSI device has two numbers in its ID: *x:n*. The *x* parameter identifies the ID of the SCSI controller the device is connected to. The first controller in the system has an ID of 0, the second has an ID of 1, and so on. The *n* parameter identifies the ID of the device on that controller's bus. So 0:0 indicates the drive is the first SCSI device on the first SCSI controller (and will be the first boot device by default). To change the boot order, you can access the CMOS Setup program and change the boot order manually, or you can change the SCSI ID assigned to the device you want to boot from. Just remember that no two SCSI devices on the same bus can share the same ID number.

The way you set the SCSI ID varies from device to device. Most SCSI hard disk drives use three jumpers to set the ID value. These three jumpers have the following values:

- Jumper 1 = 1
- Jumper 2 = 2
- Jumper 3 = 4

The SCSI ID is determined by adding together the values of all jumpers with shunts installed. For example, if you use no shunts at all (in other words, no jumpers are closed), then the SCSI ID is set to 0 + 0 + 0 = 0. If you put a shunt on jumper 2, then the SCSI ID is set to 0 + 2 + 0 = 2. If you put a shunt on jumpers 2 and 3, then the SCSI ID is set to 0 + 2 + 4 = 6. The SCSI ID may also be set using software, depending upon the device.

In addition to SCSI ID, you also need to be concerned with termination when setting up a SCSI chain. Each end of the SCSI chain must have a terminating resistor installed to absorb data signals. This prevents the signal from reflecting back down the bus.

Termination can be implemented in a variety of ways on the SCSI chain. Some terminators are implemented by attaching a terminator to the end of the SCSI ribbon cable for internal devices. For external devices, the terminator may be a special plug that is inserted in the second SCSI port on the last external device in the SCSI chain.

Termination can also be implemented on the SCSI devices themselves. This can be done in the following ways:

- **Resistor packs** Resistor packs are inserted in the SCSI device's circuit board to enable termination.
- **Jumpers** A shunted jumper is frequently used to enable termination on the device.
- **Software** SCSI controller boards usually include a software setup program run from the controller board's BIOS that can be used to turn termination off and on.
- **Active termination** Many SCSI devices use active termination, in which the device checks to see if it's the last device on the chain. If it is, it automatically enables the terminating resistor.

When configuring SCSI termination, it's important to remember that both ends of the SCSI bus must be terminated, but nothing in the middle can be terminated. Anydevices after the terminator in the SCSI chain will not be visible to the controller.

My experience has been that about 95 percent of problems encountered when working with SCSI are due to misconfigured SCSI IDs or terminators.

Over the years, a wide variety of SCSI standards have been introduced. A thorough review of all of the standards is beyond the scope of this topic; it would take an entire chapter devoted to the various SCSI standards to cover all the different flavors of SCSI available. For our purposes here, just make sure that all of the devices in your SCSI chain, including the SCSI controller, use the same SCSI standard. For example, if you're using Wide Ultra SCSI III hard disk drives, then you need to use a Wide Ultra SCSI III controller.

Optical Storage Devices

In addition to floppy diskettes and hard disks, you can also use optical storage media to store data in a PC system. Currently, you can use CD, DVD, or Blu-ray optical devices in your computer. An example of an optical storage device is shown in Figure 3-12.

Optical storage media stores binary data just like any other storage device. However, the way it stores that data is very different. Unlike hard disks, optical drives do not use magnetism. Instead they store data in the form of reflected light. The bottom surface of an optical disc is encoded using a series of pits and lands. Pits don't reflect light, but lands do. By bouncing a laser beam off the bottom surface of the disc, binary computer data is reconstructed in the form of 0's and 1's by capturing the reflections and nonreflections created by the pits and lands.

Compact Discs (CDs) are 120 mm in diameter and are 1.2 mm thick. A CD can store between 650–700MB of binary computer data or 74 minutes of digital audio. Digital Versatile Discs (DVDs) have the same physical dimensions as a CD. However, because the tracks on a DVD are thinner and closer together, a DVD can store dramatically more data than a CD (4.7GB).

Blu-ray Disc (BD) is a newer type of optical disc that has a much greater storage capacity than DVDs and CDs. Blu-ray was originally developed for video but can also be used for storing computer data in the same way a CD or DVD can.

Figure 3-12
An optical drive

The key difference between Blu-ray discs and earlier optical discs is that they use a blue laser instead of a red laser—hence the name. The light in the blue laser has a much shorter wavelength than the red laser used in CDs and DVDs, which allows more data to be stored in the same physical space on the disc. A Blu-ray disc can hold up to 25GB of data.

The key advantages of using optical media to store data in a PC are as follows:

- They can store a relatively large amount of data.
- They are highly portable.
- They are very inexpensive to manufacture.

Optical discs were originally introduced for use in PCs as read-only media. To encode the pits and lands that store binary PC data, a disc had to be pressed at a manufacturing facility. Once pressed, no more data could be added to the disc.

Today, that has all changed. In a modern PC system, you can implement writable and rewritable optical drives (usually called burners). Optical burners implement a second, high-intensity laser in addition to the standard read laser. This second laser is used to write information to the bottom side of a burnable optical disc. Once-writable discs use a special photo-reactive dye on the bottom side of the disc. When the high-intensity laser in an optical burner strikes this dye, it creates changes the pigment to a darker color. This causes binary data to be encoded on the disc using light and dark spots that operate much like the pits and lands found on factory-pressed discs.

With an "R" optical burner, such as a CD-R, DVD-R, or BD-R, the data becomes fixed as soon as it is burned, and you can't erase or modify the data. To be able to modify the data, you need to use a rewritable optical burner (called a CD-RW, DVD-RW, or BD-RE). A rewritable burner uses a high-intensity secondary laser just like an R burner. However, the bottom surface of a rewritable disc uses a photo-reactive crystalline coating. These discs can be encoded with light and dark spots just like an R disc. However, they can also be erased. Using the right intensity and frequency in the laser, a rewritable drive can reset the crystals on the bottom surface of the disc back to their original state, allowing you to burn new data.

CD burners are available in two varieties:

- **CD-R burners** Can write data once to a CD-R disc. They can also read standard CD-ROMs as well as burned CD-Rs.
- **CD-RW burners** Can write data to write-once CD-R discs or to erasable CD-RW discs. They can also read CD-RWs, CD-Rs, and CD-ROMs.

DVD burners are available in a wider array of standards:

- **DVD-R burners** DVD-R discs use organic dye technology like a CD-R. DVD-Rs are compatible with most DVD burners and players.
- **DVD+R burners** A write-once variation of DVD+RW.
- **DVD-RW burners** Use a crystalline phase change coating, allowing them to be erased and rewritten. DVD-RW discs are playable in many DVD drives and players.

- **DVD+RW burners**   An erasable disc format based on CD-RW technology. DVD+RW discs are readable in many existing DVD drives and players.

BD burners are available in two varieties:

- **BD-R burners**   Can write data once to a BD-R disc. They can also read standard BD-ROMs as well as burned BD-Rs.

- **BD-RE burners**   Can write data to write-once BD-R discs or to erasable BD-RE discs. They can also read all types of CDs and DVDs.

Flash Drives

The last type of storage device we need to discuss are flash drives. Instead of using magnetically encoded platters or optical discs to store data, flash drives use a memory chip. You may recall from our earlier discussion of system memory that one of the problems with DRAM is that it isn't persistent. If you turn off the power, you lose all of your data. You might be wondering how we can use a memory chip, then, to store persistent PC data.

This is done using a different type of memory chip. Instead of DRAM, a flash drive uses flash memory. Flash memory can be electronically erased and reprogrammed, and it is also persistent. Once written, it retains its contents even if the electrical current is turned off.

Essentially, a flash drive is little more than a printed circuit board with a flash memory chip installed that is connected to a USB or SATA interface. Once plugged into your computer, your system can read information from or write information to the flash drive as if it were a hard disk drive.

This combination makes flash drives a very useful and powerful storage solution for PCs. They can store large amounts of data in a very small package. In fact, most flash drives are so small that they can be carried on a keychain. Many times you will hear flash drives referred to as thumb drives due to their small size. An example of a flash drive is shown in Figure 3-13.

In addition to thumb drives, flash storage technology is also implemented in Solid State Drives (SSDs). SSDs look and function like traditional hard disk drives, and they even use the same SATA interface to connect to the motherboard. However, instead of spinning platters, SSDs store data using flash memory. Because they have no moving parts, SSDs typically read and write data faster than traditional hard disk drives. They also tend to last longer. The key disadvantage of SSD drives is that they usually cost quite a bit more than a comparably sized traditional hard drive.

Figure 3-13
A flash storage
device

PC Peripherals

In addition to the internal hardware of a PC system, you should also be familiar with external hardware. In this part of the chapter, we will look at:

- Removable hardware interfaces
- Display devices

Removable Hardware Interfaces

In the last decade, new hardware interfaces for PCs have been introduced that have revolutionized the way we connect external devices to the system. Prior to these interfaces, we could connect external devices to the system using serial ports, parallel ports, keyboard ports, and mouse ports. However, for most of these external devices to work correctly, you had to make sure they were properly connected and turned on (if applicable) before you powered on the PC system itself. If you didn't, the system wouldn't recognize that the device was attached. In addition, you couldn't unplug one external device and connect a new one while the system was running. That kind of change usually required a full system reboot.

With removable hardware interfaces, all of that has changed. Now, we can add or remove external devices while the system is running and have the PC automatically recognize the change. In this topic, we're going to review the following removable hardware interfaces:

- Universal Serial Bus
- FireWire IEEE1394

Universal Serial Bus

Universal Serial Bus (USB) is a high-speed removable hardware interface that has replaced serial, parallel, mouse, and keyboard ports on the PC. PC systems today include an integrated USB interface on the motherboard that can be used to connect a wide variety of external devices, including

- External hard drives
- External optical drives
- Printers
- Scanners
- Music players
- Digital cameras
- Mice
- Keyboards
- Flash storage

An example of a USB connector on a PC system is shown in Figure 3-14.

USB connects these devices into a bus. A single USB bus can include up to 127 external devices. All devices on the bus are categories grouped into one of three categories:

- **Hubs**   USB hubs are central connecting points for USB devices. USB uses a star topology. All devices on the bus connect to a USB hub. The USB interface in your PC, whether it is an expansion board or is built into the motherboard, functions as the root hub in your USB bus. The cool thing about USB is that you can cascade multiple USB hubs together to connect additional devices to the bus by simply plugging one USB hub into a USB port on another hub. This makes USB extremely scalable.

- **Functions**   Functions are individual external USB devices such as printers, scanners, hard drives, keyboards, and mice.

- **Hub and function**   Some USB devices are both a function and a hub at the same time. For example, many USB keyboards include several USB ports that you can use to connect additional USB devices.

Because all USB devices eventually connect to the PC through the root hub in your USB interface, USB eliminates the need for multiple interfaces to support multiple external devices. This is a really cool feature of USB. Back in the old days of serial and parallel ports, you had to implement a separate interface for each device you wanted to connect. For example, if you wanted to connect two parallel printers to the same PC, you had to purchase and install an additional parallel port interface for the second printer. This isn't an issue with USB. A single USB interface can support many USB devices. Some USB devices, such as a flash drive, can even draw the power they need to run directly from the USB bus. Other USB devices, such as external DVD drives, need their own power supply unit that is plugged into a wall outlet.

In addition, USB devices are self-configuring, self-identifying, and hot-swappable. You can attach a USB device to the system while it is running. When you do, the device

Figure 3-14   USB connectors

will advertise its presence to the PC, which will assign the necessary resources for it to function. When you're done using the device, you can stop the device and disconnect it without halting the system.

USB has been implemented in three different versions:

- **USB 1.1**   The oldest version, this transfers data at a rate of 12 Mbps.
- **USB 2.0**   Much faster than earlier versions, this can transfer data at 480 Mbps.
- **USB 3.0**   The latest version of USB (introduced in 2008), this increases the data rate of the bus to 5 Gbps.

The important thing to remember is that the overall speed of the entire bus is set to the speed of the slowest device. For example, if you have a USB 2.0 interface and connect a USB 1.1 hard drive to it, the entire system slows down to 12 Mbps.

FireWire IEEE 1394

FireWire is very similar to USB in that it is designed to support high-speed data transfers between external devices and your PC system. However, FireWire isn't as widely implemented as USB; most PC systems sold today do not include a FireWire interface. To use FireWire devices, you will probably have to install a FireWire expansion board in an expansion slot in your system's motherboard.

 NOTE   FireWire is also referred to as IEEE 1394 or i.Link.

Like USB, FireWire devices are PnP-compatible and hot-swappable. It is frequently used for:

- External hard drives
- External CD and DVD drives
- Digital cameras
- Digital video cameras

FireWire is extremely fast. It can transfer data at 400 Mbps or 800 Mbps. Unlike USB, FireWire does not use a star topology. Instead, FireWire connects devices in true bus fashion by running a cable from device to device to device, forming a chain. A maximum of 63 devices can be connected together in this manner.

Display Devices

After the motherboard, processor, and system RAM have loaded programs and data into memory and processed them according to the instructions they contain, we need some way to view the results as well as prompt the end user for input. Believe it or not, back in the old days, computers didn't have monitors. The output from a computer's processing was sent to a type of printer. Fortunately, today we can take this output and display it on a video monitor.

A computer's video display is composed of several components that you should be familiar with:

- Video adapters
- Monitors

Let's look at each of these components in more detail and identify how they work together to display output from the processor.

Video Adapters

The video adapter (sometimes called the video board or video interface) is the interface between the PC system and the monitor. A video board plugs into an expansion slot on the motherboard (or may be integrated directly into the motherboard). The video board has an external connector that is used to connect it to a monitor using a video cable.

When working with video adapters, you need to be familiar with the two different video interfaces commonly used in PC systems and monitors:

- Video Graphics Array (VGA)
- Digital Visual Interface (DVI)

Video Graphics Array   The Video Graphics Array (VGA) interface is an older video interface that is still commonly used in PC systems. It was originally developed by IBM. The VGA interface is connected using a VGA cable to a VGA port on a monitor. A VGA monitor connects to the VGA adapter using a DB-15 connector, shown in Figure 3-15.

The key component in a VGA video board is the Random Access Memory Digital-to-Analog Converter (RAMDAC), a small microprocessor built into the video adapter itself. Its job is to convert digital signals from the system to an analog monitor signal. The RAMDAC combines a memory chip on the video board with three digital-to-analog

Figure 3-15 A VGA video connector

converters. They convert digital video data into red, green, and blue (RGB) analog signals that are sent through a VGA cable to the VGA port on a monitor.

When working with VGA video adapters, there are several considerations to keep in mind:

- **Expansion bus type** VGA video adapters are commonly available for PCI Express expansion buses. Older video adapters may use the Accelerated Graphics Port (AGP) expansion bus, which is almost obsolete today.

- **Resolution support** Resolution is measured as the number of pixels on the X and Y axis. Common resolutions for modern systems include

  - 4:3 aspect ratios:

    1024 × 768

    1152 × 864

    1280 × 1024

  - 16:9 aspect ratios:

    1280 × 720

    1360 × 768

    1600 × 900

  The resolution supported by a VGA adapter is dependent on the amount of memory installed on the video adapter. Simply put, the higher the resolution desired, the more video memory is required to store the increased number of pixels.

  In addition, you need to ensure that your monitor supports the desired resolution. This is where things get a little tricky. Older cathode-ray tube (CRT) monitors could dynamically adjust to the signal being sent by the video adapter, allowing them to support a wide range of resolutions. However, newer LCD and LED monitors support only a single resolution (called the native resolution). In this situation, you need to ensure that the resolution you want to use matches the native resolution of the monitor.

- **Color depth support** The color depth specifies the number of colors that can be displayed on the monitor simultaneously. The color depth is controlled by the number of memory bits used for the color palette. The more bits used for the color palette, the more colors can be displayed. Common bit depths include

  - 8-bit (256 color palette)

  - 16-bit (65,536 color palette)

  - 24-bit (16.7 million color palette)

  - 32-bit (16.7 million color palette)

Digital Visual Interface (DVI) Newer video adapters and monitors use the Digital Visual Interface (DVI), a digital interface standard created by the Digital Display

Working Group (DDWG). The key advantage of DVI over VGA is that it can support both analog and digital monitors.

With DVI, data is transmitted using a digital signal from the computer's video subsystem to the monitor. It uses a single plug connector that encompass both the new digital and legacy VGA interfaces, as well as a digital-only plug connector. Most DVI video adapters use a DVI-Integrated (DVI-I) connector that is compatible with either analog or digital video signals, depending upon the type of video cable connected to it. Some DVI video adapters may use a DVI-Analog (DVI-A) or DVI-Digital (DVI-D) interface. An example of a DVI connector is shown in Figure 3-16.

Monitors

The monitor is the device that receives the video signal from the video adapter and renders the image on the screen. How this is done depends upon the type of monitor. There are two general categories of monitors commonly used today:

- CRT monitors
- LCD and LED monitors

CRT Monitors   Cathode ray tubes (CRT) monitors are an older type of computer monitor that are becoming less and less common. A CRT monitor is composed of the following components:

- Phosphor screen
- Vacuum tube
- Yoke
- Electron guns

To render images on the screen from the video signal received from the video adapter, the following actions occur:

1. Current is applied to the electron guns.
2. The electron guns emit a stream of electrons.
3. The yoke, which is a big magnet, controls the aim of the electron stream.
4. The electron stream hits the phosphor screen, causing a point of light to be emitted.
5. The phosphor glows for a second after it is hit, creating a persistence of vision (POV) effect.

Figure 3-16
A DVI video
connector

A CRT monitor uses three electron guns, one each for the colors red, green, and blue (RGB). The phosphors in the screen can glow red, green, or blue, and each electron gun is aimed at red, green, or blue phosphors. The phosphor screen implements a device called a shadow mask that prevents the wrong electron beam from hitting the wrong phosphor pixel. The electron beams can be varied in intensity, resulting in varying levels of intensity for phosphors when they are struck. Each pixel on the monitor is composed of one red, one green, and one blue phosphor.

When working with CRT monitors, you need to be aware of the concept of the refresh rate. The refresh rate identifies how fast the monitor can draw a single screen. The refresh rate is composed of the following:

- **Horizontal refresh rate (HRR)**   Specifies the speed at which the electron beam draws a single line across the screen from left to right.

- **Vertical refresh rate (VRR)**   Specifies the speed at which the electron beam moves from the top of the screen to the bottom and then returns to the top left corner.

Early CRT monitors used a fixed rate. When working with fixed rate monitors, you had to be careful to match the refresh rate of the video board to the refresh rate of the monitor to avoid damage. Later CRT monitors were designed to support multiple refresh rates. Even multirate monitors, however, have a maximum refresh rate that the video adapter shouldn't exceed because doing so will damage the monitor. However, you should also be aware that pushing the monitor too slowly causes it to flicker, inducing eye strain. Basically, you should configure the video adapter to push the monitor at the highest rate possible without damaging the monitor.

LCD and LED Monitors   Most modern computer systems will use an LCD or LED monitor instead of a CRT monitor. Liquid Crystal Display (LCD) monitors use liquid crystals instead of a CRT tube. These crystals act as polarizing filters. The crystals themselves do not emit light directly; instead light passes through them from a light source behind them. The way different colors are displayed depends upon the way the display grid is constructed.

A passive matrix LCD monitor uses a grid of conductors with pixels located at each intersection in the grid.

 NOTE   There are actually three grids, one for red, one for green, and one for blue.

In a passive matrix display grid, electrical current is sent across two conductors on the grid to control the light for any given pixel. An active matrix LCD panel, on the other hand, implements a transistor located at each pixel intersection.

NOTE Active matrix LCDs are sometimes called Thin Film Transistor (TFT) panels.

The active matrix grid is superior to a passive matrix. Because it uses transistors, the electrical current can be switched on and off more frequently, improving the screen refresh time. It also requires less electricity to control the luminance of a pixel. In addition, an active matrix panel can be viewed from a wider angle and can display more colors than a passive matrix panel.

Regardless of whether an LCD monitor uses a passive or active matrix, it must have a light source behind the panel to illuminate it. This is called the backlight. LCD monitors use cold cathode florescent (CCFL) tubes as a backlight. The backlight shines light through the panel, where the polarizing crystals determine the colors that are displayed on the screen.

In addition to LCD monitors, you can also use LED monitors with a modern PC system. LED-based monitors are still LCDs; they use liquid crystals to create images on the screen. However, they use a different type of backlight than an LCD monitor. An LED monitor replaces the CCFL tube used in an LCD monitor with an LED backlight. There are several different types of commonly used LED backlights:

- **Edge-lit using white LEDs (EL-WLED)** This is the type of backlight most commonly used in modern LED monitors. White LEDs are aligned along the edge of the monitor behind the LCD panel. The light is spread over the entire screen using a diffuser.

- **RGB LED** This type of backlight uses LEDs positioned all over behind the LCD panel. Each individual LED is capable of producing red, green, or blue light, which allows the monitor to display more colors more accurately than EL-WLEDs can. However, RGB LED monitors are more expensive than EL-WLED.

At this point, we've covered most of the internal and external computer components that you need to be familiar with to manage a Linux system. Before we end this chapter, you need to learn how the CPU in a PC system uses device drivers to communicate with all of the various components we have discussed.

Device Drivers

If you are going to be responsible for managing Linux systems, it's important that you understand how device drivers are used by the operating system. If you've used a Windows system, you're probably already familiar with the process required to load a driver to support a piece of hardware. However, the way drivers work under Linux is somewhat different.

To familiarize you with the way Linux drivers work, we're going to cover the following topics in this last part of the chapter:

- How drivers work
- How drivers are used under Linux

How Drivers Work

The key thing you need to understand is that the CPU on your motherboard doesn't natively know how to communicate with the internal and external hardware devices we discussed earlier in this chapter. It doesn't know how to play a sound through the sound interface; it doesn't know how to read data from an external USB hard drive; it doesn't know how to send visual output to the video interface.

To be able to do these things, the CPU needs instructions to tell it how to communicate with these devices. This is done using software. However, the type of software used depends on the hardware device that the CPU needs to interface with. Generally speaking, PC hardware devices can be divided into three categories:

- **Devices that are almost always present and don't have any configurable parameters** Devices in this category are usually present in most PC systems. They have no configurable parameters and aren't likely to be upgraded. Devices in this category include your system speaker, your system clock, and your keyboard. The software needed for your CPU to communicate with devices in this category is stored in your motherboard's BIOS chip.

  You can't directly configure or modify this software. The only way to update this software is to download and install an update through a process called *flashing* the BIOS. Recall that your BIOS chip is composed of flash memory that is persistent when the system is powered off. However, it can be erased and rewritten with new information.

- **Devices that are almost always present but have configurable parameters** Devices such as the system RAM and hard disk drives are always present in a given PC system. However, the amount of RAM present in the system can vary, and the size and geometry of your hard drives can vary. The BIOS alone can't handle these types of devices efficiently. For example, separate drivers for each and every type of hard disk drive would have to be stored in the BIOS chip, which really isn't practical.

  Instead, we configure parameters for these devices in the complementary metal oxide semiconductor (CMOS) chip we discussed earlier in this chapter that is integrated into the BIOS. Remember that the CMOS chip is a RAM chip that can be dynamically written to and erased. You can access the CMOS setup program and specify parameters for hardware devices in this category, as discussed earlier. For example, the CMOS setup program can store:

  - The amount of RAM installed in the system
  - The geometry of the system hard disk drives
  - The size and type of system floppy disk (if installed)

Once configured, the software in your BIOS can read the parameters stored in your CMOS chip to obtain the information it needs to allow the CPU to communicate with these devices.

- **Devices that may or may not be present in a given system**   Devices in this category include network boards, sound boards, and so on. The CPU still needs software to communicate with these devices. However, there are so many different makes and models of these devices that it would be impossible to store all the drivers needed for every hardware device within the BIOS chip. Instead, we store the software the CPU needs to communicate with on the system's hard drive. When the system boots, the operating system loads the driver from the hard disk into RAM. Once done, the CPU has the instructions it needs to communicate with the associated hardware.

In this chapter, we're primarily concerned with drivers associated with this last category of hardware.

How Drivers Are Implemented Under Linux

There are two different ways in which Linux can implement a device driver for a particular piece of hardware in your PC system. First of all, the driver can be loaded as a *kernel module*. Once the Linux kernel has been loaded into memory during system boot, it can be configured to load kernel modules, which allow the CPU and operating system to work with the hardware installed in the system.

Kernel modules have a .ko or .o extension and are stored within the /lib/modules/ *kernel_version*/kernel/drivers directory on your Linux system. Within this directory is a series of subdirectories where kernel modules for your hardware devices are stored. These are shown in Figure 3-17.

For example, the kernel modules used to support your PATA and SATA storage devices are stored in the ata subdirectory, as shown in Figure 3-18.

The second way hardware support can be implemented in Linux is to compile the necessary driver support directly within the kernel. Doing so requires that you manually recompile your kernel from its source code and specify which hardware support you want integrated directly within the kernel in the process. After you do so, kernel modules for those devices are no longer needed because the operating system will have all the software it needs within the kernel itself.

This sounds like a pretty great way to do things, right? So why don't we compile the drivers for all the hardware in the system directly into the kernel? It is a good strategy for some drivers; however, as a general rule of thumb, you should limit the drivers compiled into the kernel to only those drivers the system needs to boot up (keyboard drivers, storage drivers, and so on). The drivers needed to support the rest of the hardware in the system should be loaded as kernel modules.

There are a couple of really good reasons for doing things this way. First of all, each driver you compile into the kernel increases the overall size of the kernel. As a best practice, you should try to keep your kernel as lean and clean as possible. Second, configuring a kernel is an advanced task that shouldn't be attempted until you have a solid understanding of the Linux kernel and the hardware device you are implementing.

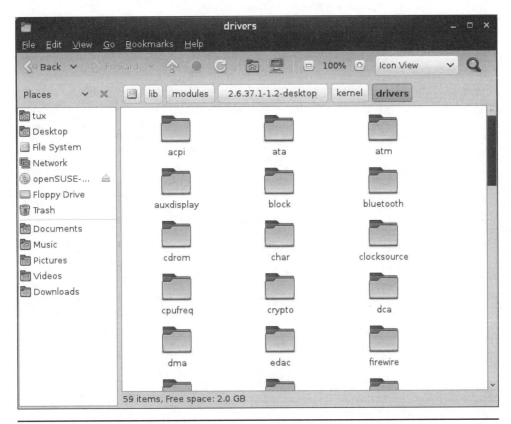

Figure 3-17 Module subdirectories

Finally, the issue of modularity comes into play. If you never modify, upgrade, or reconfigure your computer system, then compiling more drivers directly into the kernel may make sense. However, it doesn't make sense if you're the type of user (and you probably are) who is constantly adding, removing, and reconfiguring the hardware in your PCs. By loading kernel modules, you can add or remove support for hardware devices very quickly from the command line. If you compile them into the kernel, you could end up with a bloated kernel that contains unnecessary drivers for hardware that is no longer in the system. Essentially, kernel modules allow your system to be much more dynamic.

Chapter Review

In this chapter, you were introduced to the basic components that comprise a PC system. We began by reviewing the role and function of the power supply in a PC system. The power supply's job is to convert AC wall current into DC current that the PC can use. It's also responsible for cooling the internal PC components with a cooling fan.

Next, we talked about the motherboard and how the primary function of the motherboard is to tie all of the components in the PC together, including the CPU, RAM, and

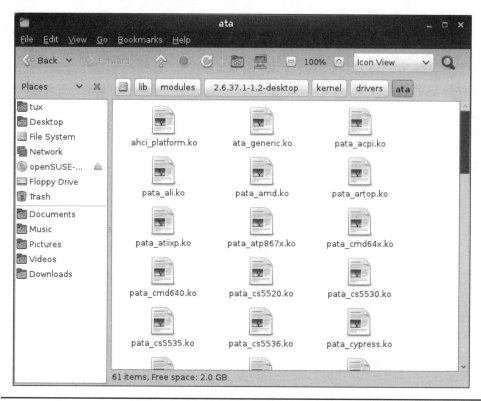

Figure 3-18 ATA kernel modules

expansion boards. We also pointed out that the motherboard includes a chip called the BIOS that contains many software programs that allow the CPU to communicate with the hard drive, the keyboard, the system memory, and so on.

After looking at the motherboard, we discussed the CPU, whose primary function is to perform arithmetic and logical functions with the data we supply. We discussed that the motherboard clock sets the tempo for the CPU. We also discussed the importance of L1 and L2 cache on a CPU and reviewed the various CPU families that have been produced by Intel and AMD.

We then turned our attention to the system memory. We first discussed how DRAM stores data using transistors and capacitors. We emphasized that DRAM must be frequently refreshed to keep the data it stores intact. We then reviewed the various memory technologies that have been used over the years and the memory module packages that have been used to implement memory technology. We pointed out that most systems today use either DDR2-SDRAM or DDR3-SDRAM.

After discussing memory, we turned our attention to the expansion bus. We emphasized that the expansion bus makes the modern PC modular in nature. We then reviewed the PCI and PCIe expansion buses and how modern PCI and PCIe boards can be automatically configured using PnP. We also reviewed the role and function of interrupts,

I/O addresses, and DMA channels as well as how the PnP system works, emphasizing that PCI expansion cards use PnP and can be configured to share interrupt channels.

Next, we discussed the various types of storage devices used in a PC system. We first reviewed how PATA and SATA hard disk drives work and how they are configured. We ended this topic by discussing how optical and flash memory storage devices work.

We then reviewed several removable hardware interfaces that are used to connect external devices to a PC. We noted that USB uses hubs to create a cascaded star topology that can connect up to 127 external devices. We then reviewed how IEEE 1394 accomplishes a similar task using a daisy-chained bus topology.

Then we discussed how the video system operates to display images on the monitor screen. We reviewed the role and function of the video interface and the different types of monitors that can be used with a modern PC system.

We ended this chapter by discussing the role and function of drivers in a Linux system. Drivers are small programs that are loaded into RAM, which enable the CPU to communicate with a particular hardware component. For basic components, this software is provided by the BIOS. For other components, the driver is stored on the hard disk and must be loaded into RAM by the operating system kernel.

On Linux, drivers can be loaded in two ways. First, they can be loaded as kernel modules after the operating system has started. Second, they can be compiled directly into the kernel itself. As a general rule of thumb, only drivers needed to boot the system should be compiled directly into the kernel. Drivers for other hardware should be loaded as kernel modules. This will keep your kernel lean and trim.

Accelerated Review

- Power supplies convert AC current to DC current and keep the PC system cool.
- The motherboard interconnects all of the PC devices, allowing them to communicate together.
- The BIOS contains many small programs that allow the CPU to communicate with basic system devices such as RAM, keyboards, floppy diskette drives, and hard disk drives.
- The BIOS is configured using the CMOS setup program.
- CPUs perform arithmetic and logical functions.
- Intel and AMD are the primary manufacturers of PC CPUs.
- Intel CPUs include the following:
  - Pentium 4
  - Core 2
  - Pentium Dual Core
  - Celeron
  - Celeron M
  - Core i3

- Core i5
- Core i7
- Xeon
- AMD CPUs include the following:
  - Opteron
  - Phenom FX
  - Phenom X4
  - Phenom X3
  - Athlon 6-series
  - Athlon 4-series
  - Athlon X2
  - Sempron
  - Phenom II
  - Athlon II
  - Turion II
- You must use the right CPU in the right CPU socket in the motherboard.
- The motherboard clock is used to drive the CPU.
- CPUs use cache memory to speed them up.
- DRAM is fast but isn't persistent.
- System memory technology includes the following:
  - DDR-SDRAM
  - DDR2-SDRAM
  - DDR3-SDRAM
- Two multichannel memory architectures are commonly used:
  - Dual channel
  - Triple channel
- System memory is packaged in the following types of modules:
  - 168-pin DIMM
  - 184-pin DIMM
  - 240-pin DIMM
- The PCI bus is typically 32 bits wide and runs at a clock speed of 33 MHz.
- PCI cards are self-configuring and can share interrupts.
- The PCI Express expansion bus provides a serial point-to-point connection for each device connected to the bus.

- Interrupts alert the CPU that a device needs attention.
- Every device in the PC must have an interrupt assigned.
- Two PCI devices can share interrupts.
- I/O addresses are like mailboxes for PC devices.
- I/O addresses are written in hex.
- All devices must have an I/O address assigned.
- Most devices will use a range of I/O addresses.
- Devices must use unique I/O ports.
- DMA channels allow a device to communicate directly with the system RAM without using the CPU.
- Devices must use unique DMA channels.
- PnP allows devices to be automatically configured with system resources when the PC is booted.
- A PnP system requires three components:
  - A PnP-compatible BIOS
  - A PnP-compatible device
  - A PnP-compatible operating system
- Hard disks use coated aluminum platters to store data.
- Drive geometry consists of the following parameters:
  - Heads
  - Cylinders
  - Sectors per track
- PATA (IDE) hard drives have the disk controller integrated into the drive itself.
- PATA uses master and slave drives.
- A PATA channel can only have one master drive.
- Most modern PCs provide one PATA channel; older systems provided two channels (Primary and Secondary).
- Optical drives use pits and lands to represent binary 0's and 1's.
- Writable optical discs use a special photo-reactive coating that can be used to encode binary data.
- Flash drives use flash memory to persistently store data.
- USB allows you to connect up to 127 external devices to the PC.
- USB devices are self-configuring and hot-swappable.
- USB hubs can be cascaded.
- FireWire allows you to connect up to 63 devices.

- FireWire devices are self-configuring and hot-swappable.
- FireWire devices are daisy-chained together.
- The video adapter is the interface between the PC system and the monitor.
- There are two different video interfaces commonly used in PC systems and monitors:
  - Video Graphics Array
  - Digital Visual Interface
- There are two general categories of monitors that are commonly used today:
  - CRT monitors
  - LCD and LED monitors
- Drivers are small programs that are loaded into RAM that enable the CPU to communicate with a particular hardware component.
- For basic system components, driver software is stored in the BIOS.
- Other components require that a driver that is stored on the hard disk be loaded into RAM.
- On Linux, drivers can be loaded in two ways:
  - Loaded as kernel modules after the operating system has started
  - Compiled directly into the kernel itself

Questions

1. What DC voltage levels does a PC power supply provide? (Choose two.)

   A. 3.3 volts

   B. 24 volts

   C. 6 volts

   D. 5 volts

   E. 18 volts

2. You need to install Linux on a workstation. The hard drive has been wiped and is ready for the new operating system. You insert your Linux installation DVD in the optical drive and boot the system. Instead of starting the installation routine, the screen displays an error message indicating that an operating system couldn't be found. What's causing the problem?

   A. Your Linux disc is damaged.

   B. The hard drive is failing and needs to be replaced.

   C. The optical drive is malfunctioning.

   D. The boot device order is set incorrectly in the BIOS.

3. Which of the following is an Intel CPU?

 A. Celeron

 B. Athlon

 C. Phenom

 D. Opteron

4. What type of memory is used to create the internal CPU cache?

 A. DRAM

 B. SDRAM

 C. SRAM

 D. DDR2-DRAM

 E. DDR3-RAM

5. Which type of memory is used in DIMM memory modules?

 A. SDRAM

 B. SRAM

 C. FPM RAM

 D. EDO RAM

6. How wide is the standard PCI expansion bus?

 A. 8 bits

 B. 16 bits

 C. 24 bits

 D. 32 bits

 E. 64 bits

7. What is the clock speed of a standard PCI expansion bus?

 A. 4.77 MHz

 B. 8.33 MHz

 C. 16 MHz

 D. 24 MHz

 E. 33 MHz

8. Which PCI component functions as an intermediary between the PCI bus and other expansion buses on the motherboard?

 A. Northbridge

 B. Southbridge

 C. PCI Gateway

 D. ISA Bridge

9. You need to install a PCI sound board and a PCI network board in a PC system. Can you do this?

    A. Yes, both boards can coexist in the system.

    B. No, only one PCI device can be installed in the PCI bus at any given time.

    C. No, network boards must use INT 2, which is the sound board used by default.

    D. No, installing both PCI boards would require both INT 2 and INT 9 to be used at the same time.

10. Which of the following hard drive parameters refers to a set of concentric, parallel tracks on all sides of all platters in a hard disk drive?

    A. Cylinders

    B. Heads

    C. Sectors per track

    D. Write precompensation

    E. Landing zone

11. How many slave drives can be configured on a PATA channel? (Choose two.)

    A. 0

    B. 1

    C. 2

    D. 4

12. If there are two hard drives on a PATA channel, how many master drives must be configured on the channel?

    A. 0

    B. 1

    C. 2

    D. 4

13. Suppose you have a PATA DVD drive and a PATA hard drive connected to the PATA channel. The DVD drive is connected to the first connector on the ribbon cable; the hard drive is connected to the second connector. Which drive must be set to be the master drive?

    A. The DVD drive.

    B. The hard drive.

    C. Either device can be the master.

    D. Neither device can be the master if dissimilar devices are connected to the same IDE channel.

14. What is the maximum number of devices that can share the same SATA bus?

    A. 1

    B. 2

    C. 4

    D. Varies by manufacturer

15. Which USB category includes devices such as printers, scanners, and hard drives?

    A. Hub

    B. Function

    C. Hub and function

    D. Terminal device

16. What is the maximum number of USB devices that can be connected to a single USB bus?

    A. 8

    B. 24

    C. 63

    D. 127

    E. 256

17. How fast does FireWire transfer data?

    A. 12 Mbps

    B. 64 Mbps

    C. 400 Mbps

    D. 480 Mbps

18. You currently have an external FireWire hard drive connected to the FireWire port in your computer. You need to disconnect the hard drive and connect a FireWire digital video camera to your FireWire port. Can you do this without rebooting the system?

    A. No, you must bring the system down to do this.

    B. No, you can't connect a FireWire digital video camera to a FireWire port used by an external hard drive.

    C. Yes, you can shut down the hard drive and connect the camera.

    D. Yes, but you must use a different port for each device.

19. Which type of monitor uses a CCFL for a backlight?

    A. LED

    B. LCD

    C. Plasma

    D. CRT

Answers

1. **A, D**. A PC power supply provides 3.3v, 5v, and 12v DC current.

2. **D**. The most likely cause of this problem is that the system is set to boot off the hard drive first. When it can't find the operating system on the hard drive, the error message is displayed.

3. **A**. The Celeron CPU is manufactured by Intel.

4. **C**. Cache memory uses a special type of RAM called static RAM.

5. **A**. DIMM modules use SDRAM memory technologies.

6. **D**. The standard PCI bus is 32 bits wide. However, there are 64-bit versions of the PCI bus used in high-end server systems.

7. **E**. The PCI bus operates at 33 MHz, although there are 66 MHz variations available in server systems.

8. **B**. The Southbridge functions as an intermediary between the PCI bus and other expansion buses on the system, such as the ISA bus.

9. **A**. Multiple devices can coexist on the PCI bus. Each device is automatically assigned system resources using the plug-and-play system.

10. **A**. Cylinders are composed of concentric, parallel tracks on all sides of all platters in a hard disk drive.

11. **A, B**. Any PATA channel can have either 0 or 1 slave drives on the channel. If no master is implemented on the channel, then no slave drives can be implemented. If a master drive is implemented, then the channel can have one slave drive.

12. **B**. If there are two hard drives on a PATA channel, one of them has to be set to be a master drive. The other must be a slave drive.

13. **C**. The location on the PATA cable has no bearing on whether a drive is a master device or a slave device.

14. **A**. Each SATA device has its own dedicated data channel to the SATA controller. The controller itself may provide multiple SATA data channels to support multiple devices, however.

15. **B**. USB functions include end devices, such as printers, scanners, and hard drives, that don't include USB hub functionality. Be aware that manufacturers of some of these devices do include hub functionality, making them a hub and function.

16. **D**. By cascading multiple USB hubs together, you can create a USB bus that can accommodate up to 127 devices. Be aware that the hubs used to create the bus, including the root hub, each count as one device.

17. **C**. A FireWire bus transfers data at 400 Mbps.

18. **C**. FireWire devices are self-identifying, self-configuring, and hot-swappable.

19. **B**. LCD monitors use a CCFL for a backlight. The backlight is positioned behind the LCD panel to illuminate it.

Open Source Software

In this chapter you will learn about:

- Open source software
- Open source software development

Today, many powerful applications are available that run on Linux. This array of powerful applications has been a key factor in helping Linux transform from a programmer's pet project to a robust tool suitable for wide deployment in the modern workplace. You will be happy to learn that most of these applications are completely free. Yes, you read that correctly: they are free.

This is because most of the software developed for Linux is created as open source software. In this chapter we will discuss what open source software is and how it is created.

Open Source Software

Software created under an open source license must make its source code freely available so that other developers can work collaboratively on the application and, hopefully, make it better.

This is the same underlying philosophy behind GNU, as discussed in Chapter 1. You may be wondering what the relationship is between the open source and free software movements. Essentially, both are trying to accomplish the same thing and have similar goals. The key differences are simply in the mechanisms used to accomplish those goals. Some common terms you may hear when discussing open source software include

- **Free Software Foundation (FSF)**   This foundation was founded by Richard Stallman, who, as you learned in Chapter 1, is responsible for launching the GNU Project and the GPL in the early 1980s. The mission of FSF is to promote the creation and proliferation of free software. In this context, the term "free" is used to describe your ability to copy and reuse the software.

- **Open Source Initiative (OSI)**   This organization, founded in the late 1990s by Bruce Perens and Eric S. Raymond, also has the goal of promoting the creation and proliferation of open source software. The focus of OSI is to make open source software a viable alternative for mainstream business use. Unfortunately, the FSF and OSI are frequently at odds with each other, even though they espouse similar principles. The main issue is one of culture. The FSF typically views the OSI as too moderate, while the OSI tends to view the FSF as too radical.

- **Free and Open Source Software (FOSS)** This acronym refers to both free software and open source software. It is designed to overcome the division that exists between the OSI and FSF by not labeling software as "open source" or "free software," but for everyone to refer to both types of software generically as FOSS.

- **Free Libre Open Source Software (FLOSS)** Like FOSS, FLOSS is an acronym designed to overcome the division between OSI and FSF by not labeling software as "open source" or "free software" and have everyone to refer to both types of software generically as FLOSS.

- **Berkeley Software Distribution (BSD)** A cousin of Linux, BSD is an operating system derived from UNIX that was developed at the University of California, Berkeley. Original versions shared source code with UNIX, and as such, were proprietary in nature and not considered open source software. However, just like Linux, BSD eventually inspired several open source versions of the operating system, most notably FreeBSD and NetBSD.

- **Creative Commons** The goal of this organization, founded in the early 2000s by Lawrence Lessig, Eric Eldred, and Hal Abelson, is to create a new option for sharing copyrighted works. Typically, most copyright owners use an "all rights reserved" model. In this situation, anyone who wants to use a copyrighted work must negotiate directly and individually with the copyright owner. As an alternative, Creative Commons introduced the Create Commons License, which uses a "some rights reserved" copyright model. Under this license, the copyright owners specify specific rights they reserve for themselves and other rights they do not, which are granted to the public to freely use. This license is frequently used for digital artwork.

Like the Linux kernel itself, free software and open source software were viewed with a skeptical eye early on. Today, however, this type of software is commonplace. In fact, you probably use one or more open source applications every day. For example, you may use the Firefox web browser to view an HTML page provided by an Apache web server on the Internet. Both Firefox and Apache are open source applications. Let's review the following:

- Desktop applications
- Server applications

Desktop Applications

Some very popular open source desktop applications include

- **OpenOffice.org** A free alternative to Microsoft's Office suite of products. OpenOffice includes word processor, spreadsheet, database, and presentation applications.

- **Audacity**   A very powerful audio editor that you can use to can record, edit, splice, and mix audio.

- **Thunderbird**   A very popular e-mail and calendaring client.

- **GIMP**   A powerful image editor that you can use as an open source alternative to Adobe PhotoShop.

- **Blender**   A very useful 3-D rendering application that you can use for modeling, skinning, particle simulation, animation, and texturing.

- **Pidgin**   An instant messaging tool that allows you to IM just about anyone, regardless of the instant messaging platform they're using.

- **Calibre**   An e-book management tool. You can use it to sort and manage your e-book collection. You can also use it to convert e-book files between various formats.

Server Applications

Common open source server applications include

- **Apache**   The most popular web server software in use today. It is managed by the apache.org project, which also manages several other very commonly used open source projects such as SpamAssassin and Tomcat.

- **MySQL**   A very popular open source database service, MySQL is one of the most commonly used database servers in the world. It can be used to power enterprise database applications as well as web sites on the Internet. It competes very well with commercial relational database systems, such as Microsoft SQL Server.

- **Zenoss**   An open source IT management application that allows you to monitor your entire network. It provides alerts, network discovery, performance monitoring, service monitoring, and network inventory.

- **Mono**   The open source implementation of Microsoft's .NET technology that allows you to develop powerful server-side applications on Linux servers.

- **CUPS**   The most common Linux printing system in use today, the Common UNIX Printing System (CUPS) was designed from the ground up to make Linux printing as easy as possible, whether printing to a locally attached printer or to a remote network printer. The CUPS service automatically announces the availability of its print queues on the local network. CUPS client systems listen to these announcements, allowing the user to select the printer he or she wants with little networking knowledge. CUPS also support network printing over the Internet Printing Protocol (IPP) on port 631.

- **Postfix**   A very widely used mail transfer agent (MTA) that can be used on a Linux server to provide e-mail services.

This list is only a sampling of the many open source applications that are available for Linux. With the proliferation of mobile phones and tablet devices that run the Android operating system, there are literally thousands of open source mobile apps now available as well (far too many to review in this book). For more information about open source applications, visit http://freeopensourcesoftware.org. The most important point to remember is that open source software is free and the source code is publicly available.

Open Source Software Development

Now that you understand what open source software is, we need to review how it is developed. Let's look at the following topics:

- Software development models
- Package management tools and repositories
- Open source business model

Software Development Models

Like free software, open source software is usually developed collaboratively. Instead of a single organization funding the development of proprietary code, open source software is developed by a loose coalition of developers around the world. In his 1998 essay, "The Cathedral and the Bazaar: Musings on Linux and Open Source by an Accidental Revolutionary," Eric S. Raymond identified two common development models used to create open source software:

- **The Cathedral Model** The Cathedral Model is a very organized software development model. As such, it is also much less collaborative and more structured in nature. In this development model, software development is restricted to a group of specific programmers for a particular open source software project. The source code is still released to the public when the project is complete, ensuring that the project really is "open source." However, during the development process itself, access to the source code is limited to this select group of developers.

- **The Bazaar Model** The Bazaar Model is much less organized. In fact, as its name implies, it's fairly chaotic in nature. That's because this development model relies on extensive collaboration from software developers around the world. The fundamental philosophy behind this model is the idea that using more developers brings in many different perspectives and results in better, less buggy software in the end. Essentially, this is the model that Torvalds used when he initially released the source code to the Linux kernel on the Internet.

Whichever model is used, the results are amazing. You may be asking, "What development language do open source developers actually use to write their programs?" There are many! Here's a short list of some of the more commonly used languages:

- C and C++
- C#
- Forth

- Java
- JavaScript
- Perl
- PHP
- Python
- Ruby

Package Management Tools and Repositories

As a Linux system administrator, you need to know how to install and manage software on a Linux system. "Ha!" you may be thinking. "How hard can it be to install software? I can install software on a Windows system with my eyes closed!" Actually, installing software on Linux can be somewhat challenging to those new to Linux. It's not that installing software on Linux is any more difficult than on other operating systems. It's just that it's different.

If you have experience installing Windows applications, you need to momentarily shelve what you already know about installing software and be prepared to approach the process from a new perspective. My past experience has been that if students new to Linux hang on too tightly to their "Windows way" of doing things, they really struggle when working with Linux software. There just aren't enough similarities. If, on the other hand, you let Windows go and learn how to do things in a new way, you're going to be just fine.

When installing software on a Linux system, you essentially have two choices to choose from:

- **Install a precompiled application or service from a software** *package*   Packages contain executables (and other files) that have been precompiled and configured for a specific hardware architecture and/or Linux distribution.
- **Install from** *source*   When you install from source, you use a compiler on your system to compile the application's source code into executables that can run on your hardware and distribution.

To install software from source, you must have a compiler (such as gcc) already installed on your Linux system. To install software from packages, you must have a package manager installed. Many distributions, including OpenSUSE and Fedora, use the Red Hat Package Manager (RPM) to install and manage RPM packages on the system. Other distributions, such as Ubuntu, use the Debian package management system.

Regardless of which package manager your distribution uses, each package manager does the following:

- Installs software
- Updates software that's already been installed
- Uninstalls software

- Queries installed software
- Verifies the integrity of installed software

To keep track of all this information, the package manager stores information about installed packages in a database file. Whenever you install, update, or uninstall a package, a corresponding entry is made in the database. The package manager also maintains a database of software dependencies and version information to prevent software mismatches and missing prerequisites.

One of the things that I love most about Linux is that there is a wealth of software available for your system from a variety of sources, most at little or no cost. Back in the early days of Linux, this wasn't the case. In fact, one of the great impediments that prevented the widespread adoption of Linux in the early days was the lack of applications, particularly office productivity applications.

Today, however, all that has changed. You name a particular task you need to complete with a Linux system, and you can probably find an application or service somewhere that can handle the job.

The availability of the OpenOffice.org productivity suite (and its derivative LibreOffice), in my opinion, has played a very important role in the acceptance and adoption of Linux on the desktop. Linux has always held an edge in the server room. Its reliability, scalability, and flexibility made it a natural fit in the server role. However, the uptake of Linux on the desktop has been much slower. One of the key issues was that less computer-savvy users needed a desktop environment similar to Windows as well as a productivity suite similar to Microsoft Office. With the KDE and GNOME desktops, the first condition is addressed. With the OpenOffice.org suite, the second condition is addressed as well. I predict that within the next five to ten years, you'll see a dramatic increase in Linux systems at users' desktops.

So where can you get Linux software? As we discussed earlier in this book, the Linux development model violates most of the accepted norms. With other operating systems, you obtain software by visiting your local computer store and purchasing a box copy of your desired application. Many vendors also allow you to purchase your application online and download a copy.

With Linux, however, this usually isn't the case. As I was writing this, I visited the web site of a well-known big-box computer store to see how many boxed applications they offer for Linux. Guess how many? Only three! In fact, two of the three were actually Linux *distributions*, not applications. The point is, most of your Linux software is obtained from alternative sources.

You can obtain software for your Linux system from a variety of sources other than the computer store. The first source you should be aware of (and a source that many Linux users overlook) is your distribution DVD. Many distributions include a cornucopia of applications and services that you can install. For example, the OpenSUSE installation DVD includes hundreds of application and service RPMs in the subdirectories of the suse directory, as shown in Figure 4-1.

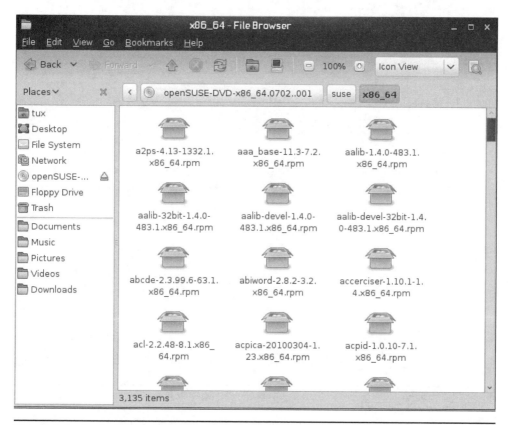

Figure 4-1 Applications and services on the distribution DVD

In addition to your distribution disc, you can also download software for your Linux system from a host of web sites on the Internet. Most open source applications have their own web sites where you can learn about the software and download the latest version. For example, you can visit www.pureftpd.org to learn about and download the pure-ftpd service, which is used to configure an FTP service on your Linux system. This web site is shown in Figure 4-2.

In addition to individual project web sites, there are several other web sites that provide you with links to many different programs from a single location. One of my favorites is www.rpmfind.net. This web site provides a repository that you can search to locate and download an application package for your Linux system.

Another great source for Linux software is the SourceForge web site (http://sourceforge .net), which is a central repository for open source software. As of the date this was written, there were over 100,000 different programs available on this site. As with the rpmfind web site, you can search SourceForge to locate and download a particular package. For example,

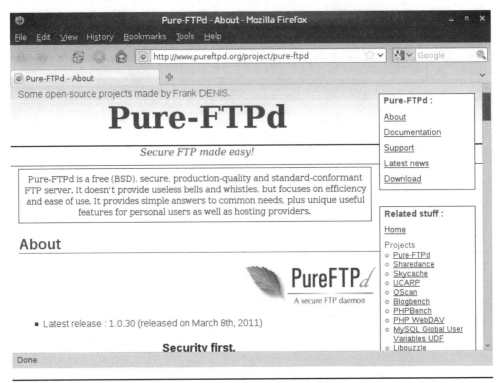

Figure 4-2   Obtaining software from an open source project web site

in Figure 4-3, I've conducted a search for the pure-ftpd package just mentioned. The results are displayed with links that allow you to download the appropriate programs.

As you can see, you can download just about anything you need from these web sites. In addition, you can also use the following web sites to download software for your Linux system:

- **Tucows**   http://linux.tucows.com
- **Freshmeat**   http://www.freshmeat.net

With some distributions, you can also go directly to the distribution's web site and download packages from there. For example, you can go to http://software.opensuse.org and download packages for your specific version of OpenSUSE, as shown in Figure 4-4.

In fact, you can typically update the software installed on your Linux system automatically from the distribution's repository using the package management system. For example, in Figure 4-5, the Software Update utility is being run on an OpenSUSE system. The utility checks the version number of each software package installed on the system and compares it with the version number of the packages available in

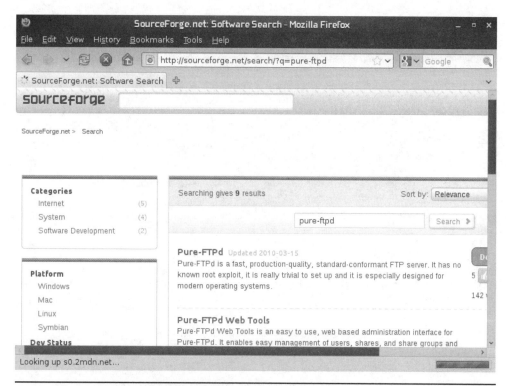

Figure 4-3   Searching for software on the SourceForge web site

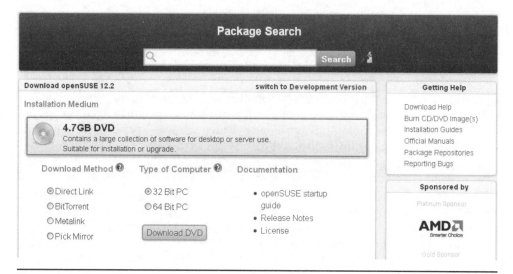

Figure 4-4   Searching for software on the OpenSUSE web site

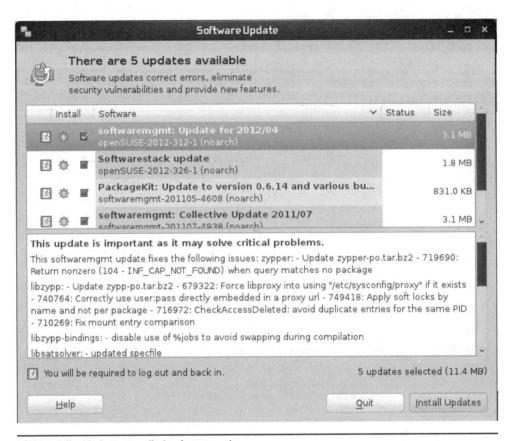

Figure 4-5   Updating installed software packages

the repository. A list of available updates is then displayed, allowing you to download and install them.

Once you've located the package you want to use, you can install it using a package management command. If your system uses the Red Hat package management system, you can use the rpm command. This is done by entering **rpm –i** *package_filename*. The –i option tells the rpm utility to install the package specified.

In addition to rpm, you can also use the yum command at the shell prompt to install RPM packages. The yum command is really useful because, unlike rpm, it checks to see what dependencies are required for the package you want to install and installs them automatically for you. It also locates packages for you by automatically searching one or more repositories on the Internet. The syntax is **yum install** *package_name*.

On the other hand, if your system uses the Debian package management system, then you must use the dpkg command to install software packages. The syntax is **dpkg -i** *package_filename*.

The point is that software is readily available for you to use on your system. Spend some time reviewing what's available on these various sites. You'll be glad you did!

Open Source Business Model

Given the nature of open source software, you may be wondering why organizations and developers put time and effort into developing open source applications if they are given away for free. Everyone likes to get a paycheck, right? Organizations that release open source applications typically use a variety of means to generate revenue so they can keep developing new products:

- **Contributions**   Some open source projects simply ask you to contribute financially so they can continue working.
- **Added functionality**   Some open source projects release a base version of their software for free but then charge a fee for highly desirable add-ons that really ratchet up what the application is capable of doing.
- **Support contracts**   Some open source projects release their software for free but then require a fee to provide technical support. This can be a very useful option for larger organizations that choose to implement open source software enterprise-wide, ensuring problems will be fixed quickly should they arise.
- **Training contracts**   Like support contracts, some open source projects also provide training for a fee.
- **Partnerships**   Sometimes an open source project will partner with a commercial organization. In this situation, two versions of an application will be created, one that is commercial and one that is open source. The commercial version is typically used to finance the development of the free version.
- **Subscriptions**   Sometimes an open source project will sell subscriptions for online accounts or server access.

Chapter Review

In this chapter, you were introduced to open source software. We discussed the open source software movement and identified how it is related to GNU. Open source offers free software whose source code must remain publicly available. We also discussed the difference between the open source and free software movements. We reviewed several key terms:

- Free Software Foundation (FSF)
- Open Source Initiative (OSI)
- Free and Open Source Software (FOSS)
- Free Libre Open Source Software (FLOSS)
- Berkeley Software Distribution (BSD)
- Creative Commons

We then reviewed several popular desktop and server open source applications. Some commonly used desktop applications include

- OpenOffice.org
- Audacity
- Thunderbird
- GIMP
- Blender
- Pidgin
- Calibre

Common open source server applications include

- Apache
- MySQL
- Zenoss
- Mono
- CUPS
- Postfix

This list is only a sampling of the many open source applications that are available for Linux. With the proliferation of mobile phones and tablet devices that run the Android operating system, there are literally thousands of open source mobile apps now available as well.

We then reviewed the two commonly used open source development models:

- The Cathedral Model
- The Bazaar Model

Some of the more commonly used languages open source developers use include

- C and C++
- C#
- Forth
- Java
- JavaScript
- Perl
- PHP
- Python
- Ruby

When installing software on a Linux system, you essentially have two choices:

- Install a precompiled application or service from a software *package*.
- Install from *source*.

To install software from packages, you must have a package manager installed. Many distributions use the Red Hat Package Manager (RPM) to install and manage RPM packages on the system. Other distributions use the Debian package management system. The package manager does the following:

- Installs software
- Updates software that's already been installed
- Uninstalls software
- Queries installed software
- Verifies the integrity of installed software

We then spent some time reviewing the various resources available to you for obtaining Linux software. These include the following:

- Your installation CD or DVD
- You distribution's web site
- Open source project web sites
- www.rpmfind.net
- www.sourceforge.net
- http://linux.tucows.com
- www.freshmeat.net
- www.linux.org

Open source applications typically use a variety of means to generate revenue so they can keep on developing new products:

- Contributions
- Added functionality
- Support contracts
- Training contracts
- Partnerships
- Subscriptions

Accelerated Review

- Open source offers free software whose source code must remain publicly available.
- The Free Software Foundation (FSF) promotes the creation and proliferation of free software.

- The Open Source Initiative (OSI) is another organization whose goal is to promote the creation and proliferation of open source software.
- Free and Open Source Software (FOSS) refers to both free software and open source software.
- Free Libre Open Source Software (FLOSS) is an acronym designed to overcome the division between OSI and FSF by not labeling software as "open source" or "free software."
- Berkeley Software Distribution (BSD) is an operating system derived from UNIX that was developed at the University of California, Berkeley.
- The goal of Creative Commons organization is to create a new option for sharing copyrighted works.
- Some commonly used desktop applications include
  - OpenOffice.org
  - Audacity
  - Thunderbird
  - GIMP
  - Blender
  - Pidgin
  - Calibre
- Common open source server applications include
  - Apache
  - MySQL
  - Zenoss
  - Mono
  - CUPS
  - Postfix
- Commonly used open source development models include
  - The Cathedral Model
  - The Bazaar Model
- Some of the more commonly used languages open source developers use include
  - C and C++
  - C#
  - Forth
  - Java
  - JavaScript

- Perl
- PHP
- Python
- Ruby
- When installing software on a Linux system, you essentially have two choices:
  - Install a precompiled application or service from a software package.
  - Install from source.
- To install software from packages, you must have a package manager installed.
- Commonly used package mangers include
  - Red Hat Package Manager (RPM)
  - Debian package management system.
- The package manager does the following:
  - Installs software
  - Updates software that's already been installed
  - Uninstalls software
  - Queries installed software
  - Verifies the integrity of installed software
- Resources available to you for obtaining Linux software include
  - Your installation CD or DVD
  - You distribution's web site
  - Open source project web sites
  - www.rpmfind.net
  - www.sourceforge.net
  - http://linux.tucows.com
  - www.freshmeat.net
  - www.linux.org
- Open source applications typically use a variety of means to generate revenue so they can keep on developing new products:
  - Contributions
  - Added functionality
  - Support contracts
  - Training contracts
  - Partnerships
  - Subscriptions

Questions

1. You are a computer programmer. Your supervisor wants you to download the source code for an open source application and modify it to support an in-house business process. Can you do this?

    A. No, the source code for open source applications is not available on the Internet.

    B. No, the copyright on the source code won't permit it.

    C. Yes, but you must pay a royalty to the GNU Project.

    D. Yes, you can create a new application from the source code and even redistribute it, as long as the source code remains freely available.

2. Which Linux service can be used to configure network printing on a Linux server for both Linux client workstations?

    A. MySQL

    B. NFS

    C. CUPS

    D. NIS

    E. OpenPrint

3. Which Linux service can be used to configure a network database application?

    A. MySQL

    B. NFS

    C. CUPS

    D. Samba

    E. NIS

4. Which software movement is considered by many to be more radical than the others?

    A. FSF

    B. OSI

    C. FOSS

    D. FLOSS

5. Which desktop application is used for instant messaging?

    A. GIMP

    B. Blender

    C. Pidgin

    D. Calibre

6. Which software development model is considered to be less structured than the others?

   A. Bazaar

   B. Cathedral

   C. Waterfall

   D. Spiral

7. You've downloaded an application package that has an extension of .rpm. What is required to install it on your Linux system?

   A. Red Hat Package Manager

   B. Debian Package Management System

   C. GCC

   D. Mono

Answers

1. **D.** With open source software, you are free to download the source code and modify the application to suit your own needs.

2. **C.** The CUPS service provides network printing to other Linux systems.

3. **A.** The MySQL service can be used to configure a network database application.

4. **A.** The Free Software Foundation (FSF) is considered by many to be more radical than the others.

5. **C.** Pidgin is an open source desktop application used for instant messaging.

6. **A.** The Bazaar software development model is considered to be less structured than the others.

7. **A.** To install an .rpm file, your system must support and have the Red Hat Package Manager installed.

Command Line Basics

In this chapter you will learn about:
- Using the Linux shell
- Working with variables
- Getting help with Linux commands
- Using Linux text editors

To use an operating system, some means must be provided for the end user to communicate with it. That is, we need a way to send commands to the operating system. For example, we may need it to run an application, copy a file from an external USB drive, or even shut the system down. You issue these commands through a user interface. Linux provides both a command line interface (CLI) and a graphical user interface (GUI).

When using the command-line interface, you communicate with the Linux operating system by typing commands at a command prompt using your keyboard. An example of the Linux CLI is shown in Figure 5-1.

Most Linux distributions also provide a graphical user interface (GUI). The Linux GUI is much easier and more comfortable for most users to use than the Linux CLI. Because of the dominance of Microsoft Windows in the home computer market, most end users have never used a command-line type of interface. To make life easier, the X Window System was developed to provide a GUI on the Linux operating system. Using the X Window System along with a window manager and a desktop environment (such as GNOME or KDE), users can interact with the Linux kernel using a mouse and keyboard. The KDE desktop environment on Linux is shown in Figure 5-2.

In this chapter, we'll focus on working with the Linux command line. Let's begin by discussing the Linux shell.

Using the Linux Shell

While graphical user interfaces are generally easier to use, many of the tasks you must perform to administer and support a Linux system must be done from the command line. Generally speaking, Linux end users primarily use the GUI, while system administrators use the command line.

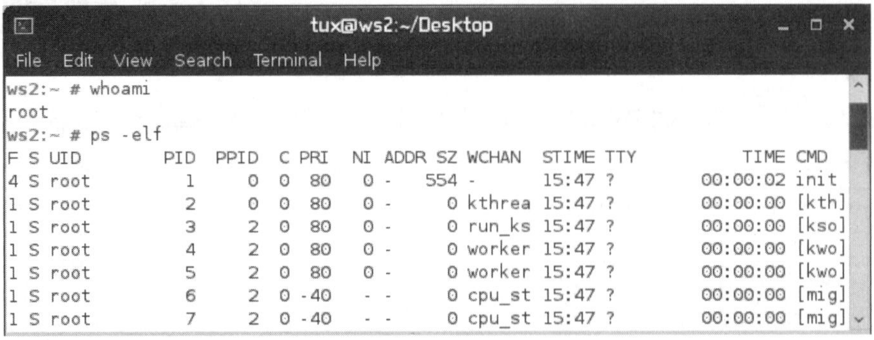

Figure 5-1 The Linux command-line interface

Figure 5-2 A typical Linux graphical user interface

NOTE   Linux administrators are expected to know how to use the Linux CLI as well as the GUI to manage the system.

Because of this, we will spend a great deal of time working with the Linux command-line interface in this book. In this part of the chapter, we will discuss the following topics:

- Linux shells
- Entering commands at the shell prompt
- Using command history
- Using tab completion
- Shell configuration files

Let's begin by discussing commonly used Linux shells.

Linux Shells

To fully understand how the command-line interface works under Linux, you need to understand the concept of a *shell*. A shell is a command interpreter that allows you to type commands at the keyboard that are sent to the operating system kernel.

Back in the days before Windows, most computer users had no choice but to be familiar with command-line shells. In the various versions of DOS that were in use back then, the only way you could communicate with the operating system was to enter commands through a command-line interpreter called COMMAND.COM.

Linux also uses a command-line shell. However, unlike DOS, Linux enables you to choose from a variety of shells. As with many other aspects of Linux, you can try out several different command-line shells and choose the one that you like the best. Some of the more popular shells include the following:

- **sh (Bourne shell)**   The sh shell was the earliest shell, developed for UNIX back in the late 1970s. While not widely used on Linux systems, it is still frequently used on UNIX systems.

- **bash (Bourne-Again shell)**   The bash shell is an improved version of the sh shell and is one of the most popular shells today. In fact, it's the shell used by default on most Linux distributions. If you're using the command line interface on a Linux system, more than likely you're using the bash shell.

- **csh (C shell)**   The csh shell was originally developed for BSD UNIX. It uses a syntax that is very similar to C programming.

- **tsch**   The tsch shell is an improved version of the C shell. It is the default shell used on FreeBSD systems.

- **zsh (Z shell)** The Z shell is an improved version of the bash shell.
- **ksh (Korn shell)** The Korn shell is an early shell that is similar in many ways to the C shell.

When you first boot your Linux system and log in, your default shell is loaded. You can identify which shell you're using by entering **echo $SHELL** at the command prompt. You can also check the /etc/passwd file to see what shell will be used by default for your user account.

The echo command is used to display text on the screen. Adding $SHELL to the echo command tells echo to display the contents of the SHELL environment variable for the currently logged in user. An example is shown in Figure 5-3, where the bash shell is set to be the default shell for the rtracy user account.

However, you're not stuck with the default shell. If you want to switch to a different shell, enter the shell's command name at the prompt. For example, if you are currently using the bash shell and want to use zsh instead, enter **zsh** at the prompt. To stop using the new shell and revert back to the original shell, enter **exit**.

EXAM TIP You can specify the default shell for your user account. We'll discuss how to do this in a later chapter in this book.

Linux is capable of running multiple shell sessions at once. Each session can run its own programs, all simultaneously. This can be very useful if you have one program running and then need access to the command prompt. Press ALT-F*x* (where *x* is a number from 2 to 6) to open a new session. For example, to switch to the third alternate console screen, press ALT-F3. You can then return to your original session by pressing ALT-F1.

As with the command prompt in Windows, you can also run terminal sessions within the Linux GUI. This is done by running a terminal program such as Konsole or GNOME Terminal. To run multiple command-line sessions, open two or more terminal windows. Each shell session runs its programs independently of the other sessions. This is shown in Figure 5-4.

This can also be accomplished in a second way. While you're within the Linux GUI, press CTRL-ALT-F*x* (where *x* is a number from 1 to 6). This will switch you to a text-based shell prompt. To switch back to your GUI environment, press ALT-F7 (on most distributions).

NOTE On Fedora systems, you press ALT-F1 to return to your GUI environment.

Figure 5-3
Viewing the current shell

```
tux@ws2:~> echo $SHELL
/bin/bash
tux@ws2:~> ▮
```

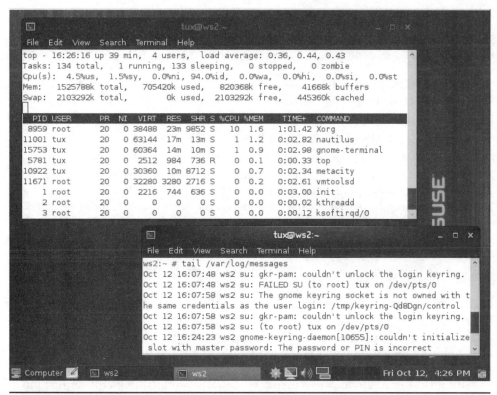

Figure 5-4   Running multiple command-line sessions within the Linux GUI

Exercise 5-1: Working with Linux Shells   In this exercise, you learn how to access the shell prompt, change shells, and access alternate console screens. Complete the following:

1. Boot your Linux system to a shell prompt.

> **NOTE**   If your system booted into a graphical system, log in and then press CTRL-ALT-F1.

2. At your login prompt, authenticate to the system.

3. View your default shell by entering **echo $SHELL** at the prompt. Your default shell is displayed. On most systems, this will be /bin/bash.

4. Open an alternate console window by pressing ALT-F2. A new login prompt is displayed.

5. Authenticate again to the system.

6. Return to the first console screen by selecting ALT-F1.

7. Load the sh shell by entering **sh** at the prompt.

8. Return to your default shell by entering **exit** at the prompt.

Now that you understand the role and function of the shell, you are ready to learn how to use it to run programs.

Running Commands from the Shell Prompt

Running a program or command from the shell prompt is relatively easy. It is done in the same manner as in DOS or within a command window in Windows. You simply type the command, script filename, or program filename at the shell prompt and press ENTER. In this example, the ls command has been entered at the shell prompt:

```
tux@ws2:~> ls
bin        Documents   Music      public_html    Templates
Desktop    Download    Pictures   resources.odp  Videos
docs       Maildir     Public     schedule.txt   widget_project.doc
tux@ws2:~>
```

The ls command is equivalent to the DIR command under DOS and Windows. It displays a listing of files and directories within the current directory on the screen.

The important issue that many new Linux users struggle with when using the shell is that Linux handles the path to the executable you want to run in a different manner than Windows or DOS.

Within DOS or a Windows command window, the command interpreter first looks in the current directory for the executable filename you entered at the prompt. If the file isn't located in the current directory, the command interpreter reads the PATH environment variable. It searches each directory listed in the PATH variable, looking for the executable filename that was entered at the command prompt. If the file is found, it will then run the executable. If not, an error message is displayed on the screen for the user.

Linux also employs a PATH environment variable. However, Linux does *not* check the current directory. This can be a real stumbling block to new Linux users, who expect to be able to switch to the directory where an executable resides and run it from the command line.

Under Linux, this doesn't work. Linux searches only for the file being run within the directories in the current user's PATH variable. A typical Linux PATH environment variable is shown in this example:

```
tux@ws2:~> echo $PATH
/usr/lib/mpi/gcc/openmpi/bin:/home/rtracy/bin:/usr/local/bin:/usr/bin:/bin:/
usr/bin/X11:/usr/X11R6/bin:/usr/games:/usr/lib/jvm/jre/bin:/usr/lib/mit/bin:/
usr/lib/mit/sbin
tux@ws2:~>
```

 NOTE You can also view the current user's PATH variable by entering env at the command prompt.

Notice that the PATH environment variable contains a list of directories separated by colons (:).

Even if the executable in question resides in the current directory, Linux won't be able to find it if the current directory is not in the PATH variable. Instead, the shell will return an error. In the following example, an executable script file named runme.sh is located in the home directory of the tux user, as evidenced by the output of the ls command.

```
tux@ws2:~> ls
bin        Documents  Music      public_html     schedule.txt  widget_project.doc
Desktop    Download   Pictures   resources.odp   Templates
docs       Maildir    Public     runme.sh        Videos
tux@ws2:~> runme.sh
If 'runme.sh' is not a typo you can use command-not-found to lookup the pack-
age that contains it, like this:
    cnf runme.sh
tux@ws2:~>
```

As you can see, when runme.sh is entered at the shell prompt, the shell can't find the file. This is because tux's home directory (/home/tux) is not listed within the PATH environment variable.

There are three ways to deal with this. First, you can enter the full path to the executable file. For the example just shown, you could enter **/home/tux/runme.sh** at the shell prompt to execute the file.

Second, you can switch to the directory where the executable file resides, then add ./ to the beginning of the command. In the preceding example, you would first verify that the current directory is /home/tux; then you could enter **./runme.sh** at the shell prompt. The ./ characters specify the current directory. By adding them to the beginning of a command, you tell the shell to look for the specified file in the command in the current directory.

Finally, you could add the directory where the executable resides to the list of directories in the PATH environment variable. We'll talk about how to do this later on in this chapter.

In addition to path issues, you also need to be aware that Linux filenames and directory names are case-sensitive! This means Linux commands are also case-sensitive. If the executable file you are going to run is named runme.sh, then you must enter **runme.sh** at the shell prompt. Entering Runme.sh, RUNME.SH, or Runme.SH won't work. The shell interprets each of those names as different files.

This rule applies to directory names as well. If you're calling /home/tux/runme.sh, then you must enter the command using the exact case. /Home/TUX/Runme.pl will point the shell to a completely different place in the file system.

As you gain experience with Linux, you'll discover that it includes some very powerful commands and utilities that you will use over and over. Some of the commands include the following:

- **halt**   Shuts down the operating system but can only be run by the root user.

- **reboot**   Shuts down and restarts the operating system and can only be run by root.

- **init 0** Shuts down the operating system and can only be run by your root user.
- **init 6** Shuts down and restarts the operating system and can only be run by root.
- **shutdown** Shuts down or reboots the system.
- **exit** Terminates the currently running process, including the current shell session. For example, if you open a terminal session within the Linux GUI and enter **exit** at the shell prompt, the terminal session is closed. Likewise, if you are working in the CLI and enter **exit**, the current shell session is ended and you are logged out.
- **su** Switches the current user to a new user account. For example, if you're logged in as tux and need to change to user account rtracy, you can enter **su rtracy** at the shell prompt. This command is most frequently used to switch to the superuser root account. In fact, if you don't supply a username, this utility assumes that you want to change to the root account. If you enter **su –**, then you will switch to the root user account and have all of root's environment variables applied. When you're done, enter **exit** to return to the original user account.

NOTE "su" stands for "substitute user." Sometimes it's also referred to as "super user" or "switch user."

- **env** Displays the environment variables for the currently logged in user.
- **echo** Echoes a line of text on the screen. It's frequently used to display environment variables. For example, if you wanted to see the current value of the PATH variable, you could enter **echo $PATH**.

TIP The $ character tells echo that the text that comes after it is a variable.

- **top** Displays a list of all applications and processes currently running on the system. You can sort them by CPU usage, memory usage, process ID number, and which user owns them.
- **which** Displays the full path to a shell command or utility. For example, if you wanted to know the full path to the ls command, you would enter **which ls**.
- **whoami** Displays the username of the currently logged in user.
- **netstat** Displays the status of the network, including current connections, routing tables, and so on.
- **route** Allows you to view or manipulate the system's routing table.

- **ifconfig** Manages network boards installed in the system. It can be used to display or modify your network board configuration parameters. This command can only be run by the root user.

- **uname** Returns information about your Linux system using several different options, including:

  - -s Displays the Linux kernel's name

  - -n Displays the system's hostname

  - -r Displays the Linux kernel's release number

  - -v Displays the Linux kernel's version number

  - -m Displays the system's hardware architecture (such as x86_64)

  - -p Displays the processor type

  - -i Displays the hardware platform

  - -o Displays the operating system

  - -a Displays all of this information

The list of commands presented here is only intended to acquaint you with common Linux commands and utilities. You will need to be very familiar with these and many other commands to manage a Linux system. Additional commands and utilities will be covered in later chapters in this book.

Let's practice using common Linux commands in the following exercise.

Exercise 5-2: Using Linux Commands In this exercise, you learn how to use common Linux commands from the shell prompt. Complete the following:

1. Boot your Linux system to a shell prompt. If your system booted into a graphical system, log in and press CTRL-ALT-F1.

2. At your login prompt, authenticate to the system.

3. At the shell prompt, determine your current directory by entering **pwd**. What is the current directory?

4. Determine the current user by entering **whoami**. Who is the current user?

5. Change to the root user by entering **su –** at the shell prompt. Enter your root user's password when prompted.

6. Create a directory listing of the files in the current directory by entering **ls**.

7. Get more information about the ls utility by entering **man ls** at the shell prompt.

8. Use the PAGE DOWN key to scroll through the man page. Which option can you use with ls to use a long listing format?

9. Press Q.

10. Create a long listing with the ls command by entering **ls –l** at the shell prompt.

11. View the type of processor installed in your system by entering **uname –p** at the shell prompt.

12. Reboot your system by entering **reboot** at the shell prompt.

Using Command History

The bash shell supports command history. Every time you enter a command at the shell prompt, that command is saved in the .bash_history file in your home directory. This file is a hidden text file that contains all of your previously entered shell commands, one on each line, and is continually updated each time you enter a shell command. You can display the contents of the .bash_history file by entering **history** at the shell prompt. An example is shown in Figure 5-5.

If you press the UP ARROW key at the shell prompt, bash will read this file and display the last command you entered. If you press the UP ARROW key repeatedly, you can scroll through a list of your last used commands. When you arrive at the one you want, press ENTER to execute the command. I love this feature, especially if I need to retype a very long or complex command.

If you don't want to arrow through all of your past commands to find the one you want, you can also enter a part of the command you need and then press CTRL-R. The bash shell will search through your command history and display the most recent matching command.

You can manage the entries in your history file using several environment variables:

- **HISTSIZE** or **HISTFILESIZE**   Configures the size of your history file. On most distributions, this is set to 1000 entries. You can customize the size of your history file by changing the value of this variable.

- **HISTCONTROL**   Controls how your command history is stored. You can set this variable to a value of ignoredups, ignorespace, ignoreboth, or erasedups. A value of ignorespace tells the shell to ignore commands in the history that start with spaces. A value of ignoredups tells the shell to ignore duplicate commands in the history. A value of ignoreboth specifies both ignorespace and ignoredups. You can also set this variable to a value of erasedups to remove all duplicate entries in the history file.

Figure 5-5

The command history file

```
tux@ws2:~> history
   1  su -
   2  cd ..
   3  clear
   4  echo $SHELL
   5  top
   6  history
   7  clear
   8  history
tux@ws2:~> █
```

NOTE We'll discuss environment variables in more depth later in this chapter.

Let's practice using command history in the following exercise.

Exercise 5-3: Using Command History   In this exercise, you will practice using command history in the bash shell. Complete the following:

1. Boot your Linux system to a shell prompt. If your system booted into a graphical system, log in and then press CTRL-ALT-F1.

2. Authenticate to your system.

3. At the shell prompt, enter **which cat**.

4. At the shell prompt, enter **pwd**.

5. At the shell prompt, enter **whoami**.

6. At the shell prompt, enter **uname –a**.

7. Run the which command in Step 3 again by pressing the UP ARROW key three times and then pressing ENTER.

8. Use the UP ARROW key to run the uname command again.

9. Use the UP ARROW key to run the whoami command again.

In addition to command history, the bash shell also offers command completion. Let's talk about this feature next.

Using Command Completion

In addition to command history, I also love the command completion feature offered by the bash shell. This feature is extremely helpful when you need to enter a very long filename in a command line. The command completion feature allows you to simply press the TAB key while entering a command at the shell prompt. When you do, the bash shell tries to predict what it is you want to type and then automatically completes the command for you. For example, suppose a file named systembackup.tar.gz exists in the /tmp directory. I need to extract this tarball archive so I can access the files it contains. If I wanted to, I could type out the full command **tar –zxvf /tmp/systembackup.tar.gz** at the shell prompt and tar would extract the file for me.

NOTE   We'll discuss how the tar command works in more detail later in this book.

However, if you're like me, your fingers don't always do what you tell them to do. I tend to make a lot of typos when I'm entering commands, especially when dealing with long filenames as in this example. To prevent this, I can use command completion to take care of the typing for me. In this example, I would enter **tar –zxvf /tmp/syst** at the shell prompt and then press the TAB key. When I do, the bash shell looks at the files in the /tmp directory that begin with syst and determines that I probably am referring to the systembackup.tar.gz file. It then tacks this filename on to the end of the command. All I then have to do is press ENTER. Command completion is great!

Let's practice using command completion in the following exercise.

Exercise 5-4: Using Command Completion   In this exercise, you will practice using command completion in the bash shell. Complete the following:

1. Boot your Linux system to a shell prompt. If your system booted into a graphical system, log in and then press CTRL-ALT-F1.

2. Authenticate to your system.

3. Change to your root user account by entering **su –** followed by your root user's password.

4. At the shell prompt, type **tail /var/log/m**, but don't press ENTER yet.

5. Press the TAB key twice. A list of all files in /var/log/ that start with *m* should be displayed.

6. Add an **e** to the command, but don't press ENTER yet. Your command prompt should display tail /var/log/me.

7. Press the TAB key. The command should automatically display tail /var/log/ messages.

8. Press ENTER to execute the command.

Shell Configuration Files

You can customize your bash shell environment using several configuration files. The files used to configure the shell depend on whether you are using a *login shell* or a *non-login shell*. A login shell is in use if your Linux system boots to a text-based login screen and you use the CLI to log in to the system. An example of this type of shell is shown in Figure 5-6.

 NOTE   A login shell is what you are using if your system boots to runlevel 3. We'll discuss runlevels in detail later in this book.

Welcome to openSUSE 11.4 "Celadon" - Kernel 2.6.37.1-1.2-desktop (tty2).

us2 login:

Figure 5-6   The login shell

Even if your system is configured to boot into a graphical environment (runlevel 5), a login shell is still created at boot; you just don't see it. However, if you open a terminal window within your desktop environment, you are *not* using a login shell. Instead, you are running a non-login shell. This is shown in Figure 5-7.

This distinction is important because the type of shell you're using dictates what configuration files are used to customize your shell environment. These files are really text-based shell scripts that contain specific commands to be run. When the configuration file is run, all of the commands in the file are run in the order they appear in the file.

 NOTE A shell script is similar to a batch file on other operating systems.

Commonly used shell configuration files are listed in Table 5-1.

If you're using a non-login shell, things are pretty straightforward. The bash shell runs /etc/bashrc for system-wide functions and aliases, and then it runs ~/.bashrc from the user's home directory for user-specific customizations.

Figure 5-7 A non-login shell

bash Configuration File	Type of Shell	Function
/etc/bashrc or /etc/bash.bashrc	Non-login shells	Contains shell system-wide functions and aliases.
~/.bashrc	Non-login shells (Although login shells on many distributions use this file as well. It is frequently called from one of the configuration files listed next)	Stores user-specific functions and aliases.
/etc/profile and the files in /etc/ profile.d	Login shells	Contains system-wide shell environment configuration parameters.
~/.bash_profile	Login shells	Stores user-specific shell preferences.
~/.bash_login	Login shells	Stores user-specific shell preferences.
~/.profile	Login shells	Stores user-specific shell preferences.
~/.bash_logout	Login shells	Stores user-specific shell preferences.

Table 5-1   Shell Configuration Files

If you're using a login shell, bash first runs /etc/profile and applies the configurations specified in that file. After that, however, things get a little more complex. As you may have noticed in Table 5-1, several of the files listed sound like they do exactly the same thing. You're right, they do. The issue is that no distribution uses *all* of these files. For example, a Fedora system uses ~/.bashrc, ~/.bash_profile, and ~/.bash_logout. Alternatively, an OpenSUSE system uses ~/.bashrc and ~/.profile.

When a login shell is run, the bash shell program searches for configuration files in the following order:

> ~/.bash_profile
> ~/.bash_login
> ~/.profile

It uses the first file it finds and ignores all of the rest. This isn't much of an issue on SUSE and Fedora. Remember that .bashrc is not read by bash when loading a login shell (although it may be called by .bash_profile or .profile). Therefore, after reading /etc/profile, the bash shell reads .bash_profile on a Fedora system. Likewise, on an OpenSUSE system bash reads .profile after reading /etc/profile.

CAUTION   If you want to make a change to the bash shell environment that will be applied to all users on a Linux system whenever a login shell is opened, you can make the change to the /etc/profile file. However, there is a chance that any changes you make could be lost if an update is applied to the operating system. Most distributions recommend that you make the change to the /etc/profile.local file to prevent this from happening.

The .bash_logout file is only used when you log out of a login shell. Most distributions don't include this file in users' home directories by default. However, most distributions do allow individual users to create their own .bash_logout file and customize it with their own commands to be run at logout.

Working with Variables

Whenever you start a shell session, several different variables are used to define critical parameters the shell needs to run properly. Because these variables define the shell environment, they are called *environment variables*. In this part of this chapter, you'll learn about environment variables and how they work. We'll cover the following topics:

- How environment variables work
- Managing environment variables
- Creating user-defined variables

How Environment Variables Work

Before you can understand how environment variables work, you must first understand what a variable is. The best way to describe them is to envision a container in which a variety of substances can be stored. This container has a name, such as "Stuff," and you can fill it with one substance at a time, whether it's rocks, water, mashed potatoes, or any other substance. If the container is already full of a particular substance, such as sand, it must emptied before you can fill it with another substance, such as rocks.

That's essentially how a variable in a Linux works. It's an area in your system's RAM that's reserved to store whatever values you want to put in it. Essentially, it's like a container in memory. Just as you must empty out a real container before you can pour a new substance in, you must also empty out a variable before you can assign a new value to it. On your Linux system, you can define and use two different types of variables:

- User-defined
- Environment

User-defined variables are just that. They are containers in memory that you create yourself. You can assign user-defined variables with a name of your choice. You can also assign whatever contents you want to them. User-defined variables can be very useful when working with shell scripts, discussed later in this book.

Environment variables, on the other hand, are created, named, and filled by the operating system itself. As the name implies, environment variables are used to configure the system's computing environment. Environment variables are frequently accessed and used by programs you run from the shell prompt. Using the information stored in these variables makes these programs much more flexible and robust.

For example, suppose you were to enter the **cd ~** command at the shell prompt. This command will switch the current directory in the shell to your home directory, no matter what your username is. A different user could enter exactly the same command on the same system and be taken to their home directory.

NOTE We will discuss file and directory management commands in depth later in this book.

For example, suppose I am logged into my Linux system as the tux user account with a home directory of /home/tux. If I enter the **cd ~** command while logged in as tux, the current directory will be changed to /home/tux. Notice that nowhere in the command do I specify the path /home/tux. The cd command just knows that the tilde (~) points to /home/tux. If I were logged in as the rtracy user, however, the same cd ~ command would not take me to /home/tux. Instead, the current directory would be changed to /home/rtracy.

How does the cd command know what directory in the file system to switch to? The cd command checked the value of an environment variable named HOME. As you can see in Figure 5-8, the value of the HOME environment variable is set to the home directory path of the current user.

Because rtracy is currently logged in, the value of HOME is set to /home/rtracy. If, however, I log in as a user named ksanders, the value of the HOME environment variable is changed by the system to /home/ksanders. This is shown in Figure 5-9.

Your Linux system defines a number of environment variables like the HOME variable we just looked at. Some of the more pertinent environment variables commonly used on most Linux distributions are listed in Table 5-2.

Managing Environment Variables

For the most part, the values assigned to your environment variables by the system are usually sufficient for most tasks. However, there may be occasions when you will need to manipulate the values assigned to your environment variables. To do this, you need to know how to manage them. In this part of this chapter, the following topics will be addressed:

- Viewing variables and their values
- Setting the value of a variable
- Making variables persistent

Let's begin by discussing how to view the value of a variable.

Figure 5-8
Viewing HOME

```
rtracy@ws2:~/Desktop> echo $HOME
/home/rtracy
rtracy@ws2:~/Desktop>
```

```
ksanders@ws2:~/Desktop> echo $HOME
/home/ksanders
ksanders@ws2:~/Desktop>
```

Figure 5-9 Viewing the value of the HOME environment variable for the ksanders user

Environment Variable	Stores	Default Value
BASH and SHELL	The full path to the shell executable	/bin/bash
CPU	The type of CPU installed in the system	Depends on your system—an Intel Pentium IV computer would have a value of i686
DISPLAY	The location where your X Window display should be sent	0.0 (the local video card and monitor)
ENV	The name of the file bash read to configure its environment	/etc/bash.bashrc
EUID	The user ID (UID) of the current user	The UID number of the current user
HISTFILE	The path to the bash command history file	~/.bash_history
HISTSIZE	The number of commands saved in the command history file	1000
HOME	The path to the current user's home directory	The current user's home directory
HOST and HOSTNAME	The hostname of the system	The hostname you assigned when you installed the system
LOGNAME	The username of the current user	The username of the current user
MAIL	The path to the current user's mailbox file	/var/spool/mail/*username* or /var/mail/*username*
MANPATH	The path to your system's man program	Depends on the distribution
OLDPWD	The path to the prior current directory	Depends on what your prior current directory was
OSTYPE	The type of operating system currently being run	Linux
PATH	A list of directories to be searched when running a command from the shell prompt	Depends on your distribution
PS1	The characters used to create the shell prompt	Depends on your distribution
PWD	The path to the current working directory	Depends on what your current directory is
USER and USERNAME	The username of the current user	The username of the current user

Table 5-2 Commonly Used Environment Variables

Viewing Variables and Their Values

If you need to see the value assigned to a variable on your system, you can use a variety of different commands from the shell prompt. If you need to see the value of a single variable, you can use the echo command. The syntax is echo $*variable*. For example, to view the value of the PATH variable, I would enter **echo $PATH** at the shell prompt. This is shown in Figure 5-10.

As you can see in Figure 5-10, the contents of the PATH variable are displayed on the screen. Notice that when you use the echo command you *must* place a dollar sign (**$**) before the name of the variable. This is very important. The $ character tells the echo command that the text that follows is not a literal string but is instead the name of a variable, and echo should retrieve the value of the variable and display it on the screen.

If you omit the $ character, the echo command will display your variable name as text on the screen. For example, if you were to enter **echo PATH** at the shell prompt, the echo command will display "PATH" on the screen because it won't know that "PATH" is the name of a variable. The echo command thinks you want the text string "PATH" displayed. Don't forget the $ character when using echo with variables!

As you just saw, the echo command works great for displaying the contents of a variable on the screen. However, it can display only the variables you specify, which means you have to know the name of the variables you want to view. What if you don't know the exact name of the variable? What if you want to view all of your variables at once?

In these situations you can use the env shell command to view your variables and their associated values. The output of env can be very long, so you should append | **more** to the command to pause the display one page at a time. In Figure 5-11, the env command has been issued.

As with set, the env command displays each variable and its current value. However, notice that env doesn't sort the variables. The set command sorts the variables alphabetically, which I really like!

These commands—echo, set, and env—can all show you variables and their values. However, what if you need to change the value assigned to a variable?

Setting the Value of a Variable

As we discussed earlier, most of the environment variables used on a Linux system work great using the values assigned to them by the system. In fact, there are many environment variables that you should not change! For example, changing the value of the HOSTNAME variable could cause problems with many services running on your system.

However, there are times when you will need to change the value assigned to an environment variable. For example, you may need to add an additional directory to the

```
tux@ws2:~> echo $PATH
/usr/lib/mpi/gcc/openmpi/bin:/home/tux/bin:/usr/local/bin:/usr/bin:/bin:/usr/bin
/X11:/usr/X11R6/bin:/usr/games:/usr/lib/jvm/jre/bin
tux@ws2:~>
```

Figure 5-10   Using echo to view the value of a variable

```
XCURSOR_THEME=DMZ
WINDOWMANAGER=/usr/bin/gnome
MACHTYPE=i686-suse-linux
LOGNAME=tux
LESS=-M -I -R
G_FILENAME_ENCODING=@locale,UTF-8,ISO-8859-15,CP1252
CVS_RSH=ssh
DBUS_SESSION_BUS_ADDRESS=unix:abstract=/tmp/dbus-ySvQuMm4d1,guid=45ef1fa5cadd58f
08e47a33100000cc5
XDG_DATA_DIRS=/usr/share
LESSOPEN=lessopen.sh %s
WINDOWPATH=8
DISPLAY=:0.0
GTK_IM_MODULE=cedilla
XAUTHLOCALHOSTNAME=localhost
LESSCLOSE=lessclose.sh %s %s
QT_IM_SWITCHER=imsw-multi
G_BROKEN_FILENAMES=1
COLORTERM=gnome-terminal
XAUTHORITY=/var/run/gdm/auth-for-tux-oNO5Co/database
JAVA_ROOT=/usr/lib/jvm/jre
OLDPWD=/home/tux/Desktop
_=/usr/bin/env
tux@ws2:~> █
```

Figure 5-11   Using env to view environment variables and their values

end of the PATH variable. This can be a handy way to make life easier for your users (and for you as well). In addition, you may need to edit the DISPLAY variable to configure the Linux GUI to redirect the display output to a remote computer. Likewise, you may want to alter the shell prompt to display different information.

To do these tasks, you need to change the value of an environment variable. This is relatively easy to do: just enter *variable=value* at the shell prompt. For example, suppose you installed an application in /var/opt/myapp named myapp. This path doesn't currently exist in your PATH variable, and you want to add it so that you won't have to use the full path when you want to run the program. To do this, you can enter **PATH=$PATH:/var/opt/myapp** at the shell prompt.

Note that I specify $PATH in the variable assignment. This includes the current value of the PATH variable in the new value assignment. I then tack :/var/opt/myapp to the end of the existing list of paths. If you don't include $PATH in the command, all of the current directories in your PATH variable will be *erased* and replaced by the new path you specify in the command! When this happens, your system will start to experience a host of problems.

NOTE   Remember that setting the value of an environment variable will erase its current contents. If you want to preserve the current contents, use the $PATH technique shown in the previous example. If you do want to erase the contents of the variable and replace it with a new value, then you can enter *variable=value* at the shell prompt.

However, I still have one more task to complete. I've assigned an additional directory the value of PATH environment variable, but the new value of the PATH variable applies only to the current shell session. If I open up another terminal session, the change that I made to PATH will not be applied. This is shown in Figure 5-12.

As you can see, the value of PATH doesn't include /var/opt/myapp even though I've logged in to the new shell session as the same user. To make the change apply to all shell sessions, I need to export the new value of the variable. To do this, I enter **export** *variable* at the shell prompt. In this example, I need to enter **export PATH** at the shell prompt. After I do, the new value assigned to PATH is made available to all other shells.

Making Variables Persistent

One additional problem you will encounter is that any new value you add to an environment variable will be lost after the system reboots. If the change you made needs to be persistently applied every time the system boots, then you need to edit one of your bash configuration files and add the variable assignment command to the file.

Let's say that in the preceding example, I want my new PATH variable value assignment to be automatically made each time the system starts; I don't want to be required to manually set the value of PATH and export it at startup.

To do this, I can insert the necessary commands in one of the following bash configuration files:

- ~/.bashrc
- /etc/profile
- ~/.bash_profile
- ~/.bash_login
- ~/.profile

 TIP Adding the commands to a global bash configuration file such as /etc/ profile will cause the change to be applied to all users. If you want to apply the change to only a single user, then you should use the appropriate bash configuration file found in that user's home directory.

You need to determine which files your particular distribution uses. For example, you could modify the following commands in the ~/.bash_profile file in the tux user's home directory:

```
PATH=$PATH:$HOME/bin:/var/opt/myapp
export PATH
```

```
tux@ws2:~> echo $PATH
/usr/lib/mpi/gcc/openmpi/bin:/home/tux/bin:/usr/local/bin:/usr/bin:/bin:/usr/bin
/X11:/usr/X11R6/bin:/usr/games:/usr/lib/jvm/jre/bin
tux@ws2:~>
```

Figure 5-12 The new variable value is not exported

Now, whenever the system boots and tux logs in, the /var/opt/myapp path is automatically added to his PATH environment variable. Because I added the command to the ~/. bash_profile file in the tux user's home directory, it will not be added to any other user's PATH variable.

Let's practice working with environment variables in the following exercise.

Exercise 5-5: Working with Environment Variables   In this exercise, you will practice working with environment variables in the bash shell. Complete the following:

1. If you haven't done so already, boot your Linux system and log in.

2. If necessary, start a terminal session.

3. Change to your root user account by entering **su** – followed by your root password.

4. At the shell prompt, view the value of the following environment variables by entering the following commands:

   echo $PWD

   echo $HOME

   echo $EUID

   echo $PATH

   echo $PS1

5. Change your shell prompt to display the currently logged in user, the name of the Linux host, the current time, the full path to the current working directory, and a colon by doing the following:

   a. At the shell prompt enter **PS1="[\u@\h \t \w]:"**. The prompt should immediately change.

   b. At the shell prompt, enter **export PS1**.

   c. At the shell prompt, enter **ls ~ –a**.

   Which file would you edit on your particular distribution if you wanted to make the changes to your PS1 environment variable persistent?

Creating User-Defined Variables

In the preceding topic, we focused on working with environment variables. These variables are automatically defined for you each time the system boots. However, you can create your own customized variables as well. This is done in exactly the same way as managing environment variables: just enter *variable=value* at the shell prompt.

For example, suppose I wanted to create a variable named ME and set it to a value of "TUX". I can do this by entering **ME="TUX"** at the shell prompt. Once I do this, a variable named ME is added to my system and set to a value of TUX. You can use the echo command to view the value of the ME variable, as shown here:

```
tux@ws2:~> ME="TUX"
tux@ws2:~> echo $ME
TUX
tux@ws2:~>
```

As with environment variables, a user-defined variable is only available to the current instance of the shell. To make it available to other shells, you need to export it with the export command. In this example, I would enter **export ME** at the shell prompt to do this. In addition to echo, you can also use env to view user-defined variables just as you did with environment variables.

As with environment variables, you can make a user-defined variable persistent by adding the appropriate commands to one of the bash configuration files discussed previously. When creating user-defined variables, keep the following rules in mind:

- Variable names can contain letters or numbers, but they may not begin with a number.
- Variable names may contain hyphens (-) or underscore characters (_).
- While not required, you should try to use all uppercase characters when naming your variables. Notice, when you enter **env**, that all of your system's environment variables use uppercase names.
- Variable names cannot contain spaces.

Getting Help with Linux Commands

One of the great things about Linux is that documentation and help information are abundantly available. Pick any Linux command, utility, or daemon and you can probably find documentation that will teach you how to use it to accomplish what you need to do. In this chapter, I'm going to teach you how to use two excellent resources for getting help with Linux.

However, before doing so, there are a few key things about Linux documentation materials that you need to understand. First of all, the vendor who provided your Linux distribution probably provides some kind of general system documentation for you to use. However, this system documentation is probably quite minimal. (For some distributions, it may be nonexistent.) This is because each service or application you install on a Linux distribution usually includes documentation for that particular program. If you think about all the different packages that are distributed with Linux, you can see that it would be an extremely daunting task for a Linux vendor to try to develop their own documentation describing how to use all of these packages. Instead, they rely on others in the open source community to document all of the various applications and services that can be used on Linux.

This brings us to the second point you need to keep in mind when working with Linux documentation: The programmer who wrote a particular service or utility is probably the person who wrote the associated documentation. Only some of the Linux software documentation is written by professional technical writers. This means there are wide variations in the quality of the documentation from one piece of software to another. Some programmers are quite good at writing documentation. They write well and they understand how to structure information in fashion that is easy to understand.

Unfortunately, other programmers aren't very good at writing documentation. In fact, many are really bad at it. Their key fault is they assume the reader has the same knowledge level as they do. This kind of documentation tends to be incomplete and generally unhelpful.

NOTE If you encounter this situation and have some extra time to spare, most programmers would love to have someone volunteer to help write documentation. As you'll see later in this chapter, most Linux help sources include a contact e-mail address that you can use to contact the author.

The third point you need to keep in mind is that most Linux documentation sources are not print-based. Back in the early days of Linux, some distributions did include a thick printed manual. The first Linux distribution I installed back in 1995 (Caldera OpenLinux version 1.0) included just such a manual. Today, however, printed manuals are nonexistent. As you can imagine, printing manuals of this size is very expensive and uses up a lot of paper. Therefore, nearly all current documentation sources for your Linux distribution are made available only in electronic format.

EXAM TIP Knowing how to get help when working with Linux is a critical part of a Linux admin's job role. When a problem happens, you need to be able to find an answer fast. You need to be very familiar with resources you can use to find information, and you need to know how to launch the utilities, navigate through the information displayed, and exit.

In this part of the chapter, we'll introduce you to the various sources for getting help when working with Linux. The following topics will be covered:

- Using man pages
- Using the info utility

Let's begin by discussing how to use man to get help with your Linux system.

Using man Pages

One of the primary ways to maintain Linux system documentation is through the use of manual (man) pages. These manual pages contain documentation about the operating system itself as well as any applications installed on the system. These man pages are viewed using a utility called *man*.

The man utility was original developed and used by the UNIX operating system. It has been ported to Linux and provides the same functionality as on a UNIX system. It can be used to display a manual page for a particular Linux command, utility, or file.

The man utility is an extremely useful tool when managing a Linux system. If you think about it, there are a lot of commands and utilities available on even the most basic Linux system. Some of the commands and utilities are used frequently; others are used very rarely. It's very difficult for the average Linux admin to remember the syntax and options of every possible command and utility, especially those you don't use frequently.

The man utility is a real lifesaver. If you ever find yourself at a loss when working with a particular command or utility, you can use man to display the appropriate man page and remind yourself of how it's used. I love man!

In addition to system commands and utilities, man pages are also maintained for most of the packages on your system. Whenever you install a package on Linux, the man pages containing the documentation for the software are also installed. This allows you to use man to view documentation for these packages as well.

In this part of the chapter, we'll review the following man-related topics:

- The man directory structure
- Manual sections
- Using man to view documentation

The man Directory Structure

The actual pages displayed by man are maintained in several directories beneath the directory specified in the MANPATH environment variable. On a 64-bit OpenSUSE Linux system, the MANPATH variable is set to the /usr/lib64/mpi/gcc/openmpi/share/man, /usr/local/man, and /usr/share/man directories.

You can check the value of the MANPATH variable on your system by entering **echo $MANPATH** at a shell prompt. When you do, a list of environment variables is displayed. The MANPATH variable lists the directories containing man pages, each separated by a colon; as shown in Figure 5-13.

It's important to note that the man utility can be implemented in different ways on different Linux distributions. For example, the Fedora distribution doesn't use the MANPATH environment variable by default. Instead, it uses the MANPATH_MAP directive in the /etc/man_db.conf file to specify the directories where man pages are stored. An example of this configuration file is shown in Figure 5-14.

Beneath the directories specified in the MANPATH variable or in the MANPATH_MAP directive in the /etc/man_db.conf file are a series of directories denoted by man1, man2,

```
tux@ws2:~> echo $MANPATH
/usr/lib64/mpi/gcc/openmpi/share/man:/usr/local/man:/usr/share/man
```

Figure 5-13 The MANPATH environment variable

```
#-----------------------------------------------------------
# set up PATH to MANPATH mapping
# ie. what man tree holds man pages for what binary directory.
#
#                  *PATH*         ->        *MANPATH*
#
MANPATH_MAP      /bin                      /usr/share/man
MANPATH_MAP      /usr/bin                  /usr/share/man
MANPATH_MAP      /sbin                     /usr/share/man
MANPATH_MAP      /usr/sbin                 /usr/share/man
MANPATH_MAP      /usr/local/bin            /usr/local/man
MANPATH_MAP      /usr/local/bin            /usr/local/share/man
MANPATH_MAP      /usr/local/sbin           /usr/local/man
MANPATH_MAP      /usr/local/sbin           /usr/local/share/man
MANPATH_MAP      /usr/X11R6/bin            /usr/X11R6/man
MANPATH_MAP      /usr/bin/X11              /usr/X11R6/man
MANPATH_MAP      /usr/games                /usr/share/man
MANPATH_MAP      /opt/bin                  /opt/man
MANPATH_MAP      /opt/sbin                 /opt/man
#-----------------------------------------------------------
```

Figure 5-14   Configuring man directories on Fedora

man3, etc., as shown in Figure 5-15. Some of the directories shown in Figure 5-15 aren't used for manual sections. Directories such as hu, it, and jp are used for man pages that have been localized into a language other than English.

Manual Sections

All of the man pages contained in the various man directories together compose the *manual.* Each of the directories shown in Figure 5-15 represents a *section* of the manual. The standards used by man page authors divide the manual into the sections shown in Table 5-3.

Manual pages are categorized and stored in the appropriate directory, depending upon the type of software they are associated with. Many of the man pages you will use in this book will be stored in Section 1: Shell Commands and Section 8: Administrative Utilities.

Using man to View Documentation

Using man to look up information is really easy. All you have to do is enter **man** followed by the name of the utility you need information about.

```
tux@ws2:~> ls /usr/share/man/
cs   fr             hu  man0p   man2   man4   man7   mann   pt_BR
de   fr.ISO8859-1   it  man1    man3   man5   man8   nl     ru
es   fr.UTF-8       ja  man1p   man3p  man6   man9   pl
tux@ws2:~> █
```

Figure 5-15   man directories

Section	Content
1	Programs and shell commands that can be used by any user
2	System functions provided by the Linux kernel
3	Library functions
4	Special files found in /dev
5	File format descriptions and conventions
6	Games
7	Miscellaneous conventions
8	Administrative utilities used by the root user
9	Kernel routine documentation

Table 5-3   Sections Used in man Pages

For example, the ls command is a very useful shell command that displays a list of files in a directory. It can be used with a variety of options that customize how it works and how the data it returns is displayed. How do you know what these options are and how to use them? You use the man utility to display the manual page for the ls command. To do this, enter **man ls** at a shell prompt. When you do, the screen shown in Figure 5-16 is displayed. Figure 5-17 shows additional sections of the man page.

```
LS(1)                           User  Commands                          LS(1)



NAME
       ls - list directory contents

SYNOPSIS
       ls [OPTION]... [FILE]...

DESCRIPTION
       List  information  about  the FILEs (the current directory by default).
       Sort entries alphabetically if none of -cftuvSUX nor --sort.

       Mandatory arguments to long options are  mandatory  for  short  options
       too.

       -a, --all
              do not ignore entries starting with .

       -A, --almost-all
              do not list implied . and ..

Manual page ls(1) line 1
```

Figure 5-16   Viewing the man page for the ls utility

```
AUTHOR
        Written by Richard M. Stallman and David MacKenzie.

REPORTING BUGS
        Report ls bugs to bug-coreutils@gnu.org
        GNU coreutils home page: <http://www.gnu.org/software/coreutils/>
        General help using GNU software: <http://www.gnu.org/gethelp/>
        Report ls translation bugs to <http://translationproject.org/team/>

COPYRIGHT
        Copyright © 2011 Free Software Foundation, Inc.   License  GPLv3+:  GNU
        GPL version 3 or later <http://gnu.org/licenses/gpl.html>.
        This  is  free  software:  you  are free to change and redistribute it.
        There is NO WARRANTY, to the extent permitted by law.

SEE ALSO
        The full documentation for ls is maintained as a  Texinfo  manual.   If
        the  info and ls programs are properly installed at your site, the com-
        mand

                info coreutils 'ls invocation'

        should give you access to the complete manual.
Manual page ls(1) line 216
```

Figure 5-17   Additional man page sections

A given man page consists of several elements, as shown in Figure 5-16. Some man pages will include many sections; others will only include a few. Most man pages will include the following:

- **Title**   The title section is the first line of the man page. It lists the name of the utility, command, or file discussed in the man page followed by the section number. In Figure 5-16, notice that the first line reads LS(1). This indicates the man page describes the ls utility and is located in Section 1 of the manual. Remember from Table 5-3 that Section 1 of the manual contains manual pages for commands and utilities that all Linux users can use.

- **NAME**   The NAME section displays the name of the command, file, or utility and a short abstract about what it does. In Figure 5-16, the NAME section indicates that the ls utility is used to list directory contents.

- **SYNOPSIS**   The SYNOPSIS section provides a brief description of the syntax for using a particular command or utility. If the manual page documents a configuration file, such as smb.conf, the SYNOPSIS section provides a brief overview of what the file is used for. In Figure 5-16, the SYNOPSIS section of the man page for the ls utility displays the syntax for using the command from the shell prompt. It tells you that you can enter ls followed by a list of possible options and filenames.

- **DESCRIPTION**   The DESCRIPTION section provides the meat of the manual page. This section describes how the command, file, or utility works in detail. It also provides a list of options that can be used. For example, in Figure 5-16, the man page specifies that you can use the –a or –all option with the ls utility to display hidden directories and files along with normal files and directories in the file system. Without a man page, you probably wouldn't have known this.

 EXAM TIP   The names of hidden Linux files and directories begin with a period.

- **AUTHOR**   The AUTHOR section displays the name of the programmer who wrote the command, utility, or service referenced in the man page. This is shown for the ls utility in Figure 5-17.

- **REPORTING BUGS**   The REPORTING BUGS section provides an e-mail address you can use to report any bugs you discover in the utility or the documentation, as shown in Figure 5-17.

- **COPYRIGHT**   The COPYRIGHT section provides you with details about who owns the copyright to the command, utility, or service referenced in the man page. It also provides you with redistribution information, as shown in Figure 5-17.

- **SEE ALSO**   The SEE ALSO section provides you with a list of man pages or other resources that are related to the current man page. For example, in Figure 5-17, the SEE ALSO section directs the user to use info to view the complete documentation for the ls command.

- **Version Number and Revision Date**   The very last line of the man page displays the version number of the program and the revision date.

All sections other than NAME are optional. Authors are free to add new sections not shown the preceding list if their particular program requires them. You may see man pages for other utilities or services that contain sections such as OPTIONS, FILES, ENVIRONMENT, or DIAGNOSTICS.

As you use man to display a manual page, a status indicator shown at the very bottom of the display tells you what manual page is being displayed, the current line displayed, and how far into the document you are. This status indicator is shown in Figure 5-17. In this example, the status indicator shows that the ls(1) manual page is being displayed. It also indicates that line 216 is the top line currently displayed.

With a man page displayed, you can use the keystrokes shown in Table 5-4 to navigate around within the page.

Some man pages are short and concise; others are quite long and extensive. When working with a man page, you may need to search for a specific term within the page itself.

For example, if you're using the ls command, you may need to view extended information about files and directories in your file system. Notice in Figure 5-16 that by default ls only displays the names of the files or directories within the current directory.

Keystroke	Function
DOWN ARROW	Scrolls down 1 line in the page.
UP ARROW	Scrolls up 1 line in the page.
PAGE DOWN	Scrolls down 14 lines in the page.
PAGE UP	Scrolls up 14 lines in the page.
SPACEBAR	Scrolls down 26 lines in the page.
HOME	Moves you to the beginning of the page.
END	Moves you to the end of the page.
Q	Unloads the current man page and exits the man utility.

Table 5-4 Sections Used in man Pages

To view extended information, such as permissions, ownership, file size, or modification dates, you'll need the long listing format.

To search for this format or any other specific information within a man page, you enter a forward-slash (/) followed by the search term you want to search for. For example, to find out how to obtain a long listing format from ls, load the man page for ls by entering **man ls**. Then, enter **/long** to search for the text string "long" in the man page. This is shown in Figure 5-18.

When you press ENTER, the first instance of "long" is located in the man page. To find the next instance, press N. After pressing N several times, the instance you want to find is located, as shown in Figure 5-18. Using the –l option with the ls utility will display its output in long format, which shows permissions, ownership, size, and modification dates for files and directories.

Many times, you will need to search for information in a man page for a utility, but you can't quite remember exactly how the command is spelled. Remember that man requires you to know the name of the command, utility, or file to view its associated manual page. If, for some reason, you can't remember, you can use the following tools to search across man pages:

- **man –k** Allows you to search across all manual page names and descriptions to find a specific keyword. For example, suppose you wanted to remove a directory from your file system, but you can't remember which utility does that. You can enter **man –k "remove empty"** at the shell prompt to view a list of man pages that include the phrase "remove empty." This is shown in Figure 5-19.

```
       -k        like --block-size=1K

       -l        use a  long  listing format

 Manual page ls(1) line 88/242 43%
```

Figure 5-18 Searching for text in a man page

```
tux@ws2:~> man -k "remove empty"
rmdir (1)              - remove empty directories
tux@ws2:~>
```

Figure 5-19 Searching across man pages

In Figure 5-19, you can see that the rmdir command can remove a directory. Now that you know the name of the command, you can enter **man rmdir** to learn how to use it.

- **apropos**   Basically the same as the man –k command: you can use this utility to search across man page names and descriptions to search for a text string. For example, to search for man pages that have the string "remove empty" in their text, you would enter **apropos remove**.

- **whatis**   Basically the same as the man –k and apropos commands: this utility searches across man page names and descriptions to search for a text string. For example, to search for man pages that have the string "remove empty" in their text, you would enter **whatis remove**.

With this in mind, let's practice using man in the following exercise.

Exercise 5-6: Using man Pages   In this exercise, you will practice using the man utility to view manual pages for Linux utilities. Complete the following:

1. Boot your Linux system to a shell prompt. If your system booted into a graphical environment, log in and then press CTRL-ALT-F1.

2. Authenticate to your system.

3. At the shell prompt, enter **man rm**.

4. Answer the following questions:
   - What does the rm utility do?
   - What does the –r option do when used with rm?
   - Who wrote the rm utility?
   - To what e-mail address can you send any bugs you discover?
   - In what man section does the rm page reside?
   - If you wanted the rm utility to prompt you before removing an existing file, what option would you use?

5. Close man by pressing Q.

Using the info Utility

In addition to man, you can use the info utility to view documentation for commands, utilities, services, and files on your Linux system. You might be asking, "Why do I need info if I've already got man?" The two utilities do serve a similar purpose; however, they do it in different ways.

The man utility is a "down-and-dirty" reference utility. Man pages are packed with information, but they aren't instructional in nature. Essentially, man says, "Here's the utility and its syntax. You go figure out how to use it."

The info utility, on the other hand, is more of a learning utility. Most info nodes contain the same information as a man page. However, info nodes are usually more verbose and can teach you how to use a particular Linux tool.

NOTE Instead of calling them pages, we refer to units of information displayed by the info utility as *nodes*. You'll see why they are called nodes later in this chapter.

Launching info is done in much the same manner as man: you enter **info** followed by the name of the command, utility, service, or file you need to learn about. For example, earlier in this chapter, you used man to view information about the ls utility. To use info to learn about the ls utility, you enter **info ls**. When you do, the information in Figure 5-20 is displayed.

Right away, you'll notice several differences between man and info. The information available in the ls man page is fairly minimal. Conversely, the information available in info is much more verbose. The info node explains what the ls utility does and what you can expect when you use it.

```
File: coreutils.info,  Node: ls invocation,  Next: dir invocation,  Up: Directo\
ry listing

10.1 `ls': List directory contents
==================================

The `ls' program lists information about files (of any type, including
directories).  Options and file arguments can be intermixed
arbitrarily, as usual.

   For non-option command-line arguments that are directories, by
default `ls' lists the contents of directories, not recursively, and
omitting files with names beginning with `.'.  For other non-option
arguments, by default `ls' lists just the file name.  If no non-option
argument is specified, `ls' operates on the current directory, acting
as if it had been invoked with a single argument of `.'.

   By default, the output is sorted alphabetically, according to the
locale settings in effect.(1) If standard output is a terminal, the
output is in columns (sorted vertically) and control characters are
output as question marks; otherwise, the output is listed one per line
and control characters are output as-is.
--zz-Info: (coreutils.info.gz)ls invocation, 58 lines --Top-----------------
Welcome to Info version 4.13. Type h for help, m for menu item.
```

Figure 5-20   Using info to view information about the ls utility

Keystroke	Function
DOWN ARROW	Scrolls down one line at a time.
UP ARROW	Scrolls up one line at a time.
PAGE DOWN	Scrolls down one page at a time.
PAGE UP	Scrolls up one page at a time.
SPACEBAR	Scrolls down one page at a time.
DEL OR BACKSPACE	Scrolls up one page at a time.
HOME	Moves you to the beginning of the node.
END	Moves you to the end of the node.
N	Takes you to the next node.
P	Takes you to the previous node.
Q	Unloads the current document and exits the utility.

Table 5-5   Keystrokes for Navigating in Info

Notice in Figure 5-20 that the top line of the info display shows information about the page currently displayed. The file that contains the information is named coreutils .info. Within the coreutils.info file, the *ls invocation* node is currently being displayed. The next node in the file is named *dir invocation.*

One of the key differences between info and man is that info divides the information into nodes, whereas man displays all information related to the particular utility or command on a single page. You can use the keystrokes listed in Table 5-5 to navigate within a node in the info utility as well as between nodes.

Just as you can search for information using the man utility, you can also search for information using info. If you want to search for information within the node displayed, press CTRL-S. When you do, the I-search prompt is displayed, as shown in Figure 5-21. At the I-search prompt, enter the text you want to search for and press ENTER. The first instance of the text you entered after your current cursor location is displayed. Pressing CTRL-S again will jump to the next instance of the string you entered.

Let's practice using info in the following exercise.

Exercise 5-7: Using info   In this exercise, you will practice using the info utility to view documentation for your Linux system. Complete the following:

1. If you haven't already, boot your Linux system and log in.

2. If necessary, start a terminal session.

3. At the shell prompt, enter **info ls**.

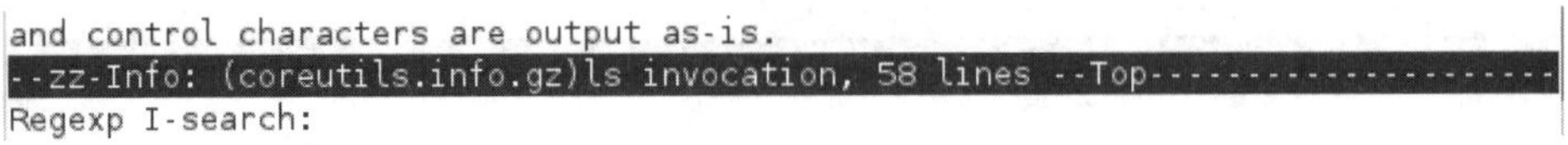

```
and control characters are output as-is.
--zz-Info: (coreutils.info.gz)ls invocation, 58 lines --Top--------------------
Regexp I-search:
```

Figure 5-21   Searching within info

4. Answer the following questions:
   - What does the ls utility do?
   - What does the –l option do when used with ls?
   - In which node does the ls documentation reside?
   - What node comes before the current node?
   - What node comes after the current node?
   - If you wanted the ls utility to list the contents of subdirectories recursively, what option would you use?

5. Close info by pressing Q.

Using Linux Text Editors

One of the key skills you will need when working with any Linux system (and for your Linux Essentials exam) is the ability to use a text editor effectively. Most system configuration tasks in Linux are completed using a text editor to edit a text file, whether you're configuring the operating system itself or configuring a service running on the system.

This represents a significant difference between Linux and other operating systems such as Windows. Under Windows, most of your configuration settings are stored in a database called the Registry, and within the Registry, information is stored in logical sections called keys. These keys are stored in a hierarchy; a given key can contain a number of subkeys. These keys contain values that store the system's configuration information.

The Registry is a good concept, but one of the problems with it is that it isn't designed with the end user in mind. While a Registry editor named Regedit.exe is supplied with Windows, you are discouraged from manually editing values in the Registry. Instead, you're supposed to let the operating system and the applications installed on the system make any and all changes to the Registry.

Linux, on the other hand, doesn't use a central database of all system configuration information. Instead, all of the configuration information is stored in text files. Most of these file are stored in the /etc directory in your Linux file system. For example, the text file used to configure which storage devices are automatically mounted when the system boots is the /etc/fstab file, shown in Figure 5-22.

```
tux@ws2:~> cat /etc/fstab
/dev/sda1            swap                swap      defaults           0 0
/dev/sda2            /                   ext4      acl,user_xattr     1 1
/dev/sda3            /home               ext4      acl,user_xattr     1 2
proc                 /proc               proc      defaults           0 0
sysfs                /sys                sysfs     noauto             0 0
debugfs              /sys/kernel/debug   debugfs   noauto             0 0
devpts               /dev/pts            devpts    mode=0620,gid=5    0 0
tux@ws2:~> 
```

Figure 5-22 Viewing the /etc/fstab file

Instead of discouraging you from manually editing these configuration files, as Windows does with the Registry, Linux *expects* you to know how to edit these files to customize the way your system runs. Therefore, you must know how to use Linux text editors to manage your system.

At this point, you may be thinking, "I know how to use text editors on other operating systems. I can use Notepad on Windows. Why are we devoting so much time to text editors in this book?" There are two reasons:

- Knowing how to use a text editor is absolutely critical to being able to manage a Linux system. If you can't use a text editor, you will struggle with the topics presented throughout the rest of this book.

- Linux editors are difficult for most new users to learn how to use, especially if they come from a Windows background.

Therefore, in this chapter, you're going to spend a significant amount of time learning how to use a variety of Linux text-editing tools.

In this part of this chapter, we'll look at the following:

- Launching vi
- Using vi to edit text files
- Using pico and nano to edit text files

Launching vi

The most commonly used Linux text editor is the vi editor. It is small, it doesn't require a graphical environment, and it is portable enough to fix on external storage media. This makes it ideal for use in emergency repair situations when you need to boot and repair a malfunctioning system from a USB flash drive.

There are two versions of vi. The older version is called simply vi; the newer version is called vim (for vi *im*proved). On older systems, you may be using the original vi when you enter **vi** at a shell prompt. However, on most modern Linux distributions, you are probably using the vim version of vi.

Using vi to Edit Text Files

The first time you run vi, you'll notice right away that its user interface is very different from what you may be used to with other text editors. We'll discuss the following vi topics here:

- Opening files in vi
- vi modes
- Working in insert mode
- Working in command-line mode
- Working in command mode

Opening a File in vi

To open a file from the shell prompt to edit in vi, enter **vi** *filename*. For example, suppose there is a file named myfile.txt in your user's home directory. If the file resides in the current directory, you can enter **vi myfile.txt** at the shell prompt to load this file into the vi editor. If the file resides in a directory other than the current directory, however, you need to include the full path to the file. For example, if your current directory is /tmp and you need to open the /home/tux/myfile.txt file in vi, you would enter **vi /home/tux/myfile.txt** at the shell prompt.

It's also possible to create a new text file using vi. To do this, enter **vi** followed by the name of the file you wish to create at the shell prompt. If you don't include a path with the filename, the file will be created in the current directory. If you do specify a path, the file will be created in that directory.

For example, Figure 5-23 shows the result of entering the command vi yourfile.txt at the shell prompt in the current directory /home/tux. Notice that a blank file has been opened in the vi editor interface, as indicated by the [New File] text at the bottom of the screen. It's important to note that when creating a new file with vi the file isn't created on disk until you save the file. Until you save it, all the lines of text you enter in the vi interface are saved only in a memory buffer. If you don't save the file, you will lose it!

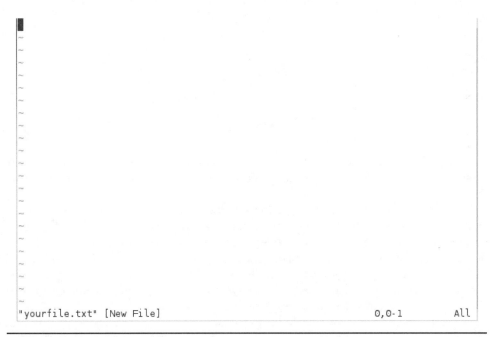

Figure 5-23   Creating a new text file

vi Modes

So far, so good, right? Most of my students can handle opening a file in vi or creating a new file. However, once the file is opened, things start to get a little confusing. That's because vi uses four different operating modes:

- Command mode
- Command-line mode
- Insert mode
- Replace mode

By default, vi opens or creates a file in command (sometimes called *normal*) mode. You probably noticed in the preceding figures that the vi interface doesn't include any pull-down menus that you can use to complete operations on the current file, such as writing, searching, or closing. Instead, you must use commands in command (and command-line) mode to accomplish these tasks.

The confusing part for most of my students is that, while in command or command-line mode, you can't edit the file! Unless you happen to hit the right key, nothing happens on the screen if you try to change the text of the file. To change text, you must first enter insert mode by pressing any one of the following (case-sensitive) keys on the keyboard:

- I
- INSERT
- S
- O
- A

Pressing one of these keys allows you to edit the text of the file. You can tell you're in insert mode by the --INSERT-- text displayed at the bottom of the vi interface, as shown in Figure 5-24.

Pressing INSERT a second time will cause vi to switch to replace mode. Insert mode is analogous to using a word processor in insert mode. Any text you type is inserted wherever the cursor is located in the file. All text that already exists after the cursor is moved down a space for each character typed.

Replace mode, on the other hand, is analogous to overtype mode in a word processor. When you type in new characters, the new characters overwrite any existing characters. You can toggle back to insert mode by pressing INSERT again.

While in insert mode, you can add text, change text, or delete text from the file. However, you can't perform any file operations. For example, if you make changes to a file and want to save them, you can't do so while in insert mode. Instead, you must first switch back to command mode by pressing ESC. Figure 5-25 shows the screen after pressing ESC to switching from insert mode back into command mode. Notice that the --INSERT-- text is no longer displayed in the bottom left corner of the screen.

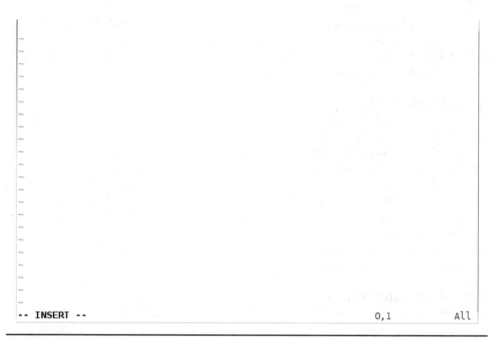

Figure 5-24   Insert mode

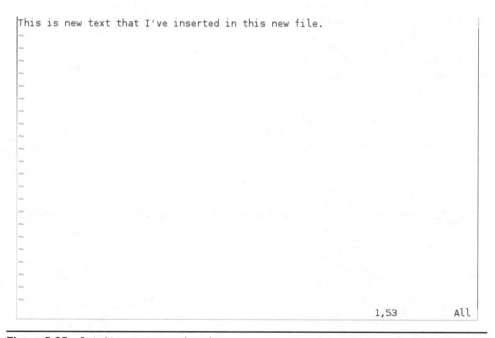

Figure 5-25   Switching to command mode

In command mode, you can enter a variety of different commands to delete lines of text or search the file for particular words. You can also enter command mode where you can save the current file or exit the editor. We'll review these commands later in this section. To switch back to insert mode, just press I, INSERT, or S.

Using Insert Mode

Once you have opened a file in vi and entered insert mode, you can edit the text as you would with any other text editor. Note that, on the left side of the screen, you see several lines of tildes (~). These characters aren't in the file; they indicate that these lines don't exist in the file. After adding lines to the file, you'll see that the tildes disappear one at a time.

You can navigate around to different insertion points in the file by pressing the arrow keys as well as the PAGE UP, PAGE DOWN, HOME, and END keys. You can add text by typing characters on the keyboard. You can remove text by pressing DELETE or BACKSPACE.

Once you're done editing the text, you can then switch back to command mode by pressing ESC. From command mode, you can also enter command-line mode.

Using Command-line Mode

As we discussed earlier, the vi editor doesn't provide menus to accomplish common file tasks. Instead, you have to enter commands in command-line mode. In this topic, we'll review some of the commands you can use and what they do.

To enter command-line mode in vi, you must first enter command mode (if you were previously in insert mode) and then enter a colon (:). When you do, a command prompt is displayed at the bottom of the screen, as shown in Figure 5-26.

Figure 5-26 The vi command prompt

You can then enter commands at this prompt to accomplish file-related tasks. Obviously, one of the most important tasks you'll need to complete in command mode is to write the file to disk. This is done by entering **w** at the command prompt. Be sure to press ENTER after entering the command. After entering **w** at the command prompt, a message is displayed at the bottom of the screen indicating that the file has been written to disk, as shown in this example:

```
"yourfile.txt" [New] 1L, 28C written                    1,26
All
```

Entering **w** *filename* at the command prompt will write the file to a different filename. You can also enter the following other commands at the command-line prompt:

- **exit** Writes the current file and then closes vi.
- **wq** Also writes the current file to disk and closes vi.
- **q** Closes vi without saving the current file. This can only be used if the file hasn't been changed. If the file has been changed, then you must enter **q!**.
- **w!** Overwrites the current file.
- **e!** Forgets changes since last write.

Another useful feature of the vi editor is that it provides a very useful syntax checker. This feature can be a real lifesaver when writing scripts or editing a configuration file. There's nothing more frustrating than having a script or daemon not work because you forgot a semicolon or closing parenthesis somewhere. The syntax checker can be enabled or disabled using the syntax command-line command. Press ESC to enter command mode, and then enter **:syntax on | off**. For example, to enable the syntax checker, you would enter the following:

```
:syntax on
```

When you do this, different elements in the script or configuration file are denoted with different colors. If you make a syntax error, the mistake will be highlighted with an alternate color, making it easy for you to spot. An example of using the vi syntax checker while editing a daemon's configuration file is shown in Figure 5-27.

In addition to commands that are entered at the command-line prompt, you can also enter commands in command mode. Let's discuss these commands next.

Using Command Mode

Command mode commands aren't entered at the command prompt. Instead, they are entered *without* entering a **:** first. If you are in insert mode, press ESC to return to command mode. Then you can enter the following commands:

- **dw** Deletes the word that comes immediately after the cursor, including the space following the word. The text is saved in a memory buffer.
- **de** Deletes the word that comes immediately after the cursor, not including the space. The text is saved in a memory buffer.

```
# default: off
# description: rsync file transfer daemon
service rsync
{
        socket_type     = stream
        protocol        = tcp
        wait            = no
        user            = root
        server          = /usr/sbin/rsyncd
        server_args     = --daemon
        disable         = yes
}
~
~
~
~
~
~
~
~
~
~
~
~
:syntax on
```

Figure 5-27 The vi syntax checker

- **d$** Deletes from the insertion point to the end of the line. The text is saved in a memory buffer.

- **dd** Deletes the entire current line. The text is saved in a memory buffer.

- **p** Inserts the text deleted in the last deletion operation after the current cursor location.

- **u** Undoes the last action.

- **D** Deletes the rest of the current line from the cursor position.

- **yy** Copies the line in which the cursor is located to the buffer.

- **a** Appends text after the cursor.

- **A** Appends text to the end of the current line.

- **C** Changes characters in the current line, until ESC is hit.

- **cw** Changes (replaces) the current word with new text, starting with the character under the cursor, until ESC is hit

- **cc** Changes (replaces) the entire current line, until ESC is hit.

- **ZZ** Saves the current file and ends vi.

- **h** Moves the cursor left one character.

- **j** Moves the cursor down one line.

- **k** Moves the cursor up one line.

- **l** Moves the cursor right one character.

- **0** Moves the cursor to the start of the current line.

- CTRL-G Displays a status line at the bottom of the interface that includes the name of the file, the status of the file, the total number of lines in the file, and the current cursor location, as in the following example:

```
"yourfile.txt" [Modified] 2 lines --100%--                    2,29        All
```

- **/search_term** Searches for the next instance of the term specified. For example, entering **/init** searches for the next instance of the text "init" after the cursor. Pressing N after executing a search will search for the next instance of the search term. In Figure 5-28, the /file command has been entered while in command mode. The first instance of *file* has been highlighted as a result.

- **?/search_term** Searches for the previous instance of the term specified.

As you can see, vi is a simple yet powerful text editor. The only complaint I have about vi is that its user interface can be difficult to learn. However, once you've used vi for a while, it will become second nature to you.

Let's spend some time practicing with vi in the following exercise.

```
# default: off
# description: rsync file transfer daemon
service rsync
{
        socket_type        = stream
        protocol           = tcp
        wait               = no
        user               = root
        server             = /usr/sbin/rsyncd
        server_args        = --daemon
        disable            = yes
}
~
~
~
~
~
~
~
~
~
~
~
~
search hit BOTTOM, continuing at TOP                    2,22        All
```

Figure 5-28 Searching for text in vi

Exercise 5-8: Using the vi Editor   In this exercise, you will practice using the vi editor to create and manipulate text files. Complete the following:

1. If you haven't already, boot your Linux system and log in using your standard (nonroot) user account.

2. If necessary, open a terminal session.

3. The current directory should be your user's home directory. You can check this by entering **pwd** at the shell prompt. In this example, the user account is named tux, so the current directory is displayed as /home/tux:

   ```
   tux@ws2:~> pwd
   /home/tux
   ```

4. At the shell prompt enter **vi test.txt**. The vi editor should run with test.txt open as a new file.

5. Press the INSERT key on your keyboard. You should now be in insert mode.

6. Enter the following text in the file:

   ```
   Usu agam legere delicata ut, per democritum scriptorem an. Nec
   te zzril possim tincidunt, at qui probo mucius gubergren. Ea mei
   paulo cetero oportere, at pertinax liberavisse pri.
   ```

7. Save your file by completing the following:

   a. Press ESC to return to command mode.

   b. Enter **:w**. You should see a message indicating that the file was written.

8. Exit vi by entering **:exit**.

9. Reload test.txt in vi by entering **vi test.txt** at the shell prompt.

10. Display the status line by pressing CTRL-G while in command mode.

11. Use the arrow keys to move the cursor to the beginning of the first word in the first line of the file.

12. Search for all occurrences of the text "at" by doing the following:

    a. While in command mode, enter **/at**. The first instance should be highlighted.

    b. Find the next instance by pressing the N key.

    c. Find the remaining instance by pressing N until you reach the end of the file.

13. Practice deleting text by doing the following:

    a. While in command mode, use the arrow keys to place the cursor on the first letter of the word *legere*.

    b. Delete the word *legere* and the space that follows it by entering **dw**.

    c. Use the arrow keys to move the cursor to the period at the end of the last line.

    d. Put the contents of the memory buffer after the period by entering **p**.

14. Exit the file without saving your changes by entering **:q!**.

Using pico and nano to Edit Text Files

In addition to vi, there are many other text editors you can use with Linux. Two of the more commonly used editors are pico and nano. Both of these editors are minimalist in nature; they only do a little bit, but they do it well.

Be aware that pico is not an open source application; its source code is protected by a proprietary license.

The syntax for using pico is pico *filename*. For example, to load a file named teammembers.txt, located in the current directory, you enter pico teammembers.txt at the shell prompt. You can then edit the file as you would in any other text editor. Some commands and shortcuts you can use while editing a file in pico include the following:

- CTRL-K/CTRL-U   Cuts and pastes text.
- CTRL-U   Undoes an action.
- CTRL-W   Searches for text in the file.
- CTRL-O   Saves the file currently open.
- CTRL-X   Exits the editor when done editing the file. If you modified the file, you'll be prompted to save your changes.

The nano editor is an open source clone of the pico editor and uses the same syntax and keystrokes that pico does. Press CTRL-G to view a complete list of available commands.

Chapter Review

We started this chapter by reviewing the two user interfaces provided by most Linux distributions: the command-line interface and the graphical user interface. We discussed the shell configuration files and pointed out that there are two types of shells on a Linux system:

- Login shells
- Non-login shells

When running a login shell, /etc/profile is read first to initially configure the shell environment. The shell then searches for the following files in the user's home directory in the following order:

- .bash_profile
- .bash_login
- .profile

The shell will read the first of these files found and use it to configure the shell environment for the current user. Different Linux distributions will use different bash configuration files.

We then discussed the command history function of the bash shell. Using command history, you can press the UP ARROW key to scroll through a list of previously entered commands. These commands are saved in the .bash_history file in each user's home directory.

The bash shell also offers command completion. Using command completion, you can enter part of a command and then press the TAB key to automatically finish the command for you.

At this point in the chapter, we turned to a discussion of environment variables. Environment variables are used to configure the shell environment. These variables are automatically populated when the bash shell is started, but you can modify many of them if needed. You can view the value of an environment variable using the following utilities:

- echo

- env

To set the value of a variable, you can enter *variable_name=value*. After assigning a new value to an environment variable, you can enter **export** *variable_name* at the shell prompt to make the new value available to other shells, including subshells launched by the current shell.

It's important to remember that any change you make to an environment variable is not persistent. To make it persistent, you need to edit one of the bash configuration files discussed in this chapter to make the value assignment to the variable each time a shell is started.

I also pointed out that you can create your own variables from the shell prompt using the same technique as described for environment variables. Like environment variables, user-defined variables have to be exported in order for them to be available to other shells.

Next, we discussed how to get help when working with the Linux shell. We first reviewed how to use the man utility to view manual pages. Most commands and utilities on your Linux system have a man page associated with them that contains information about what they do and how to use them, and all of the man pages together compose the manual. The manual is divided into sections according to the functionality of the utility or command. The files that compose the manual are stored in the directory specified by the MANPATH variable or the MANPATH directive in the /etc/man_db.conf file.

To use man, you enter **man** followed by the name of the command, utility, file, or service that you need to learn more about. We reviewed the different sections used in most man pages and the keystrokes you can use to navigate within a man page.

We also discussed how to search man pages for a word within a single man page by entering / followed by a text string . You can also use man –k or the apropos utility to search for text across man pages.

After discussing the man utility, we turned our attention to the info utility, which contains more extensive documentation than the man utility. To view information about a command or utility, you enter **info** followed by the name of the utility you want to learn about. We also discussed the keystrokes you can use to navigate within and between info nodes, and I pointed out that you can search info nodes for a string of text by pressing CTRL-S and entering a search pattern.

To end this chapter, we discussed how to use the vi text editor. I emphasized the important role text editors play in Linux system management. Unlike other operating systems that use a database to store system and application settings, Linux stores this information in text files. Therefore, to configure a Linux system, you need to know how to edit these files.

The most commonly used Linux text editor is the vi editor. It is small, it doesn't require a graphical environment, and it can fit on external storage devices. This makes it ideal for use in emergency repair situations when you need to boot and repair a malfunctioning system.

To run vi, enter **vi** at a shell prompt. To run vi and load a file, enter **vi** *filename* at a shell prompt. If the filename you specify doesn't exist, vi will create a new file for you.

We then discussed the four different modes that vi can operate in. In command mode, you can't directly edit the text of the file. Instead, you need to switch to insert mode or replace mode by pressing the INSERT, S, O, or I key. To return to command mode, you just press the ESC key. Once in insert mode or replace mode, you can edit the text file as you would with most typical word processors.

We then discussed the commands you can enter to perform file-related operations in command-line mode. To enter command-line mode, you first switch to command mode (if necessary) and then enter a full colon (:). This causes a command-line prompt to be displayed that you can use to enter vi commands, including the following:

- **w**   Writes the current file to disk.
- **exit**   Writes the current file and then closes vi.
- **wq**   Also writes the current file to disk and closes vi.
- **q**   Closes vi without saving the current file.
- **q!**   Closes vi without saving the current file even if the file has been modified.
- **w!**   Overwrites the current file.
- **e!**   Forgets changes since last write.

We then discussed the text manipulation commands that you can enter in command mode. These commands are entered without entering a colon (:). You can enter the following:

- **dw**   Deletes the word that comes immediately after the cursor, including the space following the word.
- **de**   Deletes the word that comes immediately after the cursor, but not the following space.
- **d$**   Deletes from the insertion point to the end of the line.
- **dd**   Deletes the entire current line.

- **p**   Inserts deleted text after the current cursor location.
- **u**   Undoes the last action.
- **/term**   Searches for the specified term in the file.
- **D**   Deletes the rest of the current line from the cursor position.
- **yy**   Copies the line in which the cursor is located to the buffer.
- **a**   Appends text after the cursor.
- **A**   Appends text to the end of the current line.
- **C**   Changes characters in the current line, until ESC is hit.
- **cc**   Changes (replaces) the entire current line, until ESC is hit.
- **ZZ**   Saves the current file and ends vi.
- **h**   Moves the cursor left one character.
- **j**   Moves the cursor down one line.
- **k**   Moves the cursor up one line.
- **l**   Moves the cursor right one character.
- **0**   Moves the cursor to start of current line.

Accelerated Review

- Linux offers both command-line and graphical user interfaces.
- The Linux command-line interface is created by shells.
- The bash shell is the default shell for most distributions.
- Linux shells do not search the current directory when running a file from the command prompt.
- The default shell for most Linux distributions is the bash shell.
- Shells used to log in to the system are login shells.
- Shells opened after the user has logged in are non-login shells.
- The .bashrc file is used to configure non-login shells.
- The /etc/profile file is the first file read when creating a login shell.
- After the /etc/profile file is read, the bash shell looks for one of the following configuration files in the user's home directory:
  - .bash_profile
  - .bash_login
  - .profile
- The first of these files found is the one used to configure the user's shell environment.

- The bash shell saves your command history in .bash_history.

- Pressing the UP ARROW key displays the last commands entered at the shell prompt.

- The bash shell offers command completion using the TAB key.

- Environment variables are used to define the shell environment.

- You can view the values of your environment variables using the echo, set, or env shell commands.

- You must use a dollar sign ($) when referencing an environment variable to specify that the text is a variable name, not a string.

- You can set the value of an environment variable by entering *variable_name=value* at the shell prompt.

- After setting the value of a variable, you must export it using the export command.

- The value you assign to an environment variable is not persistent.

- To make a variable assignment persistent, you need to add the appropriate commands to one of your bash configuration files.

- You can also create user-defined variables in the same manner as environment variables.

- User-defined variables need to be exported in order for them to be used by other shells.

- Manual (man) pages are one of the primary means for maintaining documentation on a Linux system.

- Manual pages are viewed using the man utility.

- Manual pages are maintained for most commands, utilities, services, and configuration files on your system.

- The location of the man pages in your file system is stored in the MANPATH environment variable or in the MANPATH directive in the /etc/man.config file.

- All of the man pages together compose the manual.

- The manual is divided into the following sections:
  - **Section 1**   User programs and shell commands
  - **Section 2**   Kernel functions
  - **Section 3**   Library functions
  - **Section 4**   Special files found in /dev
  - **Section 5**   File format descriptions and conventions
  - **Section 6**   Games
  - **Section 7**   Miscellaneous conventions
  - **Section 8**   Utilities used by root
  - **Section 9**   Kernel routines

- Man pages are categorized into the various manual sections.
- To view a man page, enter **man** followed by the name of the utility or command that you need information about.
- Man pages are divided into sections.
- Some of the more commonly used man page sections include the following:
  - NAME
  - SYNOPSIS
  - DESCRIPTION
  - AUTHOR
  - REPORTING BUGS
  - COPYRIGHT
  - SEE ALSO
- To search for text within a man page, you enter / followed by the text you want to search for.
- To search for text across man pages, you can use one of the following:
  - man –k
  - apropos
- In addition to man, you can also use the info utility to view system documentation.
- The info utility displays more in-depth information than the man utility.
- The information displayed by the info utility is called a node.
- To use info, enter **info** at the shell prompt followed by the name of the command, utility, or configuration file you need to learn about.
- To search for information in info, press CTRL-S and enter the term you want to search for.
- You must be able to use a text editor to manage a Linux system.
- Linux uses text files to store operating system and application configuration settings.
- Most of your configuration files reside in /etc.
- Many graphical configuration utilities are now available for most Linux distributions; however, you still need to be familiar with manually editing configuration files with a text editor.
- The vi editor is one of the most commonly used Linux text editors.
- The older version of vi was called *vi*; the newest version is called *vim* (for vi *im*proved).
- You can open a file with vi by entering **vi** *filename*. If the file doesn't exist, a new file will be created.

- The vi editor opens in command mode by default.
- You can't directly edit files in vi when you are in command mode.
- To switch to insert mode, press I, S, or INSERT.
- In insert mode, you can directly edit the text of a file.
- Pressing INSERT while in insert mode will cause vi to switch to replace mode.
- To switch back to command mode, press ESC.
- From within command mode, you can enter a full colon (:) to switch to command-line mode.
- In command-line mode, you can enter file-related commands:
  - Entering **:w** will write the current file to disk.
  - Entering **:exit** will write the current file to disk and exit vi.
  - Entering **:q** will exit vi.
  - Entering **:q!** will exit vi without saving changes to a modified file.
- You can enter text manipulation commands from within command mode in vi.
- Entering **dw** deletes the word that comes immediately after the cursor, including the space following the word.
- Entering **de** deletes the word that comes immediately after the cursor, not including the space.
- Entering **d$** deletes from the insertion point to the end of the line.
- Entering **dd** deletes the entire current line.
- Entering **p** inserts the text deleted in the last deletion operation after the cursor.
- Entering **u** undoes the last action.
- Pressing CTRL-G displays a status line at the bottom of the interface.
- Entering **/*search_term*** or **?*search_term*** searches for the term specified.
- In addition to the vi editor, you can also use pico or nano to edit text files.

Questions

1. Which shell is the default shell for most Linux distributions?

    A. sh

    B. csh

    C. bash

    D. zsh

2. You are working at the bash shell in a text-only environment on a Linux system. You have a program currently running when you discover that you need access to the shell prompt to perform another task. You don't want to halt the first program to do this. What can you do?

   A. Nothing, you must halt the first program to access the shell prompt.

   B. Press CTRL-PAUSE on the keyboard to pause the running program while you access the shell prompt.

   C. Press ALT-F2 to open an alternate console screen and access a new shell session.

   D. Press CTRL-SHIFT-F6 to automatically open a new shell session without pausing the running program.

3. You've copied an executable file named updatewebcontent.sh from your company's server to the ~/Downloads directory on your Linux system. You change to the ~/Downloads directory at the shell prompt. When you enter **updatewebcontent.sh**, the shell says the command is invalid. What can you do? (Choose two.)

   A. Enter the filename in all capital letters.

   B. Add a ./ before the filename when entering it at the prompt.

   C. Enter the filename without the .sh extension.

   D. Move the file to your home directory and then execute it.

   E. Include the full path to the executable in the command.

4. You need to find out what directories in the Linux file system are included in the path. What command can you use? (Choose two.)

   A. env

   B. show $PATH

   C. man path

   D. echo $PATH

   E. writeln PATH

5. You've copied an executable file named dailyupdate.sh from your company's server to /tmp on your Linux system. You open a shell and change to the /tmp directory. When you enter **./Dailyupdate.sh**, the shell indicates this is an invalid command. What should you do?

   A. Enter the filename in all lowercase letters.

   B. Add a .\ before the filename when entering it at the prompt.

   C. Enter the filename without the .sh extension.

   D. Move the file to your home directory and then execute it.

   E. Enter the full path of the executable in the command.

6. Which Linux command displays a list of all running processes on your system?

   A. env

   B. uname -a

   C. netstat

   D. top

   E. echo $PROCESSES

7. Which Linux command displays the IP address assigned to your system?

   A. netstat

   B. route

   C. ifconfig

   D. ipconfig

   E. whatis

8. Which Linux utility switches to the root user account at the shell prompt?

   A. user

   B. chuser

   C. switchuser

   D. su

9. Which configuration file is read when a non-login bash shell is run?

   A. .bashrc

   B. .bash_profile

   C. .bash_login

   D. .profile

10. Which configuration file is the first file read when a login bash shell is run?

   A. ~/.bashrc

   B. ~/.bash_profile

   C. ~/.bash_login

   D. ~/.profile

   E. /etc/profile

11. Which file contains a list of your most recently entered shell commands?

   A. ~/.history

   B. ~/.bash_history

   C. /etc/bash_history

   D. ~/.shell_command_history

12. Which keystroke is used for the command completion feature of bash?

    A. ENTER

    B. F1

    C. TAB

    D. UP ARROW

    E. HOME

13. Which utility is used to view manual pages?

    A. man

    B. manual

    C. gman

    D. Kwrite

14. Which environment variable specifies the directory where man page files are located?

    A. MANUAL

    B. MANUALPATH

    C. MPATH

    D. MANPATH

15. Which file configures the path to the man page files?

    A. /etc/man_db.conf

    B. /etc/man.conf

    C. /etc/man.txt

    D. /etc/manual.conf

    E. ~/.MANPATH

16. Which of the following manual sections contains man pages for administrative utilities used by the root user?

    A. 1

    B. 3

    C. 8

    D. 9

17. Which of the following manual sections contains man pages for utilities and commands that can be used by any user?

    A. 9

    B. 1

    C. 3

    D. 7

18. You need to learn about the options available for the cd utility. Which command will display its manual page?

    A. gman cd

    B. cat cd | man

    C. manual cd

    D. man cd

19. You need to learn about the options available for the chgrp utility. Which command will display its manual page?

    A. gman chgrp

    B. manual chgrp

    C. man chgrp

    D. man display chgrp

20. Which section in a man page provides a brief review of the syntax used for a particular command or utility?

    A. REVIEW

    B. SYNOPSIS

    C. DESCRIPTION

    D. SYNTAX

21. Which section in a man page provides a list of man pages or other resources related to the particular command or utility?

    A. DESCRIPTION

    B. VERSION

    C. SEE ALSO

    D. REFERENCES

22. You're using man to view the man page for the chmod utility. Which keystroke will unload the current man page and exit man?

    A. CTRL-U

    B. X

    C. CTRL-X

    D. Q

    E. CTRL-Z

23. You're using man to view the man page for the NTP daemon. Which keystrokes can you use to search for the term "server" in the man page?

   A. /"server"

   B. CTRL-S

   C. /server

   D. CTRL-F

24. After searching for a term within a man page, you need to jump to the next instance of the term in the page. Which keystroke will do this?

   A. Q

   B. P

   C. N

   D. S

25. You need to search for man pages that relate to the Samba daemon. Which command will do this? (Choose two.)

   A. man –s samba

   B. man –k samba

   C. search samba | man

   D. which samba

   E. apropos samba

26. You need to search for man pages that relate to the PAM service. Which command will do this?

   A. which pam

   B. man –s pam

   C. search pam | man

   D. apropos pam

   E. whatis pam

27. You need to use info to view information about using the smbpasswd utility. Which command will do this?

   A. info /smbpasswd

   B. info "smbpasswd"

   C. show info smbpasswd

   D. info smbpasswd

28. While viewing an info node, which keystroke can be used to navigate to the next node?

    A. /next

    B. P

    C. N

    D. L

29. While viewing an info node, which keystroke can be used to navigate to the previous node?

    A. P

    B. /prev

    C. N

    D. /up

30. While viewing an info node, which keystroke can be used to navigate to the beginning of the node?

    A. B

    B. /top

    C. HOME

    D. T

31. You want to add the ~/temp directory to your system's PATH environment variable. You want to be sure you don't overwrite the existing directories in your path, so you enter **PATH=PATH:~/temp** at your shell prompt. Did you do this correctly?

    A. Yes, this command will work correctly.

    B. No, you must first export the variable before you set it.

    C. No, you must use a $ before each PATH variable name in the command.

    D. No, you must use a $ before the second PATH variable name in the command.

32. Which commands can you use to view the values currently assigned to your environment variables? (Choose two.)

    A. echo

    B. display

    C. var

    D. show

    E. env

33. The current directory is /tmp. You need to use vi to edit a text file named myservice.conf in the /etc directory on your system. Which of the following commands will do this?

 A. vi myservice.conf

 B. vi /tmp/myservice.conf

 C. vi /etc/myservice.conf

 D. vi /myservice.conf

34. You've opened a text file named list.txt in vi. You move the cursor using the arrow keys to the point in the file where you need to make several changes. You try to type, but nothing happens. Why is this happening?

 A. The vi editor is in insert mode. You need to switch to command mode.

 B. The vi editor is in command mode. You need to switch to insert mode.

 C. The vi editor is in insert mode. You need to switch to replace mode.

 D. The text file is corrupt.

 E. F1

35. You're using vi to edit a text file in insert mode. You need to switch to replace mode. Which keystroke will do this?

 A. ESC

 B. CTRL-X CTRL-R

 C. :

 D. INSERT

36. You're using vi to edit a file in insert mode. You need to switch back to command mode. Which keystroke will do this?

 A. INSERT

 B. :

 C. ESC

 D. BACKSPACE

37. You're using vi to edit a file in command mode. You try to use the BACKSPACE key to delete a word, but nothing happens. What's wrong with the system?

 A. You need to switch to normal mode.

 B. You need to press CTRL-BACKSPACE.

 C. Nothing is wrong. BACKSPACE doesn't work in command mode.

 D. You need to switch to command-line mode.

38. You've created a new file using vi and need to save the file to disk and exit the program. Which command will do this? (Choose two.)

    A. :w

    B. :e!

    C. :wq

    D. :exit

    E. :q

39. You've made several changes to a configuration file using vi. You realize that you've made many mistakes and need to quit without saving the changes so that you can start over. Which command will do this?

    A. :q!

    B. :exit

    C. :q

    D. :exit!

40. You're working with a file in vi in command mode. You locate a word in the file that needs to be deleted and place your cursor at the beginning of that word. Which command will delete this word without deleting the space that follows the word?

    A. dw

    B. de

    C. d$

    D. dd

Answers

1. **C.** bash is the default shell used with most Linux distributions.

2. **C.** Pressing ALT-F2 will open an alternate console. You can use this console to perform other tasks without stopping the program running in the first console screen. You can switch back by pressing ALT-F1.

3. **B and E.** Adding ./ before the filename tells the shell that the file resides in the current directory. Including the full path to the executable in the command also tells the shell where the executable resides.

4. **A and D.** Both of these commands will print the PATH environment variable on the screen.

5. **A.** Linux is case-sensitive. The command in the question uses an uppercase *U*.

6. **D.** The top utility displays running processes.

7. **C.** The ifconfig command is used to view and modify your network board configuration.

8. **D.** The su command changes to a different user account at the shell prompt. The syntax is su *username*. If you omit the username, su assumes you want to switch to the root superuser account.

9. **A.** A non-login shell reads the ~/.bashrc file to define the user's shell environment.

10. **E.** The /etc/profile file is read when a bash login shell is first opened.

11. **B.** The ~/.bash_history file contains a list of your most recent shell commands.

12. **C.** The TAB key is used with command completion.

13. **A.** The man utility is used to view man pages. If an info node isn't available for a particular command or utility, then info may display a man page as well.

14. **D.** The MANPATH environment variable stores the path to the man pages on many Linux distributions.

15. **A.** You can use the /etc/man_db.conf file to specify the path to the man files on some Linux distributions.

16. **C.** Section 8 of the manual contains man pages for utilities and commands used by root.

17. **B.** Section 1 of the manual contains man pages for commands that can be used by any user.

18. **D.** The man cd command will display the man page for cd.

19. **C.** The man s command will display the man page for chmod.

20. **B.** The SYNOPSIS section of a man page provides a review of the syntax used for a command or utility.

21. **C.** The SEE ALSO section of a man page provides a list of related resources.

22. **D.** Pressing Q will exit man.

23. **C.** To search for the expression "server" in a man page, you enter /**server**.

24. **C.** After entering a search term, pressing N will take you to the next instance of that term in a man page.

25. **B and E.** Entering man –k samba will search across man pages for the term "samba." Entering apropos samba will accomplish the same task.

26. **D and E.** Entering apropos pam will search across man pages for the term "pam." Entering whatis pam will accomplish the same task.

27. **D.** Entering info smbpasswd will cause info to display information about the smbpasswd utility.

28. **C.** Pressing N will jump to the next node.

29. **A.** Pressing P will jump to the previous node.

30. **C.** Pressing the HOME key will take you to the first line in an info node.

31. **D.** You must reference the PATH variable using $PATH after the = sign. Otherwise, PATH will be interpreted as a literal string of text.

32. **A and E.** You can use the echo command or the env command to view your variables.

33. **C.** Because the file to be loaded doesn't reside in the current directory, you have to provide the full path to the file along with its filename when starting vi.

34. **B.** The vi editor opens by default in command mode. You must press INSERT to switch to insert mode to start editing the file.

35. **D.** Pressing INSERT while in insert mode will switch vi to replace mode.

36. **C.** Pressing ESC while in insert mode switches vi to command mode.

37. **C.** The BACKSPACE key doesn't work in command mode. You must first switch to insert or replace mode.

38. **C and D.** Entering :exit will cause vi to save the current file and exit the program, as will entering :wq.

39. **A.** Entering :q! will exit vi without saving changes to the current file.

40. **B.** Entering de in command mode will cause vi to delete the word without deleting the space that follows the word.

Working with Files and Directories

In this chapter, you will learn about

- Linux file systems and the Filesystem Hierarchy Standard (FHS)
- Managing directories from the command line
- Managing files from the command line
- Finding files in the Linux file system
- Working with link files

It's time to dig in and start working with Linux files and directories! If you're coming to Linux from a Windows background, this chapter may be challenging for you. The Linux file system is similar to the file systems used in Windows systems in many ways, but it is radically different in many others. My experience with new Linux students is that there are just enough similarities to give you a false sense of security when you initially start working with the file system. Then, as we dig deeper and start looking at more advanced tasks, confusion and frustration set in.

Hopefully, I can make things as easy to understand as possible as we work through this chapter. If I could emphasize one thing that will make your life easier, it would be to remember that Linux file and directory names are case-sensitive! New Linux users tend to really struggle with this aspect of the Linux file system. When you see a command or filename in an example or exercise in this book, remember that you must use the correct case; otherwise, you won't get the same results!

Linux File Systems and the Filesystem Hierarchy Standard (FHS)

In this part of the chapter, we're going to discuss the Linux file system in general. Specifically, we're going to review the following:

- The role of the Linux file system
- The hierarchical structure of the Linux file system

- Linux file types
- Disk file systems used on Linux

The Role of the Linux File System

So what exactly is the role of the file system? On a Linux system (or any other operating system, for that matter), the file system stores information on a storage device in such a manner that:

- Data can be saved in a persistent manner.
- Data is organized and can be easily located.
- Data can be quickly retrieved for use at a later point in time.
- Data integrity is preserved.

In other words, if you save a file to a storage device you should be able to find it later on and retrieve it, all the while assured that its contents will be exactly the same as when it was saved. It doesn't matter whether you're saving data to a hard drive or a USB drive; the goals are the same. To accomplish this, you must use some type of file system to manage stored data.

NOTE The term "file system" actually has multiple meanings in the Linux world. You may hear the terms "ext2," "ext3," "ext4," and "Reiser" referred to as *file systems*. That usage is correct, they are file systems. However, they are more properly identified as *disk file systems*. They are used to define how data is stored on your Linux system's hard disk drive. A disk file system is a specific implementation of the general file system. Specifics about each type of file system will be discussed later in this chapter.

Let's review how the Linux file system organizes the data to make it easily locatable and retrievable using the Filesystem Hierarchy Standard (FHS).

The Hierarchical Structure of the Linux File System

The Linux file system uses a hierarchical structure to organize and store data. This is shown in Figure 6-1.

The topmost directory in the structure is the / directory, also called the *root* directory, which by the way has nothing to do with your root user account. It simply indicates that this is the topmost directory (the "root") of your hierarchical file system tree.

Beneath the root directory are many subdirectories. Specifications for how these directories are to be named are contained in the *Filesystem Hierarchy Standard (FHS)*. The FHS provides Linux software developers and system administrators with a standard directory structure for the file system, ensuring consistency between systems and distributions. Can you imagine the mess if every distribution used its own proprietary file system structure? What a disaster! You wouldn't be able to find anything.

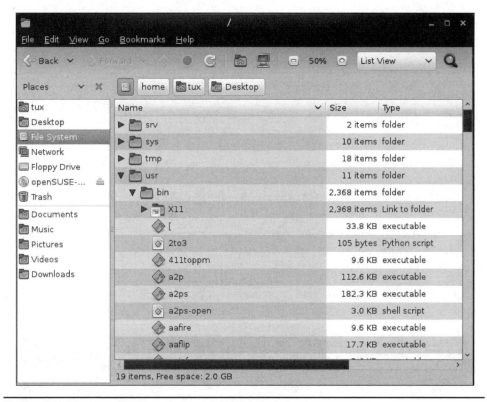

Figure 6-1 The hierarchical structure of the Linux file system

NOTE You can view more information about the FHS at www.pathname .com/fhs/.

Fortunately, we have the FHS to keep everyone in line. The FHS defines the directories that should appear under the root directory (/) as well as the directories that should appear under the /usr and /var directories. These include the following:

- **/bin** This directory contains executable files necessary to manage and run the Linux system, including shells (such as bash) and file system management utilities such as cp and rm.

- **/boot** This directory contains your bootloader files, which are required to boot your system.

- **/dev** This directory contains special files that are used to represent the various hardware devices installed in the system. For example, the first hard disk drive in your system is called sda, the second is called sdb, and so on. The partitions on each drive are identified by an additional number added to the end of the disk filename. For example, the first partition on the first hard drive in the system is sda1, the second partition is sda2, and so on. The files that represent these devices are stored in /dev, as shown in Figure 6-2. Notice in the figure that two kinds of device files are stored in /dev:

NOTE In older versions of the Linux kernel, SCSI, USB, and SATA hard drives were denoted by sdx while older PATA (IDE) hard drives were denoted by hdx. This is no longer the case. Now all hard disks are denoted by sdx.

- **Character-oriented device files** These files are used for devices that send or receive data sequentially one character at a time; such as a printer, mouse, or tape drive. These devices usually don't support random access to the data stored on them.

- **Block-oriented device files** These files are used for devices that manage data in blocks; such as floppy disks and hard drives. Block devices usually support random access to the data stored on them.

Many types of hardware devices are represented by device files in /dev. A sampling is shown in Table 6-1. The key thing to understand is the fact that the physical hardware in

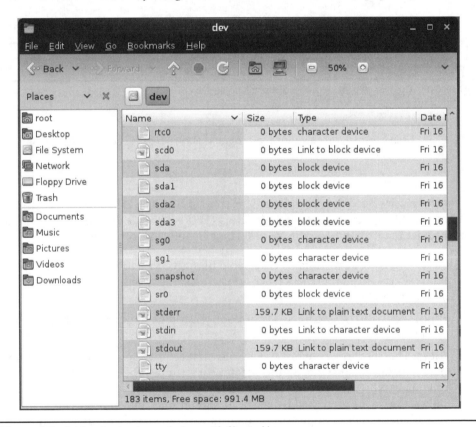

Figure 6-2 Addressing hardware devices with files in /dev

	Device	Device File in /dev
Table 6-1	Floppy drive	/dev/fd0
Hardware	Optical drive (CD or DVD)	/dev/scd0
Represented	Serial port	/dev/ttyS0
by Files in /dev	Parallel port	/dev/lp0

a Linux system is addressed by applications and services running on the system through the files in /dev. Need to save a file to disk? It goes through the appropriate file in /dev. Need to send a print job to a printer? It goes through a file in /dev. Need to open a file from a DVD? It comes in through a file in /dev.

 TIP Device files in /dev can also be used to access system resources that have no connection to any physical hardware device, such as random number generators (/dev/random).

- **/etc** This directory contains text-based configuration files used by the system as well as services running on the system. You can edit these files with a text editor to customize how Linux behaves. Some of the more important files in this directory include those shown in Table 6-2.

File	Function
/etc/aliases	Contains a table used to redirect mail to local recipients.
/etc/exports	Configures file systems to be exported to remote NFS clients.
/etc/fstab	Lists the partitions and file systems that will be automatically mounted when the system boots.
/etc/ftpusers	Controls user access to the FTP service running on the system.
/etc/group	Contains local group definitions.
/etc/grub.conf	Contains configuration parameters for the GRUB bootloader.
/etc/hosts	Contains a list of hostname-to-IP address mappings the system can use to resolve hostnames.
/etc/inittab	Contains configuration parameters for the init process.
/etc/init.d/	A subdirectory that contains startup scripts for services installed on the system. On a Fedora or Red Hat system, these are located in /etc/rc.d/init.d.
/etc/modules.conf	Contains configuration parameters for your kernel modules.
/etc/nsswitch.conf	Configures which services are to be used to resolve hostnames and to store users, groups, and passwords.
/etc/passwd	Contains your system user accounts.
/etc/resolv.conf	Specifies the DNS server and domain suffix used by the system.
/etc/services	Maps port numbers to named services on the system.
/etc/shadow	Contains encrypted passwords for your user accounts.
/etc/X11/	Contains X Window configuration files.

Table 6-2   Some of the Configuration Files in /etc

- **/home** This directory contains subdirectories that serve as home directories for each user account on your Linux system.

- **/lib** This directory contains code libraries used by programs in /bin and /sbin. Your kernel modules are also stored in the modules subdirectory of /lib.

- **/media** This directory is used by some Linux distributions (such as OpenSUSE and Fedora) to mount external devices, including optical drives, USB drives, and floppy diskettes (if you're still using them). This is done using a series of subdirectories, shown in Figure 6-3.

- **/mnt** This directory is used by some Linux distributions to mount external devices, including CD drives, DVD drives, USB drives, and floppies. As with the /media directory on other distributions, a series of subdirectories is used to do this.

- **/opt** This directory contains files for some programs you install on the system.

- **/proc** This directory is a little different from the other directories in this list. /proc doesn't actually exist in the file system. Instead, it's a pseudo–file system that is dynamically created whenever it is accessed. It's used to access process and other system information from the Linux kernel.

  Within /proc are a number of different subdirectories, as shown in Figure 6-4. Notice that each of these subdirectories is identified with a number, not a name.

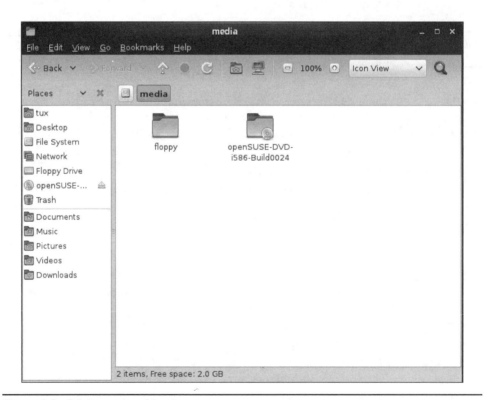

Figure 6-3 Subdirectories of /media

These numbers correspond to the process ID (PID) number of the associated software process running on the system. In Figure 6-5, the *top* program is being run to display the running processes on the system.

The PID column, on the far-left side of the display, lists the PID number of each software process. The actual name of the command that was run to create the process is displayed in the far-right column of the display. For example, the process associated with the top program itself has a PID of 10178. Therefore, if you were to look in the /proc/10178 directory, you could view information about the top process running on the system, as shown in Figure 6-6.

- **/root** This directory is the root user's home directory. Notice that it is located separately from the home directories for other users in /home.

- **/sbin** This directory contains important system management and administration files, such as fdisk, fsck, ifconfig, init, mkfs, shutdown, and halt.

- **/srv** This directory contains subdirectories where services running on the system (such as httpd and ftpd) save their files.

- **/sys** This directory contains information about the hardware in your system.

- **/tmp** This directory contains temporary files created by you or by the system.

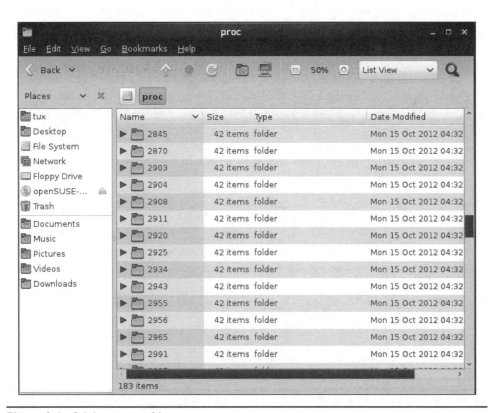

Figure 6-4 Subdirectories of /proc

```
tux@ws2:~/Desktop                          _  □  ×
File   Edit   View   Search   Terminal   Help
top - 16:39:35 up 8 min,  3 users,  load average: 0.19, 0.56, 0.38
Tasks: 127 total,   2 running, 125 sleeping,   0 stopped,   0 zombie
Cpu(s):  3.6%us,  1.2%sy,  0.0%ni, 94.9%id,  0.2%wa,  0.0%hi,  0.2%si,  0.0%st
Mem:   1525788k total,   569804k used,   955984k free,    31772k buffers
Swap:  2103292k total,        0k used,  2103292k free,   392472k cached

  PID USER      PR  NI  VIRT  RES  SHR S %CPU %MEM    TIME+  COMMAND
 1180 root      20   0 37724  22m 9768 S    8  1.5  0:37.95 Xorg
 2841 tux       20   0 30296  10m 8688 S    1  0.7  0:01.14 metacity
 2934 tux       20   0 91092  22m  15m S    0  1.5  0:09.20 nautilus
 7507 tux       20   0 60116  13m  10m S    0  0.9  0:00.54 gnome-terminal
10178 tux       20   0  2512  976  736 R    0  0.1  0:00.11 top
    1 root      20   0  2216  724  620 S    0  0.0  0:03.12 init
    2 root      20   0     0    0    0 S    0  0.0  0:00.02 kthreadd
    3 root      20   0     0    0    0 S    0  0.0  0:00.03 ksoftirqd/0
    4 root      20   0     0    0    0 S    0  0.0  0:00.00 kworker/0:0
    5 root      20   0     0    0    0 S    0  0.0  0:00.01 kworker/u:0
    6 root      RT   0     0    0    0 S    0  0.0  0:00.00 migration/0
    7 root      RT   0     0    0    0 S    0  0.0  0:00.00 migration/1
    9 root      20   0     0    0    0 S    0  0.0  0:00.00 ksoftirqd/1
   10 root      20   0     0    0    0 S    0  0.0  0:00.72 kworker/0:1
   11 root       0 -20     0    0    0 S    0  0.0  0:00.00 cpuset
   12 root       0 -20     0    0    0 S    0  0.0  0:00.00 khelper
   13 root       0 -20     0    0    0 S    0  0.0  0:00.00 netns
```

Figure 6-5   Using top to display running processes

 CAUTION   The system will periodically delete old files out of the /tmp directory. Don't save anything in /tmp that you want to keep!

- **/usr**   This directory contains application files. In fact, most of the application files used on your system are stored in a subdirectory of /usr. These subdirectories include those shown in Table 6-3.

- **/var**   This directory contains variable data, including your system log files. Some of the typical subdirectories contained in /var are shown in Table 6-4.

```
tux@ws2:/proc/10178 ls
attr            coredump_filter  io        mounts        pagemap       stack
autogroup       cpuset           latency   mountstats    personality   stat
auxv            cwd              limits    net           root          statm
cgroup          environ          loginuid  numa_maps     sched         status
clear_refs      exe              maps      oom_adj       schedstat     syscall
cmdline         fd               mem       oom_score     sessionid     task
comm            fdinfo           mountinfo oom_score_adj smaps         wchan
tux@ws2:/proc/10178
```

Figure 6-6   Viewing information about the top process in /proc

Subdirectory	Contents
bin	Most of your executable programs
lib	Library files
lib64	64-bit library files
local	Locally installed software that you created yourself (used to prevent it from being overwritten during a system update)
sbin	System administration programs
share	Documentation and man page files

Table 6-3 Subdirectories of /usr

Types of Files Used by Linux

When working with Linux, you need to be aware of the fact that there are a number of different file types used by the file system. This is another area where the Linux file system differs significantly from the Windows file system. With a Windows file system you basically have two entry types in the file system:

- Directories
- Files

Granted, you can have normal files, hidden files, shortcut files, word processing files, executable files, and so on. However, these are all simple variations of the basic file type.

On Linux, however, there are a variety of different file types used by the file system. These include the file types listed in Table 6-5.

Linux Disk File Systems

In the previous chapter, we discussed how a hard disk drive works. The drive is made up of multiple aluminum platters, each with two read-write heads that are used to read and write data. When conducting disk I/O operations, the operating system needs to know where data is stored, how to access it, and where it is safe to write new information.

This is the job of the *disk file system*. It reliably stores data on the hard drive and organizes it in such a way that it is easily accessible. When you use a file browser to navigate through the directories on a hard disk drive and open a file, it's the disk file system that makes the entire process possible.

Subdirectory	Contents
lib	Library files created by various services and applications running on the system
log	Log files from your system and from services running on the system
spool	Print queues

Table 6-4 Subdirectories of /var

File Type	Description
Regular files	These files are similar to those used by the file systems of other operating systems—for example, executable files, word processing files, images, text files, etc.
Links	These files are pointers that point to other files in the file system.
FIFOs	FIFO stands for *First In First Out.* These are special files used to move data from one running software process on the system to another. A FIFO file is basically a queue where the first chunk of data added to the queue is the first chunk of data removed from the queue. Data can only move in one direction through a FIFO.
Sockets	Sockets are similar to FIFOs in that they are used to transfer information between processes. Unlike FIFOs, however, sockets can move data bidirectionally.

Table 6-5   Linux File Types

Most Linux distributions offer a wide variety of disk file systems that you can choose from. In this topic, we'll review some of the most widely used types:

- ext2
- ext3
- Reiser
- ext4

 NOTE   You can also use many other disk file systems with Linux. For example, you can use the XFS file system from Silicon Graphics. You can even use Windows VFAT or NTFS file systems such that the data is readable under either Linux or Windows (although complete NTFS support isn't fully baked yet).

ext2

The ext2 file system is one of the oldest Linux file systems still available. The acronym *ext2* stands for *Second Extended File System.* Originally introduced back in 1993, ext2 stores data in the standard hierarchical fashion used by most other file systems. Data is stored in files; files are stored in directories. A directory can contain either files or other directories (subdirectories).

The maximum file size supported in the ext2 file system is 2 terabytes (TB). An ext2 volume can be up to 4TB. Filenames can be up to 255 characters long. The ext2 file system supports Linux file system users, groups, and permissions (called POSIX permissions). It also supports file compression.

The ext2 file system is a fantastic file system. It's been around long enough for most of its bugs to be worked out. In fact, it's probably the most widely used Linux file system ever implemented. It's also reputed to be the fastest Linux file system available.

However, ext2 has one key weakness that has led to the development of other file systems. This is the fact that ext2 takes a long time to recover if the system shuts down abruptly. When shutting down the Linux system, the operating system first cleanly dismounts the file system, ensuring all pending file system transactions are written to disk before the system shuts off.

The problem arises when the system halts without completing this clean dismount procedure. For example, suppose a power outage occurs and the Linux system shuts off suddenly without going through the proper shutdown procedure. When this happens, it is possible that pending disk transactions weren't completed.

 TIP You're using an uninterruptible power supply to keep power outages from shutting down your system uncleanly, right? If not, do so! I lost data once due to a power outage, and I've sworn to never let it happen again.

To clean up the file system, the ext2 file system will automatically run a program called e2fsck the next time the system is booted. This utility tries to fix any problems that were created when the system went down without properly dismounting the disk. If it finds nonallocated files or unclaimed blocks of data, it will write this information in a directory called lost+found. By doing this, ext2 tries to ensure that data integrity is maintained in spite of the improper shutdown.

The issue here is that e2fsck will analyze the entire file system when this happens, not just the last few files that were in the process of being modified. On a basic Linux system, this can take from 10 to 15 minutes. On an extensive system that has a lot of file system data (such as a network file server), this process can take several hours. It's bad enough that the system went down unexpectedly in the first place; now you have to wait hours for it to start back up again!

Because of this issue, two other Linux file systems have started replacing ext2. The first of these is ext3.

ext3

The ext3 file system is an updated version of ext2. In fact, *ext3* stands for *Third Extended File System*. The two are so similar that most of the file system utilities used by ext2 are also used by ext3. You can easily upgrade ext2 file systems to ext3. You can even downgrade an ext3 file system to ext2.

However, the ext3 file system offers one key advantage that makes it highly preferable over ext2: *journaling*. Remember that the main disadvantage of ext2 is the fact that it must check the entire file system if the system goes down uncleanly. Journaling eliminates this problem.

Before committing a transaction to the hard disk drive, the ext3 file system records the transaction to a journal and marks it as *incomplete*. After the disk transaction is complete, the ext3 file system marks the transaction as *complete* in the journal. By doing this, the ext3 file system can keep a log (a *journal*) of the most recent file transactions and whether or not they were actually completed.

If an event such as a power outage occurs that causes the system to shut down without properly dismounting the disk, the ext3 file system will replay the journal when the system comes back up. This allows the file system to verify the data on the disk and bring it back to a consistent state (if possible) using the information stored in the journal. Unlike ext2, the ext3 file system doesn't need to check the entire file system.

Because it has a log of the most recent transactions in the journal, the ext3 file system simply checks the transactions that are listed as incomplete.

Using journaling, disk recovery time after an improper shutdown takes dramatically less time than that experienced using ext2. Instead of taking hours, the ext3 file system can replay the journal in only a few seconds or minutes, even if the file system is very large.

The disadvantage of ext3 is the fact that the journaling process uses up more system memory and slows down disk I/O operations slightly. However, because it does a better job of ensuring data integrity and does it faster, most system administrators prefer ext3 over ext2 in spite of the slightly decreased performance.

In addition to ext3, you can also choose from a third journaling file system called Reiser.

Reiser

The Reiser file system is an alternative to the ext3 file system. Like ext3, Reiser utilizes journaling to make crash recovery very fast. However, Reiser is a completely different file system from ext2 and ext3, using a dramatically different internal structure. This allows the Reiser file system to support a larger maximum file size of 8TB and maximum volume size of 16TB. In addition, the structure of Reiser allows it to perform much faster than ext2 or ext3.

ext4

The ext4 file system was released in late 2008. As you might guess, ext4 (Fourth Extended File System) is an updated version of ext3. Just as ext3 is backward-compatible with ext2, ext4 is backward-compatible with ext3 (and ext2, for that matter). The ext4 file system supports volumes up to 1 exabyte in size and files up to 16TB in size. You can have a maximum of four billion files in an ext4 file system. As with ext2 and ext3, the maximum length of a file or directory name is 256 bytes. Ext4 also uses checksums to verify the journal file itself. This helps improve the overall reliability of the system, since the journal file is one of the most heavily used files on the disk. As you can see, ext4 represents a dramatic leap forward over ext3 and Reiser.

You need to choose which file system you want to implement after you partition a storage device, such as a hard drive. So which disk file system should you use? It depends upon your personal preferences and the needs of your deployment. My choice for many years was the Reiser file system. However, ext4 is now my file system of choice.

With this introduction to the Linux file system in mind, you're ready to start learning how to complete common file system tasks. Just as with any other operating system, you need to be able to create, copy, and move files and directories in the Linux file system. In the next part of this chapter, we're going to spend some time reviewing how this is done.

If you have any experience working with the command line in other operating systems, such as Windows, you may be thinking that these tasks are trivial in nature. Believe it or not, these tasks can be difficult for many of my students when they are first learning how to use Linux. The key mistake I see is students trying to use Windows commands when working with the file system at the Linux shell prompt.

I even catch myself doing this on occasion. I was presenting a demo for students recently and needed to copy some files on a Linux system. Without thinking, I entered *copy* instead of *cp* at the shell prompt and, of course, it didn't work. Boy, was I was red-faced! My students had a great time razzing me about that for the rest of the class!

As with Windows, you can perform file system manipulation tasks either from the shell prompt or from within the Linux GUI. Many who are coming to Linux from a Windows background are tempted to perform these tasks solely using the GUI utilities provided with most distributions.

While these graphical utilities are handy and easy to use, you still need to learn how to do these tasks from the shell prompt. I realize that this goes against standard practice with Windows systems. I've worked with many Windows users who don't know that the command prompt even exists on their systems. With Linux, however, you need to first become proficient with shell commands and then use the GUI utilities for convenience. I say this for the following reasons:

- Most employers and coworkers won't take you seriously as a Linux administrator if you can't manage the system from the shell prompt. It just goes with the territory.

- Many Linux systems, especially those deployed as servers, don't run a GUI. Running a GUI environment requires a lot of CPU overhead. Many server admins prefer to allocate those CPU cycles to network services instead of moving the mouse cursor on the screen or running a screensaver. In this situation, you need to know how to do things from the shell prompt.

Let's begin by learning how to manage directories in the file system using shell prompt commands.

Managing Directories from the Command Line

Now that you understand how the Linux file system is structured, you're ready to start managing the file system. In this part of the chapter, we're going to focus on managing directories from the shell prompt. The following topics are addressed:

- Navigating the file system
- Viewing directory contents
- Creating new directories
- Copying, moving, and deleting directories

Navigating the File System

As you work with the Linux file system from the shell prompt, one of the most common tasks you will complete is to move around between the different directories on your storage devices. Your Linux system provides the following shell commands that you can use to do this:

- pwd
- cd

Using the pwd Command

The pwd command is a relatively simple utility. The name of the command, *pwd*, stands for *Print Working Directory*.

This command simply displays the current directory on the screen.

This utility can be useful if your shell profile hasn't been configured to display the current directory as a part of the shell prompt. To use pwd, simply enter **pwd** at the shell prompt; as shown here:

```
tux@ws2:~> pwd
/home/tux
```

In this example, you can see that the current directory is set to /home/tux.

 TIP The ~ character in the shell prompt points to the current user's home directory. Because we're logged in as the user tux in the preceding example, ~ points to the /home/tux directory.

At this point, you know how to identify what directory you're in. Frequently, you're going to need to change to a different directory in the file system. You do this with the cd command.

Using the cd Command

The cd command is used from the Linux shell prompt to change directories in the file system. To use this command, simply enter **cd** followed by the name of the directory you want to switch to. There are two ways you can do this. If you enter **cd** and then the name of a directory *without* specifying the full path to the directory, cd will assume that the directory is a subdirectory of the current directory. For example, in the example that follows the **cd Documents** command has been issued:

```
tux@ws2:~> cd Documents/
tux@ws2:~/Documents>
```

Because the command was issued from /home/tux, cd changed directories to /home/tux/Documents. This is called using a *relative path*. The path specified with the command is relative to some other point in the file system, in this case, the /home/tux directory.

You can also use *absolute paths* with the cd command. When you use an absolute path, you specify the full path, starting from / to the directory you want to change to. For example,

```
tux@ws2:~> cd /var/log
tux@ws2:/var/log>
```

Because we specified an absolute path (/var/log), the cd command knew that the /var/log directory didn't exist in the current directory. Instead, the path was determined from the root directory (/) and the current directory was changed to it.

TIP If you enter **cd** at the shell prompt without specifying a path, it will automatically change to the home directory of the currently logged-in user.

You can also use the cd command to move up the file system hierarchy by entering **cd ..** This will change the current directory to the next directory higher in the hierarchy. Consider the following example:

```
tux@ws2:/var/log> cd ..
tux@ws2:/var>
```

In this example, the **cd ..** command has been issued, changing from /var/log to the /var directory. To go up two directories, you can enter the cd ../.. command at the shell prompt:

```
tux@ws2:/var/log> cd ../..
tux@ws2:/>
```

TIP You can use **..** to move up one level in the hierarchy and **...** to move up two levels. Most distributions define these two aliases (.. and ...) automatically for you in one of your bash configuration files.

Viewing Directory Contents

To this point, you've learned how to view the current directory and change to other directories in the file system. Now you need to learn how to list the files and subdirectories that may exist within a directory. This is done using the ls command. If you enter **ls** at the shell prompt, the contents of the current directory are listed on the screen, as shown here:

```
tux@ws2:~> ls
bin        Documents  Music    Public       Templates  test.txt  words
Desktop    Downloads  Pictures public_html  test2.txt  Videos    yourfile.txt
tux@ws2:~>
```

As with the cd command, you can also provide an absolute path when using ls. This will cause ls to display the contents of the directory you specify. Consider this example:

```
tux@ws2:~> ls /var/log
acpid         cups          mail           ntp                Xorg.0.log.old
apparmor      faillog       mail.err       pk_backend_zypp    YaST2
audit         firewall      mail.info      pm-powersave.log   zypp
boot.log      gdm           mail.warn      samba              zypper.log
boot.msg      krb5          messages       warn
boot.omsg     lastlog       NetworkManager wtmp
ConsoleKit    localmessages news           Xorg.0.log
tux@ws2:~>
```

In this example, the **ls /var/log** command has been issued, causing the contents of /var/log to be displayed.

When working with ls, you can use a variety of options to customize how it works. Some of these options include the following:

- **–a**   Displays all files, including hidden files. In the next example, the **ls –a** command has been issued in the /home/tux directory:

```
tux@ws2:~> ls -a
.                  .esd_auth          .inputrc           test2.txt
..                 .fontconfig        .local             test.txt
.bash_history      .fonts             .mozilla           .themes
.bashrc            .gconf             Music              .thumbnails
bin                .gconfd            .nautilus          Videos
.cache             .gnome2            Pictures           .viminfo
.config            .gnome2_private    .profile           .vimrc
.dbus              .gstreamer-0.10    Public             words
Desktop            .gtk-bookmarks     public_html        .xim.template
.dmrc              .gvfs              .pulse             .xinitrc.template
Documents          .hplip             .pulse-cookie      .xsession-errors
Downloads          .ICEauthority      .recently-used.xbel .xsession-errors.old
.emacs             .icons             Templates          yourfile.txt
tux@ws2:~>
```

- **–l**   Displays a long listing of the directory contents. This is a very useful option. You can use it to see the filenames, ownership, permissions, modification dates, and sizes. A sample is shown here.

```
tux@ws2:~> ls -l
total 56
drwxr-xr-x 2 tux users 4096 2011-01-19 10:41 bin
drwxr-xr-x 2 tux users 4096 2011-01-19 10:42 Desktop
drwxr-xr-x 2 tux users 4096 2011-01-19 10:42 Documents
drwxr-xr-x 2 tux users 4096 2011-01-19 10:42 Downloads
drwxr-xr-x 2 tux users 4096 2011-01-19 10:42 Music
drwxr-xr-x 2 tux users 4096 2011-01-19 10:42 Pictures
drwxr-xr-x 2 tux users 4096 2011-01-19 10:42 Public
drwxr-xr-x 2 tux users 4096 2011-01-19 10:41 public_html
drwxr-xr-x 2 tux users 4096 2011-01-19 10:42 Templates
-rw-r--r-- 1 tux users   37 2011-01-20 11:04 test2.txt
-rw-r--r-- 1 tux users  182 2011-01-21 11:48 test.txt
drwxr-xr-x 2 tux users 4096 2011-01-19 10:42 Videos
-rw-r--r-- 1 tux users   23 2011-01-20 11:32 words
-rw-r--r-- 1 tux users  121 2011-01-21 11:46 yourfile.txt
tux@ws2:~>
```

- **–R**   Displays directory contents recursively; that is, it displays the contents of the current directory as well as the contents of all subdirectories. Depending on the number of entries in the directory, you may want to append | **more** after using this option. This will cause the more utility to pause the display one page at a time. An example is shown in Figure 6-7, where the **ls –R** command has been issued from the /var/log directory.

This list is only a sampling of the different options you can use with ls. You can view the ls man page or info node to learn more.

Most distributions define several aliases that you can use for the ls command. For example, on OpenSUSE the **dir** or **ll** alias runs the **ls –l** command while the **la** alias runs the **ls –la** command.

Let's practice navigating the file system in the following exercise.

Figure 6-7

Using the –R
option with the
ls command

```
./ConsoleKit:
history

./cups:
access_log
ls: cannot open directory ./gdm: Permission denied
ls: cannot open directory ./krb5: Permission denied
ls: cannot open directory ./news: Permission denied
ls: cannot open directory ./samba: Permission denied
ls: cannot open directory ./YaST2: Permission denied

./zypp:
history
tux@ws2:/var/log> █
```

Exercise 6-1: Navigating the File System   In this exercise, you will practice using shell commands to navigate the Linux file system. Complete the following:

1. Boot your Linux system and log in as a standard user.

2. If necessary, open a terminal session.

3. Determine your current working directory by entering **pwd** at the shell prompt. What's the current directory?

4. Change directories to /etc by entering **cd /etc** at the shell prompt.

5. Generate a listing of the current directory by entering **ls**.

6. Generate a long listing of the current directory by entering **ls –l**.

7. Generate a long list and pause the output a page at a time by entering **ls –l | more**. Page your way through the listing.

8. Switch back to your home directory by entering **cd ~**.

9. Enter **ls**.

10. View the hidden files in your user's home directory by entering **ls –a**. Which files are displayed by ls –a that are not displayed by ls?

Let's now shift gears and discuss shell commands that you can use to manage directories in the Linux file system. Let's first look at how you create new directories.

Creating New Directories

You can use shell commands to create new directories. This is done using the mkdir command. You enter **mkdir** from the shell prompt followed by the name of the directory you want to create. In the next example, the **mkdir MyFiles** command has been issued from the home directory of the tux user.

```
tux@ws2:~> mkdir MyFiles
tux@ws2:~> ls
bin        Downloads  Pictures    Templates  Videos
Desktop    Music      Public      test2.txt  words
Documents  MyFiles    public_html test.txt   yourfile.txt
tux@ws2:~>
```

Notice in the output from the ls command that a new directory named MyFiles was created in /home/tux. Of course, you could use an absolute path with the directory name if you wanted to create it somewhere other than the current directory. For example, if you wanted to create a new directory named backup in the /tmp directory, you would enter **mkdir /tmp/backup** at the shell prompt.

On many distributions, an alias named md is defined by one of the shell configuration files that runs the mkdir –p command. The –p option specifies that the entire directory path specified in the command be created if it doesn't exist. For example, **md ~/temp/backups/daily** would create the temp and backups directories, if they didn't already exist, before creating the daily directory.

Copying, Moving, and Deleting Directories

In addition to creating and viewing directories in the Linux file system, you can also copy, move, or delete them using shell commands. You use the following utilities to accomplish these tasks:

- **cp** This utility is used to copy entire directory structures from one location in the file system to another.

  To copy an entire directory structure, you need to include the –R option, which specifies that the directory contents be recursively copied. For example, in the example that follows the **cp –R ~/MyFiles ~/backup** command was issued in the tux user's home directory. This caused the MyFiles directory and all of its files and subdirectories to be copied to the backup directory in the user's home directory.

 NOTE Because cp *copies* the directory, the original directory is left intact.

```
tux@ws2:~> cp -R ~/MyFiles ~/backup
tux@ws2:~> ls
backup    Documents  MyFiles    public_html test.txt   yourfile.txt
bin       Downloads  Pictures   Templates   Videos
Desktop   Music      Public     test2.txt   words
tux@ws2:~>
```

- **mv** The mv command is used much like cp. However, it copies the specified directory to the new location in the file system and then *deletes* the original. For example, to move a directory named backup from your home directory to

/tmp, you enter **mv ~/backup /tmp**. The mv command can also be used to rename directories. Simply enter **mv** followed by the directory to be renamed and then the new directory name. For example, to rename the backup directory in your home directory to temp, you enter **mv ~/backup ~/temp**.

- **rmdir**   This utility can be used to delete an existing directory. To use it, simply enter **rmdir** *directory_name*—for example, **rmdir MyFiles**. Be aware, however, that rmdir requires that the directory be empty before it will delete it. On many distributions, an alias named rd is defined by one of your shell configuration files that runs the rmdir command.

- **rm**   The rm utility is a more powerful deletion utility that can be used to delete a populated directory. To delete a directory, enter **rm –r** *directory_name*.

So, that's how you manage directories from the shell prompt. With this in mind, we next need to discuss how to manage files within those directories from the shell prompt.

Managing Files from the Command Line

In addition to managing directories in the file system, there will be many occasions when you need to manage the files they contain. In this part of the chapter, you will learn how to complete the following tasks:

- Creating files
- Deleting files
- Copying and moving files

Creating New Files

From time to time, you will need to create new files in your Linux file system. Creating a new file can be accomplished using the touch command from the shell prompt. To use touch, enter **touch** followed by the name of the file you want to create. In the next example, the command **touch myfile.txt** was issued from within the home directory of the tux user:

```
tux@ws2:~> touch myfile.txt
tux@ws2:~> ls -l my*
-rw-r--r-- 1 tux users 0 2011-02-01 11:36 myfile.txt
tux@ws2:~>
```

After entering touch, the ls command was entered. You can see that a 0-byte file was created named myfile.txt in /home/tux. If you wanted to create the file elsewhere in the file system, you would use an absolute path with the filename.

In addition to creating files, you will also need to know how to delete existing files.

Deleting Files

As with directories, there will be times when you will need to delete an existing file from the Linux file system. Deleting files can be accomplished with the rm command. This is the same command we used previously to delete directories. The rm utility is a powerful deletion utility that can be used to delete either a file or a populated directory. To delete a file, simply enter **rm** *filename*. In the next example, the myfile.txt file is deleted using the rm command:

```
tux@ws2:~> rm myfile.txt
tux@ws2:~>
```

You need to be very careful when using the rm utility! As you can see in the preceding example, it doesn't prompt you to confirm a deletion operation. It assumes that you really mean to delete the file or directory and does the deed. And by the way, the deleted file doesn't get moved to the Recycle Bin. If you delete a file or directory with rm, it is gone! If you want rm to prompt you before deleting a file or directory, include the –i option.

Copying and Moving Files

In addition to creating and deleting files in the Linux file system, you can also copy or move them. You use the same utilities that you used to manage directories to copy or move files:

- **cp** This utility is used to copy files from one location in the file system to another. For example, to copy a file named /tmp/schedule.txt to your home directory, you enter **cp /tmp/schedule.txt** ~. Remember, cp makes a copy of the file, so the original file is left intact.

- **mv** The mv command copies a file to the new location in the file system and then deletes the original. For example, to move a file named mylog.txt from /tmp to /var/log, you enter **mv /tmp/mylog.txt /var/log**.

  As with directories, the mv command can also be used to rename files. Simply enter **mv** followed by the file to be renamed and then the new filename. For example, to rename schedule.txt to schedule.old, you enter **mv schedule.txt schedule.old**.

Let's practice managing files in the following exercise.

Exercise 6-2: Managing Files and Directories In this exercise, you will practice managing files and directories using shell commands. Complete the following:

1. With your Linux system running and authenticated as a regular user, open a terminal session and switch to your home directory by entering cd at the shell prompt.

2. Create a new directory in your home directory by entering **mkdir MyFiles**.

3. Enter **ls** and verify that the new directory exists.

4. Create a new file in the MyFiles directory called myfile.txt by entering **touch ~/MyFiles/myfile.txt**.

5. Enter **ls ~/MyFiles** and verify that the file exists.

6. Delete the MyFiles directory in your home directory by entering **rm –r ~/MyFiles**.

7. Enter **ls** and verify that the directory and its contents are gone.

8. Make a copy of your home directory files and subdirectories in /tmp by entering **cp –R ~ /tmp**.

9. View the contents of /tmp by entering **ls /tmp**. Verify that your home directory was copied.

Finding Files in the Linux File System

One of my great weaknesses is the fact that I have a terrible memory. You can call me on the phone and relate some bit of important information and I am pretty much guaranteed to forget what you told me by the time I hang up. This problem can be very embarrassing when I run into someone I've known and worked with for years and find myself unable to recall that person's name.

This fallibility, unfortunately, carries over into my work life. I can't tell you how many times I've created a file, saved it, and then promptly forgot where I saved it. To help people like me, Linux includes utilities that you can use to search for files in the file system. In this part of the chapter, you'll learn the following:

- Using find
- Using locate
- Using which
- Using whereis
- Using type

Let's begin by learning how to use the find utility.

Using find

The find utility is fantastic tool that you can use to search the Linux file system. To use find, simply enter **find** *path* **–name** *"filename"* at the shell prompt. Replace *path* with the place in the file system where you want to start looking. Replace *filename* with the name of the file you want to search for.

 TIP Don't forget to use quotation marks!

You can use regular expressions such as * to broaden your search results. For example, suppose you wanted to find all of the log files stored in your file system that have a .log extension. You could enter **find / –name "*.log"**. The find utility would then locate all files with an extension of .log starting in the root directory of the file system and searching all subdirectories. This is shown in Figure 6-8.

 NOTE This process of filename expansion is called *globbing*. We'll look at globbing in more detail later in the next chapter when we discuss regular expressions.

The find utility is flexible. You can also use the **–user** *"username"* option to search for files owned by a specific user, or use the **–size** *"size"* option to search for files of a specified size. You can use a + sign before the size value to search for files larger than the specified size, or a – sign before the size value to search for files smaller than the specified size. The find utility has many other options. You can use the man page for find to see everything it has to offer.

Using locate

You can also use the locate utility to search for files in the file system. The locate utility functions in much the same manner as find. However, it has one distinct advantage over find. Here's the issue: Whenever you run a search with find, it manually walks through each directory in the path you specify in the command looking for matching files. This process can take a really long time, especially if you're doing a top-down search from the root of the file system.

The locate utility, on the other hand, works in a much more efficient way. Instead of walking the file system each time you run a search, it builds an index of the files in the file system. Then, when you run a search, locate simply queries the index. It doesn't actually search the file system directly. The result is that locate runs *much* faster than find in most situations.

To use locate, you must first install the findutils-locate package on your system. With the package installed, an index (named locatedb) of all the files in your file system will be created in /var/log. This index will be updated each day with the latest changes to the file system. However, you can also manually update the index using the **updatedb** command from the shell prompt. Be aware that updatedb does all the leg work for the locate utility; it can take some time to complete and will use up a lot of system resources in the process.

Figure 6-8

Using the find utility to search for files

```
ws2:~ # find / -name "*.log"
/root/.local/share/tracker/tracker-miner-fs.log
/root/.local/share/tracker/tracker-extract.log
/root/.local/share/gvfs-metadata/root-c2aec5a6.log
/root/.local/share/gvfs-metadata/home-0394ef01.log
/root/.config/tomboy/tomboy-panel.log
/root/.config/tomboy/tomboy.log
/var/log/Xorg.0.log
```

With the index updated, you can search for files by simply entering **locate** *filename* at the shell prompt. For example, if you wanted to search for a file named snmp.conf, you could enter **locate snmp.conf**. This is shown here:

```
ws2:/ # locate snmp.conf
/etc/cups/snmp.conf
/usr/share/man/man5/cups-snmp.conf.5.gz
ws2:/ #
```

Notice that locate found two files that had the text string *snmpd.conf* somewhere in the filename.

Using which

The which command is used to display the full path to a shell command or utility. For example, if you want to know the full path to the ls command, you enter **which ls** at the shell prompt. When you do, the full path to ls is displayed on screen, as shown here:

```
ws2:/ # which ls
/bin/ls
ws2:/ #
```

Using whereis

The whereis command locates the source code, binary files, and manuals pages for specified files. The –b option returns the location of the binaries for the specified command. The –m option returns the location of the command's manual pages. To see the location of the command's source code, use the –s option with the whereis command. If no option is used, all information is returned.

For example, if you enter **whereis –b ls** at the shell prompt, the location of the ls command's binary executable file is returned, as shown here:

```
ws2:/ # whereis -b ls
ls: /bin/ls
```

Likewise, the whereis –m ls command returns the location of the ls command's man page file; as shown next:

```
ws2:/ # whereis -m ls
ls: /usr/share/man/man1p/ls.1p.gz /usr/share/man/man1/ls.1.gz
```

Using type

The type command returns what type of command is executed when you enter it. The values returned will be one of the following:

- **A command that is hard-coded into the shell itself**   For example, the **cd** command is a built-in shell command:

  ```
  ws2:/ # type cd
  cd is a shell builtin
  ```

- **An external command that is called by the shell**   If the command has been run recently in the shell, the output of type says that the command is *hashed*. This indicates the location of the external command in the file system has been stored in the shell's hash table. If you run the same command again, the shell will execute it without searching for it in the directories in the PATH environment variable. An example is shown here:

```
ws2:/ # type cat
cat is hashed (/bin/cat)
```

- **An alias**   An alias is essentially a shortcut to another file in the Linux file system. Aliases are frequently used for commonly used commands, such as the ls command. This is shown in this example:

```
ws2:/ # type ls
ls is aliased to 'ls $LS_OPTIONS'
```

- **A function**   You can also use the –**a** option with the type command. This option causes type to return all instances of the specified command in the file system. For example, entering the **type –a ip** command shows that there are two executables named ip:

```
ws2:/ # type -a ip
ip is /sbin/ip
ip is /bin/ip
```

Let's practice using Linux search tools in the following exercise.

Exercise 6-3: Using Linux Search Tools   In this exercise, you will practice using Linux search tools. Complete the following:

1. Verify that you are logged in to your Linux system.

2. If necessary, open a terminal session.

3. Change to your root user account by entering **su** – at the shell prompt and entering your root user's password.

4. Search for a file named fstab by entering **find / –name "fstab"** at the shell prompt. Where is this file located?

5. Perform the same search using locate by entering **locate fstab** at the shell prompt.

 CAUTION   The locate command will not work if the findutils-locate package hasn't been installed on your system.

6. Find the location of the init executable by entering **which init** at the shell prompt. Where is it located?

7. Enter **whereis init** at the shell prompt. Where is the file that contains the manual sections for the init command located?

8. At the shell prompt, display the last few lines of your messages log file by entering
   tail /var/log/messages.

9. At the shell prompt, see if the tail command is now hashed by the shell session
   by entering **type tail**. Is it? What does this mean?

Thus far, we've been working primarily with files, directories, and aliases in the Linux
file system. However, there's a fourth type of Linux file that is used a lot and that you
need to be familiar with. These files are called *links*.

Working with Link Files

As we discussed earlier in this chapter, the Linux file system supports a file type called
a *link file*. Link files don't contain content in the way that regular files do. Instead, they
are redirectors that point you to a different file or directory in the file system. On Linux
you can create two different types of link files:

- **Hard**   A hard link is a file that points directly to the inode of another file. An
  inode stores basic information about a file in the Linux file system, including its
  size, device, owner, and permissions. Because the two files use the same inode,
  you can't actually tell which file is the pointer and which is the pointee after the
  hard link is created. It is as if the two files were the same file, even though they
  may exist in different locations in the file system.

- **Symbolic**   A symbolic link file also points to another file in the file system.
  However, a symbolic link has its own inode. Because the pointer file has its own
  inode, the pointer and the pointee in the file system can be easily identified. For
  example, in the preceding chapter, you saw that the /usr/bin/vi file is actually a
  symbolic link that points to the /bin/vim file. This is shown in this example:

```
ws2:/usr/bin # ls -l vi
lrwxrwxrwx 1 root root 8 Jan 19 10:24 vi -> /bin/vim
ws2:/usr/bin #
```

To create a link file, you use the ln command. The syntax is **ln *pointee_file pointer_file***.
Using ln without any options creates a hard link. If you want to create a symbolic link,
you use the **–s** option. In the example that follows, the ln command has been used to
create a symbolic link between a file named myapp in the bin subdirectory of my user's
home directory and an executable file named myapp located in /var/opt:

```
tux@ws2:~/bin> ln -s /var/opt/myapp myapp
tux@ws2:~/bin> ls -l
total 0
lrwxrwxrwx 1 tux users 14 2011-02-01 13:15 myapp -> /var/opt/myapp
tux@ws2:~/bin>cd ..
tux@ws2:~> myapp
This is my new executable script file.
tux@ws2:~>
```

Using the **ls –l** command, you can see that myapp actually points to the /var/opt/ myapp executable file. This can be a useful trick if the /var/opt/myapp program is one that I need to use frequently. Because the /var/opt directory is not in my user's PATH environment variable, I would need to supply the full path to the myapp executable each time I wanted to run it (or switch to the /var/opt directory first). However, the bin subdirectory of my home directory is automatically added to the PATH environment variable by my bash configuration files. By placing the symbolic link in this directory, I can run the /var/opt/myapp executable by simply entering myapp at the shell prompt. The symbolic link file redirects the shell to the appropriate file in /var/opt and runs it from there, as shown in the preceding example.

Exercise 6-4: Working with Link Files In this exercise, you will practice using link files. Complete the following:

1. Verify that you are logged in to your Linux system.
2. If necessary, open a terminal session.
3. Create a symbolic link from a directory named docs in your home directory to the /usr/share/doc directory by entering ln –s /usr/share/doc/ ~/docs.
4. Enter ls –l. Verify that the docs file points to /usr/share/doc/.
5. Enter cd docs.
6. Enter pwd. What directory are you in?
7. Enter ls. You should see the contents of the /usr/share/doc/ directory even though you are still in ~/docs.

You are now a file system pro! You have to be humble when you know this much!

Chapter Review

In this chapter, we reviewed a variety of topics related to managing the Linux file system. I began by introducing you to the Linux file system and then differentiated between a general file system and a specific disk file system such as Reiser or ext4. I then pointed out that the role of the Linux file system is to organize data such that it can be easily located and retrieved as well as reliably preserved.

I then related that Linux uses a hierarchical file system. The topmost directory of this hierarchy is the root directory (/). We discussed the role of the various standard directories used in a typical Linux system as specified in the Filesystem Hierarchy Standard (FHS). These include

- /bin
- /boot
- /dev

- /etc
- /home
- /lib
- /media
- /mnt
- /opt
- /proc
- /root
- /sbin
- /srv
- /sys
- /tmp
- /usr
- /var

We also discussed the four different types of files used on a Linux system: regular files, links, FIFOs, and sockets.

With this background information in hand, we turned our attention to common Linux file system tasks. I emphasized that, while most of these tasks can be performed using graphical utilities, you need to know how to complete them from the shell prompt.

We next reviewed how to navigate through the Linux file system using the pwd and cd commands. We then discussed how to manage files and directories. I pointed out that you could create new files using the touch command. You can also create new directories using the mkdir command.

We also reviewed the utilities you can use to delete files and directories, including rmdir and rm. To copy and move files and directories, you can use the cp and mv utilities. I pointed out that mv can also be used to rename files or directories.

We then discussed utilities that you can use to search for files or directories in the Linux file system. We reviewed how to use the find and locate commands to find specific files or directories. I pointed out that find manually walks the file system hierarchy to conduct its searches, which can be somewhat slow. As an alternative, the locate utility creates a database of files in the file system. When you search with locate, it queries its database instead of walking the file system hierarchy, which is much faster.

I also pointed out that you can use the which command to find out where the executables for system utilities, such as ls, cp, and man, reside in the file system. We also looked at the whereis command, which displays information such as executable file, source file, and man page file locations for a particular shell command. We reviewed how to use the type command to determine a file's type.

We ended this chapter by discussing link files. I pointed out that link files point to other files or directories in the file system. I related that you can create either hard links or symbolic links using the ln command.

Accelerated Review

- The role of the file system is to store and organize data such that it can be easily located and retrieved.
- The file system must also preserve data intact.
- Linux uses a hierarchical file system.
- The Linux file system hierarchy is based on the Filesystem Hierarchy Standard (FHS).
- The topmost directory is / and is called the root directory.
- Other standard directories are created beneath / and serve functions defined in the FHS.
- The Linux file system uses regular files, links, FIFOs, and sockets.
- Most file system management tasks can be completed using either graphical or command-line tools.
- The pwd command is used to display the current directory.
- The cd command is used to change directories.
- The ls command is used to display directory contents.
- Using ls with the –l option displays additional details about files and directories.
- Using ls with the –R option displays directory contents recursively.
- The touch command is used to create new files.
- The mkdir command is used to create new directories.
- You can use rmdir to delete an empty directory.
- You can use rm to delete populated directories or files.
- The cp command is used to copy files.
- The mv command is used to move files.
- You can use the find utility to locate files or directories in the file system.
- The find utility manually walks the file system hierarchy to search for files.
- You can use locate to search for files or directories.
- The locate utility maintains a database of all files in the file system.
- When locate conducts a search, it searches the database instead of the file system.
- The which command is used to display the location of files in the file system.

- The whereis command displays information about a command's executable file, source code file, and man page file.
- The type command displays a file's type.
- The Linux file system allows you to create link files that point to other files or directories in the file system.
- Hard links point directly to the inode of another file.
- Symbolic links have their own inode.
- Links are created using the ln command.

Questions

1. Which of the following are roles of the Linux file system? (Choose two.)

   A. To create automatic backups of system data

   B. To make data easily locatable

   C. To preserve data integrity

   D. To provide the user with a command-line interface

   E. To provide the user with a graphical user interface

2. Which directory contains file system management utilities such as cp or rm?

   A. /bin

   B. /dev

   C. /var

   D. /usr

3. Which directory is a pseudo–file system that is dynamically created when it is accessed?

   A. /var

   B. /opt

   C. /proc

   D. /srv

4. Which directory does the ~ character represent when used with file system commands?

   A. /var

   B. The current directory

   C. The current user's home directory

   D. The root user's home directory

   E. /home

5. You need to generate a listing of files and directories within the /var directory, including files in subdirectories. Which command will do this?

   A. ls /var

   B. ls –l /var

   C. ls –f /var

   D. ls –R /var

6. You need to delete the Temp directory within your user's home directory. Given that Temp has files in it, which is the best command to do this?

   A. rmdir Temp

   B. rmdir ~/Temp

   C. rm Temp

   D. rm –r ~/Temp

7. You need to copy the Documents directory within your user's home directory to the /tmp directory. Given that Documents has files and subdirectories within it, which is the correct command to do this?

   A. cp ~/Documents /tmp

   B. cp –R ~/Documents /tmp

   C. cp ~/Documents ~/tmp

   D. cp –R ~/Documents ~/tmp

8. You want to create a symbolic link in your home directory that will link the manual file to the /usr/share/doc/manual directory. Which is the correct command to do this?

   A. ln –s /usr/share/doc/manual ~/manual

   B. ln /usr/share/doc/manual ~/manual

   C. ln –s ~/manual /usr/share/doc/manual

   D. ln ~/manual /usr/share/doc/manual

9. You need to find a file named myfile.txt somewhere in your Linux file system. Which is the correct command to do this?

   A. find / –name "myfile.txt"

   B. find "myfile.txt"

   C. find / –name myfile.txt

   D. find –name "myfile.txt"

10. You need to find a file named myfile.txt somewhere in your Linux file system. Which is the correct command to do this?

   A. locate –name myfile.txt

   B. locate –find myfile.txt

   C. locate –file myfile.txt

   D. locate myfile.txt

Answers

1. **B, C.** The role of the file system is to make data easily locatable and to preserve its integrity.

2. **A.** File system utilities are located in /bin.

3. **C.** The /proc file system is a pseudo–file system.

4. **C.** The ~ character points to the home directory of the current user.

5. **D.** The ls –R /var command will generate a listing of /var and its subdirectories.

6. **D.** The rm –r command will delete the Temp directory and its contents.

7. **B.** The –R switch copies data recursively.

8. **A.** The –s option creates a symbolic link with the ln command.

9. **A.** The find / –name "myfile.txt" command uses the correct syntax.

10. **D.** The locate myfile.txt command uses the correct syntax.

Extracting Data from Files

In this chapter, you will learn about
- Viewing file contents
- Finding content within files
- Using redirection and piping
- Processing text streams

In the previous chapter, you learned how to manage files and directories in the Linux file system. In this chapter, we're going to go a step further and discuss how you can extract data from files in the Linux file system.

As you learned in Chapter 5, Linux is configured primarily with text files. Therefore, it's critical that you understand how to view the contents of files in the Linux file system. In addition, there will be many instances when you need to locate a particular term or parameter within a text file. You may even need to extract that text and write to a new file or send it to another Linux command as input for processing.

In this chapter, we're going to discuss how to do this. By the time we are done, you should have a number of cool tools added to your Linux utility belt that you can use to manipulate the contents of files on Linux. Let's begin by discussing how to view the contents of a file.

Viewing File Contents

As you learned in Chapter 5, your Linux system and the services that run on it are configured using simple text files usually stored in the /etc directory in the file system. In addition, many of your system log files are saved as text files. Because Linux uses text files to configure and manage just about everything, you will frequently need to view the contents of files.

In Chapter 5, you also learned how to use text editors to open a file for viewing and editing. This works very well. However, there will be many occasions when you simply want to quickly view a text file onscreen and don't need or want to load up a text editor.

Figure 7-1

Viewing a text file
with cat

```
tux@ws2:~> cat /etc/xinetd.conf
#
# xinetd.conf
#
# Copyright (c) 1998-2001 SuSE GmbH Nuernberg, Germany.
# Copyright (c) 2002 SuSE Linux AG, Nuernberg, Germany.
#

defaults
{
        log_type          = FILE /var/log/xinetd.log
        log_on_success    = HOST EXIT DURATION
        log_on_failure    = HOST ATTEMPT
#        only_from         = localhost
        instances         = 30
        cps               = 50 10
```

Linux provides you with a variety of command-line tools that you can use to do this. These include the following:

- **cat** The **cat** *filename* command will display the contents of the specified text file onscreen. For example, if you needed to view the /etc/xinetd.conf configuration file, you would enter **cat /etc/xinetd.conf** at the shell prompt. This is shown in Figure 7-1.

TIP The cat command doesn't pause the output, so if you use it to view a long file, you may need to pipe it to the more program (**| more**) to pause the output one page a time. We'll discuss piping and redirection in more detail later in this chapter.

- **less** The **less** *filename* command can also be used to display the specified text file onscreen, much like cat. However, the less command automatically pauses a long text file one page at time. You can use the SPACEBAR, PAGE UP, PAGE DOWN, and ARROW keys to navigate around the output. When you're done, you can press Q to exit out of less. In Figure 7-2 the /var/log/messages file is displayed with the less command.

```
Oct 12 21:47:34 linux kernel: [   15.132337] type=1400 audit(1350100038.784:5):
apparmor="STATUS" operation="profile_load" name="/sbin/syslogd" pid=778 comm="ap
parmor_parser"
Oct 12 21:47:34 linux kernel: [   17.227400] type=1400 audit(1350100040.882:6):
apparmor="STATUS" operation="profile_load" name="/usr/lib/apache2/mpm-prefork/ap
ache2" pid=783 comm="apparmor_parser"
Oct 12 21:47:34 linux kernel: [   17.228017] type=1400 audit(1350100040.883:7):
apparmor="STATUS" operation="profile_load" name="/usr/lib/apache2/mpm-prefork/ap
ache2//DEFAULT_URI" pid=783 comm="apparmor_parser"
Oct 12 21:47:34 linux kernel: [   17.228283] type=1400 audit(1350100040.883:8):
apparmor="STATUS" operation="profile_load" name="/usr/lib/apache2/mpm-prefork/ap
/var/log/messages lines 1-9/778 1%
```

Figure 7-2 Viewing a text file with less

Figure 7-3

Viewing a text file
with head

```
tux@ws2:~> head /etc/xinetd.conf
#
# xinetd.conf
#
# Copyright (c) 1998-2001 SuSE GmbH Nuernberg, Germany.
# Copyright (c) 2002 SuSE Linux AG, Nuernberg, Germany.
#

defaults
{
        log_type        = FILE /var/log/xinetd.log
tux@ws2:~>
```

- **head**   The **head** *filename* command is used to display the first couple of lines of a text file on the screen. In Figure 7-3, the head command is being used to view the /etc/xinetd.conf file. Notice that only the first portion of the file is displayed by the command.

- **tail**   The **tail** *filename* command is used to display the last couple of lines of a text file onscreen. By default, the last 10 lines are displayed. The tail command is particularly useful when displaying a log file onscreen, when you typically only want to see the latest entries at the end of the file. You probably don't care about earlier log entries made several days or weeks ago. You can use tail to see just the last few log entries added to the end of the file. If you want to view more than 10 lines, you can use the –n option with the tail command followed by the number of lines you want it to display.

The tail command also includes the –f option, which is very useful. You can use it to monitor the file specified in the command. If new content is added to the end of the file (such as a log file) the new lines will be displayed onscreen. In Figure 7-4, the **tail –f /var/log/messages** command has been issued to monitor the file for new entries.

Using –f with the tail command can be very helpful when troubleshooting a misbehaving service or configuration problem on the system. You can start monitoring the appropriate log file with the tail –f command, then run or use

```
ws2:~ # tail -f /var/log/messages
Oct 16 16:00:00 ws2 dhclient: XMT: Solicit on eth0, interval 64950ms.
Oct 16 16:01:05 ws2 dhclient: XMT: Solicit on eth0, interval 121060ms.
Oct 16 16:01:45 ws2 su: The gnome keyring socket is not owned with the same cred
entials as the user login: /tmp/keyring-VKbaKI/control
Oct 16 16:01:45 ws2 su: gkr-pam: couldn't unlock the login keyring.
Oct 16 16:01:45 ws2 su: (to root) tux on /dev/pts/0
Oct 16 16:03:06 ws2 dhclient: XMT: Solicit on eth0, interval 129310ms.
Oct 16 16:05:16 ws2 dhclient: XMT: Solicit on eth0, interval 129570ms.
Oct 16 16:06:48 ws2 su: The gnome keyring socket is not owned with the same cred
entials as the user login: /tmp/keyring-VKbaKI/control
Oct 16 16:06:48 ws2 su: gkr-pam: couldn't unlock the login keyring.
Oct 16 16:06:48 ws2 su: (to root) tux on /dev/pts/0
```

Figure 7-4   Using tail with the –f option to monitor a log file

the service. The tail –f command will display error messages on the screen as they are written to the log file. That's helpful! When you're done, you can break out of tail by pressing CTRL-C.

In addition to creating and viewing files, you will also need to know how to delete existing files.

Finding Content Within Files

In the previous chapter, we discussed shell commands that can you can use to search for files in the file system. However, there will be many occasions when you need to look for information *within* a file itself. Linux provides a utility called **grep** that you can use to search for specific content within a file. The grep utility is extremely useful; in fact, I dare say that most Linux admins use it on a daily basis. Using grep, you can search through a file for a particular text string. This can come in handy when you want to search a very large log file for a specific message or when you need to find a specific directive within a configuration file. You can even use grep to search through multiple files at once to locate a particular piece of information.

To use grep, you enter **grep** *search_expression file_name* at the shell prompt. For example, suppose you want to search through your /var/log/messages file for any log entries related to the VNC service running on your Linux system. You would enter **grep vnc /var/log/messages**. The grep utility would then display each line from the file that contained your search term, as shown here:

```
ws2:~ # grep vnc /var/log/messages
Feb  1 13:47:25 ws2 xinetd[7134]: Reading included configuration file: /etc/
xinetd.d/vnc [file=/etc/xinetd.d/vnc] [line=15]
ws2:~ #
```

Likewise, if you needed to find a line in your /etc/ntp.conf file that contains the directive "server", you could enter **grep server /etc/ntp.conf** at the shell prompt. This is shown in the next example:

```
ws2:~ # grep server /etc/ntp.conf
# server 127.127.8.0 mode 5 prefer
server 127.127.1.0
## # rcntp addserver <yourserver>
server bigben.cac.washington.edu iburst
# key (7) for accessing server variables
# controlkey 15          # key (6) for accessing server variables
ws2:~ #
```

When working with grep at the command line, you can use the following options:

- **-i** Ignores case when searching for the search text.
- **-l** Displays only the names of the files that contain the matching text. It doesn't display the actual matching line of text.
- **-n** Displays matching line numbers.

- **-r**   Searches recursively through subdirectories of the path specified.
- **-v**   Displays all lines that *do not* contain the search string.

The grep utility works great when you need to search for a specific text string within a file. However, there may be times when you need to search for more complex patterns. In this situation, you can use the egrep command instead.

 NOTE   The egrep command is the same as using the grep –E command.

The key advantage of egrep is that it can search files for extended *regular expressions*. Regular expressions are strings consisting of *metacharacters*, regular characters, and numerals.

 NOTE   Regular characters (A–Z and numerals) are called *literals*.

Metacharacters are characters that do not represent themselves but represent other characters instead. They can also be used to specify a character's location within a text string. Some commonly used regular expressions are listed in Table 7-1.

In addition to egrep, you can also use the fgrep (fixed-string grep) utility to search for content within files.

 NOTE   Running fgrep is the same as running grep –F.

The fgrep utility searches files for lines that match a fixed string. Unlike egrep, it does not perform searches for regular expressions. Instead, fgrep uses direct string comparisons to find matching lines of text in the input. The syntax is **fgrep** *pattern filename*. For example, running the fgrep server *.c command searches for the string "server" in all files in the current directory whose filename has a ".c" extension.

Let's practice using Linux search tools in the following exercise.

Exercise 7-1: Using grep   In this exercise, you will practice using Linux search tools. Complete the following:

1. With your Linux system running and authenticated as a regular user, switch to root by entering **su –** followed by your root user's password at the shell prompt.

2. Locate references to the inittab file in your system log file by entering **grep inittab /var/log messages**. What can you learn about this file from the output of grep?

Metacharacter	Function	Example
*	Matches any number of any characters.	**Myfile*** would match Myfile1, Myfile2, Myfiles, Myfiles23, etc.
?	Matches zero or one of the preceding characters.	**Fou?r** would match both For and Four.
.	Matches a single character	**Myfile.** would match Myfile1, Myfile2, and Myfiles, but would not match Myfiles23.
^	Matches an expression if it appears at the beginning of a line.	**^server** would match any instance of "server" as long as it appears at the beginning of a line.
$	Matches an expression if it appears at the end of a line.	**server$** would match any instance of "server" as long as it appears at the end of a line.
|	Matches the expressions on either side of the pipe character.	**Server|server** would match either "Server" or "server".
[nnn]	Matches any one character between the braces.	**[xyz]** would match any one of "x", "y", or "z".
[^nnn]	Matches an expression that does not contain any one of the characters specified.	**[^aei]** would not match the characters "a", "e", or "i".
[n-n]	Matches any single character in the range.	**[1-5]** would match any number between 1 and 5.

Table 7-1   Regular Expressions

3. Use egrep to find information about the init process in your system log file by entering **egrep init* /var/log/messages** at the shell prompt.

4. Use egrep again to find information about all the Ethernet interfaces installed in your system by entering **egrep eth[0-3] /var/log/messages** at the shell prompt.

5. Find all lines in your system log file that end with "Enabled" by entering **egrep Enabled$ /var/log/messages** at the shell prompt.

Using Redirection and Piping

The bash shell (as well as most other Linux shells) is extremely powerful and flexible. One of the features that makes it this way is its ability to manipulate command input and output. In this part of this chapter, we're going to explore how to do this. Specifically, we're going to cover the following:

- Standard bash file descriptors
- Redirecting output and input for shell commands

- Piping information
- Using command substitution

Standard bash File Descriptors

Before you can learn how to redirect or pipe outputs from a bash command, you must first understand bash shell *file descriptors*. There are three file descriptors that are available for every command you enter at a shell prompt. These are shown in Figure 7-5.

These three file descriptors include the following:

- **stdin** This file descriptor stands for *standard input*. Standard input is the input provided to a particular command to process. The stdin for a command is represented by the number 0.

- **stdout** This file descriptor stands for *standard output*. Standard output is simply the output from a particular command. For example, the directory listing generated by the ls command is its stdout. The stdout for a command is represented by the number 1.

- **stderr** This file descriptor stands for *standard error*. Standard error is the error code generated, if any, by a command. The stderr for a command is represented by the number 2.

Not all commands will use all three of these descriptors, but many do. Let's take a look at some examples. Suppose you display the contents of a file in my home directory by entering **cat ~/test2.txt**, as shown here:

```
tux@ws2:~> cat ~/test2.txt
This is a text file named test2.txt.
tux@ws2:~>
```

The cat command displays the contents of the file on the screen. This is the stdout of the cat command. Now suppose you enter the same command but specify a file that doesn't exist, as shown here:

```
tux@ws2:~> cat ~/test1.txt
cat: /home/tux/test1.txt: No such file or directory
tux@ws2:~>
```

Because the file doesn't exist, the cat command generates an error. This is the stderr of the cat command. Knowing these descriptors, you can redirect where each one goes when the command is executed.

Figure 7-5
bash shell file
descriptors

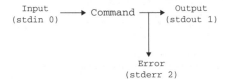

Redirecting Output and Input for Shell Commands

Using the three descriptors, you can manipulate where a command gets its input from and where it sends its outputs. In this part of this chapter, we're going to review how you can do this from the command line. We'll discuss the following:

- Redirecting output
- Redirecting input

Redirecting Output

The bash shell allows you to manipulate where the output from a command goes after it is generated. By default, it is displayed on the screen. However, you can specify that it be sent elsewhere. For example, it is very common to redirect output from a command from the screen to a text file in the file system, especially if the output from the command is very long.

Redirection is accomplished using the > character in the command line. The syntax for redirecting output is *command output> filename_or_device*. For example, suppose you want to use the tail command to view the last few lines of your system log file /var/log/messages and you want to save the output to a file named lastmessages in the current directory. You could do this by entering **tail /var/log/messages 1> lastmessages**. This tells the shell to redirect the stdout (1) to a file named lastmessages. The output from the command is truly redirected. It isn't displayed on the screen at all. All stdout text is sent to the file specified, as shown in Figure 7-6.

If you don't enter a file descriptor number in the command, the shell will assume that you want to only redirect the stdout from the command. In the example in Figure 7-6, you could enter **tail /var/log/messages > lastmessages** and get the same result.

You can use the same technique to redirect stderr from the screen to a file. For example, if you were to use the cat command to try to display a file that doesn't exist, you could redirect any error messages generated to a file by entering **cat myfiles.odt 2> errorfile**. Because the file doesn't exist, the cat command generates an error message (stderr) instead of regular output (stdout). This is shown in Figure 7-7.

```
ws2:~ # tail /var/log/messages 1> lastmessages
ws2:~ # cat lastmessages
Oct 16 16:16:20 ws2 su: gkr-pam: couldn't unlock the login keyring.
Oct 16 16:16:20 ws2 su: (to root) tux on /dev/pts/2
Oct 16 16:17:05 ws2 dhclient: XMT: Solicit on eth0, interval 130810ms.
Oct 16 16:19:16 ws2 dhclient: XMT: Solicit on eth0, interval 130880ms.
Oct 16 16:21:27 ws2 dhclient: XMT: Solicit on eth0, interval 128450ms.
Oct 16 16:23:35 ws2 dhclient: XMT: Solicit on eth0, interval 118750ms.
Oct 16 16:25:34 ws2 dhclient: XMT: Solicit on eth0, interval 119950ms.
Oct 16 16:27:34 ws2 dhclient: XMT: Solicit on eth0, interval 131700ms.
Oct 16 16:29:09 ws2 unix2_chkpwd: gkr-pam: unlocked login keyring
Oct 16 16:29:46 ws2 dhclient: XMT: Solicit on eth0, interval 109840ms.
ws2:~ # █
```

Figure 7-6 Redirecting output from the tail command

Figure 7-7

Redirecting stderr

to a text file

```
ws2:~ # cat myfiles.odt 2> errorfile
ws2:~ # cat errorfile
cat: myfiles.odt: No such file or directory
ws2:~ #
```

This command specifies that the stderr (2) from the cat command be redirected to a file named errorfile in the current directory. Because it's redirected, the stderr output is not displayed on the screen but is instead written to the specified file.

When you redirect output to a file that doesn't exist, the shell will automatically create it for you. This is what happened in the preceding examples. However, if the file already exists, be warned that the shell will erase the existing file and replace it with the new output by default. If you want to *append* the new output to an existing file without erasing its contents, then you should use >> instead of >. For example, if you wanted to write the stdout from the ps command to a file named myprocesses without overwriting the existing contents of that file, you would enter **ps 1>> myprocesses**. An example of appending with >> is shown in Figure 7-8. In this figure the stdout of the ps command has been written twice to the myprocesses file.

You can even redirect both stderr and stdout to text files at the same time. To do this, you add two redirection instructions to the command, one for the stdout and one for the stderr. The syntax for doing this is *command* **1>** *stdout_filename* **2>** *stderr_filename*. This will send stdout to one file and stderr to a different file. For example, if you wanted to write the stdout from the mount command to a file named mntok and the stderr to a file named mnterr, you would enter **mount 1> mntok 2> mnterr**.

You can also send both outputs to the same file. To do this, use the syntax of *command* **1>** *filename* **2>** **&1**. This syntax causes the stdout to first be sent to the specified file, and then stderr (2) output is redirected to the stdout output (&1). If you're going to use this option, it's very important to remember to use the & symbol before the 1. This tells the shell that the character that follows is a file descriptor and not a filename. If you omit this character, then the shell will write stderr output to a separate file named 1.

Now that you know how to redirect output from a command, we next need to discuss how to redirect command inputs. Let's do that next.

Redirecting Input

Just as you can specify where output from a command is sent, you can also specify where a command's inputs (stdin) come from as well. To do this, you simply reverse

Figure 7-8

Appending

content to the

end of a file

```
ws2:~ # ps 1>> myprocesses
ws2:~ # cat myprocesses
    PID TTY          TIME CMD
   9577 pts/0     00:00:00 su
   9581 pts/0     00:00:00 bash
  10278 pts/0     00:00:00 ps
    PID TTY          TIME CMD
   9577 pts/0     00:00:00 su
   9581 pts/0     00:00:00 bash
  10287 pts/0     00:00:00 ps
ws2:~ #
```

the character that you used previously for redirecting output. The syntax you use is *command < input_text_or_file*.

For example, you can enter **tail < /var/log/messages** at the shell prompt. This sends the text string "/var/log/messages" to the tail command as an input. For most commands, however, this isn't a terribly useful option. In the preceding example, it would probably be easier to simply enter **tail /var/log/messages**. Where this option really shines is when you need to send a lot of text to a command that is expecting it.

For example, you can send a list of words from a text file to the **sort** command and have it sort them for you. In the example that follows, I've used a text editor to create a file named **words** that contains several lines of text:

```
tux@ws2:~> cat words
Who
What
Why
Where
How
tux@ws2:~>
```

With this file created, I can specify that it be used as an input with the sort command. This is done by entering **sort < words** at the shell prompt. The sorted output is then displayed on the screen, as shown here:

```
tux@ws2:~> sort < words
How
What
Where
Who
Why
tux@ws2:~>
```

Let's practice working with redirection in the following exercise.

Exercise 7-2: Redirecting Input and Output   In this exercise, you will practice redirecting input and output. Complete the following:

1. If necessary, boot your Linux system and log in as a standard user.

2. Change to your root user account by entering **su –** followed by your root password.

3. Use tail to view the last lines of your /var/log/messages file and redirect the standard output to a text file in your home directory by entering **tail /var/log/ messages 1> lastlines**.

4. Enter **ls l*** and verify that the lastlines file was created.

5. Use the **cat** command to view the lastlines file by entering **cat lastlines** at the shell prompt.

6. Append the last lines of the content of your /var/log/firewall log file to lastlines by entering **tail /var/log/firewall 1>> lastlines** at the shell prompt.

7. Use the **cat** command to view the lastlines file again by entering **cat lastlines** at the shell prompt. You should see the lines from the firewall log file added to the end of the file.

8. Send standard error to a log file by entering **tail /var/log/mylog 2> errorout** at the shell prompt.

9. View the errorout file by entering **cat errorout** at the shell prompt. Why was an error generated by the preceding command?

10. Send the lastlines file to the stdin of the sort command by entering **sort < lastlines** at the shell prompt. The sort command should send the words from the file to the stdout (the screen) in alphabetical order.

In addition to redirecting input or output from a command, you can pipe outputs.

Piping Information

Redirection is great, but it has one weakness. It only allows us to redirect to or from a file in the file system or a system device. What if we need to redirect the output from one command to the input of another command? This is done using *pipes*. In this part of the chapter, I'm going to explain how this is done.

Pipes are extremely useful when you're working at the shell prompt. For example, we mentioned earlier in this book that you can use | **more** with commands such as cat or env. The pipe character (|) in the command tells the shell to take the output of the first command and send it to the input of the second program specified.

For example, if you enter **cat /var/log/messages** | **more** at the shell prompt, the cat command reads the contents of the /var/log/messages file and sends it to the stdout. Normally, this would be displayed on the screen. However, because you are using a pipe, the shell knows that it should not display the stdout from cat on the screen. Instead, it takes the stdout from cat and sends it as the stdin for the next command listed—in this case, the more command. The more command then takes the output from cat and performs its manipulations on it, which is to display the text on the screen one line at a time.

Pipes can be used with any commands that produce output of some sort and accept input of some sort. A great example is the grep command. You can use grep alone at the command line, of course. However, it's very handy when used in a pipe in conjunction with another command. The syntax of the command is *command* | **grep** *expression*. Doing this pipes the output of the first command to the input of grep, which then searches for information that matches the specified expression.

For example, suppose you are using the cat command to display the contents of the /var/log/messages file on the screen. You're only interested in displaying log file entries created when the network interfaces in the system were brought up. You could filter out the output of cat by piping it to grep and searching for the expression "ifup" in the output of cat. To do this, you enter **cat /var/log/messages** | **grep ifup**, as shown here:

```
ws2:~ # cat /var/log/messages | grep ifup
Jan 19 10:39:42 linux ifup:    lo
```

```
Jan 19 10:39:42 linux ifup:      lo
Jan 19 10:39:42 linux ifup: IP address: 127.0.0.1/8
Jan 19 10:39:42 linux ifup:
Jan 19 10:39:42 linux ifup:
Jan 19 10:39:42 linux ifup: IP address: 127.0.0.2/8
Jan 19 10:39:42 linux ifup:
Jan 19 10:39:42 linux ifup:      eth0      device: Intel Corporation 82545EM
Gigabit Ethernet Controller (Copper) (rev 01)
Jan 19 10:39:43 linux ifup-dhcp:      eth0      Starting DHCP4+DHCP6 client
Jan 19 10:39:43 linux ifup-dhcp: .
```

Only the entries in the output of cat that match the expression "ifup" are displayed on the screen by grep.

NOTE   Remember that when you are piping information, only the last command in the pipe actually displays output on the screen. The output from all of the other commands is redirected to the input of the next command in the pipe and is not displayed on the screen.

In this example, there are actually too many matching entries to fit on a single screen, but you can include multiple commands within a pipe to address this. In this situation you need to use cat to generate the initial output, then filter it through grep to find only those entries that have "ifup" in them, and then send the output of grep to the more command so that the display is paused one screen at a time. To do this, you enter **cat /var/log/messages | grep ifup | more** at the shell prompt.

Occasionally, you may need the output from a command to be displayed on the screen *and* written to a file at the same time. This can be done using the **tee** command. The syntax for using tee is *command* | **tee** *filename*. For example, if you wanted to output the stdout from the ls –l command to be displayed on the screen and written to a file named output.txt, you could use the following command:

```
ls -l | tee output.txt
```

Using Command Substitution

The bash shell allows you to use *command substitution*, which allows you to run a command and have its output pasted back on the command line as an argument for another command. Command substitution allows you perform multiple tasks at once. Essentially, command substitution is an alternative way to pipe the output from one command to the input of another.

Command substitution works by first creating a child process that runs the first command. The stdout from this command is then piped back to the bash shell. The shell parses the output from the first command into words separated by whitespace. After the pipe from the first command closes (indicating the first command is done running) the shell starts another child process to run the second command using the stdout from the first command as arguments.

For example, suppose you wanted to use the tail command to view the last few lines of all the files in /etc that contained the text "192.168". You could use the following command substitution:

```
tail $(fgrep -l 192.168 /etc/*)
```

First the **fgrep –l** command is run to search through all of the files in the /etc directory for the text string "192.168". Using the –l option with fgrep causes the command to return a list of filenames only, not the actual matching text. This list of files is then piped to the input of the tail command, which then displays the last few lines of each file it receives.

Let's practice working with pipes in the following exercise.

Exercise 7-3: Using Pipes   In this exercise, you will practice using pipes to send stdout from one command to the stdin of another. Complete the following:

1. If necessary, boot your Linux system and log in as a standard user.

2. If necessary, open a terminal session.

3. Change to your root user account by entering **su –** followed by your root password.

4. View all entries in your system log that contain the word "kernel" by piping the output from cat to grep. Enter **cat /var/log/messages | grep kernel** at the shell prompt to do this.

5. The output from the preceding command was probably very long. Pipe the output from cat to grep to more by entering **cat /var/log/messages | grep kernel | more** at the shell prompt.

6. Send the output from the preceding command to the screen and to a file named kernel.txt in your home directory by entering **cat /var/log/messages | grep kernel | tee ~/kernel.txt** at the shell prompt.

7. Verify the information was written to kernel.txt by entering **cat ~/kernel.txt** at the shell prompt.

Now that you understand how piping and redirection works, let's discuss how to process text streams.

Processing Text Streams

The processes of piping and redirection create text streams. Imagine a stream of text characters flowing from the output of one command to the input of another.

When processing a text stream within a script or when piping output at the shell prompt, there may be times when you need to filter the output of one command such that only certain portions of the text stream are actually passed along to the stdin of the next command. There is a variety of tools you can use to do this. In the last part of this chapter, we'll look at using the following commands:

- cut
- fmt
- join and paste
- nl
- pr
- sort
- split
- tr
- uniq
- wc

cut

The cut command is used to print columns or fields that you specify from a file to the standard output. By default, the Tab character is used as a delimiter. The following options can be used with cut:

- **–c***list*   Select only these characters.
- **–d***delim*   Use the specified character instead of Tab for field delimiter.
- **–f***list*   Select only the specified fields. Print any line that contains no delimiter character, unless the –s option is specified.
- **–s**   Do not print lines that do not contain delimiters.

For example, you could use the cut command to display all group names from the /etc/group file. The name of each group is contained in the first field of each line of the file, as shown next:

```
tux@ws2:~> cat /etc/group
...
video:x:33:ksanders,rtracy,tux
wheel:x:10:
www:x:8:
xok:x:41:
users:x:100:
tux@ws2:~>
```

Notice that the group file uses colons as a delimiter between fields, so you must specify a colon instead of a Tab as the delimiter. The command to do this is **cut –d: –f1 /etc/group**. An example is shown in Figure 7-9.

Figure 7-9

Using the cut
command to
extract a field
from /etc/group

```
ws2:~ # cut -d: -f1 /etc/group
video
wheel
www
xok
users
```

fmt

You can use the fmt command to reformat a text file. It is commonly used to change
the wrapping of long lines within the file to a more manageable width. The syntax for
using fmt is **fmt** *option filename*.

You can use the –w option with the fmt command to specify how many characters
(columns) wide the output text should be. For example, you can narrow the text of a
file to 80 columns by entering **fmt –w 80** *filename*. An example is shown in Figure 7-10.

join and paste

The join command prints a line from each of two specified input files that have identical join fields. The first field is the default join field, delimited by white space. You can
specify a different join field using the –j *fieldnumber* option.

For example, suppose you have two files. The first file (named firstnames) contains
the following content:

```
1 Mike
2 Jenny
3 Joe
```

The second file (named lastnames) contains the following content:

```
1 Johnson
2 Doe
3 Jones
```

```
tux@ws2:~> cat longfile.txt
Greetings everyone. I welcome you to this session today. I hope your travel was
pleasant.
We have a number of very talented speakers lined up for this session. I hope you
 find their topics information.
tux@ws2:~> fmt -w 80 longfile.txt
Greetings everyone. I welcome you to this session today. I hope your travel
was pleasant.  We have a number of very talented speakers lined up for this
session. I hope you find their topics information.
tux@ws2:~> █
```

Figure 7-10   Using fmt to change the number of columns in a text file

You can use the join command to join the corresponding lines from each file by entering **join –j 1 firstnames lastnames**. This is shown here:

```
tux@ws2:~> join -j 1 firstnames lastnames
1 Mike Johnson
2 Jenny Doe
3 Joe Jones
tux@ws2:~>
```

The paste command works in much the same manner as the join command. It pastes together corresponding lines from one or more files into columns. By default, the Tab character is used to separate columns. You can use the –d*n* option to specify a different delimiter character. For example, you could use the paste command to join the corresponding lines from the firstnames and lastnames files above by entering **paste firstnames lastnames**. An example is shown here:

```
tux@ws2:~> paste firstnames lastnames
1 Mike    1 Johnson
2 Jenny   2 Doe
3 Joe     3 Jones
tux@ws2:~>
```

nl

The nl command determines the number of lines in a file. When you run the command, the output is written with a line number added to the beginning of each line in the file. The syntax is **nl** *filename*.

For example, in the example shown here, the nl command is used to add a number to the beginning of each line in the myfile.txt file.

```
tux@ws2:~> nl myfile.txt
     1 Hello everyone.
     2 We welcome you today.
     3 I hope your travel was pleasant.
     4 Refreshments will be served after this session.
tux@ws2:~>
```

pr

The pr command is used to format text files for printing. It formats the file with pagination, headers, and columns. The header contains the date and time, filename, and page number. You can use the following options with pr:

- **–d**   Double-space the output.

- **–l** *page_length*   Set the page length to the specified number of lines. The default is 66.

- **–o** *margin*   Offset each line with the specified number of spaces. The default margin is 0.

sort

The sort command sorts the lines of a text file alphabetically. The output is written to the standard output. Some commonly used options for the sort command include the following:

- −f   Change lowercase characters to uppercase characters.
- −M   Sort by month.
- −n   Sort numerically.
- −r   Reverse the sort order.

The sort command can be used to sort the output of other commands by piping the standard output of the first command to the standard input of the sort command. In the example shown in Figure 7-11, the output of the ps −e command (which generates a list of running processes on the system) is piped to the input of the sort command. Because the −r option is used with sort, the output from ps is sorted by process ID number from highest to lowest.

split

The split command splits an input file into a series of files (without altering the original input file). The default is to split the input file into 1000-line segments. You can use the −n option to specify a different number of lines.

For example, the **split −1 firstnames outputfile_** command can be used to split the firstnames file into three separate files, each containing a single line. This is shown in Figure 7-12.

tr

The tr command is used to translate or delete characters. However, be aware that this command does not work with files. To use it with files, you must first use a command such as cat to send the text stream to the standard input of tr. The syntax is **tr** *options X Y*. Some commonly used options for the tr command include the following:

- −c   Use all characters not in *X*.
- −d   Delete characters in *X*; do not translate.

Figure 7-11

Sorting lines in a file

```
tux@ws2:~> ps -e | sort -n -r
 7193 pts/3    00:00:00 sort
 7192 pts/3    00:00:00 ps
 7085 ?        00:00:02 packagekitd
 4149 tty6     00:00:00 mingetty
 4148 tty5     00:00:00 mingetty
 4147 tty4     00:00:00 mingetty
 4146 tty3     00:00:00 mingetty
 4145 tty2     00:00:00 mingetty
 4144 tty1     00:00:00 mingetty
```

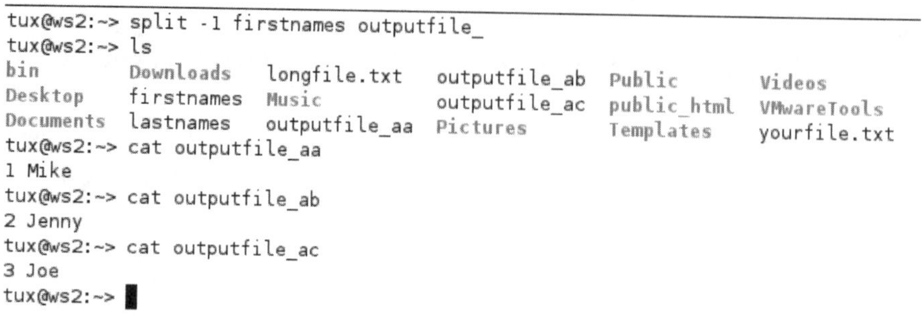

```
tux@ws2:~> split -1 firstnames outputfile_
tux@ws2:~> ls
bin          Downloads    longfile.txt   outputfile_ab  Public       Videos
Desktop      firstnames   Music          outputfile_ac  public_html  VMwareTools
Documents    lastnames    outputfile_aa  Pictures       Templates    yourfile.txt
tux@ws2:~> cat outputfile_aa
1 Mike
tux@ws2:~> cat outputfile_ab
2 Jenny
tux@ws2:~> cat outputfile_ac
3 Joe
tux@ws2:~> █
```

Figure 7-12   Splitting a file

- **–s**   Replace each input sequence of a repeated character that is listed in X with a single occurrence of that character.
- **–t**   First truncate X to length of Y.

For example, to translate all lowercase characters in the lastnames file to uppercase characters, you could enter **cat lastnames | tr a-z A-Z**, as shown in this example:

```
tux@ws2:~> cat lastnames | tr a-z A-Z
1 JOHNSON
2 DOE
3 JONES
tux@ws2:~>
```

uniq

The uniq command reports or omits repeated lines. The syntax is **uniq** *options input output*. You can use the following options with the uniq command:

- **–d**   Only print duplicate lines.
- **–u**   Only print unique lines.

For example, suppose our lastnames file contained duplicate entries:

```
1 Johnson
1 Johnson
2 Doe
3 Jones
```

You could use the **uniq lastnames** command to remove the duplicate lines, as shown in the example here:

```
tux@ws2:~> uniq lastnames
1 Johnson
2 Doe
3 Jones
tux@ws2:~>
```

Be aware that the uniq command only works if the duplicate lines are adjacent to each other. If the text stream you need to work with contains duplicate lines that are not adjacent, you can use the sort command to first make them adjacent and then pipe the output to the standard input of uniq.

wc

The wc command prints the number of newlines, words, and bytes in a file. The syntax is **wc** *options files*. You can use the following options with the wc command:

- **−c** Print the byte counts.
- **−m** Print the character counts.
- **−l** Print the newline counts.
- **−L** Print the length of the longest line.
- **−w** Print the word counts.

For example, to print all counts and totals for the firstnames file, you would use the **wc firstnames** command, as shown in this example:

```
tux@ws2:~> wc firstnames
  3 6 21 firstnames
tux@ws2:~>
```

Let's practice processing text streams in the following exercise.

Exercise 7-4: Processing Text Streams In this exercise, you will practice processing text streams. Complete the following:

1. If necessary, boot your Linux system and log in as a standard user.
2. At the shell prompt, use the ls command to verify that the test.txt file we created in Chapter 5, Exercise 5-7 still exists in your home directory.

   If it doesn't exist, use vi to create the file and enter the following as its contents:
   ```
   Usu agam legere delicata ut, per democritum scriptorem an. Nec
   te zzril possim tincidunt, at qui probo mucius gubergren. Ea mei
   paulo cetero oportere, at pertinax liberavisse pri.
   ```
3. Open test.txt in the vi editor.
4. Add a carriage return, if it doesn't already exist, to the end of each line of text.
5. Save your changes and exit vi.
6. View the contents of the file by entering **cat test.txt** at the shell prompt.
7. Change the formatting of the text to 80 characters wide by entering **fmt −w 80 test.txt** at the shell prompt. Note that the output is written to the stdout, not to the file. The original file is unaltered.
8. Number each line of text by entering **nl test.txt** at the shell prompt. Again, the output is written to the stdout, not to the file. The original file is unaltered.

9. Sort each line of the file alphabetically by entering **sort test.txt** at the shell prompt.

10. Translate all characters to uppercase characters by entering **cat test.txt | tr a-z A-Z** at the shell prompt.

Chapter Review

In this chapter, we examined a variety of topics related to managing the contents of text files in the Linux file system. We began this chapter by discussing utilities you can use to view the contents of text files onscreen. I pointed out that you can use cat, less, head, or tail to do this. I also pointed out that you can use the –f option with tail to monitor changes to a text file, such as a log file, as they are made. We then discussed how to use grep to find specific content within text files.

We then shifted gears and addressed the issue of managing the inputs and outputs of shell commands. Most shell commands have three file descriptors:

- stdin (0)
- stdout (1)
- stderr (2)

You can redirect stdout and stderr output from a command to a file by adding **1>** *filename* or **2>** *filename* to any command. If the specified file doesn't exist, the shell will create it. If it does exist, its contents will be overwritten. If you want to preserve the existing contents of the file, use >> instead of >. You can also send input from a file to a command's stdin using the < character.

In addition to redirecting to a file, you can also use a pipe to redirect stdout from one command to the stdin of another. This is done by entering *command | command* at the shell prompt. In fact, you can include many different commands in the same pipe.

We then discussed command substitution. I related that the bash shell allows you to run a command and have its output pasted back on the command line as an argument for another command. This is command substitution.

We ended this chapter by discussing how to process text streams and text files to manipulate and modify text, either within a script or within a pipe. We looked at the following utilities:

- **cut**   Prints columns or fields that you specify from a file to the standard output. By default, the Tab character is used as a delimiter.

- **fmt**   Reformats a text file.

- **join and paste**   The join command prints a line from each of two specified input files that have identical join fields. The first field is the default join field, delimited by white space. The paste command works in much the same manner. It pastes together corresponding lines from one or more files into columns. By default, the Tab character is used to separate columns.

- **nl**   Determines the number of lines in a file. When you run the command, the output is written with a line number added to the beginning of each line in the file.

- **pr**   Formats text files for printing with pagination, headers, and columns. The header contains the date and time, filename, and page number.

- **sort**   Sorts the lines of a text file alphabetically.

- **split**   Splits an input file into a series of files (without altering the original input file).

- **tr**   Translates or deletes characters.

- **uniq**   Reports or omits repeated lines.

- **wc**   Prints the number of newlines, words, and bytes in a file.

Accelerated Review

- You can use cat to view a text file onscreen.

- You can also use less to view a text file onscreen.

- The less command pauses the display one line at a time.

- The head command can be used to display the first few lines of a text file.

- The tail command can be used to display the last few lines of a text file.

- The tail command used with the –f option can monitor a text file for changes.

- You can use grep to search for text within a file.

- To use grep, you enter **grep** *search_expression file_name* at the shell prompt.

- egrep can search files for extended *regular expressions.*

- Regular expressions are strings consisting of *metacharacters,* regular characters, and numerals.

- Metacharacters are characters that do not represent themselves but represent other characters instead.

- Metacharacters can be used to specify a character's location within a text string.

- The fgrep utility search files for lines that match a fixed string.

- Most Linux shell commands have three standard file descriptors:

  - stdin (0)

  - stdout (1)

  - stderr (2)

- You can redirect output (stdout and stderr) from the screen to a file using the > character after the command.

- Using 1> *filename* redirects stdout to the specified file.

- Using 2> *filename* redirects stderr to the specified file.

- Using > causes the specified file to be created if it doesn't exist. If it does exist, the file's contents will be overwritten.
- Using >> will cause the specified file's existing contents to be preserved and the new output appended to the end.
- You can use < to specify a file to be used as the stdin for a command.
- Using pipes allows you to move the stdout from one command to the stdin of another command.
- The syntax for using pipes is *command1 | command2*.
- You can use multiple commands within a single pipe.
- Command substitution allows you to run a command and have its output pasted back on the command line as an argument for another command.
- You can process text streams to manipulate and modify text within a script or within a pipe.
- You can use the following utilities to process a text stream:
  - cut
  - fmt
  - join
  - paste
  - nl
  - pr
  - sort
  - split
  - tr
  - uniq
  - wc

Questions

1. You need to view the last few lines of your /var/log/warn file. Which is the best command to do this?

   A. tail /var/log/warn

   B. cat /var/log/warn | more

   C. head /var/xinetd.log

   D. less /var/xinetd.log

2. You need to find all entries in your /var/log/messages file that contain the term "scsi". Which is the correct command to do this?

   A. grep /var/log/messages "scsi"

   B. grep scsi "/var/log/messages"

   C. grep /var/log/messages scsi

   D. grep scsi /var/log/messages

3. Which file descriptor refers to the text that a command displays on the screen after the command has finished processing? (Choose two.)

   A. stdin

   B. stdout

   C. stdisplay

   D. stdoutput

   E. stderr

4. You want to send the standard output and the standard error from the tail /var/log/firewall command to a file named lastevents in the current directory. Which command will do this?

   A. tail /var/log/firewall 1> lastevents 2> lastevents

   B. tail /var/log/firewall > lastevents

   C. tail /var/log/firewall 1> lastevents 2> &1

   D. tail /var/log/firewall 1&2>lastevents

5. You want to send the contents of the logfile.txt file in the current directory to the sort command to sort them alphabetically and display them on the screen. Which command will do this?

   A. sort < ./logfile.txt

   B. sort –i ./logfile.txt

   C. sort < ./logfile.txt –d "screen"

   D. sort < ./logfile.txt > screen

6. Which command can be used to print columns or fields that you specify from a file to the standard output using the Tab character as a delimiter?

   A. cut

   B. pr

   C. fmt

   D. sort

7. Which command can process a file or text stream and add a number to the beginning of each new line?

A. join

B. paste

C. fmt

D. nl

8. You want to send the contents of the logfile.txt file in the current directory to the sort command to sort them alphabetically and display them on the screen. Which commands will do this? (Choose two.)

A. sort < logfile.txt

B. sort logfile.txt

C. sort < logfile.txt –o ""screen""

D. sort < logfile.txt > screen

E. sort –n logfile.txt

9. You used the less command to view the contents of the /etc/mtab file. You found the information you needed and now need to exit less so you can continue to work at the shell prompt. What keystroke can you use to do this?

A. q

B. x

C. CTRL+X

D. CTRL+Z

10. You need to use grep to find all instances of the text string *eth0* in your /var/log messages file. Which command can you use to do this?

A. grep /var/log/messages "eth0"

B. grep "eth0" /var/log/messages

C. grep /var/log/messages –name "eth0"

D. grep –find "eth0" /var/log/messages

11. Which regular expression would match the text strings *eth0*, *eth1*, and *eth2*? (Choose two.)

A. eth*

B. eth.

C. ^eth

D. eth$

E. eth[^1-2]

12. Which regular expression would match either *eth0* or *Eth0*? (Choose two.)

    A. eth*

    B. .th0

    C. ^eth0

    D. $th0

    E. eth0|Eth0

13. Which file descriptor refers to the text a command will accept for processing?

    A. stdin

    B. stdout

    C. stdisplay

    D. stdoutput

    E. stderr

14. You want to use the last command to write the last login times for the users on your Linux system to a file in your home directory named last_logins.txt. You want to run the command on a regular schedule and have the output appended to the end of the last_logins.txt file. Which command will do this?

    A. last < ~/ last_logins.txt

    B. last 1> ~/ last_logins.txt

    C. last 2>> ~/ last_logins.txt

    D. last 1>> ~/ last_logins.txt

15. You want to run the ps –e command to locate a process running on your Linux system that has a process ID number of 3978. To avoid manually searching the output of the command, you want to send the output of ps to the grep command to automatically find the line that contains the PID number you are looking for. Which command will do this?

    A. ps –e | grep "3978"

    B. ps –e 1> grep "3978"

    C. ps –e < grep "3978"

    D. ps –e 2> grep "3978"

Answers

1. **A.** The tail utility is the best choice to display the last few lines of the file.

2. **D.** The grep scsi /var/log/messages command uses the correct syntax.

3. **B and E.** The stdout and stderr file descriptors represent output displayed onscreen (by default) by most commands.

4. **C.** The **tail /var/log/firewall 1> lastevents 2> &1** command will send both stdout and stderr to the same file.

5. **A.** The **sort < ./logfile.txt** command will send the file to the stdin of the sort command.

6. **A.** The cut command can be used to print columns or fields that you specify from a file to the standard output using the Tab character as a delimiter.

7. **D.** The nl command can be used to process a file or text stream and add a number to the beginning of each new line.

8. **A, B.** The sort < logfile.txt command and the sort logfile.txt command will both send the contents of the logfile.txt file to the sort command to sort its lines alphabetically and display them on the screen.

9. **A.** Pressing the Q key will exit out of less. You can also press zz.

10. **B.** The **grep "eth0" /var/log/messages** command can be used to find all instances of the text string *eth0* in the /var/log messages file.

11. **A, B.** The eth* and eth. regular expressions match the text strings *eth0*, *eth1*, and *eth2*. The * regular expression matches any number of characters, while the . regular expression matches exactly one character.

12. **B, E.** The .th and eth0|Eth0 regular expressions match either the *eth0* or the *Eth0* text strings.

13. **A.** The stdin file descriptor refers to the text a command will accept as input for processing.

14. **D.** The **last 1>> ~/ last_logins.txt** command will append the output of last to the end of the last_logins.txt file in your home directory. Because >> is used instead of > , the output will be added to the end instead of overwriting the file's contents.

15. **A.** The **ps –e | grep "3978"** command will send the output of ps to the grep command to automatically find the line that contains the number 3978.

Managing Users and Groups

In this chapter, you will learn about

- Managing Linux user accounts
- Managing Linux group accounts
- Managing user account security

One of the great things about Linux is the fact that it is a true multiuser operating system. A single Linux system can be configured with one, two, five, ten, or more user accounts. Each user on the system is provided with his or her own computing environment that is unique to the user. For example, in Figure 8-1, the current user is named tux.

Notice that tux has his own directory in /home named tux.

Within his home directory, he has a variety of subdirectories, including the following:

- **Desktop** Contains the files and icons displayed on the desktop.
- **Documents** Contains documents.
- **public_html** Contains personal Web pages.
- **bin** Contains executable files and scripts that tux may need to run. This directory is automatically added to the PATH environment variable for the tux user, so he doesn't need to specify the full path to any executable stored here.
- **Downloads** Contains files downloaded from the Internet by ksanders' web browser.
- **Music** Contains music files.
- **Pictures** Contains image files.
- **Videos** Contains video files.

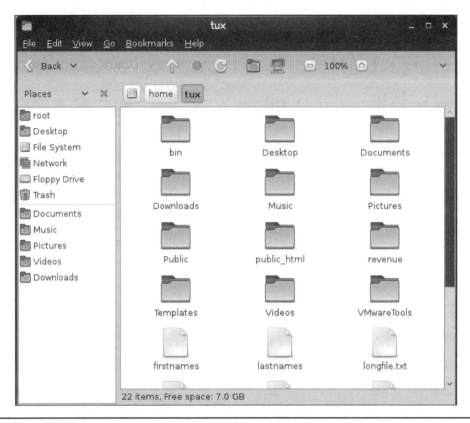

Figure 8-1 The tux user's system environment

When tux logs in to the system, his own desktop preferences are loaded and he has access to his files stored in /home/tux. If a different user logs in, his or her desktop preferences are loaded and access is provided to that user's home directory. If the system has been configured to work on a computer network, then users can log in to the system remotely and access their desktop and home directory as if they were sitting in front of the computer. In this scenario, multiple users can be logged in and using the same computer at the same time.

Because Linux is a multiuser operating system, we need some way to control who has access to what in the system. For example, suppose you have a Linux system with five user accounts:

- ksanders
- jelison
- hsaez
- ebuchannan
- aebbert

You need some way to make sure each of these users can access what he or she needs in the file system and nothing more. For example, you need to ensure that hsaez can access her files but can't access jelison's files and directories. Imagine what a nightmare it would be if one user on the system could access and tinker with files owned by a different user.

Linux uses file system access controls that prevent users from accessing files and directories they shouldn't. This is done using users, groups, ownership, and permissions.

EXAM TIP You must know Linux users, groups, ownership, and permissions inside and out. These concepts are central to the management of a Linux system. You should understand how users are implemented on Linux, the difference between system and regular users, and how to manage accounts from the command line. You should also know how groups are used on Linux and how to manage them from the command line.

To control access to a Linux system and the data it contains, we need to do two things:

- Require users to supply a set of credentials before they will be granted access to the system. This is called *authentication*.
- Set up access controls that specify what individual users can do with files and directories in the file system after they have logged in. These are called *permissions*.

We're going to address the first action in this chapter. To control overall access to the system itself, we need to implement users and groups. (Permissions will be addressed in the next chapter.) Let's begin by discussing how Linux user accounts work.

Managing Linux User Accounts

One of the key problems with MS-DOS and early versions of Windows (such as Windows 3.1) is the fact that they didn't implement individual user accounts. Because of this, there was no authentication mechanism required to access the system. Whoever sat down in front of the computer and turned it on had full access to all of the data on the hard drive *without a password*. It didn't matter if it was the user, a coworker, a boss, a custodian, or (of more concern) a corporate spy from a competitor. This was a great weakness with these operating systems.

To remedy this problem, a workstation operating system that used true user accounts was required. Fortunately, the days of the "userless" operating system are all but gone. Most modern operating systems include some type of user authentication system based on user accounts. Linux in particular performs this function very well. In this part of this chapter, we're going to discuss the following:

- How Linux user accounts work
- Where Linux user accounts are stored
- Creating and managing user accounts from the command line

How Linux User Accounts Work

You've probably noticed as we've worked through the various exercises in this course that you must log in (or *authenticate*) before you can use your Linux system. Authentication is the process of proving to the system that you are who you say you are. To authenticate, you must supply the following credentials:

- Username
- Password

NOTE There are a variety of other authentication methods available for Linux systems. Instead of manually entering usernames and passwords, you can configure Linux to use smart cards, proximity cards, biometric readers, and so on. This is made possible because Linux uses *Pluggable Authentication Modules (PAM)* to manage authentication to the system. PAM makes Linux authentication extremely flexible.

After logging in, your user's unique system environment is created. In Figure 8-2, the tux user has logged in to the local system. His customized desktop preferences have been loaded and access has been granted to his home directory in /home/tux.

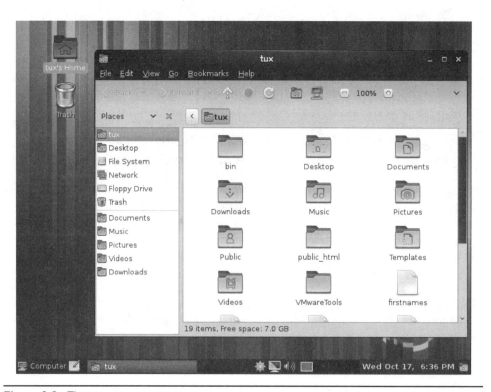

Figure 8-2 The tux system environment

If another user were to log in to the same system, her preferences would be loaded instead of tux's preferences. That user would also be provided with access to her home directory. An important point to remember is that files saved in a given user's home directory are protected from all other users on the system. For example, if tux were to save files in /home/tux, the ksanders user on this system would not be able to access them.

By default, all user home directories are created and maintained in the /home directory. For example, in Figure 8-3 three user accounts have been created on the Linux system, tux, rtracy, and ksanders.

All users have home directories created for them in /home. There is one exception to this rule, however. Remember that all Linux systems use a superuser account named *root*. Notice in Figure 8-3 that there is no home directory in /home for the root user account. Is root homeless? Actually, no. The root user account is given a home directory too. However, it isn't maintained in /home. Instead, the root user's home directory is /root. If you look carefully in Figure 8-3, you'll see a directory named root at the top of the file system. This is root's home directory and, of course, only root can access it.

You can view information about any user account on your system using the **finger** *username* command from the shell prompt.

For example, if I want to view information about the ksanders account on my Linux system, I enter **finger ksanders**. When I do, useful information about the ksanders account is displayed, as shown here:

```
ws2:~ # finger ksanders
Login: ksanders                    Name: Kimberly Sanders
Directory: /home/ksanders           Shell: /bin/bash
Last login Thu Mar 10 16:44 (MST) on :0 from console
No Mail.
No Plan.
```

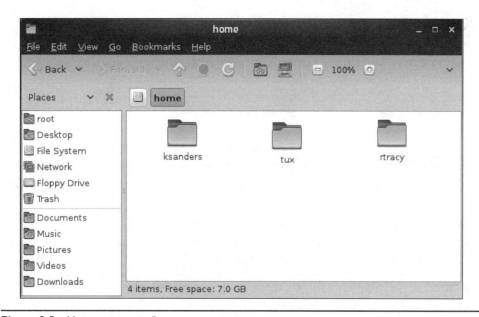

Figure 8-3 User accounts in /home

Notice that finger displays the following information about the ksanders account:

- **Login**   This is the username that is used to authenticate to the system.
- **Name**   This is the user's full name.
- **Directory**   This is the user's home directory.
- **Shell**   This is the default shell that will be started by the user.
- **Last Login**   This displays the last time the user logged in and where from.

In addition to having a home directory and default shell assigned, each user account is also assigned a unique user ID (UID) number when they are created. No two user accounts on the system will have the same UID. To view the UID for a given user account, you can use the **id** *username* command from the shell prompt. For example, to view information about the tux user account, we can enter **id tux** at the shell prompt. Here is the output from this command:

```
ws2:~ # id tux
uid=1000(tux) gid=100(users) groups=100(users),33(video)
```

Notice that on this system, the tux user account has been assigned a UID of 1000. On a SUSE Linux system, the first regular user account created on the system is always assigned a UID of 1000. The next user account will be assigned a UID of 1001, and so on.

Other distributions may use a different numbering scheme for the UID, however. For example, UIDs on a Fedora system start at 500 instead of 1000. Next, you can see that the rtracy user on this Fedora system has a UID of 500 because it was the first standard user account created:

```
[root@fs3 ~]# id rtracy
uid=500(rtracy) gid=500(rtracy) groups=500(rtracy)
```

Notice that the preceding paragraphs refer to UIDs assigned to standard user accounts. What about the root user? The root user account is always assigned a UID of 0 on most Linux distributions. This is shown next:

```
[root@fs3 ~]# id root
uid=0(root) gid=0(root) groups=0(root),1(bin),2(daemon),3(sys),4(adm),6(disk),
10(wheel)
```

It's the UID that the operating system actually uses to control access to files and directories in the file system. We'll discuss this in more detail in the next chapter. For now, however, we need to discuss where Linux user accounts are saved in the system.

Where Linux User Accounts Are Stored

Linux is a very flexible operating system. One of its flexible features is how user accounts are stored in the system. When you originally installed the system, your distribution may have given you several options for where you wanted to store your user accounts. For example, the User Authentication Method selection screen from the SUSE Linux Enterprise Server installer is shown in Figure 8-4.

Figure 8-4
Selecting a user
authentication
method

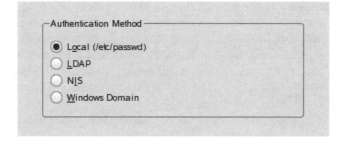

Notice that this screen allows you to choose from the following authentication methods:

- **Local**   This option stores user accounts in the /etc/passwd file. This has been the default configuration used by Linux systems for many years.

- **LDAP**   This is an option that many Linux administrators are starting to adopt more and more. Instead of storing user accounts in a file in the file system, user accounts are stored in a directory service and accessed via the Lightweight Directory Access Protocol (LDAP). Unlike local authentication, which stores accounts in a simple flat file, the directory service is hierarchical in nature; allowing you to sort and organize your user accounts by location, function, or department. The directory database can also be replicated among several different Linux systems, providing fault tolerance. The key benefit of this option is that it allows you to maintain a single set of user accounts that can be used to authenticate to many different Linux systems in your network.

 NOTE   Essentially, the LDAP option moves Linux in the direction of other server operating systems that use directory services, such as Novell's eDirectory or Microsoft's Active Directory.

- **NIS**   This option stands for *Network Information Service.* NIS is also designed to provide centralized user account management when you have multiple systems that all need the same user accounts. To do this, NIS configures systems to all use a common passwd and shadow file.

- **Windows Domain**   If you have an Active Directory domain controller in your network (or another Linux server running the Samba service), you can configure your Linux system to use the user accounts in the domain to authenticate to the local system.

Which of these options is best? It depends on what you need your system to do. If the system is a standalone workstation, the Local option is usually sufficient. You could also optionally use the LDAP option as well.

If your system is going to participate on a network where lots of different users will need access to your system, then you may want to consider using LDAP, NIS, or Windows Domain authentication.

For our purposes here, we're going to focus on the Local option. This option stores user and group information in the following files in the file system:

- **/etc/passwd**   This file contains the user account information for your system.
- **/etc/shadow**   This file contains passwords for your user accounts.
- **/etc/group**   This file contains your system's groups. (We'll discuss groups later in this chapter.)

The /etc/passwd File

If configured to use local authentication, your /etc/passwd file contains your system's user accounts. Each user account on your system is represented by a single line in the file, as shown in this example:

```
ws2:~ # cat /etc/passwd
...
root:x:0:0:root:/root:/bin/bash
sshd:x:100:102:SSH daemon:/var/lib/sshd:/bin/false
uucp:x:10:14:Unix-to-Unix CoPy system:/etc/uucp:/bin/bash
wwwrun:x:30:8:WWW daemon apache:/var/lib/wwwrun:/bin/false
ksanders:x:1002:100:Kimberly Sanders:/home/ksanders:/bin/bash
rtracy:x:1001:100:Robb Tracy:/home/rtracy:/bin/bash
tux:x:1000:100:Tux Penguin:/home/tux:/bin/bash
```

Each account record is composed of several different fields in the line, separated by a colon (:). These are organized as follows:

```
Username:Password:UID:GID:Full_Name:Home_Directory:Default_Shell
```

For example:

```
ksanders:x:1002:100:Kimberly Sanders:/home/ksanders:/bin/bash
```

Here's what these fields contain:

- **Username**   The Username field simply identifies the username the user will supply when logging in to the system. In this example, it is ksanders.
- **Password**   This is a legacy field. At one time, the user's password was stored in encrypted form in this field in the passwd file. However, for security reasons, the password has been moved from /etc/passwd to /etc/shadow. (We'll look at this file in more detail later.) Therefore, only the character *x* is shown in this field.
- **UID**   This is the user ID for the user account. We discussed the UID earlier in this chapter. In this example, the UID for the ksanders account is 1002.
- **GID**   This field references the group ID number of the user's default group. In this example, the GID for the ksanders account is 100. As you'll see later in this chapter, this references the users group.

- **Full_Name**   This field contains the user's full name. In this example, it's Kimberly Sanders.

- **Home_Directory**   This field contains the path to the user's home directory. In this case, the home directory is /home/ksanders.

- **Default_Shell**   This field specifies the shell that will be used by default. For ksanders, this is /bin/bash (the Bourne-Again SHell).

There are actually a lot of user accounts listed in the /etc/passwd file on any Linux system, even if you've only created one or two accounts. All of the other user accounts are *system* user accounts. Three sample system user accounts are shown here:

```
sshd:x:100:102:SSH daemon:/var/lib/sshd:/bin/false
uucp:x:10:14:Unix-to-Unix CoPy system:/etc/uucp:/bin/bash
wwwrun:x:30:8:WWW daemon apache:/var/lib/wwwrun:/bin/false
```

System user accounts aren't used for login. Instead, they are used by services running on the system. When one of these services needs to do something in the Linux file system, it does so as its associated user account from /etc/passwd. Notice that the system user accounts have a much lower UID number as compared to standard user accounts. UIDs between 0 and 999 are typically reserved for system accounts, depending upon the distribution.

For example, suppose I've logged in to the ftp service on my Linux system as an anonymous user and uploaded a file. This file needs to be written to the ftp service's default directory in the file system. When it writes, it does so as the ftp user. By doing this, we can use permissions (discussed in the next chapter) to control what a given service can or can't do.

The /etc/shadow File

With most Linux distributions that use local authentication, your users' passwords will be stored in encrypted format in the /etc/shadow file. This file is linked to the /etc/passwd file we discussed previously. Each of the user accounts listed in /etc/passwd has a corresponding entry in /etc/shadow, as shown in this example:

```
ws2:~ # cat /etc/shadow
...
root:$2a$05$h03HfGFSi2i8GlotOYgreeBelUlHc.z/2KxyQQF7RSo./TdLOrDJa:15035::::::
sshd:*:14796:0:99999:7:::
uucp:*:14796::::::
wwwrun:*:14796::::::
ksanders:$2a$05$KL1DbTBqpSEMiL.2FoI3ue4bdyR.eL6GMKs7MU6.nZl5SCC7/
REUS:15043:0:99999:7:::
rtracy:$2a$05$03HfGFSi2i8J8wlmjPVSS881j7TBqpSEMiL.2FoI3ue4bdyR.yHw-
pC:15041:0:99999:7:::
tux:$2a$05$45SO5ui0J8wlmjPVSS881ekzk4MD9pj725evpCeIdDivHxQ.yHw-
pC:15041:0:99999:7:::
```

As with /etc/passwd, each user account is represented by a single line in the /etc/shadow file. Each record is composed of the following fields, each separated by a colon:

Username:Password:Last_Modified:Min_Days:Max_Days:Days_Warn:Disabled_Days:Expire

For example, the record for ksanders is as follows:

```
ksanders:$2a$05$KL1DbTBqpSEMiL.2FoI3ue4bdyR.eL6GMKs7MU6.nZl5SCC7/
REUS:15043:0:99999:7:::
```

Here's what each of these fields contain:

- **Username**   This is the user's login name from /etc/passwd.
- **Password**   This is the user's password in encrypted format. In the preceding example, the password for ksanders is M3linux273. However, to prevent someone from accessing the /etc/shadow file and grabbing your user passwords from it, they are stored in encrypted format. You may notice that all of the system user accounts in the above example have a simple asterisk in this field (*). This indicates that these accounts aren't allowed to log in to the system. For example, if a user tried to log in to a system as ftp, they would be denied access even though the ftp user account exists.
- **Last_Modified**   This field displays the number of days since January 1, 1970 that the password was last changed. In this example, it's been 15043 days.
- **Min_Days**   This field displays the minimum number of days required before a password can be changed. In this example, it is set to 0 days.
- **Max_Days**   This field displays the maximum number of days before a password must be changed. In this example, it is set to 99999 days. Effectively, this means a password change isn't required.
- **Days_Warn**   This field displays the number of days prior to password expiration that the user will be warned of the pending expiration. In this case, it's set to 7 days.
- **Disabled_Days**   This field displays the number of days to wait after a password has expired to disable the account. In this example, it's set to a null value.
- **Expire**   This field displays the number of days since January 1, 1970 after which the account will be disabled. In this example, it is set to a null value, indicating the account never expires.

As you can see, it is very important that these two files stay synchronized with each other. If they get out of whack, then it's possible that a user may not be able to log in or a service may not be able to access the file system correctly.

The good news is that these files usually stay in sync as they are supposed to without any intervention on the part of the administrator. The only times I've seen these two files become unsynchronized is when the administrator decides to manually edit these files with a text editor. I strongly discourage this practice. Your Linux system includes a wide variety of utilities that are used to manage user accounts and passwords on your system. (We'll discuss how to use these utilities later in this chapter.) You should always use these utilities instead of a text editor to manage user accounts. Doing so will ensure that both files are edited appropriately and stay synchronized with each other.

To verify your /etc/passwd and /etc/shadow files, you can use the pwck command at the shell prompt. This utility will verify each line in the two files and make sure they are valid. Any errors are reported on the screen, as shown in this example:

```
ws2:/ # pwck
Checking '/etc/passwd'
User 'pulse': directory '/var/lib/pulseaudio' does not exist.
User 'suse-ncc': directory '/var/lib/YaST2/suse-ncc-fakehome' does not exist.
Checking '/etc/shadow'.
```

As you can see, pwck found that the home directories specified for the pulse and suse-ncc system user accounts don't exist. Everything else checked out. If, for some reason, the /etc/passwd and the /etc/shadow files were out of synchronization, you could use the pwconv command at the shell prompt to fix the files. This utility will add any missing user accounts from /etc/passwd to /etc/shadow.

Creating and Managing User Accounts from the Command Line

As with many of the other tasks discussed in this book, you can manage user accounts on your Linux system with either graphical utilities or from the command line. For example, OpenSUSE includes the YaST User and Group Management module, shown in Figure 8-5, to manage user accounts.

Likewise, Fedora includes the User Manager utility, which can also be used to manage user accounts graphically. This utility is shown in Figure 8-6.

As with everything else, these graphical utilities are just fine to use. I'll admit that I use them the majority of the time. However, you must know how to use the command-line user management utilities to be a truly effective Linux admin. Therefore, we're going to focus on command-line tools in this chapter. Once you're comfortable with them, feel free to experiment with their graphical equivalents.

In this chapter, we're going to cover the following tools:

- useradd
- passwd
- usermod
- userdel

Figure 8-5   Using YaST to manage user accounts

Figure 8-6
Using User Manager to manage user accounts

useradd

As its name implies, the useradd utility is used to add users to the Linux system. The syntax for useradd is useradd *options username.* For example, suppose I wanted to create a user account named lmorgan using default parameters. I would enter **useradd lmorgan** at the shell prompt, as shown here:

```
ws2:/ # useradd lmorgan
```

The lmorgan account is created using the default parameters contained in the following configuration files:

- **/etc/default/useradd** This file contains defaults used by the useradd utility. Here is a sample:

```
ws2:/ # cat /etc/default/useradd
GROUP=100
HOME=/home
INACTIVE=-1
EXPIRE=
SHELL=/bin/bash
SKEL=/etc/skel
GROUPS=video
CREATE_MAIL_SPOOL=no
UMASK=022
ws2:/ #
```

Notice that this file specifies that the default group for new users is the group with a GID of 100 (that's the users group). It also specifies that a home directory for the user be created in /home. The inactive account parameter is set to −1, and the account is set to never expire. The default shell is set to /bin/bash. In addition, the user is also made a member of the video group in addition to the default group. The skeleton directory is /etc/skel, and a mail spool directory is not created for the user. As with any Linux configuration file, if you don't like these values, you can simply edit the useradd file with a text editor to customize it the way you like.

TIP You can also view new user default values by entering **useradd –D** at the shell prompt.

- **/etc/login.defs** This file contains values that can be used for the GID and UID parameters when creating an account with useradd. It also contains defaults for creating passwords in /etc/shadow. A portion of this file follows:

```
ws2:/ # cat /etc/login.defs
# /etc/login.defs - Configuration control definitions for pwdutils pack-
age.
# Comment lines (lines beginning with "#") and blank lines are ignored.
# Please read the manual page for more information (login.defs.5).
DEFAULT_HOME           yes
...
PASS_MAX_DAYS          99999
PASS_MIN_DAYS          0
PASS_WARN_AGE          7
SYSTEM_UID_MIN           100
SYSTEM_UID_MAX           499
UID_MIN                 1000
UID_MAX                 60000
SYSTEM_GID_MIN           100
SYSTEM_GID_MAX           499
GID_MIN                 1000
GID_MAX                 60000
UMASK                  022
GROUPADD_CMD                /usr/sbin/groupadd.local
USERADD_CMD                  /usr/sbin/useradd.local
USERDEL_PRECMD          /usr/sbin/userdel-pre.local
USERDEL_POSTCMD             /usr/sbin/userdel-post.local
ws2:/ #
```

  Notice that this file specifies default values for the fields we reviewed earlier in /etc/shadow for each user account. It also specifies defaults used when useradd is assigning a UID to a new account. Remember that, earlier in this chapter, we noted that SUSE Linux starts UIDs at 1000 while Fedora starts UIDs at 500. This file is where this behavior comes from. It also defines the UID number range for system user accounts, as well as which executable to run when you run useradd or userdel from the shell prompt. If you don't like the defaults, you can always edit this file to match your preferences.

- **/etc/skel** The useradd command copies files from the skeleton directory (/etc/skel by default) into a newly created home directory when you create a new user. Typically, /etc/skel also contains several user configuration files, such as .bashrc and .profile. Here is an example:

```
ws2:/ # ls /etc/skel
.bash_history  bin      .fonts    .mozilla  public_html  .xim.template
.bashrc        .emacs  .inputrc  .profile  .vimrc       .xinitrc.tem-
plate
ws2:/ #
```

- You can add any files and directories to this directory that you want each and every user to have by default when their account is created on the system.

You can override these defaults when running useradd by specifying a list of options in the command line. You can use the following:

- **–c**   Includes the user's full name.

- **–e**   Specifies the date when the user account will be disabled. Format the date as *yyyy-mm-dd*.

- **–f**   Specifies the number of days after password expiration before the account is disabled. Use a value of **–1** to disable this functionality, e.g., **useradd –f –1 jmcarthur**.

- **–g**   Specifies the user's default group.

- **–G**   Specifies additional groups that the user is to be made a member of.

- **–M**   Specifies that the user account be created without a home directory.

- **–m**   Specifies the user's home directory.

- **–n**   Used only on Red Hat or Fedora systems. By default, these distributions create a new group with the same name as the user every time an account is created. Using this option will turn *off* this functionality.

- **–p**   Specifies the user's password.

- **–r**   Specifies that the user being created is a system user.

- **–s**   Specifies the default shell for the user.

- **–u**   Manually specifies a UID for the user.

For example, suppose I wanted to create a new user account for a user named Jackie McArthur on a Linux system. Further suppose that I want to specify a user name of jmcarthur, a full name of Jackie McArthur, a password of tux123, and that a home directory be created. To do this, I would enter **useradd –c "Jackie McArthur" –m –p "tux123" –s "/bin/bash" jmcarthur** at the shell prompt. After doing so, the account will be created in /etc/passwd, as shown here:

```
ws2:/ # useradd -c "Jackie McArthur" -m -p "tux123" -s "/bin/bash" jmcarthur
ws2:/ # cat /etc/passwd
...
jmcarthur:x:1003:100:Jackie McArthur:/home/jmcarthur:/bin/bash
ws2:/ #
```

Notice that useradd used the parameters we specified in the command line. For parameters we didn't specify, such as the GID and UID, the defaults from /etc/default/useradd were used instead.

Let's next look at the passwd utility.

passwd

The passwd utility is used to change an existing user's password. For example, earlier we created a new user named lmorgan with useradd. However, because we didn't use the –p option in the command line, the lmorgan account doesn't have a password and is

locked. You can see this using the –S option with passwd. For example, we could enter
passwd –S lmorgan at the shell prompt; as shown here:

```
ws2:/ # passwd -S lmorgan
lmorgan LK 10/14/2012 0 99999 7 -1
```

Notice that LK is displayed in the output. This indicates that the account is locked.
The remaining parameters are various other password parameters, such as the date of
the last password change, the minimum number of days required before a password
can be changed, the maximum number of days before a password must be changed,
the number of days prior to password expiration when the user will be warned of the
pending expiration, and the number of days to wait after a password has expired to
disable the account.

In short, this account is unusable. To enable this account, we need to add a password. We can do this using passwd. The syntax is **passwd** *username*. In this case, you
enter **passwd lmorgan** (as root). When you do, you are prompted to enter a password for the specified user, as shown here:

```
ws2:/ # passwd lmorgan
Changing password for lmorgan.
New Password:
Reenter New Password:
Password changed.
ws2:/ #
```

Enter the password you want to use at the prompts. After doing so, you can enter
passwd –S lmorgan again to view the account status, as shown next:

```
ws2:/ # passwd -S lmorgan
lmorgan PS 10/14/2012 0 99999 7 -1
```

Notice that the account status is set to PS, indicating that the password has been set
and is valid. When working with passwd, you can also use the following options:

- **–l** Locks the user's account. This option invalidates the user's password.

- **–u** Unlocks a user's account.

- **–d** Removes a user's password.

- **–n** Sets the minimum number of days required before a password can be
changed.

- **–x** Sets the maximum number of days before a password must be changed.

- **–w** Sets the number of days prior to password expiration when the user will
be warned of the pending expiration.

- **–i** Sets the number of days to wait after a password has expired to disable the
account.

Now that you know how to create a new user and how to set a user's password, we'll
next review how you go about modifying an existing user account.

usermod

From time to time, you will need to modify an existing user account. This can be done from the command line using the usermod utility. The syntax for usermod is very similar to that used by useradd. You enter **usermod** *options username* at the shell prompt. The options for usermod are likewise similar to those used by useradd. They include the following:

- **–c** Edits the user's full name.
- **–e** Sets the date when the user account will be disabled. Format the date as *yyyy-mm-dd.*
- **–f** Sets the number of days after password expiration before the account is disabled. Use a value of –1 to disable this functionality.
- **–g** Sets the user's default group.
- **–G** Specifies additional groups that the user is to be made a member of.
- **–l** Changes the username.
- **–L** Locks the user's account. This option invalidates the user's password.
- **–m** Sets the user's home directory.
- **–p** Sets the user's password.
- **–s** Specifies the default shell for the user.
- **–u** Sets the UID for the user.
- **–U** Unlocks a user's account that has been locked.

For example, suppose my jmcarthur user has recently married and changed her last name to Sanders. I could update her user account to reflect this change by entering **usermod –l jsanders –c "Jackie Sanders" jmcarthur** at the shell prompt. When I do, the user's account information is updated in /etc/passwd, as shown here:

```
ws2:/ # usermod -l jsanders -c "Jackie Sanders" jmcarthur
ws2:/ # cat /etc/passwd
...
jsanders:x:1003:100:Jackie Sanders:/home/jmcarthur:/bin/bash
ws2:/ #
```

 TIP If there's a space in the name, you will need to enclose it in quotes when using the usermod command. For example, we used the **jsanders –c "Jackie Sanders" jmcarthur** command to set the full name of the user.

The last user-related topic we need to cover here is that of deleting user accounts.

userdel

From time to time, you will need to remove a user account from your Linux system. This can be done from the shell prompt using the userdel utility. To delete a user, simply enter **userdel** *username*. For example, if we wanted to delete the lmorgan account we created earlier, we would enter **userdel lmorgan** at the shell prompt.

It's important to note that, by default, userdel will *not* remove the user's home directory from the file system. If you do want to remove the home directory when you delete the user, you need to use the –r option in the command line. For example, entering **userdel –r lmorgan** will remove the account and delete her home directory.

Let's practice managing users in the following exercise.

Exercise 8-1: Managing User Accounts from the Command Line   In this exercise, you will practice creating and modifying user accounts from the shell prompt of your Linux system. Complete the following:

1. Boot your Linux system and log in as a standard user. If you used the lab exercise in Chapter 3 to install your system, you can log in as **tux** with a password of **M3linux273**.

2. Open a terminal session and change to your root user account by entering **su –** at the shell prompt and entering your root user's password.

3. Create a user account for yourself by doing the following:

   a. Determine a username and password for yourself. A common convention is to use your first initial with your last name.

   b. At the shell prompt, enter useradd –c "your_full_name" –m –p "your_password" –s "/bin/bash" your_username.

   c. At the shell prompt, enter tail /etc/passwd. Verify that your new user account was created.

4. Create a user account using your system's default settings by entering **useradd dtracy** at the shell prompt.

5. At the shell prompt, enter **tail /etc/passwd**. Verify that your new user account was created. Notice that the new user is missing many parameters.

6. Enter a full name for the dtracy user account by entering **usermod –c "Richard Tracy" dtracy** at the shell prompt.

7. At the shell prompt, enter **tail /etc/passwd**. Verify that the full name was added to the dtracy account.

8. Give dtracy a password by entering **passwd dtracy** at the shell prompt.

9. When prompted, enter a new *password* for dtracy.

Now that you know how to manage users, we need to discuss how to manage groups.

Managing Linux Group Accounts

Like other operating systems, Linux uses groups to make managing the system easier. In this part of this chapter, we're going to discuss the following:

- How Linux groups work
- Managing groups from the command line

How Linux Groups Work

Groups make our lives as system administrators easier. To understand why, let's take a look at a scenario. Suppose you have seven users on a Linux system. Of these users, five of them need almost the same level of access to files in the file system. Without groups, you would need to assign the necessary permissions separately to each of the five user accounts. That means you would be doing the same exact task five times over. That may not sound so bad, but suppose you had 100 users that all needed the same level of access. What a waste of time!

Instead, you can implement groups on your Linux system. With groups, you assign permissions to the group and then make all the users that need that same level of access members of the group. That's much easier! You only need to make one set of assignments. If something changes in the level of access needed, you only need to make the change once to the group. All of the group members then automatically receive the change. Once again, this is much easier than the alternative!

If your Linux system has been configured to use local authentication, your groups are defined in the /etc/group file. A sample of this file follows:

```
ws2:~ # cat /etc/group
...
mail:x:12:
maildrop:!:59:
man:x:62:
messagebus:!:104:
modem:x:43:
news:x:13:
nobody:x:65533:
nogroup:x:65534:nobody
ntadmin:!:71:
ntp:!:103:
polkituser:!:111:
postfix:!:51:
public:x:32:
pulse:!:108:
pulse-access:!:109:
root:x:0:
rtkit:!:107:
shadow:x:15:
sshd:!:102:
suse-ncc:!:106:
sys:x:3:
tape:!:101:
```

```
trusted:x:42:
tty:x:5:
utmp:x:22:
uucp:x:14:
video:x:33:ksanders,tux,lmorgan,jsanders,rtracy,dtracy
wheel:x:10:
www:x:8:
xok:x:41:
users:x:100:
ws2:~ #
```

As with the /etc/passwd and the /etc/shadow files, each line in /etc/group is a single record that represents one group. Each record is composed of the following four fields:

```
Group:Password:GID:Users
```

For example, in the preceding example the record for the video group reads as follows:

```
video:x:33:ksanders,tux,lmorgan,jsanders,rtracy,dtracy
```

- **Group** Specifies the name of the group. In the example, the name of the group is **video**.

- **Password** Specifies the group password, if one is assigned.

- **GID** Specifies the group ID (GID) number of the group. In this example, the GID of the video group is 33.

- **Users** Lists the members of the group. In this case, the ksanders, tux, lmorgan, jsanders, rtracy, and dtracy users are members of the video group.

Some distributions use an additional group file to store group passwords. Just as /etc/shadow is used to store encrypted passwords for users defined in /etc/passwd, the /etc/gshadow file is used to define group passwords for groups defined in /etc/group. Here is a sample /etc/gshadow file:

```
[root@fs3 ~]# cat /etc/gshadow
root:::root
bin:::root,bin,daemon
...
nobody:::
users:::
...
[root@fs3 ~]#
```

As with /etc/shadow, each line in /etc/gshadow represents a record for a single group. Each record is composed of the following fields:

```
Group_Name:Password:Group_Admins:Group_Members
```

With this in mind, let's review how you can manage your groups with command-line tools.

Managing Groups from the Command Line

As with users, you can manage groups with either command-line or graphical tools. However, for the reasons specified earlier, we're going to focus on managing groups from the shell prompt in this chapter. We will review the following tools:

- groupadd
- groupmod
- groupdel

groupadd

As you can probably guess from its name, the groupadd utility is used to add groups to your Linux system. The syntax for using groupadd at the shell prompt is relatively simple. Just enter **groupadd** *options groupname*. For example, if I wanted to add a group named dbusers, I would enter **groupadd dbusers** at the shell prompt. When I do, a group is added to /etc/group using default parameters specified in /etc/login.defs.

When using groupadd, you can override the defaults in /etc/login.defs and customize the way the group is created using the following options:

- **–g** Specifies a GID for the new group
- **–p** Specifies a password for the group
- **–r** Specifies that the group being created is a system group

groupmod

You may have noticed that the groupadd command didn't add one key component to the new group: Users! What good is a group if you don't have any users occupying it?

To modify a group, including adding users to the group membership, you use the groupmod utility. The syntax for using groupmod is similar to that used by usermod. Enter **groupmod** *options group* at the shell prompt. You can use the following options with the command:

- **–g** Changes the group's GID number
- **–p** Changes the group's password
- **–A** Adds a user account to the group
- **–R** Removes a user account from the group

For example, if we wanted to add ksanders to the dbusers group, we would enter **groupmod –A "ksanders" dbusers** at the shell prompt.

Finally, let's look at deleting groups.

groupdel

If, for some reason, you need to delete an existing group from the system, you can do so using the groupdel command at the shell prompt. For example, to delete the dbusers group, you enter **groupdel dbusers**.

Let's practice managing groups in the following exercise.

Exercise 8-2: Managing Groups from the Command Line   In this exercise, you will practice creating and modifying groups from the shell prompt of your Linux system.

Suppose your company is putting together a new research and development team that will be using your Linux system. You need to create a new group for users who will be members of this team. Complete the following:

1. Verify that you are logged in to your system.

2. If necessary, switch to your root user account with the **su –** command.

3. Create a new group named research by doing the following:

    a. At the shell prompt, enter **groupadd research**.

    b. Add your user account and the dtracy user account (created in the previous exercise) to the research group by entering **groupmod –A "dtracy,**_your_username_**" research** at the shell prompt.

    c. Verify the users were added to the group by entering **tail /etc/group** at the shell prompt. You should see the following:

    ```
    research:!:1000:dtracy,rtracy
    ```

Managing User Account Security

A key aspect of both Linux workstation and Linux server security is to implement and use user access controls to constrain what users can do with the system. As we've already discussed earlier in this book, every Linux system, whether a workstation or a server, includes a default superuser account named root. This account has full access to every aspect of the system. As such, it should be used with great care. In this part of this chapter, we'll discuss the following:

- Proper use of the root user account
- Using su
- Using sudo
- Using log files to detect intruders

Let's begin by discussing the proper way to use the root user account.

Proper Use of the root User Account

One of the key mistakes made by new Linux users is excessive use of the root user account. There's a time and a place when the root user account should be used. However, most of your work on a Linux system should be done as a non-root user account. The rule of thumb is this: Only use root when absolutely necessary. If a task can be completed as a non-root user, then it should be.

Why is the proper use of the root user account of concern? A few pages back, we discussed the risks of leaving a logged-in system unattended. Imagine the havoc an intruder could wreak if he or she were to happen upon an unattended system that was logged in as root! All of the data on the system could be accessed and copied. Major configuration changes could be made to the daemons running on the system. Heaven only knows what kind of malware could be installed.

In addition, you should never be logged in as root while browsing the web or reading email. If a security exploit were to be delivered to your system through your browser from a compromised web site or through a malicious email attachment, the exploit would have elevated superuser privileges on the system. By completing these tasks as a standard user, you limit the damage a potential exploit can perform.

In a nutshell, a system logged in as root represents a serious security risk. Leaving such a system unattended represents a critical security risk. Everyone, including the system administrator (that's you!), should have a standard user account that he or she *always* uses to log in to the system.

If you find that you need root-level access while working on the system, you can use the su command to temporarily gain root-level privileges to the system.

Using su

By now, you should already know how su works. We've used it countless times in this book's exercises. This command allows you to change to a different user account at the shell prompt. The syntax for using su is **su** *options user_account*. If no user account is specified in the command, su assumes you want to switch to the root user account. Some of the more useful options you can use with su include the following:

- **–**   Loads the user's environment variables. Notice that we've always used the su – command to switch to the root user account. This changes to root and loads root's environment variables.

- **–c** *command*   Switches to the user account and runs the specified *command*.

- **–m**   Switches to the user account but preserves the existing environment variables.

The su command will be your best friend as a Linux administrator. However, there are times when other users may temporarily need root-level access. You can use sudo to give them limited root access.

Using sudo

Suppose you have a power user on your Linux system. This user may be a programmer, a project manager, or a database administrator. Users in this category may frequently need to run some root-level commands. But do you really want to give them your root password? Probably not. You want them to be able to run a limited number of commands that require root privileges, but you don't want them to have full root access. This can be done using sudo.

The sudo command allows a given user to run a command as a different user account. As with su, it can be any user account on the system; however, it is most frequently used to run commands as root. The sudo command uses the /etc/sudoers file to determine what user is authorized to run which commands. This file uses the following aliases to define who can do what:

- **User_Alias**   Specifies the users who are allowed to run commands
- **Cmnd_Alias**   Specifies the commands that users are allowed to run
- **Host_Alias**   Specifies the hosts users are allowed to run the commands on
- **Runas_Alias**   Specifies the usernames that commands may be run as

To edit your /etc/sudoers file, you need to run the visudo command as your root user. The /etc/sudoers file is loaded in your default editor, which is usually vi. Your changes are written to /etc/sudoers.tmp until committed. This is shown in Figure 8-7.

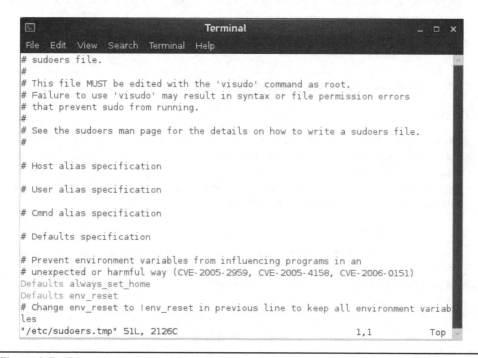

Figure 8-7   Editing /etc/sudoers with visudo

On most distributions, the sudoers file is configured by default such that users must supply the root password when using sudo. Obviously, this configuration doesn't accomplish anything. If the user already knows the root password, what's the point of configuring sudo? This configuration is specified by the following lines in sudoers:

```
# In the default (unconfigured) configuration, sudo asks for the root pass-
word.
# This allows use of an ordinary user account for administration of a freshly
# installed system. When configuring sudo, delete the two
# following lines:
Defaults targetpw   # ask for the password of the target user i.e. root
ALL      ALL=(ALL) ALL   # WARNING! Only use this together with 'Defaults tar-
getpw'!
```

To fix this, comment out the two lines specified here in the sudoers file. Then you can begin your sudoers configuration in the file. First, you need to use User_Alias to define an alias containing the user accounts (separated by commas) you want to allow to run commands. The syntax is

```
User_Alias alias = users
```

For example, to create an alias named PWRUSRS that contains the tux, rtracy, and ksanders user accounts, you would enter the following in the /etc/sudoers file:

```
User_Alias PWRUSRS = tux, ksanders, rtracy
```

 TIP All alias names must start with a capital letter.

You next need to use Cmnd_Alias to define an alias that contains the commands (using the full path) that you want the users you just defined to be able to run. Separate multiple commands with commas. For example, if your users were programmers who need to be able to kill processes, you could define an alias named KILLPROCS that contained your kill command, as shown here:

```
Cmnd_Alias KILLPROCS = /bin/kill, /usr/bin/killall
```

Then you need to use Host_Alias to specify what systems the users can run the commands on. For example, to let them run the commands on a system named WS1, you would use the following:

```
Host_Alias MYHSTS = WS1
```

Finally, you need to glue these aliases together to define exactly what will happen. The syntax is

```
User_Alias Host_Alias = (user) Cmnd_Alias
```

Using the aliases just defined, you could allow the specified users to run the specified commands on the specified hosts as root by entering

```
PWRUSRS     MYHSTS = (root) KILLPROCS
```

To exit the editor, press ESC and then enter **:exit**. The visudo utility will check your syntax and inform you if you've made any errors. At this point, the users you defined can execute the commands you specified as root by entering **sudo** *command* at the shell prompt. For example, the rtracy user could kill a process named vmware-toolbox (owned by root) by entering **sudo killall vmware-toolbox** at the shell prompt. After the rtracy user supplies his password, the process will be killed.

You can use the user-related log files on your Linux system to detect unauthorized intrusion attempts.

Using Log Files to Detect Intruders

Detecting intruders involves looking for clues they left behind in the system. One of your best resources in this regard is the log files your Linux system maintains for you. Much like a CSI detective, you need practice and experience to develop an intuitive sense that lets you know when something looks suspicious. The best way to develop this intuition is to spend a lot of time reviewing your log files. This will help you develop a feel for what is "normal" for your system. Once you know what is normal, you can spot that which is not normal.

With this in mind, let's look at several log files you can analyze to identify suspicious activities. The first is the /var/log/wtmp file. This log file contains a list of all users who have authenticated to the system. The file is saved in binary format. You can't use cat, less, or a text editor, such as vi, to view it. Instead, you must use the last command at the shell prompt. Output from the last utility is shown in Figure 8-8.

The last utility displays the user account, login time, logout time, and where users authenticated from. When you review this file, look for anything that appears unusual—for example, logins that occurred in the middle of the night when no one is at work are suspicious.

You can also view the /var/log/faillog file. This log file contains a list of failed authentication attempts. This file is very effective at detecting *dictionary attacks*, which run through a list of words (called the *dictionary*), trying each one as a password for a user account. Like wtmp, faillog is a binary file. To view it, you need to use the faillog utility.

```
ws2:~ # last
root     pts/0       :0.0              Wed Oct 17 18:47   still logged in
root     console     :0                Wed Oct 17 18:44   still logged in
root     tty8        :0                Wed Oct 17 18:44   still logged in
tux      pts/3       :0.0              Wed Oct 17 16:27 - 18:20  (01:53)
tux      console     :0                Wed Oct 17 16:26 - 18:43  (02:16)
tux      tty7        :0                Wed Oct 17 16:26 - 18:43  (02:16)
```

Figure 8-8   Using last to review login history

Figure 8-9

Using lastlog to view last login times

```
ksanders          :0        Fri Oct 12 16:38:38 -0600 2012
rtracy            :0        Fri Oct 12 16:36:24 -0600 2012
tux               :0        Wed Oct 17 16:26:57 -0600 2012
```

This utility displays the user who tried to authenticate, how many times that user failed to log in, and when the last unsuccessful attempt occurred. You can use the –u option to view login attempts for a specific user account. For example, you could enter **faillog –u rtracy** to view failed logins for the rtracy user account.

When reviewing this log file, look at unusual login attempts, such as an abnormally high number of failed logins, especially if they occurred late at night. You can also use the faillog utility to specify how the system handles failed login attempts. This is done using the following options with the faillog command:

- **–l seconds** Locks the account for the specified number of seconds after a failed login attempt.

- **–m number** Sets the maximum number of failed login attempts before the user account is disabled.

The next log file is /var/log/lastlog. This file contains a list of all the users in the system and when they last logged in. As with the other log files we've looked at, you can't view lastlog with less, cat, or a text editor. To view lastlog, you must use the lastlog utility from the shell prompt, as shown in Figure 8-9.

The last log file you can use to detect intrusion attempts is /var/log/messages. This log file contains messages from all services running on the system. As such, it contains a lot of data that may or may not be related to intrusion attempts. You can use grep to isolate the relevant entries. For example, you could use the **cat /var/log/messages | grep login | more** command to view login-related entries in the file.

In addition to viewing log files, you can also use the who command to see who is currently using the system. In Figure 8-10 you can see that the root user is logged in to the system. The root user is logged in to the first X server session (:0) and has a terminal session open (:0.0).

You can also use the w command to view who is logged in and what they are doing on the system. The w command displays information about the users logged in, the processes they are running, and system load averages. An example is shown in Figure 8-11.

Figure 8-10

Using who

```
ws2:~ # who
root      :0           2012-10-17 18:44 (console)
root      console      2012-10-17 18:44 (:0)
root      pts/0        2012-10-17 18:47 (:0.0)
```

```
ws2:~ # w
 20:00:42 up  3:34,  3 users,  load average: 0.00, 0.01, 0.08
USER     TTY       LOGIN@   IDLE   JCPU   PCPU WHAT
root     :0        18:44   ?xdm?   7:12  0.20s /usr/lib/gdm/gdm-simple-slave -
root     console   18:44   3:34m  0.00s  0.20s /usr/lib/gdm/gdm-simple-slave -
root     pts/0     18:47   1.00s  4.74s  0.02s w
```

Figure 8-11   Using w

Chapter Review

We started this chapter discussing the need for a basic level of file system security on a Linux system. We reviewed a scenario where multiple users on the same system were able to access each other's files and the problems that were encountered as a result. The way to prevent these problems is to first control who can access the system and then control what they can access once they are in.

The first part is accomplished by using Linux user accounts. With user accounts, users must supply a valid username and password (called credentials) before they are allowed to access the system. This is called "logging in" or "authentication." I pointed out that the Linux operating system will customize the system environment based on the username of the user who logged on. Users will have access to their own home directory and a customized desktop environment. I also pointed out that, by default, user home directories are located in /home, except for the root user, whose home directory is located in /root. You can view specific information about a particular user using the finger *username* command at the shell prompt.

I also told you that each Linux user account has a unique ID number called the UID. No two users on the system have the same UID on the same system. Some distributions, such as OpenSUSE, start UIDs for standard users at 1000 by default. Other distributions, such as Fedora, start UIDs at 500. No matter what distribution you're using, the root user's UID is always set to 0. You can view a user's UID (as well as group membership) using the id *username* command.

We then discussed the various locations where user accounts can be saved on a Linux system. Using local authentication, user accounts are saved in /etc/passwd and /etc/shadow. Using LDAP authentication, user accounts are saved in an LDAP-compliant directory service. Using NIS authentication, user account files are distributed among several systems using the NIS service. Using Windows Domain authentication, user accounts are stored in a central database on a Windows (or Linux Samba) domain controller.

I pointed out that, for our purposes, you only need to be familiar with the local authentication method. In this configuration, the /etc/passwd file contains your user account information while the /shadow file contains your users' encrypted passwords. The /etc/passwd file stores user accounts in the following format:

Username:Password:UID:GID:Full_Name:Home_Directory:Default_Shell

I also told you that the /etc/passwd file contains both standard and system user accounts. Standard user accounts are used for login. System user accounts can't be used for login. Instead, they are used by system services when they need to access the file system.

The /etc/shadow file stores user password information in the following format:

```
Username:Password:Last_Modified:Min_Days:Max_Days:Days_Warn:Disabled_
Days:Expire
```

The /etc/passwd and /etc/shadow files must stay synchronized. To do this, you should avoid editing these files directly with a text editor. Instead, you should use the various user and password management tools on your system. To check your files, you can use the pwck command. If you suspect the files are out of sync, you can use the pwconv command to add accounts from /etc/passwd to /etc/shadow.

We then discussed the different utilities you can use from the shell prompt to manage user accounts on your Linux system. To add a user, you use the useradd utility. If you don't supply any options when creating a user with useradd, the defaults contained in the /etc/default/useradd and /etc/login.defs files are used.

To set a user's password, you use the passwd utility at the shell prompt. To view the status of a user's account, you use the –S option with passwd. To modify an existing user account, you use the usermod utility. To remove a user account, you use the userdel utility. By default, userdel will not remove a user's home directory when deleting an account. If you want to remove the user's home directory, you can use the –r option with userdel.

We then shifted gears and discussed the role of Linux groups. Groups ease system administration by allowing you to group together users who need a common level of access to files and directories in the file system. Linux groups are stored in /etc/group. Group records in /etc/group are represented using the following syntax:

```
Group:Password:GID:Users
```

Some distributions store group passwords in /etc/group. Other distributions store them in a separate file (in encrypted format) in /etc/gshadow, much in the same manner as user accounts are stored in /etc/passwd and /etc/shadow. You create groups in your Linux system using the groupadd command. If you don't specify any options with the groupadd command, the group is created using default parameters found in /etc/login.defs.

To add users to a group, you must use the –A option with the groupmod command at the shell prompt. You can also remove groups using the groupdel command.

We then discussed user access controls you can use to constrain what users can and can't do in the system. Users, groups, and permissions are the main means of controlling access to the system. However, there are other things you can do to increase the security of the system. First of all, you need to use your root user account judiciously. The root user should be used only to complete root tasks. All other tasks should be completed using a standard user account. The system should never be left unattended while the root user is logged in. You can use the su command to switch to the root user account when you need to complete tasks that require root-level access. You can use the exit command to switch back to your regular user account when done.

If you have users who occasionally need to run commands as root, but you don't want to give them your root password, you can use the sudo command. You use the /etc/sudoers file to specify which users can run which commands as root. You edit this file using the visudo utility. This utility will load the /etc/sudoers file in the vi editor. When you exit vi, it will check your syntax to make sure you didn't make syntax errors in the file.

We ended this chapter by discussing how to detect intrusion attempts using your Linux log files. You should periodically review your log files, looking for anomalies that indicate an intrusion attempt. The log files best suited to this task include

- /var/log/wtmp
- /var/log/faillog
- /var/log/lastlog
- /var/log/messages

You can also use the who and w utilities to see who is currently using the Linux system and what they are doing.

Accelerated Review

- You need to control who can access a Linux system and what users can do with files and directories in the file system after they are in.
- To authenticate to a system, a user must supply a username and password (called *credentials*).
- Linux restores user-specific information when a user logs in, such as a home directory and desktop environment.
- User home directories are created in /home by default.
- The root user's home directory is /root.
- You can use the finger command to view information about a user account.
- Every Linux user account has a unique user ID (UID) number assigned to it.
- The root user's UID is 0.
- The starting UID for standard users is 1000 on some distributions and 500 on others.
- You can use the id command to view a user's UID.
- You can use many different authentication methods with a Linux system.
- For your Linux+/LPIC 1 exam, you need to know how to use local authentication.
- Using local authentication, user accounts are stored in /etc/passwd and /etc/shadow.

- The /etc/passwd file stores user account information.
- The /etc/shadow file stores encrypted user passwords.
- You can use the pwck utility to verify that /etc/passwd and /etc/shadow are synchronized.
- You can use the pwconv utility to copy missing users from /etc/passwd to /etc/shadow.
- You can use the useradd utility to add users to a Linux system.
- When used without any options, useradd uses the system defaults contained in /etc/default/useradd and /etc/login.defs to create user accounts.
- You can use the passwd utility to set a user's password.
- The passwd utility can also be used to check the status of a user account.
- You can use the usermod utility to modify an existing user account.
- You can use the userdel utility to delete an existing user account.
- By default, userdel will not remove a user's home directory unless you specify the –r option with the command.
- Linux groups can be used to ease administration by grouping similar user accounts together.
- User accounts are stored in /etc/group.
- Some distributions store group passwords in /etc/gshadow.
- You use the groupadd utility to add a new group to your system.
- You use the groupmod utility to add or remove users to an existing group.
- You use the groupdel utility to delete an existing group.
- Users, groups, and permissions are the main means of controlling access to the system. The root user should be used only to complete root tasks; all other tasks should be completed using a standard user account.
- The system should never be left unattended while the root user is logged in.
- You can use the su command to switch to the root user account when you need to complete tasks that require root-level access.
- You can use the exit command to switch back to your regular user account.
- You can use the sudo command to allow specific users to run commands as root without giving them your root password.
- You use the /etc/sudoers file to specify which users can run what commands as root.
- You edit /etc/sudoers using the visudo utility, which will check your syntax to make sure you didn't make syntax errors in the file.
- Linux log files can be used to detect intrusion attempts.

- You should periodically review your log files, looking for anomalies that indicate an intrusion attempt:
  - /var/log/wtmp
  - /var/log/faillog
  - /var/log/lastlog
  - /var/log/messages
- You can use the who and w utilities to see who is currently using the Linux system.

Questions

1. Which of the following commands will display the UID of a user named dcoughanour when entered at the shell prompt?

   A. id dcoughanour

   B. finger dcoughanour

   C. UID dcoughanhour

   D. info dcoughanour

2. Which of the following files is used to store user accounts on a Linux system that has been configured to use local authentication?

   A. /etc/shadow

   B. /etc/users

   C. /etc/passwd

   D. /etc/local/accounts

3. Which of the following files is used to store user passwords on a Linux system that has been configured to use local authentication?

   A. /etc/shadow

   B. /etc/users

   C. /etc/passwd

   D. /etc/local/accounts

4. Consider the following entry in /etc/passwd:

   ```
   ksanders:x:1001:100:Kimberly Sanders:/home/ksanders:/bin/bash
   ```

   What is the primary group for this user? (Choose two.)

   A. ksanders

   B. home

   C. 1001

   D. 100

   E. users

   F. video

5. Consider the following entry in /etc/shadow:

```
ksanders:$2a%05$fHzL5vsuk3ilLIuispxqKuCFEPg50ZhF8KshQyIZH7SDERJooEJ
TC:13481:30:60:7:-1::
```

How often must this user change her password?

A. Every 30 days.

B. Every 60 days.

C. Every 7 days.

D. This feature is disabled. The user isn't required to change her password.

6. You need to create a new user account on a Linux system for Mike Huffman named mhuffman. Mike's password should be set to "Panguitch," and he needs a home directory created in /home/mhuffman. Which of the following commands will do this?

A. useradd –c "Mike Huffman" –m –p "Panguitch" mhuffman

B. usermod "Mike Huffman" –p "Panguitch" mhuffman

C. useradd mhuffman

D. useradd mhuffman –c "Mike Huffman" –m –p Panguitch

7. A user named Diana Grow has recently married and changed her last name to Nelson. You need to change her username on her Linux system. Which command will do this?

A. usermod –l "dgrow" –c "Diana Nelson" dnelson

B. usermod –l "dnelson" –c "Diana Nelson" dgrow

C. useradd dnelson

D. usermod –c "dgrow" –l "dnelson" Diana Grow

8. You need to delete a user account named jcarr from your Linux system and remove his home directory contents. Which of the following commands will do this?

A. userdel jcarr

B. usermod --delete --rmhome jcarr

C. userdel –r jcarr

D. userdel --rmhome jcarr

9. Which file is used to store group information on a Linux system that has been configured to use local authentication?

A. /etc/groups

B. /etc/local/group

C. /etc/groupinfo

D. /etc/group

10. Which of the following commands can be used to add the users mhuffman, dnelson, and jcarr to a group named editors on a Linux system?

    A. groupadd –A "mhuffman,dnelson,jcarr" editors

    B. groupmod –A "mhuffman,dnelson,jcarr" editors

    C. groupmod editors –A "mhuffman,dnelson,jcarr"

    D. groupmod –R "mhuffman,dnelson,jcarr" editors

11. Which of the following commands will remove a user named dnelson from a group named editors?

    A. groupadd –R "dnelson" editors

    B. groupmod –A "dnelson" editors

    C. groupmod editors –R "dnelson"

    D. groupmod –R "dnelson" editors

12. Which of the following commands can be used to switch to the root user account and load root's environment variables?

    A. su –

    B. su root

    C. su root –e

    D. su –env

13. Which log file contains a list of all users who have authenticated to the Linux system, when they logged in, when they logged out, and where they logged in from?

    A. /var/log/faillog

    B. /var/log/last

    C. /var/log/wtmp

    D. /var/log/login

14. Which log file contains a list of failed login attempts?

    A. /var/log/faillog

    B. /var/log/last

    C. /var/log/wtmp

    D. /var/log/login

15. Which utility can you use to view your /var/log/lastlog file?

    A. cat

    B. last

    C. grep

    D. lastlog

Answers

1. **A.** Entering **id dcoughanour** will display the UID of that user account.

2. **C.** The /etc/passwd file stores user account information.

3. **A.** The /etc/shadow file stores user passwords.

4. **D, E.** The GID of ksander's primary group is 100. On most distributions, this is the users group.

5. **B.** The user must change her password every 60 days. The value of 60 in the record shown specifies that the maximum age of a password is 60 days. After that, the user must change to a new password.

6. **A.** Entering **useradd –c "Mike Huffman" –m –p "Panguitch" mhuffman** will create the user mhuffmann, set its full name to Mike Huffman, create a home directory (–m), and set the user's password to Panguitch.

7. **B.** Entering **usermod –l "dnelson" –c "Diana Nelson" dgrow** at the shell prompt will rename the dgrow user account to dnelson.

8. **C.** Entering **userdel –r jcarr** will delete jcarr's account and remove his home directory.

9. **D.** The /etc/group file stores group information.

10. **B.** Entering **groupmod –A "mhuffman,dnelson,jcarr" editors** at the shell prompt will add the mhuffman, dnelson, and jcarr user accounts to the editors group.

11. **D.** Entering **groupmod –R "dnelson" editors** will remove the dnelson user account from the editors group.

12. **A.** The su – command switches to the root user account and loads root's environment variables.

13. **C.** The /var/log/wtmp log file contains a list of all users who have authenticated to the Linux system, when they logged in, when they logged out, and where they logged in from.

14. **A.** The /var/log/faillog log file contains a list of failed login attempts.

15. **D.** The lastlog command can be used to view your /var/log/lastlog file.

## CHAPTER 9

Managing File Ownership and Permissions

In this chapter, you will learn about
- Managing file ownership
- Mounting file and directory permissions

Recall that in an earlier chapter we identified two tasks for you to accomplish when managing user access to a Linux system:

- Control who can access the system.
- Define what users can do after they have logged in to the system.

We addressed the first point earlier. We control who accesses the system by implementing users and groups. In this part of this chapter, we're going to address the second point. We need to define what users can do after they have logged in to the system. Let's begin by discussing file and directory ownership.

Managing File Ownership

To effectively control who can do what in the file system, you need to first consider who "owns" files and directories. We're going to discuss the following in this regard:

- How ownership works
- Managing ownership from the command line

How Ownership Works

Any time a user creates a new file or directory, his or her user account is assigned as that file or directory's "owner." For example, suppose the tux user logs in to his Linux system and creates a file named project_tasks.odt using LibreOffice in his home directory. Because he created this file, tux is automatically assigned ownership of project_tasks.odt. By right-clicking this file in the system's graphical user interface and selecting Properties | Permissions, you can view who owns the file. This is shown in Figure 9-1.

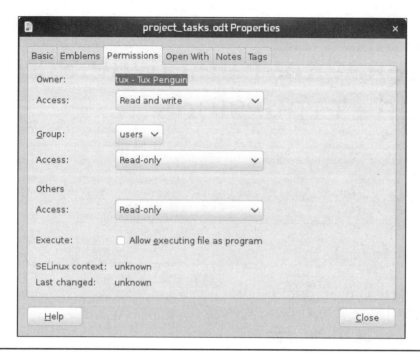

Figure 9-1 Viewing file ownership

Notice in Figure 9-1 that there are actually two owners for project_tasks.odt. The first is the name of the user who owns the file. In this case, it's tux, but the users group owns the file as well. That's because users is the primary group that tux belongs to.

You can also view file ownership from the command line using the ls –l command. This has been done in tux's home directory in this example:

```
tux@ws2:~> ls -l
total 88
drwxr-xr-x 2 tux users 4096 Oct 12 21:57 bin
drwxr-xr-x 2 tux users 4096 Oct 12 21:59 Desktop
drwxr-xr-x 2 tux users 4096 Oct 12 22:00 Documents
drwxr-xr-x 2 tux users 4096 Oct 12 21:59 Downloads
drwxr-xr-x 2 tux users 4096 Oct 12 21:59 Music
drwxr-xr-x 2 tux users 4096 Oct 12 21:59 Pictures
-rw-r--r-- 1 tux users 9177 Oct 17 20:30 project_tasks.odt
drwxr-xr-x 2 tux users 4096 Oct 12 21:59 Public
drwxr-xr-x 2 tux users 4096 Oct 12 21:57 public_html
drwxr-xr-x 2 tux users 4096 Oct 12 21:59 Templates
drwxr-xr-x 2 tux users 4096 Oct 12 21:59 Videos
drwxr-xr-x 3 tux users 4096 Oct 16 16:13 VMwareTools
tux@ws2:~>
```

Notice that the third column in the output displays the name of the file or directory's owner (tux) while the fourth column displays the name of the group that owns it (users). While file and directory ownership is automatically assigned at creation, it can be modified.

Managing Ownership from the Command Line

File and directory ownership isn't a fixed entity. Even though ownership is automatically assigned at creation, it can be modified. You can specify a different user and/or group as the owner of a given file or directory. To change the user who owns a file, you must be logged in as root. To change the group that owns a file, you must be logged in as root or as the user who currently owns the file.

This can be done with either graphical or command-line tools. Staying true to the form of this book, we're going to focus on command-line utilities, including the following:

- chown
- chgrp

Using chown

The chown utility can be used to change the user or group that owns a file or directory. The syntax for using chown is chown *user.group file* or *directory*. For example, suppose you wanted to change the project_tasks.odt file's owner to the ksanders user. You would enter **chown ksanders /home/tux/myfile.txt**, as shown here:

```
ws2:~ # ls -l /home/tux/project_tasks.odt
-rw-r--r-- 1 tux users 9177 Oct 17 20:30 /home/tux/project_tasks.odt
ws2:~ # chown ksanders /home/tux/project_tasks.odt
ws2:~ # ls -l /home/tux/project_tasks.odt
-rw-r--r-- 1 ksanders users 9177 Oct 17 20:30 /home/tux/project_tasks.odt
ws2:~ #
```

Notice that this command changed the user who owns the file to ksanders. However, also notice that the group that owns the file is still users. This was assigned when the file was created because tux's primary group is named users. If you wanted to change this to the root group, of which the root user is a member, you would enter **chown .root /home/tux/project_tasks.odt**. The period (.) before the group name tells chown that the entity specified is a group, not a user account. After executing this command, the owning group is changed to root, as shown here:

```
ws2:~ # chown .root /home/tux/project_tasks.odt
ws2:~ # ls -l /home/tux/project_tasks.odt
-rw-r--r-- 1 ksanders root 9177 Oct 17 20:30 /home/tux/project_tasks.odt
ws2:~ #
```

You could actually change both the user and the group that owns the file all at once with a single chown command. To do this in this example, you would enter **chown ksanders.root /home/tux/project_tasks.odt**. This tells chown that the user to change ownership to is ksanders and the group to change ownership to is root.

NOTE You can use the –R option with chown to change ownership on many files at once recursively.

Using chgrp

In addition to chown, you can also use chgrp to change the group that owns a file or directory. Simply enter **chgrp** *group file* or *directory*. For example, to change the group ownership of the /home/tux/project_tasks.odt file discussed in the previous examples from users to root, you would enter **chgrp root /home/tux/project_tasks.odt**.

Let's practice managing ownership in the following exercise.

Exercise 9-1: Managing Ownership   In this exercise, you will practice modifying file and directory ownership from the shell prompt of your Linux system. Complete the following:

1. Verify that you are logged in to your system.

2. Open a terminal session.

3. If necessary, switch to your root user account with the **su** – command.

4. Verify that your user account is a member of the research group by doing the following:

   a. At the shell prompt, enter **cat /etc/group**.

   b. Verify that your current user is a member of the research group, as shown here:

   ```
   research:!:1000:dtracy,rtracy,tux
   ```

   c. If your user is not a member of the research group, add it using the groupmod command.

5. Change to the / directory by entering **cd /** at the shell prompt.

6. Create a new directory named RandD by entering **mkdir RandD** at the shell prompt.

7. At the shell prompt, enter **ls –l**. Notice that the root user account and the root group are the owners of the new directory.

8. Change ownership of the directory to your user account and the research group by entering **chown** *your_username*.**research RandD** at the shell prompt.

9. Enter **ls –l** again at the shell prompt. Verify that ownership of the RandD directory has changed to your user account and the research group. This is shown here:

   ```
   ws2:/ # ls -l
   total 105
   drwxr-xr-x   2 tux   research   4096 Mar 18 09:45 RandD
   ```

    NOTE   The research group was configured in Chapter 8, Exercise 8-2.

Now that you understand users, groups, and owners, you are finally ready to work with Linux file system permissions.

Managing File and Directory Permissions

Managing ownership represents only a part of what needs to be done to control access to files and directories in the Linux file system. Ownership only specifies who *owns* what. It doesn't say *what* you can or can't do with files and directories. To do this, you need to set up and manage *permissions.* You need to understand the following:

- How permissions work
- Managing permissions from the command line
- Working with default permissions
- Working with special permissions

How Permissions Work

Unlike ownership, permissions are used to specify exactly what a particular user may do with files and directories in the file system. These permissions may allow a user to view a file but not modify it. They may allow a user to open and modify a file. They may even allow a user to run an executable file. Permissions may also be configured to prevent a user from seeing a file within a directory.

Each file or directory in your Linux file system stores the specific permissions assigned to it. These permissions together constitute the *mode* of the file. Any file or directory can have the permissions shown in Table 9-1 in its mode.

These permissions are assigned to each of three different entities for each file and directory in the file system:

- **Owner**   This is the user account that has been assigned to be the file or directory's owner. Permissions assigned to the owner apply only to that user account.

- **Group**   This is the group that has been assigned ownership of the file or directory. Permissions assigned to the group apply to all user accounts that are members of that group.

- **Others**   This entity refers to all other users who have successfully authenticated to the system. Permissions assigned to this entity apply to these user accounts.

Permission	Symbol	Effect on Files	Effect on Directories
Read	r	Allows a user to open and view a file. Does not allow a file to be modified or saved.	Allows a user to list the contents of a directory.
Write	w	Allows a user to open, modify, and save a file.	Allows a user to add or delete files from the directory.
Execute	x	Allows a user to run an executable file.	Allows a user to enter a directory.

Table 9-1   Linux Permissions

Be aware that permissions are additive. That means it is possible for one user account to receive permissions assigned to more than one entity. For example, suppose I assign the read and write permissions to a file to Owner and the execute permission to Group. If ksanders is the file Owner, users is the Group, and ksanders is a member of users, then ksanders receives *both* the permissions assigned to Owner and Group, and her effective permissions would be rwx.

Also, be very careful about what permissions you assign to Others. Basically, every user on the system belongs to Others; therefore, any permission you grant to Others gets assigned to anyone who successfully authenticates to the system. In some cases, this can be very useful. However, in others, it can get you in a lot of trouble! Just ask yourself before assigning permissions, "Do I really want everyone to have this kind of access to this file or directory?"

You can use the ls –l command to view the permissions assigned to each of these entities for any file or directory in the file system. Consider the example shown in Figure 9-2.

The first column displayed is the mode for each file and directory. The first character is either a *d* or a –. This simply indicates whether or not the associated entry is a directory or a file. As you can see, longfile.txt is a file, while Desktop is a directory.

The next three characters are the permissions assigned to the entry's owner. For example, longfile.txt has rw– assigned to its owner (which is the tux user). This means tux has read and write permissions to the file but not execute. Because the file isn't an executable, that permission isn't needed anyway. If the file were an executable and the execute permission were assigned, an *x* would have replaced the – in this part of the mode. Because the owner has read and write permissions to the file, tux can open the file, edit it, and save the changes.

The next three characters are the permissions assigned to the owning group. In this case, it is the users group. Any user on the system who is a member of the users group is granted r– – access to longfile.txt. This means they have the read right, allowing them to open a file and view its contents, but they aren't allowed to save any changes to the file.

Figure 9-2

Viewing the file mode with ls –l

```
tux@ws2:~> ls -l
total 88
drwxr-xr-x 2 tux       users 4096 Oct 12 21:57 bin
drwxr-xr-x 2 tux       users 4096 Oct 12 21:59 Desktop
drwxr-xr-x 2 tux       users 4096 Oct 12 22:00 Documents
drwxr-xr-x 2 tux       users 4096 Oct 12 21:59 Downloads
-rw-r--r-- 1 tux       users   21 Oct 17 16:27 firstnames
-rw-r--r-- 1 tux       users   24 Oct 17 16:28 lastnames
-rw-r--r-- 1 tux       users  202 Oct 17 16:30 longfile.txt
drwxr-xr-x 2 tux       users 4096 Oct 12 21:59 Music
-rw-r--r-- 1 tux       users    7 Oct 17 16:38 outputfile_aa
-rw-r--r-- 1 tux       users    8 Oct 17 16:38 outputfile_ab
-rw-r--r-- 1 tux       users    6 Oct 17 16:38 outputfile_ac
drwxr-xr-x 2 tux       users 4096 Oct 12 21:59 Pictures
-rw-r--r-- 1 ksanders  root  9177 Oct 17 20:30 project_tasks.odt
drwxr-xr-x 2 tux       users 4096 Oct 12 21:59 Public
drwxr-xr-x 2 tux       users 4096 Oct 12 21:57 public_html
drwxr-xr-x 2 tux       users 4096 Oct 12 21:59 Templates
-rw-r--r-- 1 tux       users  179 Oct 17 16:44 testfile.txt
drwxr-xr-x 2 tux       users 4096 Oct 12 21:59 Videos
drwxr-xr-x 3 tux       users 4096 Oct 16 16:13 VMwareTools
-rw-r--r-- 1 tux       users   54 Oct 12 17:13 yourfile.txt
tux@ws2:~>
```

	Permission	Value
Table 9-2	Read	4
Numeric Values	Write	2
Assigned to	Execute	1
Permissions		

The last three characters in the mode are the permissions assigned to others, meaning any legitimately authenticated user on the system who isn't the owner and isn't a member of the owning group. In this example, these users are also assigned r- - rights to longfile.txt, granting them read access.

Before we progress any further, you should know that permissions for each entity can also be represented numerically. This is done by assigning a value to each permission, as shown in Table 9-2.

Using these values, you can represent the permissions assigned to the Owner, Group, or Others with a single number. Simply add up the value of each permission. For example, suppose Owner is assigned read and write permissions to a file. To determine the numeric value of this assignment, simply add the values of read and write together (4 + 2 = 6). You will often see a file or directory's mode represented by three numbers. Consider the example shown in Figure 9-3.

In this example, the associated file owner has read and write permissions (6), the owning group has the read permission (4), and others also have the read permission (4). Using the ls –l command, this mode would be represented as –rw–r– –r– –.

If these permissions aren't correct, you use the chmod utility to modify them.

Managing Permissions from the Command Line with chmod

I realize that I sound like a broken record, but, just as with most of the other tasks in this chapter, you can modify permissions either graphically or from the command line. For example, using the file browser in the GNOME desktop environment, you can right-click any file or directory and then select Properties | Permissions. The screen in Figure 9-4 is displayed.

You then use Access drop-down lists for Owner, Group, and Others to specify what each entity can do with the file or directory. When you apply the changes, the file or directory's mode is changed to match what you specified.

Figure 9-3

Representing permissions numerically

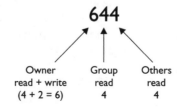

644

Owner
read + write
(4 + 2 = 6)

Group
read
4

Others
read
4

Figure 9-4

Setting permissions graphically

However, you need to be able to accomplish the same task using command-line tools. You use chmod to modify permissions. To do this, either you must own the file or you must be logged in as root. Any other user will not be allowed to do this.

There are several different syntaxes that can be used with chmod. The first is to enter **chmod** *entity=permissions filename* at the shell prompt. You substitute **u** for Owner, **g** for Group, and **o** for Others in the entity portion of the command. You substitute **r**, **w**, and/or **x** for the permissions portion of the command. For example, suppose I wanted to change the mode of longfile.txt to –rw–rw–r– – (giving the Owner and Group read and write permissions while giving Others only read access). I would enter **chmod u=rw,g=rw,o=r longfile.txt** at the shell prompt (assuming the file resides in the current directory). After doing so, the mode is adjusted with the permissions assigned by chmod, as shown here:

```
ws2:/home/tux # chmod u=rw,g=rw,o=r longfile.txt
ws2:/home/tux # ls -l longfile.txt
-rw-rw-r-- 1 tux users 202 Oct 17 16:30 longfile.txt
ws2:/home/tux #
```

You can also use chmod to toggle a particular permission on or off using the + or – signs. For example, suppose I want to turn off the write permission I just gave to Group for the longfile.txt file. If I enter **chmod g–w longfile.txt** at the shell prompt, the specified permission is turned off, as shown next:

```
ws2:/home/tux # chmod g-w longfile.txt
ws2:/home/tux # ls -l longfile.txt
-rw-r--r-- 1 tux users 202 Oct 17 16:30 longfile.txt
ws2:/home/tux #
```

If I wanted to turn the permission back on, I would enter **chmod g+w longfile.txt**. You can substitute **u** or **o** to modify the permission to the file or directory for Owner and Others as well.

Finally, you can also use numeric permissions with chmod. This is the option I use most often. You can modify all three entities at once with only three characters. To do this, enter **chmod** *numeric_permission filename*.

Going back to our earlier example, suppose I wanted to grant read and write permissions to Owner and Group, but remove all permissions to Others. That would mean Owner and Group's permissions would be represented numerically as 6. Because Others gets no permissions, its permissions would be represented by 0. I could implement this by entering **chmod 660 longfile.txt** at the shell prompt. When I do, the appropriate changes are made, as shown here:

```
ws2:/home/tux # chmod 660 longfile.txt
ws2:/home/tux # ls -l longfile.txt
-rw-rw---- 1 tux users 202 Oct 17 16:30 longfile.txt
ws2:/home/tux #
```

 TIP You can use the –R option with chmod to change permissions on many files at once recursively.

Let's practice managing permissions in the following exercise.

Exercise 9-2: Managing Permissions In this exercise, you will practice modifying permissions from the shell prompt of your Linux system. You will create a design document for your hypothetical Research and Design team and modify its permissions to control access.

Complete the following:

1. Verify that you are logged in to your system.

2. If necessary, switch to your root user account with the **su –** command.

3. Change to the /RandD directory by entering **cd /RandD** at the shell prompt.

4. Create a design document for your team and restrict access to it by doing the following:

   a. Create a new file named design_doc.odt by entering **touch design_doc.odt** at the shell prompt.

   b. At the shell prompt, enter **ls –l**. Notice that the root user account and the root group are the owners of the new file.

   c. Change ownership of the file to your user account and the research group using the chown command.

   d. Enter **ls –l** again at the shell prompt. Verify that ownership of the file directory has changed to your user account and the research group. Notice that Owner has rw– permissions to the file, but Group only has r-- permission.

e. Grant Owner rw– permissions by entering **chmod g+w design_doc.odt** at the shell prompt.

f. Enter **ls –l** again at the shell prompt. Notice that Owner and Group now both have read/write access to the file.

g. Notice that Others have read access to the file. You need to keep this document confidential, so remove this access by entering **chmod 660 design_doc.odt** at the shell prompt.

h. Enter **ls –l** again. Verify that Others have no permissions to this file.

5. Next, you need to control access to the research directory itself using permissions. Do the following:

a. At the shell prompt, enter **cd ...**

b. At the shell prompt, enter **ls –l**. Notice that Owner has full access to the RandD directory, but Group is missing the write permission to the directory. Also notice that Others can read the directory contents (r) and can enter the directory (x).

c. Grant Group full access to the directory and remove Others access to the directory completely by entering **chmod 770 RandD** at the shell prompt.

d. Enter **ls –l** at the shell prompt. Verify that Owner and Group have full access while Others has no access.

Working with Default Permissions

You may have noticed as we've worked through exercises and examples in this course that whenever you create a new file or directory in the file system, a default set of permissions is automatically assigned without any intervention on your part.

By default, Linux assigns rw–rw–rw– (666) permissions to every file whenever it is created in the file system. It also assigns rwxrwxrwx (777) permissions to every directory created in the file system. However, these aren't the permissions the files or directories actually end up with. Let's take a look at an example.

Suppose tux created a new directory named revenue in his home directory and a file named projections.odt in the revenue directory. Based on what we just discussed, the revenue directory should have a mode of rwxrwxrwx and the projections.odt file should have a mode of rw–rw–rw–. However, this isn't the case, as shown here:

```
tux@ws2:~> ls -l
total 92
drwxr-xr-x 2 tux      users 4096 Oct 12 21:57 bin
drwxr-xr-x 2 tux      users 4096 Oct 12 21:59 Desktop
drwxr-xr-x 2 tux      users 4096 Oct 12 22:00 Documents
drwxr-xr-x 2 tux      users 4096 Oct 12 21:59 Downloads
drwxr-xr-x 2 tux      users 4096 Oct 12 21:59 Music
drwxr-xr-x 2 tux      users 4096 Oct 12 21:59 Pictures
drwxr-xr-x 2 tux      users 4096 Oct 12 21:59 Public
drwxr-xr-x 2 tux      users 4096 Oct 12 21:57 public_html
drwxr-xr-x 2 tux      users 4096 Oct 17 21:13 revenue
```

```
tux@ws2:~> ls -l r*
total 0
-rw-r--r-- 1 tux users 0 Oct 17 21:13 projections.odt
tux@ws2:~>
```

Notice that the revenue directory has a mode of rwxr–xr–x (755). This means the directory owner has read, write, and execute permissions to the directory. Group and Others have read and execute permissions to the directory. Likewise, notice that the projections.odt file has a mode of rw–r– –r– – (644). The Owner has read and write permissions, while Group and Others have only the read permission.

These aren't the default permissions Linux is supposed to assign! Why did this happen? It's because the default permissions are too liberal. Think about it. The default directory mode would allow anyone on the system to enter any directory and delete any files they wanted to! Likewise, the default file mode would allow any user on the system to modify a file you created. What a nightmare!

To increase the overall security of the system, Linux uses a variable called *umask* to automatically remove permissions from the default mode whenever a file or directory is created in the file system. The value of umask is a three-digit number, as shown next (ignoring the first 0):

```
ws2:~ # umask
0022
ws2:~ #
```

For most Linux distributions, the default value of umask is 022. Each digit represents a numeric permission value to be *removed*. The first digit references Owner, the second references Group, the last references Others. Because a 0 is listed for Owner, no permissions are removed from the default mode for a file or directory owner. However, because a 2 is listed for Group and Others, the write permission is removed from the default mode whenever a file or directory is created in the file system. The function of umask is shown in Figure 9-5.

The default value of umask works for most Linux admins. However, there may be situations where you need to tighten up or loosen the permissions assigned when a file or directory is created in the file system. To do this, you can change the value assigned to umask.

Figure 9-5

How umask works

```
                                    Files
                    Default Mode : rw-rw-rw-
              Subtracted by umask : ----w--w-
                                    ─────────
                           Result:  rw-r-r--


                                    Directories
                    Default Mode:   rwxrwxrwx
              Subtracted by umask:  ----w--w-
                                    ─────────
                           Result:  rwxr-xr-x
```

This can be done in two ways. First, if you only need to make a temporary change to umask, you can enter **umask** *value* at the shell prompt. For example, if you wanted to remove the execute permission that is automatically assigned to Others whenever a new directory is created, you could enter **umask 023**. This would cause the write permission (2) to be removed from Group upon creation as well as write (2) and execute (1) from Others. This will effectively disallow anyone from entering the new directory except for the directory owner or members of the owning group. This is shown here:

```
ws2:~ # umask 023
ws2:~ # umask
0023
ws2:~ # mkdir /home/ksanders/temp
ws2:~ # ls -l /home/ksanders
drwxr-xr-x 2 ksanders users  4096 Mar 10 16:43 bin
-rw-rw---- 1 ksanders users     0 Mar 18 08:02 contacts.odt
drwxr-xr-x 2 ksanders users  4096 Mar 10 16:43 public_html
drwxr-xr-x 2 ksanders users  4096 Mar 18 11:06 revenue
drwxr-xr-- 2 root     root   4096 Mar 18 11:14 temp
ws2:~ #
```

Notice that, because the value of umask was changed, the execute permission (x) was removed from Others in the mode when the temp directory was created.

This method for modifying umask works great; however, it isn't persistent. If you were to restart the system, umask would revert to its original value. That's because the value of umask is automatically set each time the system boots using the umask parameter in the /etc/profile file or the /etc/login.defs file, depending upon your distribution.

If you want to make your change to umask permanent, simply edit the appropriate configuration file in a text editor and set the value of umask to your desired value.

Working with Special Permissions

Most of the tasks you will complete with permissions will be with the read, write, and execute permissions. However, there are several other special permissions that you can assign to files and directories in your file system. These are shown in Table 9-3.

These special permissions are referenced as an extra digit added to the *beginning* of the file or directory's mode. As with regular permissions, each of these special permissions has a numerical value assigned to it, as shown here:

- SUID: 4
- SGID: 2
- Sticky Bit: 1

You can assign these special permissions to files or directories using chmod. Just add an extra number to the beginning of the mode that references the special permissions you want to associate with the file or directory.

For example, suppose you wanted to apply the SUID and SGID permissions to a file named runme that should be readable and executable by Owner and Group. You would enter **chmod 6554 runme** at the shell prompt. This specifies that the file have SUID (4)

Permission	Description	Effect on Files	Effect on Directories
SUID	Set User ID Can be applied only to binary executable files (not shell scripts).	When an executable file with the SUID set is run, the user who ran the file temporarily becomes the file's owner.	None.
SGID	Set Group ID Can be applied to binary executable files (not shell scripts).	When a user runs an executable file with SGID set, the user temporarily becomes a member of the file's owning group.	When a user creates a file in a directory that has SGID set, the file's owner is set to the user's account (as per normal). However, the owning group assigned to the new file is set to the owning group of the parent directory.
Sticky Bit		None.	When the Sticky Bit is assigned to a directory, users can only delete files within the directory for which they are the owner of the file or the directory itself. This negates the effect of having the write permission to a directory, which could allow a user to delete files in a directory that he or she doesn't own.

Table 9-3   Special Permissions

and SGID (2) permissions assigned (for a total of 6 in the first digit). It also specifies that Owner and Group have read (4) and execute permissions (1) assigned (for a total of 5 in the second and third digits). It also specifies that Others be allowed to read (4) the file but that they can't modify or run it (for a total of 4 in the last digit).

Let's practice managing default and special permissions in the following exercise.

Exercise 9-3: Managing Default and Special Permissions   In this exercise, you will practice modifying default permissions with umask and creating files. You will also practice adding special permissions to directories. Complete the following:

1. Verify that you are logged in to your system.

2. If necessary, switch to your root user account with the **su –** command.

3. Change to the /RandD directory by entering **cd /RandD** at the shell prompt.

4. You need to create several Research and Development documents in the RandD directory. However, you need to make sure these documents are secure from prying eyes. Recall from the previous exercise that Others are automatically

granted read access to files when you create them. You don't want this to happen. You need Others to have no access at all to any documents created. Do the following:

   a. Change the default permissions by entering **umask 027** at the shell prompt.

   b. Verify the value of umask by entering **umask** at the shell prompt. It should display 0027.

   c. Create a new file named schedule.odt by entering **touch schedule.odt** at the shell prompt.

   d. Enter **ls –l** at the shell prompt. Verify that Owner has rw–, Group has r– –, and Others has – – – permissions.

5. In a previous exercise we granted Owner and Group rwx permissions to the RandD directory. However, having the write permission to the directory allows anyone in the research group to delete any file in the directory. We want to configure the directory such that users in the research group can only delete files they actually own. Do the following:

   a. At the shell prompt, enter **cd /**.

   b. At the shell prompt, add the Sticky Bit permission to the RandD directory by entering **chmod 1770 RandD**.

   c. At the shell prompt, enter **ls –l**. Notice that a *T* has been added to the last digit of the Others portion of the mode of the RandD directory. This indicates that the sticky bit has been set:

```
ws2:/ # ls -l
total 105
drwxrwx--T   2 tux   research   4096 Mar 18 11:25 RandD
...
```

6. Experiment with the new permissions you just added by logging in as different users in the system and testing what the permissions will and won't allow you to do.

7. In a previous exercise, we created a user named dtracy. However, because we didn't use the –m option when we created him, he doesn't have a home directory. Using what you've learned, do the following:

   a. Create the appropriate home directory for dtracy in /home.

   b. Look at the other home directories and determine the ownership and permissions that should be assigned.

   c. Use command-line utilities to set the ownership and permissions for dtracy's home directory.

   d. Run pwck when you're done to verify that the account is configured correctly.

You are now an expert at working with Linux users, groups, and permissions!

Chapter Review

In this chapter, we discussed ownership and permissions. I pointed out that users and groups only control who can access the system. They don't control what the user can do with files or directories in the file system. To do this, we need to implement ownership and permissions.

I also pointed out that, whenever a user creates a file or directory, that user is automatically assigned to be its owner. In addition, the group the user belongs to becomes the file or directory's group owner. These defaults can be changed; however, you must be logged in as root to change a file or directory's owner or be logged in as its owner to change its group.

To modify ownership, you use the chown command. This command can change both the user and/or the group that owns a file or directory. If you only want to change the group, you can also use the chgrp command.

I then pointed out that ownership alone can't control user access to files and directories. To fully control access, we need Linux file system permissions. Permissions define what a user can and cannot do with a given file or directory. Linux uses the following permissions:

- Read
- Write
- Execute

Linux assigns permissions to the following entities:

- Owner
- Group
- Others

The permissions assigned to Owner, Group, and Others together constitute a file or directory's mode. I emphasized that Linux permissions are additive. If a given user is both an owner and member of the owning group, then he or she receives permissions assigned for a file or directory to Owner and Group.

I then pointed out that permissions can be represented numerically for Owner, Group, and Others using the following values:

- Read: 4
- Write: 2
- Execute: 1

By adding up each permission assigned to a given entity, you can represent all of the permissions assigned with a single number. For example, a value of 7 indicates that all permissions have been assigned. A value of 5 indicates read and execute permissions have been assigned.

We then discussed the chmod tool that is used to manage permissions from the shell prompt. The chmod utility can use any of the following syntaxes to assign permissions to Owner, Group, and/or Others:

- chmod u=rw,g=rw,o=r *file_or_directory*
- chmod u+rw,g+rw,o+r *file_or_directory*
- chmod 664 *file_or_directory*

At this point, we began a discussion of default Linux permissions. I told you that, by default, Linux automatically assigns new files with rw–rw–rw– permissions and new directories with rwxrwxrwx permissions upon creation. However, to increase security, the umask variable is used to automatically remove some permission. The default umask value is 022, which removes the write permission from Group and Others when a file or directory is created. We pointed out that you can change the value of umask by entering **umask *value*** at the shell prompt.

We also briefly discussed the special permissions that you can assign, including

- SUID: 4
- SGID: 2
- Sticky Bit: 1

We pointed out that you assign these permissions with chmod by adding an extra digit before the Owner digit in the command using the values just shown.

Accelerated Review

- Ownership defines which user and group owns a particular file or directory in the file system.
- You can use the ls –l command to view ownership.
- You can use the chown utility to configure user and group ownership of a file or directory.
- You can use the chgrp utility to change group ownership.
- You must be logged in as root to change user ownership.
- You must be logged in as root or as the file/directory owner to change group ownership.
- Permissions are used to define what users may or may not do with files or directories in the file system.
- Linux uses the read, write, and execute permissions for files and directories.
- Linux permissions are assigned to Owner, Group, and Others.

- Linux permissions are additive.
- The permissions assigned to Owner, Group, and Others constitute the file or directory's mode.
- Permissions can be represented numerically: read=4, write=2, and execute=1.
- Summing all permissions assigned to an entity, such as Owner, allows you to represent all assigned permissions with a single number.
- You use the chmod utility to modify permissions.
- Linux assigns rw–rw–rw– permissions by default to new files and rwxrwxrwx permissions to new directories.
- These permissions are too relaxed for most situations, so the umask variable is used to subtract specific permissions from the defaults.
- The default value of umask is 022, which subtracts the write permission (2) from Group and Others.
- You can modify the value of umask to change the default permissions assigned upon creation.
- Linux also includes three default special permissions: Sticky Bit, SUID, and SGID.
- You assign special permissions with chmod by adding an additional digit before the Owner digit in the command.

Questions

1. You need to change the owner of a file named /var/opt/runme from mireland, who is a member of the users group, to dnelson, who is a member of the editors group. Assuming you want to change both user and group owners, which command will do this?

   A. chown mireland dnelson /var/opt/runme

   B. chown –u "dnelson" –g "editors" /var/opt/runme

   C. chown dnelson /var/opt/runme

   D. chown dnelson.editors /var/opt/runme

2. Which permission, when applied to a directory in the file system, will allow a user to enter the directory?

   A. Read

   B. Write

   C. Execute

   D. Access Control

3. A user needs to open a file, edit it, and then save the changes. What permissions does he need to do this? (Choose two.)

    A. Read

    B. Write

    C. Execute

    D. Modify

4. A file named employees.odt has a mode of rw–r– –r– –. If rtracy is the file's owner, what can he do with it?

    A. He can open the file and view its contents, but he can't save any changes.

    B. He can open the file, make changes, and save the file.

    C. He can change ownership of the file.

    D. He can run the file if it's an executable.

5. A file named employees.odt has a mode of rw–r– –r– –. If mhuffman is not the file's owner but is a member of the group that owns this file, what can he do with it?

    A. He can open the file and view its contents, but he can't save any changes.

    B. He can open the file, make changes, and save the file.

    C. He can change ownership of the file.

    D. He can run the file if it's an executable.

6. A file named employees.odt has a mode of rw–r– –r– –. If mireland is not the file's owner and is not a member of the group that owns this file, what can she do with it?

    A. She can open the file and view its contents, but she can't save any changes.

    B. She can open the file, make changes, and save the file.

    C. She can change ownership of the file.

    D. She can run the file if it's an executable.

7. A file named myapp has a mode of 755. If dnelson doesn't own this file and isn't a member of the group that owns the file, what can she do with it?

    A. She can change the group that owns the file.

    B. She can open the file, make changes, and save the file.

    C. She can change ownership of the file.

    D. She can run the file.

8. You need to change the permissions of a file named schedule.odt such that the file owner can edit the file, users who are members of the group that owns the file can edit it, and users who are not owners and don't belong to the owning group can view it but not modify it. Which command will do this?

   A. chmod 664 schedule.odt

   B. chmod 555 schedule.odt

   C. chmod 777 schedule.odt

   D. chmod 644 schedule.odt

9. You just created a new script file named myapp.sh. However, when you try to run it from the command prompt, the bash shell generates an error that says -bash: ./myapp.sh: Permission denied. Which command will fix this problem?

   A. chmod u+r myapp.sh

   B. chmod u+x myapp.sh

   C. chmod u+w myapp.sh

   D. chmod u+T myapp.sh

10. Your Linux system's umask variable is currently set to a value of 077. A user named jcarr (who is a member of the users group) creates a file named mythoughts.odt. What can users who are members of the users group do with this file?

    A. They can view the file, but they can't modify or save it.

    B. They can open, modify, and save the file.

    C. They can open, modify, and save the file. They can also execute the file if it is an executable.

    D. They have no access to the file at all.

11. An executable file has the SUID permission set. If this file is run on the system, who owns the file?

    A. The user who created the file remains the owner.

    B. The user who ran the file becomes the file's permanent owner.

    C. The user who ran the file becomes the file's temporary owner.

    D. The root user becomes the file's owner.

12. The /Projects directory has the SGID special permission set. What effect does this have when a user tries to create a file in this directory? (Choose two.)

    A. The file's owner is set to the user who created the file.

    B. The file's owner is set to the user who owns the directory.

    C. The owning group of the file is set to the owning group of the directory.

    D. The owning group of the file is set to the primary group of the user who created the file.

    E. The file's owner is set to root.

    F. The owning group of the new file is set to the root group.

13. Which special permission can't be assigned to a file?

   A. SUID

   B. SGID

   C. Sticky Bit

   D. None of the above. All special permissions can be assigned to a file.

14. A directory is owned by the users group and has a mode of rwxrwxr– – permissions assigned to that group. It also has the Sticky Bit permission set. What effect does this have on files within the directory?

   A. Users who are members of the users group can only delete files within the directory for which they are the owner.

   B. No user is allowed to delete files in this directory.

   C. Users who are members of the users group can delete any file within the directory.

   D. Others can enter the directory and delete files within the directory for which they are the owner.

Answers

1. **D.** Entering **chown dnelson.editors /var/opt/runme** will change the user and group owners of the runme file to dnelson and editors.

2. **C.** The execute permission allows a user to enter a directory in the file system.

3. **A, B.** The user must have read and write permissions to open and modify a file.

4. **B.** In the mode shown, Owner is given read and write permissions (rw–). Because rtracy is the file's owner, he can open and view file contents (r). He can also modify and save changes to the file (w).

5. **A.** In the mode shown, Group is given the read permission only. Because mhuffman is a member of the group, he can only open and view file contents. He can't modify and save the file.

6. **A.** In the mode shown, Others are given the read permission only (r). Because mireland is neither the file's owner nor a member of the owning group, she can only open and view file contents. She can't modify and save changes to the file.

7. **D.** Because dnelson isn't the owner and isn't a member of the owning group, she is granted the rights assigned to Others, which are read (4) and execute (1). This allows her to run the file.

8. **A.** Entering **chmod 664 schedule.odt** will grant Owner and Group read (4) and write (2) permissions. It will also grant Others read (4) permission.

9. **B.** Entering **chmod u+x myapp.sh** will grant the file's Owner the execute permission (x). The script file can then be run at the shell prompt.

10. **D.** Because umask is set to 077, all permissions (read=4, write=2, execute=1) are removed from Group and Others. Therefore, members of the owning group have no access to the file.

11. **C.** The SUID permission causes the user who runs the file to temporarily become the file's owner.

12. **A, C.** Because the file's parent directory has the SGID permission set, the file's owner is set to the user who created the file while the owning group is set to the owning group of the directory where the file resides.

13. **C.** The Sticky Bit special permission can't be assigned to a file. It can only be assigned to directories.

14. **A.** The Sticky Bit permission negates the effect of the group write permissions. As a result, users who are members of the users group can only delete files within the directory for which they are the owner.

## CHAPTER 10

Archiving Files

In this chapter, you will learn about
- Selecting a backup medium
- Selecting a backup strategy
- Using Linux backup utilities

One of the key roles you must perform as a Linux system administrator is to ensure that the data on the systems you are responsible for is protected. One of the best ways you can do this is to back up the data by archiving the files and folders in your file system. Creating an archive creates a redundant copy of the data so that if a disaster occurs, the data can be restored.

It's important that you remember that data is stored, for the most part, on mechanical devices in your Linux system. Hard drives have motors and other moving parts that slowly wear out over time. In fact, hard drives usually have a mean time between failures (MTBF) value assigned to them by the manufacturer. This MTBF basically gives you an estimate of how long a drive will last before it fails. Basically, it's not a matter of *if* a hard drive will fail; it's a matter of *when*.

I relate this because I want you to take backing up seriously. Many system administrators, frankly, get very lazy about running backups. It's an easy task to blow off, thinking "I'll run a backup tomorrow." Before you know it, it's been weeks since the last time you ran a backup.

If you're employed by an organization to maintain their systems and you fail to run backups, I can just about guarantee that you will lose your job if a disaster happens. Several years ago, I participated in a support call with a system administrator whose server had completely died. He called us in a last-ditch effort hoping that we would have some kind of magic solution that would get his data back. When we told him that we couldn't and that he would have to reinstall and restore from his backups, there was silence on the other end of the phone for a long time. He got a little choked up and whispered, "I don't have any backups. I'm going to lose my job over this." Take my advice: develop a backup plan and stick to it religiously.

Selecting a Backup Medium

Back in the "old days," we really only had two choices for backing up data: floppy diskettes or a tape drive. Floppies didn't hold much and were notoriously unreliable, so most system admins opted for tape drives.

Today, many Linux admins still use tape drives to back up their data. Tape drives use magnetic tape, much like the tape used in an 8mm video camera, to store data. Tape drives store a lot of data and are relatively inexpensive. They are still a great choice for backing up data on your Linux system.

However, tape drives have several limitations. First of all, tape drives employ a lot of mechanical parts that wear out over time. The tape itself is run over the top of a read/write head in the tape drive, so it also wears out over time due to friction. Second, tapes are relatively slow. Backing up large quantities of data can take hours. Restoring that data from tape can take days.

As a result, many admins are exploring other media for backing up system data. For a while, read/write DVDs were in vogue for backups. As long as hard drives didn't get much larger than 4–8GB, they worked just fine. However, modern hard drives are dramatically larger than that. Backing up a 1TB hard drive with DVDs today is similar to backing up a 100MB hard drive with floppy diskettes 15 years ago. Yes, it can be done, but it's a painful, time-consuming process. Unless the amount of data you're backing up is relatively small, I don't recommend this option. Even rewritable Blu-ray discs (BD-RE) hold only 25GB (single layer) or 50GB (double layer) of data. That's not enough for a typical modern system.

Another option that many system administrators are exploring (and one that I really like) is the use of removable USB or FireWire hard drives. Back in the old days, we used tape drives to back up our hard drives because hard disks were extremely expensive. The general rule of thumb back in the early 1990s was "$1 per megabyte" when buying a hard disk. It was just too expensive to use hard drives for backups. In addition, we didn't have a hot-swappable external interface for hard drives. Therefore, tape was one of the few viable options.

Today, however, the price of hard drives has dropped dramatically. You can buy a removable USB or FireWire hard drive for less than a $0.10 per gigabyte. Using external hard drives for backups has two distinct advantages. First, they are much, much faster than tapes. Backups that took hours on a tape drive take minutes on a hard disk. Second, hard drives tend to be more reliable than tape drives.

Of course, using hard drives for backups isn't a perfect solution. One of the key disadvantages is the fact that the disk partition on the removable drive must be mounted to run a backup. If something bad were to happen to the system that destroyed data on the main hard drive while the removable drive was connected, it could potentially destroy data on the removable drive as well.

As with any backup medium, you have to weigh the benefits and drawbacks when deciding to use external hard drives for backups.

TIP I prefer a hot backup solution over standard backups. A hot-backup involves creating a duplicate system that can be brought online very quickly in the event the original system goes down. I use the rsync utility on my mission-critical Linux systems to synchronize data to standby Linux systems over the network; essentially creating mirrored systems. In my office, I synchronize every hour, but you could do this more or less frequently as needed. If one of my mainline systems goes down, I can simply switch over to the associated standby backup system, and I'm back up and running in less than a minute!

As with anything else, you'll need to balance the cost of the solution you select with its reliability, speed, and ease of management. For example, a hot backup solution may provide the fastest performance, but it also costs considerably more to implement. Alternatively, using an external hard disk drive for backups is much less expensive to implement and provides reasonable performance, but it will require a little more work on your part to manage.

After you select the backup medium you want to use, you will need to purchase the appropriate equipment and connect it to your system. Once that's in place, you next need to select a backup strategy.

Selecting a Backup Strategy

When creating a backup plan, you have several different options. You need to decide upon the following:

- A backup type
- A backup schedule
- What to back up

Selecting a Backup Type

Depending upon the backup utility you choose to use, you will usually have at least three different types of backups that you can use (sometimes more). These include the following:

- **Full** All specified files are backed up, regardless of whether or not they've been modified since the last backup. After being backed up, each file is flagged as having been backed up.
- **Incremental** Only the files that have been modified since the last backup (full or incremental) are backed up. Each file is flagged as having been backed up.
- **Differential** Only the files that have been modified since the last full backup are backed up. Even though they have been backed up during a differential backup, the files involved are *not* flagged as having been backed up.

To determine your backup strategy, you need to select from the preceding backup types. For example, you could run a full backup every time. This strategy is thorough and exhaustive. It's also the fastest strategy when you need to restore data from a backup.

However, full backups can take a very long time to complete because every single file is backed up regardless of whether or not it has changed since the last backup. Therefore, many administrators mix full backups with incremental or differential backups.

If you use a full/incremental strategy, you run a full backup once a week, usually when the system load is lightest, such as Friday night. Then you run incremental backups each of the other six days in the week. Using this strategy, you should end up with one full backup and six incremental backups for each week. The advantage of this strategy is primarily speed. Because incrementals only back up files that have changed since the last full *or* incremental backup, they usually run very fast. The drawback to this strategy is that, if a disaster happens, you must restore all of your backups in the rotation in exactly the correct order: the full backup first, followed by the first incremental, then the second incremental, and so on. This can be a slow process.

Alternatively, you can also use full with differential backups. With this strategy, you typically run a full backup when things are slow, such as Friday night. Then you run a differential each of the other nights of the week. Remember that a differential backup only backs up files that have changed since the last full backup, *not* since the last differential. Therefore, each day's backup gets progressively bigger. The main advantage to this strategy is that restores are really fast. Instead of seven backups to restore, you only have to restore two: the last full backup first, followed by the last differential backup—and no others! The disadvantage to this method is that the differential backups start out very fast but can become almost as long as a full backup by the time you reach the last day in the cycle.

 CAUTION Whatever you do, don't mix incremental and differential backups together! Your backups will miss data, as the files to be backed up will be flagged inconsistently.

Whichever strategy you choose, you should be sure to keep a rotation of backups. Many administrators will rotate their backup media such that they have three to four weeks worth of past backups on hand. You never know when a file that was deleted two weeks ago will suddenly be needed again!

In addition, you should be sure to verify your backups. Most backup utilities provide you with the option of checking your backup against the original files after the backup completes. If you don't do this, you may have errors in your backup. One of my mentors told me many years ago that if you don't verify your backups, you really aren't backing up your system at all. If a disaster occurs and your backup or your backup media is bad, you will have no way to restore data.

Selecting a Backup Schedule

You can use whatever backup schedule works best for you. However, most admins work on a weekly rotation, as discussed previously. Pick one day for your full backup and the remaining days of the week for your incremental or differential backups.

You should schedule your backups to occur when the load on the system is at its lightest. Late in the evening or in the early morning are usually best, depending on your organization's schedule.

Determining What to Back Up

Most Linux systems you're going to be working with will probably consume a fairly large amount of disk space, depending on the applications and services you've installed. You need to decide how much of this consumed disk space is going to be backed up.

One option is to back up the entire system. This is a safe, thorough option. However, it's also somewhat slow due to the sheer amount of data involved. Many administrators choose not to do this. Instead, they back up only the critical data on the system, such as user data and configuration information. The theory behind this strategy is that you could, in the event of a disaster, simply re-install a new system and then restore the critical data to it. If you choose this strategy, you should consider backing up the following directories in your Linux file system:

- /etc
- /home
- /opt
- /root
- /var
- /srv

Notice that this strategy doesn't back up your Linux operating system or its utilities. Instead, it backs up only your configuration files, your user data, your log files, and your web/ftp files.

Once you've determined what to back up, the next part of your plan is to determine what you'll back it up with.

Using Linux Backup Utilities

When working with Linux, you have a host of different utilities at your disposal to conduct a backup. Many come with the operating system; others can be obtained from third parties. You should be familiar with the tools that are common to most Linux distributions and are run from the shell prompt. In this part of the chapter, we'll look at the following utilities:

- tar
- cpio
- dd

Using tar

The tar utility has been around for a very long time and is a very commonly used Linux backup tool. The acronym "tar" stands for tape archive. The tar utility takes a list of specified files and copies them into a single archive file (.tar). The .tar file can then be compressed with the gzip utility on your Linux system, resulting in a file with a .tar.gz extension. This is called a *tarball*.

The tar utility can be used to send backup jobs to a variety of backup media, including tape drives and removable hard disk drives. The syntax for using tar to create backups is **tar –cvf** *filename directory*. The –c option tells tar to create a new archive. The –v option tells tar to work in verbose mode, displaying each file being backed up on screen. The –f option specifies the name of the tar archive to be created.

For example, if you wanted to create a backup of the /home directory named backup.tar on an external USB hard drive mounted in /media/usb, you would enter **tar –cvf /media/usb/backup.tar /home**, as shown in this example:

```
ws2:/ # tar -cvf /media/usb/backup.tar /home
tar: Removing leading '/' from member names
/home/
/home/tux/
/home/tux/.gftp/
/home/tux/.gftp/gftp.log
/home/tux/.gftp/bookmarks
/home/tux/.gftp/gftprc
/home/tux/.nautilus/
/home/tux/.local/
/home/tux/.local/share/
...
```

Notice in this example that a message stating *tar: Removing leading '/' from member names* is displayed. When a tar archive is created, absolute paths are converted to relative paths by default. As a result, the leading / is removed.

You can use the options shown in Table 10-1 with tar.

If you wanted to back up to a tape drive instead of a USB drive, you could do this by replacing the filename parameter in the tar command with the device name for your tape drive. On most distributions, the first SCSI tape drive in the system is referenced through /dev/st0. Therefore, you could enter **tar –cvf /dev/st0 /home** if you wanted to run the same backup as in the previous example, but send it to a SCSI tape drive instead.

To restore a tar archive, simply enter **tar –xvf** *filename*. For example, to extract the archive you just created, you would enter **tar –xvf /media/usb/backup.tar**. This will extract the archive into the current working directory. If the archive has been zipped, you can also use the –z option to unzip the archive before extracting it.

You can also compress/decompress tar archives (or any other file, for that matter) directly from the shell prompt using the gzip and gunzip utilities or the bzip2 and bunzip2 utilities. The gzip utility uses the Lempel-Ziv compression algorithm, while bzip2 uses the Burrows-Wheeler compression algorithm. Archive files compressed with bzip2 instead of gzip will usually have an extension of .bz2 instead of .gz.

Option	Function
–A --concatenate	Appends (adds) tar files to an existing archive.
–c --create	Creates a new archive file.
–d --compare	Identifies differences between an archive file and files in the file system.
–P --absolute-names	Causes tar to *not* strip leading "/" from filenames.
–r --append	Adds files to the end of a tar archive.
–t --list	Lists the contents of an archive file.
–u --update	Appends files only if they are newer than the existing files in an archive.
–x --extract	Extracts files from an archive.
–z --gzip --gunzip	Does one of two things. During archive creation, it compresses the new tar archive by running it through the gzip utility. During extraction, it first decompresses the tar archive using the gunzip utility.
–j --bzip2	Does one of two things. During archive creation, it compresses the new tar archive by running it through the bzip2 utility. During extraction, it first decompresses the tar archive using the bzip2 utility.
–X *filename* --exclude-from	Causes tar to exclude files listed in the text file specified.

Table 10-1   tar Command Options

The syntax for using gzip to compress a file is **gzip *options filename***. For example, to compress a file named longfile.txt located in the current directory, you would enter **gzip longfile.txt** at the shell prompt, as shown in this example:

```
tux@ws2:~> gzip longfile.txt
tux@ws2:~> ls longfile.*
longfile.txt.gz
tux@ws2:~>
```

Notice in the preceding example that the original file (longfile.txt) has been compressed and renamed to longfile.txt.gz. Any time you see a file with an extension of ".gz", you know that file has been compressed with the gzip utility and must be decompressed before you can access its contents. For example, to decompress the longfile.txt.gz file, you could enter one of two commands:

- gunzip longfile.txt.gz
- gzip –d longfile.txt.gz

This is shown in the following example:

```
tux@ws2:~> gunzip longfile.txt.gz
tux@ws2:~> ls longfile.*
longfile.txt
tux@ws2:~>
```

As mentioned earlier, you can also use bzip2 to compress and decompress files. The syntax for using bzip2 is the same as with gzip. For example, to compress the longfile.txt file with bzip2, you would enter **bzip2 longfile.txt** at the shell prompt. When you do, the file is compressed and renamed to longfile.txt.bz2, as shown next:

```
tux@ws2:~> bzip2 longfile.txt
tux@ws2:~> ls longfile.*
longfile.txt.bz2
tux@ws2:~>
```

If you see a file with an extension of ".bz2", then you know that the file was compressed with bzip2 and it must be decompressed before you can access the contents of the file. As with gzip, there are two options for decompressing a file compressed with bzip2:

- bunzip2 *filename*
- bzip2 –d *filename*

An example of this is shown next:

```
tux@ws2:~> bunzip2 longfile.txt.bz2
tux@ws2:~> ls longfile.*
longfile.txt
tux@ws2:~>
```

Using cpio

Like tar, the cpio utility can also be used to make archive files. A key difference between tar and cpio is the fact that you must provide cpio with a list of files and directories to back up from the standard input. This can be done using cat to display the contents of a file or by generating a listing using find or ls.

For example, suppose you wanted to back up the contents of the /home/tux/myproject directory on your Linux system. To use cpio to do this, you must somehow generate a listing of files and directories in this directory and send it to cpio. Then you must redirect the output from cpio to a file. This can be done using the ls utility, discussed earlier. You could switch to /home/tux/myproject and then enter **ls | cpio –ov > /media/usb/ backup.cpio**. The ls utility will generate a listing of all files in the current directory and pipe it to the input of the cpio command, which will then create an archive file and save it as /media/usb/backup.cpio.

However, this command won't work if there are subdirectories in the MyProjects directory. If this is the case, then you can use the find command instead to create a list of files for cpio to archive. The syntax is **find . –print –depth | cpio –ov > /media/usb/**

backup.cpio. The –print option causes find to print the full name of each file to the screen (the standard output). Because the –depth option was also used, find checks the contents of each directory before processing the directory itself.

Either way, you've piped the standard output from find to the standard input of cpio. The cpio utility uses this as a list of files and directories to archive. The –o option tells cpio to create a new archive. The –v option simply tells cpio to run verbosely, displaying the name of each file and directory as it's processed. Finally, we have to redirect the standard output from cpio (the archive) to a file in the file system. This is done by entering > followed by the name of the archive file.

You can also compress a cpio archive by adding the gzip utility to the pipe. For example: **ls | cpio –ov | gzip > /media/usb/backup.cpio.gz**.

To restore files from a cpio archive, you run cpio from the shell prompt using the –i option and specifying the name of the archive to process. When you do, the archive files will be extracted into the current working directory. For example, you could extract the archive you just created by entering **cpio –iv < /media/usb/backup.cpio**, like this:

```
ws2:/tmp # cpio -iv < /media/usb/backup.cpio
acpidump
accessdb
acpisrc
.
341 blocks
ws1:/tmp #
```

If the cpio archive was compressed with gzip, you will have to run it through the gunzip command to decompress the archive before you can extract files from it with cpio, as shown here:

```
ws2:/media/usb # ls
backup.cpio.gz  backup.tar
ws1:/media/usb # gunzip backup.cpio.gz
ws1:/media/usb # ls
backup.cpio  backup.tar
ws1:/media/usb #
```

As you can see, the backup.cpio.gz file is decompressed by the gunzip command into the backup.cpio file, which can now be manipulated with the cpio command. Another way to do this is to add the –c option to the gunzip command and then pipe the results to cpio –i. The –c option tells gunzip to write the output of the command to the standard output, leaving the original file intact. Essentially, this just writes the uncompressed filename to the standard out, which is then sent to cpio for processing. Here is an example:

```
ws2:/media/usb # ls
backup.cpio.gz  backup.tar
ws1:/media/usb # gunzip -c backup.cpio.gz | cpio -i
341 blocks
ws1:/media/usb # ls
accessdb  acpidump  acpisrc  backup.cpio.gz  backup.tar
ws1:/media/usb #
```

As you can see, the gunzip command extracted the name of the file compressed in the gzip archive and sent it to the cpio –i command, which then extracted the three files out of the archive to the local directory.

Creating an Archive with dd

You can use the dd command to copy files. You can copy all kinds of Linux data with this command, including entire partitions. You may be thinking "Big deal, I already know how to use cp and mv." Actually, the dd utility is quite useful. The key difference between dd and other file copy utilities is the fact that it copies data using *records*. The default size for a record is 512 bytes.

Let's first look at how you copy a file with dd. The syntax is **dd if=***input_file* **of=***output_file*. Use the if= (input file) option to specify the file to be copied. Use the of= (output file) option to specify the name of the new file. Here is an example:

```
ws2:/ # dd if=/home/tux/MyProject/acpidump of=/home/tux/acpidump.copy
29+1 records in
29+1 records out
15112 bytes (15 kB) copied, 0.000263331 s, 57.4 MB/s
ws2:/ #
```

NOTE   You can modify the default record size using the bs=*block_size* option.

One of the cool things about dd is that, because it uses records, it can copy an entire partition to a single file. This is powerful. Essentially, dd is a simple command-line tool that you can use to archive an entire partition into a single file, creating an image of the partition or even the entire hard disk drive. I have a friend (who is Mr. Uber Linux Admin), and he uses the dd command in a script to create his own drive imaging application. Cool stuff!

To copy an entire partition, you enter **dd if=***device_file* **of=***output_file* at the shell prompt. The device file of the partition is used as the input file. All of the contents of the partition are written to the output file specified. In the example that follows, the dd command is used to copy the /dev/sdb1 partition to a file named partitionbackup in the root user's home directory:

```
ws2:/ # dd if=/dev/sdb1 of=/root/partitionbackup
dd: writing to '/root/partitionbackup':
7500249+0 records in
7500248+0 records out
3840126976 bytes (3.8 GB) copied, 108.441 s, 35.4 MB/s
ws2:/ #
```

The dd command can even create an image file of an entire hard disk. The syntax again is **dd if=***device_file* **of=***output_file*. The difference is that you simply specify the device file of the hard disk itself instead of a partition. In the next example, the entire /dev/sdb hard drive is archived into the drivebackup file:

```
ws2:~ # dd if=/dev/sdb of=/mnt/bigdrive/drivebackup
16777216+0 records in
16777216+0 records out
8589934592 bytes (8.6 GB) copied, 157.931 s, 54.4 MB/s
ws2:~ #
```

Another useful feature of dd is that it can create a backup copy of your hard drive's master boot record (MBR) and partition table. Again, this is possible because it looks at data as records. The syntax is **dd if=***device_file* **of=***output_file* **bs=512 count=1**. This tells dd to grab just the first 512K block of the hard drive, which is where your MBR and partition table reside. This is shown in the following example:

```
ws2:/tmp # dd if=/dev/sda of=/root/mbrbackup bs=512 count=1
1+0 records in
1+0 records out
512 bytes (512 B) copied, 0.0123686 s, 41.4 kB/s
ws2:/tmp #
```

Let's practice backing up in the following exercise.

Exercise 10-1: Backing Up Data   In this exercise, you will practice backing up data. Complete the following:

1. With your system up and running, open a terminal session.

2. Change to your root user account.

3. At the shell prompt, create a new directory named backup by entering **mkdir /backup** at the shell prompt.

4. At the shell prompt, create an archive of all users' home directories by entering **tar –cvf /backup/backup.tar /home**.

5. Enter **ls /backup**. Verify that the backup file exists.

6. Change to the /tmp directory by entering **cd /tmp** at the shell prompt.

7. Extract the tar file to the current directory by entering **tar –xvf /backup/backup .tar**.

8. Enter **cd home**.

9. Use the **ls** command to verify that the files from the tar archive were extracted to the current directory.

10. Switch back to your regular user account by entering **exit**.

Chapter Review

In this chapter, we discussed how to back up your Linux file system. We emphasized the importance of conducting backups on a regular schedule. We then discussed the elements required to create a backup plan for your systems. The first step is to select a backup medium. We discussed the advantages and disadvantages of tape drives, recordable optical drives, and removable hard drives.

The next step is to select a backup strategy. We discussed how full, incremental, and differential backups work and how to combine them to design your own backup strategy. We also emphasized the importance of rotating your backup media as well as verifying your backup.

The next step is to determine your backup schedule and then to decide what to back up. We reviewed the directories in the file system that are commonly backed up, including /etc, /home, /opt, /root, /var, and /srv.

We ended the chapter by reviewing some of the Linux backup utilities that you can use to back up your system. We first reviewed the syntax for using tar, both with hard disks and with tape drives. We then reviewed the syntax for using cpio to create file archives. We discussed how to use gzip and bzip2 to compress/decompress tar and cpio archives. We also discussed how you can use dd to copy files and even create image files from entire disk partitions.

Accelerated Review

- It is absolutely critical that you regularly back up your system.
- Tape drives are commonly used to back up data.
- Tape drives hold a large amount of data and are relatively inexpensive.
- Tape drives are also slow and tend to wear out.
- Rewritable CDs and DVDs can be used for backups, but they really don't hold enough information.
- Removable hard drives are becoming a popular solution for running backups.
- Removable hard drives are very fast and hold a lot of data; however, they are also susceptible to the same corruption issues as the hard disk being backed up.
- Full backups back up everything and flag the files as having been backed up.
- Incremental backups back up everything that has been modified since the last full or incremental backup and flag the files as having been backed up.
- Differential backups back up everything that has been backed up since the last full backup. It doesn't flag the files as having been backed up.
- You can mix full backups with incremental or differential backups, but you can't mix incremental and differential backups.
- You should keep a three- to four-week rotation of backups.

- You should verify your backups.
- You should set a schedule for your backups.
- You should carefully determine which directories to back up.
- You should consider backing up /etc, /home, /opt, /root, /var, and /srv.
- You can use tar to create backup files.
- The tar utility works with most backup media.
- You can use gzip and gunzip to compress and decompress tar archives (or any other files).
- You can use bzip2 and bunzip2 to compress and decompress tar archives (or any other files).
- You can also use cpio to archive data.
- You can use the dd command to convert and copy files.
- The dd utility can copy an entire partition or even an entire hard drive to a single file.

Questions

1. Which type of backup backs up all files modified since the last full backup and does not flag the files as having been backed up?

   A. Full

   B. Incremental

   C. Differential

   D. Partial

2. You need to create a backup of /etc to a removable hard disk drive mounted at /mnt/USB. Which tar command will do this?

   A. tar –cvf /mnt/USB/backup.tar /etc

   B. tar –xvf ~/backup.tar /etc

   C. tar –xzf /mnt/USB/backup.tar /etc

   D. tar –cvf /mnt/USB/backup.tar ~/etc

3. You want to create a compressed cpio archive of all the files in the Projects directory within your home directory to /mnt/usbdrive/Projectsbackup.cpio.gz. Which command will do this?

   A. cpio –ov ~/Projects | gzip > /mnt/usbdrive/Projectsbackup.cpio.gz

   B. ls ~/ Projects | cpio –ovz | > /mnt/usbdrive/Projectsbackup.cpio.gz

   C. ls ~/ Projects | cpio –ov | gzip > /mnt/usbdrive/Projectsbackup.cpio.gz

   D. cpio –ovz ~/Projects > /mnt/usbdrive/Projectsbackup.cpio.gz

4. Which command can be used to create an image of your /dev/sda2 partition in the /mnt/usb/volback file?

   A. dd if=/dev/sda2 of=/mnt/usb/volback

   B. cp /dev/sda2 /mnt/usb/volback

   C. dd if=/mnt/usb/volback of=/dev/sda2

   D. dd if=/dev/sda of=/mnt/usb/volback

5. You manage a Linux system with a 1TB hard disk installed. Currently, 33 percent of the available space on the hard disk has been consumed. Which backup device should you choose to protect the data on the system?

   A. Floppy diskette

   B. CD-RW

   C. DVD-RW

   D. BD-RE

   E. 500GB USB external hard drive

6. Which type of backup backs up all specified files, regardless of whether or not they've been modified since the last backup, and flags each file as having been backed up?

   A. Full

   B. Incremental

   C. Differential

   D. Daily

7. You are designing a backup strategy for a Linux system that is used by an architect to create architectural drawings. Construction schedules are tight, so the information on the system needs to be made available as soon as possible should a disaster occur. Which backup strategy would be the best choice in this scenario?

   A. Full only

   B. Full with differential

   C. Full with incremental

   D. Full with differential and incremental

8. You need to create a backup of /etc to a removable hard disk drive mounted at /mnt/USB. To save space, you want to compress the archive with gzip after it is created. Which tar command will do this?

   A. tar –cvjf /mnt/USB/backup.tar.gz /etc

   B. tar –cvzf /mnt/USB/backup.tar.gz /etc

   C. tar –xvf ~/backup.tar.gz /etc

   D. tar –xzf /mnt/USB/backup.tar.gz /etc

   E. tar –cvf /mnt/USB/backup.tar.gz /etc

9. You need to create a backup of /etc to a removable hard disk drive mounted at /mnt/USB. To save space, you want to compress the archive with bzip2 after it is created. Which tar command will do this?

   A. tar –cvjf /mnt/USB/backup.tar.bz2 /etc

   B. tar –xvf ~/backup.tar.bz2 /etc

   C. tar –xzf /mnt/USB/backup.tar.bz2 /etc

   D. tar –cvbf /mnt/USB/backup.tar.bz2 /etc

   E. tar –cvzf /mnt/USB/backup.tar.bz2 /etc

10. You've created a backup of /etc named backup.tar.gz on a removable hard disk drive mounted at /mnt/USB. You now need to extract all files from the archive to the current directory. Which tar command will do this?

   A. tar –xvf /mnt/USB/backup.tar.gz

   B. tar –xvzf /mnt/USB/backup.tar.gz

   C. tar –xvbf /mnt/USB/backup.tar.gz

   D. tar –cvzf /mnt/USB/backup.tar.gz

Answers

1. **C.** A differential backup backs up all files modified since the last full backup and does not flag the files as having been backed up.

2. **A.** The **tar –cfv /mnt/USB/backup.tar /etc** command uses the correct syntax to create a backup of /etc to a removable hard disk drive mounted at /mnt/USB.

3. **C.** The **ls ~/ Projects | cpio –ov | gzip > /mnt/usbdrive/Projectsbackup.cpio.gz** command will generate a listing of files in the Projects directory, send the list to the cpio command to create an archive, and send the archive to gzip for compression.

4. **A.** The **dd if=/dev/sda2 of=/mnt/usb/volback** command creates an image of the /dev/sda2 partition in the /mnt/usb/volback file.

5. **E.** Because the system has roughly 333GB of consumed hard disk space, a 500GB external hard drive is the only storage device listed that is big enough to back up the system efficiently.

6. **A.** A full backup backs up all specified files, regardless of whether or not they've been modified since the last backup, and flags each file as having been backed up.

7. **A.** A full-only backup strategy would be the fastest strategy to restore data from. Only the last full backup would need to be restored. However, this strategy would also require the most time to run each day.

8. **B.** The **tar –cvzf /mnt/USB/backup.tar.gz /etc** command will create a backup of /etc to /mnt/USB and compress the archive with gzip after it is created.

9. **A.** The **tar –cvjf /mnt/USB/backup.tar.bz2 /etc** command will create a backup of /etc to /mnt/USB and compress the archive with bzip2 after it is created.

10. **B.** The **tar –xvzf /mnt/USB/backup.tar.gz** command will decompress the archive with gzip and then extract all files from it to the current directory.

Managing Linux Processes and Log Files

In this chapter you will learn about:
- Understanding Linux processes
- Managing running processes
- Managing Linux log files

You've learned a great deal about Linux so far in this book. We started off easy, learning about the historical origins of Linux and the different roles it can play in your organization. As we've progressed through each chapter, you've been introduced to increasingly more challenging Linux concepts and skills. In this chapter, we're going to look at how the Linux operating system handles executable programs and scripts when they are run. Then we'll spend some time learning how to manage executables while they are running on the system. We'll end this chapter by looking at how logging information on Linux works.

Understanding Linux Processes

The key to being able to effectively manage Linux processes is to first understand how processes function within the operating system. For our purposes, a *process* is a program that has been loaded from a long-term storage device, usually a hard disk drive, into system RAM and is currently being processed by the CPU on the motherboard.

Many different types of programs can be executed to create a process. On your Linux system, the types of programs listed in Table 11-1 can be loaded into RAM and executed by the CPU.

Remember that the Linux operating system can run many processes "concurrently" on a single CPU. Depending on how your Linux system is being used, it may have only a few processes running at a given point in time or it may have hundreds of processes running concurrently.

In the preceding paragraph, I put the term *concurrently* in quotes because most CPUs can't truly run multiple processes at the same time. Instead, the Linux operating system quickly switches between the various processes running on the CPU, making it appear as if the CPU is working on multiple processes concurrently. However, the CPU only executes a single process at a time. All other processes currently "running" wait in the background for their turn. The operating system maintains a schedule that

Type of Program	Description
Binary executables	Programs that were originally created as a text file using a programming language, such as C or C++. The text file was then run through a compiler to create a binary file that can be processed by the CPU.
Internal shell commands	Some of the commands you enter at the shell prompt are binary files in the file system that are loaded and run by the CPU. For example, when you enter **top** at the shell prompt, you load the top binary file into memory. Other commands, however, are not binary executables. Instead, they are commands that are rolled into the shell program itself. For example, if you enter **exit** at a shell prompt, you are running an internal shell command. There is no executable file in the file system named "exit." Instead, the computer code associated with the exit function is stored within the shell program code itself.
Shell scripts	Text files that are executed through the shell itself. You can include commands to run binary executables within the text of any shell script. You will learn how to create shell scripts in a later chapter.

Table 11-1 Linux Programs Types

determines when each process is allowed access to the CPU. This is called *multitasking*. Because the switching between processes happens so fast, it appears, to you and me at least, that the CPU is executing multiple processes at the same time.

Be aware, however, that there are two exceptions to this rule. First of all, multicore CPUs can execute more than one process at a time because each core in the processor package is a separate CPU. For example, if there are two cores within the CPU, one core can execute one process while the other core works on another. The second exception to this rule is hyperthreading CPUs, which are designed such that a single processor can run more than one process at a time. Hyperthreading CPUs were once popular, but they have been pretty much replaced by multicore CPUs.

The Linux operating system uses several types of processes. Not all processes on your Linux system are the same. Some processes are created by the end user when he or she executes a command from the shell prompt or though the graphical desktop. These processes are called *user processes*. User processes are usually associated with some kind of end-user program running on the system.

For example, if you run the LibreOffice suite (using the **libreoffice** command) from the shell prompt, a user process for the LibreOffice program is created. This is shown in Figure 11-1.

Figure 11-1 User processes created by LibreOffice

The main point to remember about user processes is that they are called from within a shell and are associated with that shell session.

However, not all processes running on your system are user processes. In fact, most processes executing on a given Linux system will probably be of a different type called *system processes* or *daemons*. Unlike a user process, a system process does not usually provide an application or an interface for an end user to use. Instead, it provides system services such as a Web server or an FTP server, a file service such as Samba, a print service such as CUPS, a logging service, and so on. These processes run in the background and usually don't provide any kind of user interface.

For example, consider the processes shown in Figure 11-2.

 NOTE Some system processes (but not all of them) are noted with a *d* at the end of the name, which stands for *daemon*.

Notice that the system has many system processes running. System processes are usually (but not always) loaded by the system itself when it is booted up. Therefore, they are not associated with a particular shell instance. This is another key difference between user processes and system processes. User processes are tied to the particular shell instance they were called from. System processes are not.

```
                           tux@ws2:~                          _  □  x
 File  Edit  View  Search  Terminal  Help
14718 ?        00:00:00 main-menu
14722 ?        00:00:01 tomboy
14726 ?        00:00:00 gvfsd-trash
14735 ?        00:00:00 polkit-gnome-au
14736 ?        00:00:00 nm-applet
14737 ?        00:00:06 tracker-store
14739 ?        00:00:00 applet.py
14741 ?        00:00:01 tracker-miner-f
14742 ?        00:00:00 bluetooth-apple
14743 ?        00:00:00 gpk-update-icon
14744 ?        00:00:00 gnome-volume-co
14747 ?        00:00:00 gdu-notificatio
14748 ?        00:00:00 gnome-power-man
14759 ?        00:00:00 gnome-do
14763 ?        00:00:00 evolution-alarm
14766 ?        00:00:00 gvfsd-burn
14768 ?        00:00:00 gnome-screensav
14777 ?        00:00:01 gnome-do
14801 ?        00:00:01 gnome-terminal
14804 ?        00:00:00 gnome-pty-helpe
14805 pts/0    00:00:00 bash
14846 pts/0    00:00:02 soffice.bin
14895 pts/0    00:00:00 ps
tux@ws2:~>
```

Figure 11-2 System processes

By default, most Linux distributions boot with many daemons configured to automatically start at boot. Some of these daemons are critical to the overall functioning of the system; others are not. One of the first things I do after implementing a new Linux system, whether as a server or as a workstation, is to turn off all the daemons that aren't needed. Running unnecessary daemons consumes memory and CPU time. More seriously, it can also open up gaping security holes in the system. You need to be very aware of what system services are running on any Linux system you're responsible for. If the service is needed, keep it. If not, get rid of it!

To understand what daemons are critical to the overall function of the system and which aren't, you need to understand the heredity of Linux processes.

How Linux Processes Are Loaded

All Linux process are directly or indirectly loaded by one single process called *init* that is started by the Linux kernel when the system boots.

Any process running on a Linux system can launch additional processes. The process that launched the new process is called the *parent process*. The new process is called the *child process*.

This parent/child relationship constitutes the *heredity* of Linux processes. Because any process, including child processes, can launch additional processes, it is possible to have many generations of processes running on a system, as shown in Figure 11-3.

In Figure 11-3, the first parent process started (or *spawned*) three child processes. Each of these three child processes spawned child processes of their own, making the first parent process a grandparent! Do you see now why we call it the "heredity" of processes?

For any process on a Linux system, we need to be able to uniquely identify it as well as its heredity. Whenever a process is created on a Linux system, it is assigned two numbers:

- **Process ID (PID) Number**   A number assigned to each process that uniquely identifies it on the system.

- **Parent Process ID (PPID) Number**   The PID of the process's parent process (that is, the process that spawned it).

Figure 11-3
The generations
of Linux
processes

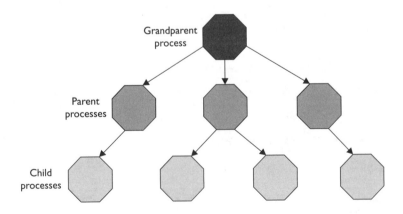

By assigning these two numbers to each process, we can track the heredity of any process through the system. The Linux kernel uses the *process table* to keep track of the processes running on the system. The process table is maintained in memory by the operating system to facilitate switching between processes, scheduling processes, and prioritizing processes. Each entry in the table contains information about one specific running process, such as the process name, the state of the process, the priority of the process, and the memory addresses used by the process.

Notice in Figure 11-3 that I've depicted a grandparent process that spawned all of the other processes. This figure is drawn from a conceptual standpoint to illustrate the nature of the parent/child relationships between processes. However, it also describes the hierarchy of generations in a Linux system. There really is a grandparent process that spawns all other processes: the *init* process. The kernel loads the init process automatically during bootup. The init process then launches child processes, such as a login shell, that in turn launch other processes, such as that used by the vi utility, as shown in Figure 11-4.

While other processes are assigned a PID randomly from the operating system's table of available PID numbers, the init process is always assigned a PID of 1. This brings up an interesting point. If the init process is the first process from which all other processes descend, what is its PPID? Does it even have one? Actually, it does. Because the init process is launched directly by the Linux kernel (which always has a PID of 0), the PPID of the init process is always 0. This is shown in Figure 11-5.

The init process is responsible for launching all system processes that are configured to automatically start on boot. It also creates a login shell that is used for login.

This brings up an important point. Notice in Figure 11-4 that I've placed a second bash shell beneath the login shell. You might wonder why I didn't just run vi from within the login shell.

Figure 11-4
The init process as the grandparent of all other processes

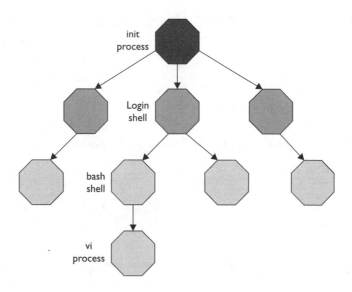

Figure 11-5
The PPID of the
init process

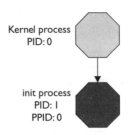

Kernel process
PID: 0

init process
PID: 1
PPID: 0

Actually, in this figure, vi was, in fact, launched from the login shell. It shows a second shell between the vi process and the login shell because any time you run a command from within any shell (whether it's a login shell or a standard shell session), a second shell session is created, called a *subshell*. The process for the command you entered is run within it. The subshell is a separate process in and of itself and has its own PID assigned. The PPID of the subshell is the PID of the shell where the command was entered.

The subshell process remains active for as long as the command that was entered at the shell prompt is in use. The process for the command runs within the subshell and is assigned its own PID. The PPID of the command's process is, of course, the PID of the subshell it's running within. When the command process is complete and has exited, the subshell is terminated and control is returned back to the original shell session. This process of creating a new subshell and running the command process within it is called *forking*.

For example, in Figure 11-6, the user issues the vi command at the shell prompt of a bash shell. A new subshell is created and the vi process is run within it. When the user exits vi, the subshell is destroyed and control is returned to the original shell instance.

Managing Running Processes

Managing running processes is one of the most important tasks to perform on the Linux systems you support. In this part of this chapter, we'll discuss the following topics:

- Starting system processes
- Viewing running processes
- Prioritizing processes

Figure 11-6
Running a process
from the shell
prompt

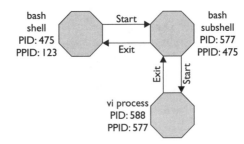

bash
shell
PID: 475
PPID: 123

Start

Exit

bash
subshell
PID: 577
PPID: 475

Exit   Start

vi process
PID: 588
PPID: 577

- Managing foreground and background processes
- Ending a running process

Starting System Processes

There are two basic ways to start a process on a Linux system. For a user process, you enter the command or script name at the shell prompt. For example, to run the vi program, you enter **vi** at the shell prompt. When you do, the vi process is created, as shown here:

```
tux@ws2:~/Desktop> ps -a
  PID TTY          TIME CMD
 3523 pts/3    00:00:00 vi
 4782 pts/0    00:00:00 ps
```

For system processes, however, you use an *init script*. An init script is used by the init process to start processes on system boot. These scripts are stored in a specific directory on your Linux system. Which directory they are stored in depends on your Linux distribution. Most Linux distributions use one of two types of init scripts:

- **System V** Linux distributions that use System V init scripts store them in the /etc/rc.d directory. Within /etc/rc.d are a series of subdirectories named rc0.d through rc6.d. Each of these directories is associated with a particular runlevel. Within each of these subdirectories are symbolic links that point to the init scripts for your system daemons, which reside in /etc/rc.d/init.d. Red Hat Linux and Fedora use System V–type init scripts.

- **BSD** Other Linux distributions use BSD-style init scripts. These scripts reside in the /etc/init.d directory. Within /etc/init.d are a series of directories named rc0.d through rc6.d. As with System V init scripts, these directories are associated with specific runlevels. These directories contain links that point to the init scripts in /etc/init.d. OpenSUSE uses this type of init script.

In addition to using the init process to run these scripts, you can run these scripts from the command prompt. Simply enter **/etc/init.d/**<i>script_name</i> at the shell prompt (on a BSD-style system) or **/etc/rc.d/init.d/**<i>script_name</i> (on a System V–style system). If you're not sure of which script name you should use, you can use the ls command to generate a listing of scripts in the script directory, as shown in Figure 11-7.

The actual scripts in your init directory depend on which services you've installed on your particular system. Whenever you install a service on your system, a corresponding init script is automatically installed in your init script directory. Once installed, you can run a service by running its init script from the command prompt. The syntax is (on a BSD-style system):

```
/etc/init.d/script_name start | stop | restart
```

For example, to run the smb service, you would enter **/etc/init.d/smb start** at the shell prompt. To stop it, you would enter **/etc/init.d/smb stop**. To restart it, you would enter **/etc/init.d/smb restart**.

```
tux@ws2:~
File  Edit  View  Search  Terminal  Help

tux@ws2:~> ls /etc/init.d/
aaeventd             boot.local           joystick           rc6.d
acpid                boot.localfs         kbd                rcS.d
after.local          boot.localnet        kexec              reboot
alsasound            boot.lvm             lirc               rpcbind
atd                  boot.md              mdadmd             rpmconfigcheck
auditd               boot.multipath       microcode.ctl      rsyncd
autofs               boot.proc            multipathd         setserial
autoyast             boot.rootfsck        network            single
avahi-daemon         boot.startpreload    network-remotefs   skeleton
avahi-dnsconfd       boot.swap            nfs                skeleton.compat
before.local         boot.sysctl          nmb                smartd
bluez-coldplug       boot.udev            nscd               smb
boot                 boot.udev_retry      ntp                smolt
boot.apparmor        cifs                 openvpn            splash
boot.cgroup          cpufreq              pm-profiler        splash_early
boot.cleanup         cron                 postfix            sshd
boot.clock           cups                 powerd             stoppreload
boot.crypto          dbus                 powerfail          SuSEfirewall2_init
boot.crypto-early    dnsmasq              random             SuSEfirewall2_setup
boot.cycle           earlysyslog          raw                svnserve
boot.d               earlyxdm             rc                 syslog
boot.device-mapper   fbset                rc0.d              vmware-tools
boot.dmraid          gpm                  rc1.d              xdm
boot.ipconfig        halt                 rc2.d              xfs
boot.klog            halt.local           rc3.d              xinetd
boot.ldconfig        haveged              rc4.d              ypbind
boot.loadmodules     inputattach          rc5.d
tux@ws2:~> 
```

Figure 11-7 Init scripts in /etc/init.d

On some distributions, you can also use the rc script to start, stop, or restart a service process without having to specify the full path to the script file. The syntax is rc*script_name* start | stop | restart. For example, to start the smb service, you could enter **rcsbm start** at the shell prompt. To stop it, you could enter **rcsmb stop**. You could also use the restart option to restart it.

Viewing Running Processes

In this part of the chapter, we're going to discuss how to view running processes on your system. We'll cover the following tools:

- Using top
- Using ps
- Using free

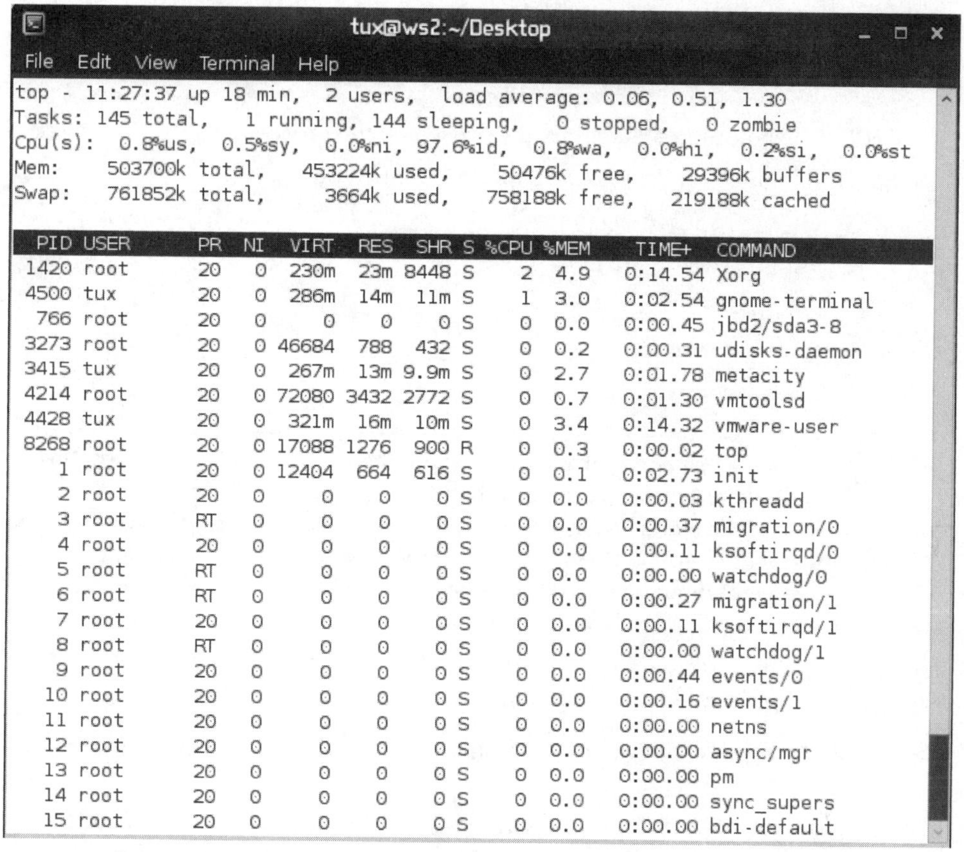

```
                              tux@ws2:~/Desktop                    _  □  x
 File   Edit   View   Terminal   Help
top - 11:27:37 up 18 min,  2 users,  load average: 0.06, 0.51, 1.30
Tasks: 145 total,   1 running, 144 sleeping,   0 stopped,   0 zombie
Cpu(s):  0.8%us,  0.5%sy,  0.0%ni, 97.6%id,  0.8%wa,  0.0%hi,  0.2%si,  0.0%st
Mem:    503700k total,   453224k used,   50476k free,    29396k buffers
Swap:   761852k total,     3664k used,  758188k free,   219188k cached

  PID USER      PR  NI  VIRT  RES  SHR S %CPU %MEM    TIME+  COMMAND
 1420 root      20   0  230m  23m 8448 S    2  4.9  0:14.54 Xorg
 4500 tux       20   0  286m  14m  11m S    1  3.0  0:02.54 gnome-terminal
  766 root      20   0     0    0    0 S    0  0.0  0:00.45 jbd2/sda3-8
 3273 root      20   0 46684  788  432 S    0  0.2  0:00.31 udisks-daemon
 3415 tux       20   0  267m  13m 9.9m S    0  2.7  0:01.78 metacity
 4214 root      20   0 72080 3432 2772 S    0  0.7  0:01.30 vmtoolsd
 4428 tux       20   0  321m  16m  10m S    0  3.4  0:14.32 vmware-user
 8268 root      20   0 17088 1276  900 R    0  0.3  0:00.02 top
    1 root      20   0 12404  664  616 S    0  0.1  0:02.73 init
    2 root      20   0     0    0    0 S    0  0.0  0:00.03 kthreadd
    3 root      RT   0     0    0    0 S    0  0.0  0:00.37 migration/0
    4 root      20   0     0    0    0 S    0  0.0  0:00.11 ksoftirqd/0
    5 root      RT   0     0    0    0 S    0  0.0  0:00.00 watchdog/0
    6 root      RT   0     0    0    0 S    0  0.0  0:00.27 migration/1
    7 root      20   0     0    0    0 S    0  0.0  0:00.11 ksoftirqd/1
    8 root      RT   0     0    0    0 S    0  0.0  0:00.00 watchdog/1
    9 root      20   0     0    0    0 S    0  0.0  0:00.44 events/0
   10 root      20   0     0    0    0 S    0  0.0  0:00.16 events/1
   11 root      20   0     0    0    0 S    0  0.0  0:00.00 netns
   12 root      20   0     0    0    0 S    0  0.0  0:00.00 async/mgr
   13 root      20   0     0    0    0 S    0  0.0  0:00.00 pm
   14 root      20   0     0    0    0 S    0  0.0  0:00.00 sync_supers
   15 root      20   0     0    0    0 S    0  0.0  0:00.00 bdi-default
```

Figure 11-8   Using top to view running processes

Using top

Linux provides a wide variety of tools for viewing running processes on your system. One of my favorites is the venerable top utility. You run top by entering **top** at the shell prompt. When you do, the interface shown in Figure 11-8 is displayed.

In Figure 11-8, you can see that top displays some of your running processes, one on each line. The following columns display information about each process:

- **PID**   The process ID of the process.
- **USER**   The name of the user that owns the process.
- **PR**   The priority assigned to the process. (We'll discuss process priorities later in this chapter.)
- **NI**   The nice value of the process. (We'll talk about what this means later in this chapter.)

- **VIRT**   The amount of virtual memory used by the process.

- **RES**   The amount of physical RAM the process is using (its resident size) in kilobytes.

- **SHR**   The amount of shared memory used by the process.

- **S**   The status of the process. Possible values include

    - **D**   Uninterruptibly sleeping

    - **R**   Running

    - **S**   Sleeping

    - **T**   Traced or stopped

    - **Z**   Zombied

NOTE   A *zombied* process is one where the process has finished executing and exited, but the process's parent didn't get notified that it was finished and hasn't released the child process's PID. A zombied process may eventually clear up on its own. If it doesn't, you may need to manually kill the parent process. We'll talk about how to do this later in the chapter.

- **%CPU**   The percentage of CPU time used by the process.

- **%MEM**   The percentage of available physical RAM used by the process.

- **TIME+**   The total amount of CPU time the process has consumed since being started.

- **COMMAND**   The name of the command that was entered to start the process.

What I like best about top is that it's dynamic. The screen is constantly updated to reflect the latest information about each process, and you can sort the information as well. Pressing H while top is running displays the help screen, which provides you with the keystrokes required to sort by a particular category, as shown in Figure 11-9.

This screen also shows you how to use other options with top. For example, you can press F to display a list of columns that you can add to the display, as shown in Figure 11-10.

Fields that will be displayed are indicated with an asterisk (*). To add or remove a field, just press the appropriate letter. This will toggle the asterisk on or off to determine whether or not the field is displayed. You can also press U to specify that only the processes associated with a specific user be displayed.

The only thing I don't like about top is that it shows a limited number of processes running on your system. There will be times when you need to see everything running on your system. In this situation, top just doesn't cut it, and you need to use the ps utility.

Using ps
The ps utility displays running processes on your system. Unlike top, which displays processes dynamically, ps displays a snapshot of the current processes running.

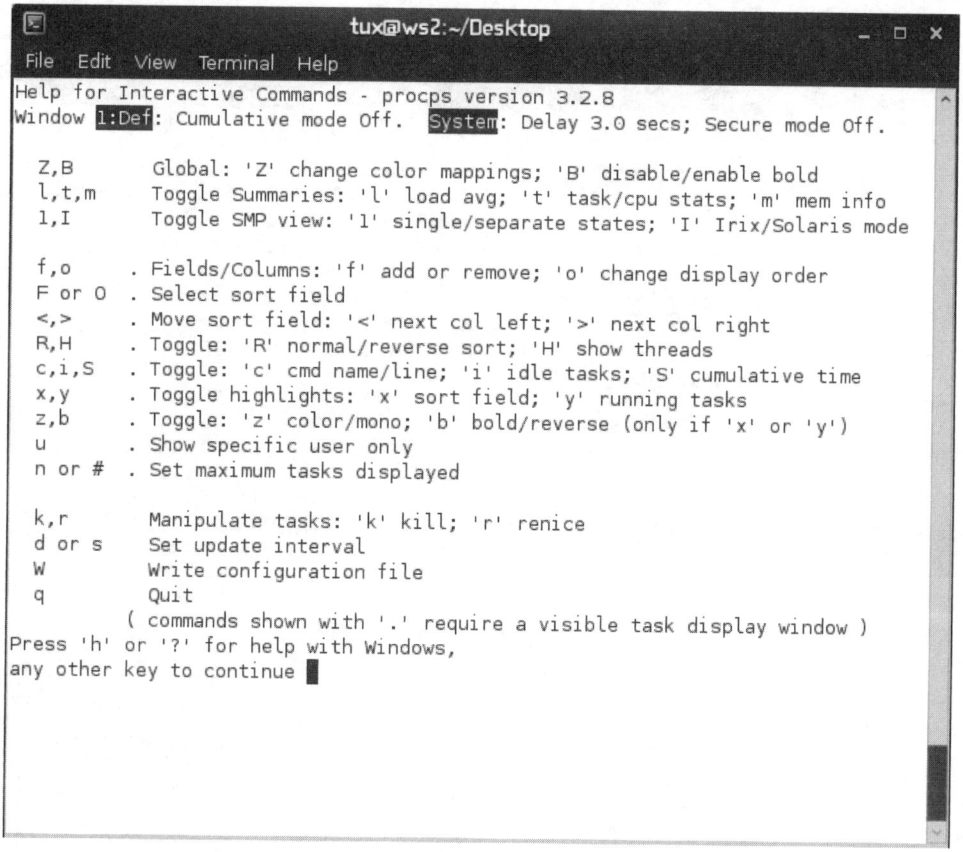

Figure 11-9 Viewing the top help screen

By entering **ps**, you can view the processes associated with the *current* shell, as shown here.

```
ws2:~ # ps
  PID TTY          TIME CMD
 8359 pts/2    00:00:00 su
 8363 pts/2    00:00:00 bash
 8396 pts/2    00:00:00 ps
ws2:~ #
```

In this example, the following processes are displayed by ps:

- **su**   The su utility is in use inside this shell to switch to the root user account.
- **bash**   The current bash shell session.
- **ps**   Because ps is in use to list current processes, its process is also listed.

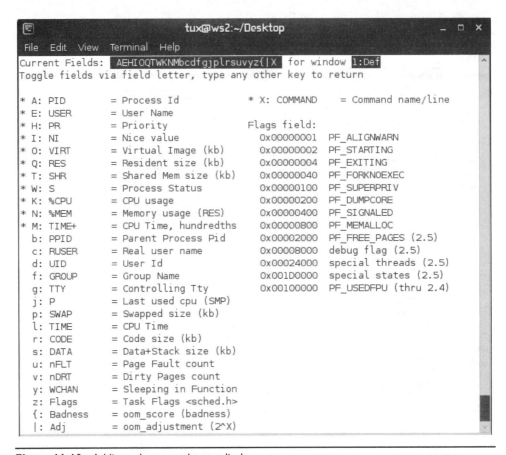

Figure 11-10 Adding columns to the top display

Notice that the following information is displayed by default:

- **PID** The process ID of the process.

- **TTY** The name of the terminal session (shell) that the process is running within.

- **TIME** The amount of CPU time used by the process.

- **CMD** The name of the command that was entered to create the process.

Notice that only three processes are listed even though many different processes were running on this system. I had top running in a separate shell, and the X server and the GNOME desktop environment were running as well. Why didn't they show up in the list? It's because, by default, ps only shows processes associated with the current shell. Hence, only the shell, su, and ps processes are displayed.

To see all processes running on the system, you need to use the –e option with ps. Here is an example:

```
ws2:~ # ps -e
   PID TTY           TIME CMD
     1 ?         00:00:02 init
     2 ?         00:00:00 kthreadd
     3 ?         00:00:00 migration/0
     4 ?         00:00:00 ksoftirqd/0
     5 ?         00:00:00 watchdog/0
     6 ?         00:00:00 migration/1
     7 ?         00:00:00 ksoftirqd/1
     8 ?         00:00:00 watchdog/1
     9 ?         00:00:00 events/0
    10 ?         00:00:00 events/1
    11 ?         00:00:00 netns
...
```

As you can see in this example, the –e option results in many more processes being displayed by the ps command. Also notice that most of the processes shown have a ? in the TTY column. This indicates the process is a system process. Remember, system processes (daemons) are loaded by the init process at startup and therefore are not associated with any shell. Because of this, a ? is displayed in the TTY column in the output of ps.

Another thing you may notice in the two preceding examples is that the amount of detail displayed by ps is rather limited as compared to top. You can use the –f option with ps to display more detail. In the next example, the –e and –f options have been used together in the ps command to display extended information about every process running on the system:

```
ws2:~ # ps -ef
UID         PID  PPID  C STIME TTY          TIME CMD
root          1     0  0 11:09 ?        00:00:02 init [5]
root          2     0  0 11:09 ?        00:00:00 [kthreadd]
root          3     2  0 11:09 ?        00:00:00 [migration/0]
root          4     2  0 11:09 ?        00:00:00 [ksoftirqd/0]
root          5     2  0 11:09 ?        00:00:00 [watchdog/0]
root          6     2  0 11:09 ?        00:00:00 [migration/1]
root          7     2  0 11:09 ?        00:00:00 [ksoftirqd/1]
root          8     2  0 11:09 ?        00:00:00 [watchdog/1]
root          9     2  0 11:09 ?        00:00:00 [events/0]
root         10     2  0 11:09 ?        00:00:00 [events/1]
root         11     2  0 11:09 ?        00:00:00 [netns]
...
```

With the –f option, you can view additional information, including the following:

- **UID**   The user ID of the process's owner.
- **PPID**   The PID of the process's parent process.
- **C**   The amount of processor time utilized by the process.
- **STIME**   The time that the process started.

If you really want to crank things up, you can also use the –l option with the ps command to display the long format of the ps output. Here is an example:

```
ws2:~ # ps -efl
F S UID        PID  PPID  C PRI  NI ADDR SZ WCHAN  STIME TTY         TIME CMD
4 S root         1     0  0  80   0 -  3101 3959   11:09 ?       00:00:02 init
1 S root         2     0  0  80   0 -     0 kthrea 11:09 ?       00:00:00 [kth]
1 S root         3     2  0 -40   - -     0 migrat 11:09 ?       00:00:00 [mig]
1 S root         4     2  0  80   0 -     0 run_ks 11:09 ?       00:00:00 [kso]
5 S root         5     2  0 -40   - -     0 watchd 11:09 ?       00:00:00 [wat]
1 S root         6     2  0 -40   - -     0 migrat 11:09 ?       00:00:00 [mig]
1 S root         7     2  0  80   0 -     0 run_ks 11:09 ?       00:00:00 [kso]
5 S root         8     2  0 -40   - -     0 watchd 11:09 ?       00:00:00 [wat]
1 S root         9     2  0  80   0 -     0 worker 11:09 ?       00:00:00 [eve]
1 S root        10     2  0  80   0 -     0 worker 11:09 ?       00:00:00 [eve]
1 S root        11     2  0  80   0 -     0 worker 11:09 ?       00:00:00 [net]
...
```

With the –l option, you can view the following information about processes running on your system:

- **F**   The flags associated with the process. This column uses the following codes:
  - **1**   Forked but didn't execute
  - **4**   Used root privileges
- **S**   The state of the process. This column uses the following codes:
  - **D**   Uninterruptible sleep
  - **R**   Running
  - **S**   Interruptible sleep
  - **T**   Stopped or traced
  - **Z**   Zombied
- **PRI**   The priority of the process.
- **ADDR**   The memory address of the process.
- **NI**   The nice value of the process. We'll talk about what this means in the next section.
- **SZ**   The size of the process.
- **WCHAN**   The name of the kernel function in which the process is sleeping. You will see a dash (–) in this column if the process is currently running.

Using free

Part of managing processes on your Linux system is knowing how much memory has been used and how much is available. As we discussed earlier, you can use the output of top to view this information.

You can also use the free command to do this. The free command displays the amount of free and allocated RAM and swap memory in your system. You can use the

–m option to display memory statistics in megabytes. You can also use the –t option to display totals for each category of information. In the following example, the free –mt command has been issued to view memory statistics:

```
tux@ws2:~> free -mt
             total      used      free    shared    buffers    cached
Mem:          1490      1401        88         0         35      1209
-/+ buffers/cache:       157      1332
Swap:         2053         0      2053
Total:        3544      1401      2142
tux@ws2:~>
```

Prioritizing Processes

Recall from the first part of this chapter that Linux is a multitasking operating system. It rotates CPU time between each of the processes running on the system, creating the illusion that all of the processes are running concurrently.

Because Linux is a multitasking operating system, you can specify a priority level for each process to determine how much CPU time a given process gets in relation to other processes on the system.

By default, Linux tries to equalize the amount of CPU time given to all of the processes on the system. However, depending on how the system is deployed, you may want a particular process to have a higher priority than other processes. This can be done using several Linux utilities. In this part of the chapter, we'll review the following:

- Setting priorities with nice
- Setting priorities of running processes with renice

Setting Priorities with nice

The nice utility can be used on Linux to launch a program with a different priority level. Recall from our previous discussion of top and ps that each process running on your system has a PR and NI value associated with it. This is shown in Figure 11-11.

The PR value is the process's kernel priority. The higher the number, the lower the priority of the process. The lower the number, the higher the priority of the process. The NI value is the nice value of the process, which is factored into the kernel calculations that determine the priority of the process. The nice value for any Linux process can range between –20 and +19. The lower the nice value, the *higher* the priority of the process.

You can't directly manipulate the priority of a process, but you can manipulate the process's nice value. The easiest way to do this is to set the nice value with the nice command when you initially run the command that launches the process. The syntax for using nice is nice –n *nice_level command*.

For example, suppose I wanted to launch the vi program and increase its priority on the system by decreasing its nice level to a value of –5. Before I do so, vi runs on my system with a priority of 80, as shown in this example:

```
ws2:~ # ps -el | grep vi
0 S  1000  8435  8425  2  80   0 - 6823 -        pts/0    00:00:00 vi
```

```
┌─────────────────────────────────────────────────────────────────────────┐
│ 🖳                          tux@ws2:~/Desktop                     _ □ ✕   │
├─────────────────────────────────────────────────────────────────────────┤
│ File  Edit  View  Terminal  Help                                         │
│ top - 11:27:37 up 18 min,  2 users,  load average: 0.06, 0.51, 1.30      │
│ Tasks: 145 total,   1 running, 144 sleeping,   0 stopped,   0 zombie     │
│ Cpu(s):  0.8%us,  0.5%sy,  0.0%ni, 97.6%id,  0.8%wa,  0.0%hi,  0.2%si, 0.0%st│
│ Mem:    503700k total,   453224k used,   50476k free,   29396k buffers   │
│ Swap:   761852k total,     3664k used,  758188k free,  219188k cached    │
│                                                                          │
│   PID USER      PR  NI  VIRT  RES  SHR S %CPU %MEM   TIME+  COMMAND       │
│  1420 root      20   0  230m  23m 8448 S    2  4.9  0:14.54 Xorg          │
│  4500 tux       20   0  286m  14m  11m S    1  3.0  0:02.54 gnome-terminal│
│   766 root      20   0     0    0    0 S    0  0.0  0:00.45 jbd2/sda3-8   │
│  3273 root      20   0 46684  788  432 S    0  0.2  0:00.31 udisks-daemon │
│  3415 tux       20   0  267m  13m 9.9m S    0  2.7  0:01.78 metacity      │
│  4214 root      20   0 72080 3432 2772 S    0  0.7  0:01.30 vmtoolsd      │
│  4428 tux       20   0  321m  16m  10m S    0  3.4  0:14.32 vmware-user   │
│  8268 root      20   0 17088 1276  900 R    0  0.3  0:00.02 top           │
│     1 root      20   0 12404  664  616 S    0  0.1  0:02.73 init          │
│     2 root      20   0     0    0    0 S    0  0.0  0:00.03 kthreadd      │
│     3 root      RT   0     0    0    0 S    0  0.0  0:00.37 migration/0   │
│     4 root      20   0     0    0    0 S    0  0.0  0:00.11 ksoftirqd/0   │
│     5 root      RT   0     0    0    0 S    0  0.0  0:00.00 watchdog/0    │
│     6 root      RT   0     0    0    0 S    0  0.0  0:00.27 migration/1   │
│     7 root      20   0     0    0    0 S    0  0.0  0:00.11 ksoftirqd/1   │
│     8 root      RT   0     0    0    0 S    0  0.0  0:00.00 watchdog/1    │
│     9 root      20   0     0    0    0 S    0  0.0  0:00.44 events/0      │
│    10 root      20   0     0    0    0 S    0  0.0  0:00.16 events/1      │
│    11 root      20   0     0    0    0 S    0  0.0  0:00.00 netns         │
│    12 root      20   0     0    0    0 S    0  0.0  0:00.00 async/mgr     │
│    13 root      20   0     0    0    0 S    0  0.0  0:00.00 pm            │
│    14 root      20   0     0    0    0 S    0  0.0  0:00.00 sync_supers   │
│    15 root      20   0     0    0    0 S    0  0.0  0:00.00 bdi-default   │
└─────────────────────────────────────────────────────────────────────────┘
```

Figure 11-11 Viewing PR and NI values

Notice that the vi process has a default nice level of 0. The kernel uses this value to calculate the overall priority of the process, which comes out to a value of 80. I could adjust this process's priority level to a higher level by entering **nice –n –15 vi** at the shell prompt. After doing so, the priority and nice values of the vi process are decreased, increasing its priority level on the system. This is shown in the next example:

```
ws2:~ # ps -el | grep vi
4 S    0  8488  8455   0  65 -15 -  6533 -        pts/0     00:00:00 vi
```

Notice that the nice value was decreased to a value of –15. This caused the overall priority of the process to be reduced to a value of 65.

Be aware that Linux is hesitant to allow you to reduce the value of nice for processes running on the system. Because Linux is a true multiuser operating system, it's possible for multiple users on the same system to adjust the nice values of their own processes. Naturally, every user on the system thinks that his or her process is much more important than anyone else's and may be tempted to crank that nice value clear down to –20 for just about everything he or she runs.

To keep this from happening, Linux won't let you adjust the nice value of a process below 0 unless you are logged in as root. Basically, if you aren't root, you won't be allowed to use a negative number with the nice command.

The nice command works great for modifying the nice value when running a command to start a process. But what can you do if the process you want to modify is already running? You can't use nice in this situation; you have to use the renice command instead.

Setting Priorities of Running Processes with renice

Instead of having to kill a process and restart it with nice to set its nice value, you can use the renice command to adjust the nice value of a process that is currently running on the system. The syntax for using this command is renice *nice_value PID*.

For example, in the last example, the PID of the vi process is 8488. If I wanted to adjust the priority of the vi process to a lower level without unloading the program, I could enter **renice 4 8488** at the shell prompt, as shown in this example:

```
ws2:~ # renice 4 8488
8488: old priority -15, new priority 4
ws2:~ # ps -elf | grep vi
4 S root       8488  8455  0  84   4 -  6533 -       08:40 pts/0   00:00:00 vi
```

As you can see in this example, the nice value of the vi process was increased from –15 to 4. This caused the overall priority of the process to go from 65 to 84, decreasing the process's overall priority level. Just as with nice, you must be logged in as root to adjust the nice level of a running process to a negative number.

Managing Foreground and Background Processes

In this part of the chapter, we'll discuss running processes in the foreground and background. We'll address the following topics:

- Running processes in the background
- Switching processes between the background and the foreground

Running Processes in the Background

Recall from our earlier discussion of processes that, when you enter any command at the shell prompt, a subshell is created and the process is run within it. As soon as the process exits, the subshell is destroyed. During the time that the process is running, the shell prompt of the parent shell disappears. You can't do anything at the shell prompt unless you open a new terminal session.

This happens because the process runs in the *foreground*. This behavior is even more apparent when running a graphical application from the shell prompt. In Figure 11-12, the LibreOffice application has been launched from the shell prompt using the libreoffice command.

Notice in Figure 11-12 that the cursor in the shell is unavailable. It will remain so until LibreOffice is closed. Only then can additional commands be entered at this shell prompt.

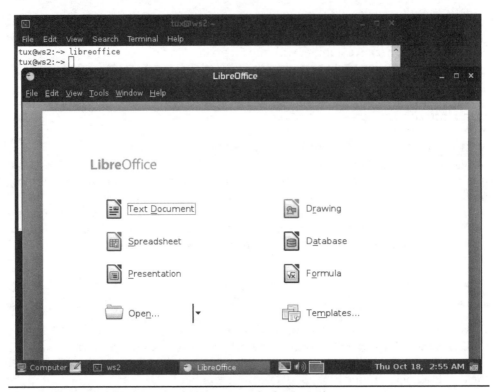

Figure 11-12 Launching a graphical application in the foreground

This is the default behavior for all commands entered at the shell prompt, whether the program is a text-based shell program or a graphical X Window program. However, it is possible to run the program in the *background*. If you do this, the program you launch will run normally. However, control will be returned immediately to the shell. You can then use the shell to launch other programs or perform other shell tasks.

Running a program in the background is very easy. All you have to do is append an ampersand (&) character to the command. This tells the shell to run the program in the background. In Figure 11-13, the LibreOffice application has been launched again. However, this time an ampersand was appended to the end of the command, causing it to run in the background.

Notice in Figure 11-13 that two values were displayed on the screen after the process was run in the background. The first value [1] is the background job ID that was assigned to the background job. The second value is the PID of the process. You can view all background jobs running on the system by entering **jobs** at the shell prompt, like this:

```
tux@ws2:~/Desktop> jobs
[1]+  Done                          libreoffice
tux@ws2:~/Desktop>
```

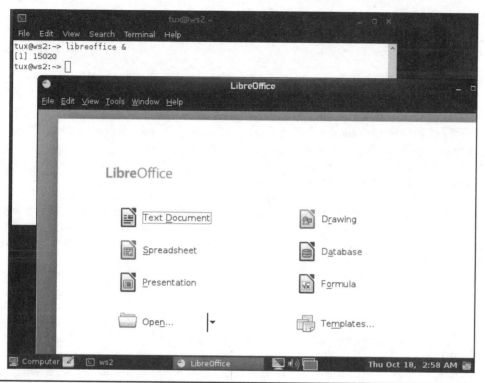

Figure 11-13 Running an application in the background

In this example, the output of the jobs command displays the status of the job as well as the name of the command that was run to create the background job. Let's next discuss how to move jobs from the background to foreground and vice versa.

Switching Processes Between the Background and the Foreground

Just because a process was started in the background or the foreground doesn't mean it has to stay there. You can switch a process between the foreground and the background while it's running. This is done using the following commands:

- **fg** Moves a background process to the foreground. The syntax is fg *job_ID*.
- **bg** Moves a foreground process to the background. To use this utility, you must first assign the foreground job a background job ID by pressing CTRL-Z. When you do this, you'll see the process stop and a background job ID assigned to the process. You can then enter **bg *job_ID*** to move the process to the background.

In the next example, the vi program was loaded as per normal into the foreground. It was then stopped using CTRL-Z, where it was assigned a job ID of 1. It was then sent to the background using the bg 1 command.

```
tux@ws2:~/Desktop> vi

[1]+  Stopped                    vi
tux@ws2:~/Desktop> bg 1
[1]+ vi &
tux@ws2:~/Desktop>
```

Ending a Running Process

To this point in this chapter, we've done just about everything you can think of to processes on a Linux system. We've loaded them, viewed them, prioritized them, and moved them to the background and to the foreground. The one task we've yet to cover is how to end a process that is running on the system.

Normally, you use the exit function that is coded into nearly all programs to end a running process. For example, you enter :**exit** in vi to exit the editor and end its process. Sometimes, however, processes hang and, no matter what you do, you can't get them to close properly. In this situation, you may need to manually kill the hung process. This can be done in two ways:

- Using kill
- Using killall

The kill command terminates a process. The syntax for using kill is kill *–signal PID*. The *PID* parameter is the PID of the process you want to kill. You can also send a specific kill signal to the process. This is one of the things about kill that I love. There are about 64 different types of kill signals you can send to the process. The most useful of these include the following:

- **SIGHUP**   Kill signal 1. This signal restarts the process. After a restart, the process will have exactly the same PID it had before. This is a very useful option for restarting a service for which you've made changes in a configuration file.
- **SIGINT**   Kill signal 2. This signal sends a CTRL-C key sequence to the process.
- **SIGKILL**   Kill signal 9. This is a brute-force signal that kills the process. If the process was hung badly, this option will force it to stop. However, the process may not clean up after itself if this signal is used, and the resources allocated to the process may remain allocated until the system is restarted.
- **SIGTERM**   Kill signal 15. This signal tells the process to terminate immediately. This is the default signal sent by kill if you omit a signal in the command line. This signal allows the process to clean up after itself before exiting.

When using kill, you can use the text of the signal, such as SIGTERM, or you can use the signal's number, such as 15. You will need to use ps or top to first identify the PID of the process before you can use kill to stop it. Here, for example, the vi process is running with a PID of 8312:

```
ws2:~ # ps
  PID TTY          TIME CMD
 8278 pts/0    00:00:00 su
```

```
 8279 pts/0    00:00:00 bash
 8312 pts/0    00:00:00 vi
 8313 pts/0    00:00:00 ps
ws2:~ # kill -SIGTERM 8312
ws2:~ #
```

In this example, I entered **kill –SIGTERM 8312** to kill the vi process. I could have also entered **kill –15 8312** and accomplished exactly the same task. Because the SIGTERM signal allows the process to return its resources before exiting, the vi process ends cleanly.

This brings up a mistake I've seen many new Linux admins make when working with kill. They frequently go for the jugular before trying less forceful signals first. Yes, using SIGKILL will work, but it's best if you try other, cleaner signals first. Only if these signals fail should you try a harsher signal. If you experience a hung process that needs to be killed, I suggest you use the following sequence:

1. Send a SIGINT first. If it doesn't respond, go to Step 2.

2. Send a SIGTERM. Usually, this will fix the problem and allow the process to exit cleanly. If it doesn't, go to Step 3.

3. Send a SIGKILL.

In addition to kill, you can also use the killall command to kill processes, which is very similar to the kill command. The syntax is almost the same. The main difference is that killall uses the command name of the process to be killed instead of its PID. For example, if I wanted to kill the vi process in the preceding example with killall instead of kill, I would have entered **killall –15 vi**. This command sends the SIGTERM signal to the process named vi.

I strongly suggest you spend some time reviewing the man page for killall. It's quite extensive and contains excellent information. For example, it will show you how to use the –u option with killall to end processes owned by a specific user.

Let's practice working with Linux processes in the following exercise.

Exercise 11-1: Working with Linux Processes In this exercise, you will practice using shell commands to manage processes running on your system. Complete the following:

1. Boot your Linux system and log in as a standard user.

2. Open a terminal session.

3. Switch to your root user account by entering **su –** followed by your root user's password.

4. Practice starting system processes by doing the following:

   a. At the shell prompt, enter **rcatd status**. What's the status of your at daemon? (For most distributions, the atd daemon is not configured to run by default.)

   b. Start the atd daemon by entering **rcatd start** at the shell prompt.

   c. Enter rcatd status again at the shell prompt. The atd service should now be shown as running.

5. Practice using top by doing the following:

   a. At the shell prompt, enter **top**.

   b. View your running processes.

   c. Press H to access the top help screen. Which keystroke will sort the display by CPU stats?

   d. Press T to sort the display by CPU stats. Which processes are using the most CPU time on your system?

   e. Press M to sort the display by memory usage. Which processes are using the most memory?

   f. Add columns by pressing F.

   g. Add the PPID column to the display by pressing B, then press SPACEBAR. You should now see the PPID of each process added to the display.

   h. Exit top by pressing Q.

6. Practice using the ps utility to view processes by doing the following:

   a. At the shell prompt, enter **ps**. What processes are associated with the current shell session?

   b. View all running processes on the system by entering **ps –ef | more** at the shell prompt.

   c. Press SPACEBAR until you find the atd service. What user name does atd run under? (On most distributions, it should run under the at user.)

   d. At the shell prompt, enter **ps –el | less**.

   e. Locate the Status (S) column.

   f. Press SPACEBAR until you find the atd service. What is the status of the service? (Because it isn't being used at the moment, it's probably sleeping.)

7. Practice managing process priorities by completing the following:

   a. At the shell prompt, enter **top**.

   b. What are the priority (PR) and nice (NI) values associated with the top processes? (For most distributions, these values should be 16 and 0.)

   c. Press Q to stop the top process.

   d. At the shell prompt, enter **nice –n –20 top**. Now what are the PR and NI values for the top process?

   e. Note the PID for the top process.

   f. Open a new terminal window and use su to switch to root.

   g. At the shell prompt, adjust the nice value of the top process while it's running by entering **renice 1 top_PID**.

   h. Switch back to the first terminal session where top is running. What are its PR and NI values now?

   i. Press Q to exit top.

8. Practice switching processes between the foreground and the background by doing the following:

   a. Load top again by entering **top** at the shell prompt.

   b. In the terminal where top is running, press CTRL-Z.

   c. Note the background job ID number assigned to the process.

   d. At the shell prompt, enter **bg** *background_job_ID*. The output from top disappears while the process runs in the background.

   e. Press CTRL-C.

   f. At the shell prompt, enter **fg** *background_job_ID*. The output from top reappears as the process now runs in the foreground.

9. Practice killing processes by completing the following:

   a. Ensure that top is still running.

   b. Switch to your other terminal session where you're logged in as root.

   c. At the shell prompt, enter **ps –e | grep top**.

   d. Note the PID of the top process.

   e. At the shell prompt, enter **kill –SIGTERM top_PID**.

   f. Switch back to the terminal session where top was running. Verify that top has exited.

   g. Load top again at the shell prompt.

   h. Switch back to your other terminal session where you're logged in as root.

   i. Kill the top process by entering **killall –15 top**.

   j. Switch back to your first terminal window and verify that top has exited.

Well done! You now know how to manage Linux processes on your system! Not many can make that claim. We'll shift gears at this point and spend the rest of the chapter learning about Linux log files.

Managing Linux Log Files

Log files are a goldmine of information for the system administrator. You can use your log files to detect intruders into your system or to troubleshoot problems with your system. In this part of the chapter, we'll teach you how to manage and use your system log files. We'll cover the following topics:

- Configuring log files
- Using log files to troubleshoot problems

Configuring Log Files

Your system log files are stored in the /var/log directory, shown in Figure 11-14.

Notice in Figure 11-14 that there are a number of subdirectories in /var/log where system daemons, such as mysql, apparmor, audit, samba, and cups, store their log files. Some of these log files are simple text files that can be read with text manipulation utilities. Others are binary files that require the use of a special utility, such as lastlog. As you can see in Figure 11-14, there are quite a number of files within /var/log and its subdirectories, and some log files are much more useful than others. Table 11-2 contains a list of some of the more important log files.

The files shown in Table 11-2 are the log files used on a SUSE Linux system. Other distributions may use different files by default. You can customize your logging using the syslog.conf file.

Logging on a Linux system is handled by the syslogd daemon. Instead of each daemon maintaining its own individual log file, most of your Linux services are configured to write log entries to /dev/log by default. This device file is maintained by the syslogd daemon. When a service writes to this socket, the input is captured by syslogd. The syslogd daemon then uses the entries in the /etc/syslog.conf file, shown in Figure 11-15, to determine where the information should go.

TIP Some Linux distributions use syslog-ng or rsyslogd instead of syslogd to manage logging. The logging daemon your system uses is configured in /etc/sysconfig/syslog by the SYSLOG_DAEMON= directive.

The syntax for the syslog.conf file is

```
facility.priority        file
```

```
tux@ws2:~
File  Edit  View  Search  Terminal  Help
tux@ws2:~> ls /var/log
acpid         cups          mail.err        pk_backend_zypp    Xorg.1.log
apparmor      faillog       mail.info       pk_backend_zypp-1  YaST2
audit         firewall      mail.warn       pm-powersave.log   zypp
boot.log      gdm           messages        samba              zypper.log
boot.msg      krb5          NetworkManager  warn
boot.omsg     lastlog       news            wtmp
btmp          localmessages nscd.log        Xorg.0.log
ConsoleKit    mail          ntp             Xorg.0.log.old
tux@ws2:~>
```

Figure 11-14 Contents of the /var/log directory

Log File	Description
boot.log	Contains log entries from daemons as they were started during bootup.
boot.msg	Contains all of the messages displayed on screen during system boot. This can be a very valuable troubleshooting tool when trying to rectify startup problems. The messages displayed on screen usually fly by too quickly to be read.
faillog	Contains failed authentication attempts.
firewall	Contains firewall log entries.
lastlog	Contains last login information for users.
mail	Contains messages generated by the postfix or sendmail daemons.
messages	Contains messages from most running processes. This is probably one of the most useful of all log files. You can use it to troubleshoot services that won't start, services that don't appear to work properly, etc.
warn	Contains warning messages.
wtmp	Contains a list of users who have authenticated to the system.
xinetd.log	Contains log entries from the xinetd daemon.

Table 11-2 Useful Linux Log Files

```
# Log all kernel messages to the console.
# Logging much else clutters up the screen.
#kern.*                                          /dev/console

# Log anything (except mail) of level info or higher.
# Don't log private authentication messages!
*.info;mail.none;authpriv.none;cron.none         /var/log/messages

# The authpriv file has restricted access.
authpriv.*                                       /var/log/secure

# Log all the mail messages in one place.
mail.*                                           -/var/log/maillog


# Log cron stuff
cron.*                                           /var/log/cron

# Everybody gets emergency messages
*.emerg                                               *

# Save news errors of level crit and higher in a special file.
uucp,news.crit                                   /var/log/spooler
./syslog.conf
```

Figure 11-15 The /etc/syslog.conf file

A *facility* refers to a subsystem that provides a message. Each process on your Linux system that uses syslog for logging is assigned to one of the following facilities:

- **authpriv** Facility used by all services associated with system security or authorization.
- **cron** Facility that accepts log messages from cron and at.
- **daemon** Facility that can be used by daemons that do not have their own facility.
- **kern** Facility used for all kernel log messages.
- **lpr** Facility that handles messages from the printing system.
- **mail** Facility for log messages from the mail MTA (such as postfix or sendmail).
- **news** Facility for log messages from the news daemon.
- **syslog** Facility for internal messages from the syslog daemon itself.
- **user** Facility for user-related log messages (such as failed login attempts).
- **uucp** Facility for log messages from the uucp daemon.
- **local0–local7** Facilities that you can use to capture log messages from your own applications that you develop.

In addition to facilities, the syslogd daemon also provides *priorities* that you can use to customize how logging occurs on your system. Prioritization is handled by the klogd daemon on most distributions, which runs as a client of syslogd. You can use the following priorities with syslogd:

- **debug** All information
- **info** Informational messages
- **notice** Issues of concern, but not yet a problem
- **warn** Noncritical errors
- **err** Serious errors
- **crit, alert, or emerg** Critical errors

For example, in Figure 11-15, the syslog.conf file directs messages of all priority levels (*) from the cron facility to the /var/log/cron file. If desired, you could customize your syslog.conf file to split messages of different priority levels to different files.

Your Linux distribution should also include a utility named logrotate. The logrotate utility is run daily, by default, by the cron daemon on your system. You can customize how your log files are rotated using the /etc/logrotate.conf file, shown in Figure 11-16.

This file contains default global parameters used by logrotate to determine how and when log files are rotated. However, these defaults can be overridden for specific daemons using the configuration files located in the /etc/logrotate.d/ directory. For example, in Figure 11-17, the /etc/logrotate.d/apache2 file is used to customize logging for the apache2 daemon.

```
# see "man logrotate" for details
# rotate log files weekly
weekly

# keep 4 weeks worth of backlogs
rotate 4

# create new (empty) log files after rotating old ones
create

# use date as a suffix of the rotated file
dateext

# uncomment this if you want your log files compressed
#compress

# comment these to switch compression to use gzip or another
# compression scheme
compresscmd /usr/bin/bzip2
uncompresscmd /usr/bin/bunzip2

# former versions had to have the compressext set accordingly
#compressext .bz2

# RPM packages drop log rotation information into this directory
include /etc/logrotate.d

# no packages own wtmp and btmp -- we'll rotate them here
#/var/log/wtmp {
#     monthly
#     create 0664 root utmp
#        minsize 1M
#     rotate 1
#}
#
# /var/log/btmp {
#    missingok
#     monthly
#     create 0600 root utmp
#     rotate 1
#}
/etc/logrotate.conf lines 1-41/43 93%
```

Figure 11-16 Configuring log file rotation in /etc/logrotate.conf

In Figure 11-17, the /var/log/apache2/access_log file will be compressed. It can have a maximum age of 365 days, after which it will be removed (maxage 365). Old versions of the file will be archived using a date extension (dateext). The log file will go through 99 rotations before being removed (rotate 99). If the file grows larger than 4096KB, it will be rotated (size=+4096k). The file will not be rotated if it is empty (notifempty). No error message will be generated if the file is missing (missingok). The file will be created with 644 permissions, will have the root user as owner, and will be owned by the root group (create 644 root root). After rotating a log file, the /etc/init.d/apache2 reload command will be run (postrotate /etc/init.d/apache2 reload). There are many

Figure 11-17

Configuring
Apache web
server logging

```
/var/log/apache2/access_log {
    compress
    dateext
    maxage 365
    rotate 99
    size=+4096k
    notifempty
    missingok
    create 644 root root
    postrotate
     /etc/init.d/apache2 reload
    endscript
}

/var/log/apache2/error_log {
    compress
    dateext
    maxage 365
    rotate 99
    size=+1024k
    notifempty
    missingok
    create 644 root root
    postrotate
     /etc/init.d/apache2 reload
apache2 lines 1-25/69 38%
```

other directives that can be used in a logrotate configuration file; see the logrotate man page for a comprehensive list.

Once done, you can test your logging configuration using the logger utility. This command-line tool allows you to manually make entries in your logging system. The syntax is logger –p *facility.priority* "*log_message*".

Using Log Files to Troubleshoot Problems

As I mentioned earlier in this chapter, your log files can be an invaluable resource when troubleshooting Linux problems. If the kernel or a service encounters a problem, it will be logged in a log file. Reviewing these log files can provide you with a wealth of information that may not necessarily be displayed on the screen.

Some log files are binary files that must be read with a special utility. However, most of your log files are simple text files that you can view with standard text manipulation utilities. Earlier in this book, you learned how to use the cat, less, and more utilities to view text files on a Linux system. These utilities can, of course, be used to view text-based log files as well. However, there's a problem with these utilities: log files are usually way too long to be viewed effectively with these utilities.

For example, the /var/log/messages file may have 10,000 or more lines in it. That's a lot of text! The less utility only displays 24 lines at a time. You're going to have to press the SPACEBAR a lot of times to get to the end of the file.

There are two strategies you can use to get around this. You can redirect the output of the cat command to the grep command to filter out a specific term within a log file. For example, suppose you want to locate information within /var/log/messages related to logins. You could enter **cat /var/log/messages | grep login | more** at the shell prompt. Then, only entries containing the term "login" would be displayed.

In addition to grep, you can also use the head and tail utilities to view log file entries. Understand that most log files record entries chronologically, usually oldest to newest. If you want to view the beginning of a log file, you can enter **head** *filename* at the shell prompt to display the first lines of the file. For example, in Figure 11-18, the beginning of the /var/log/messages file has been displayed with head.

The tail utility works in a manner opposite of head: instead of displaying the first lines of a file, it displays the last lines. This is very useful. Usually when troubleshooting, you need to see only the last few lines of a log file. To do this, enter **tail** *filename* at the shell prompt. In Figure 11-19, the /var/log/messages file is being viewed using tail.

The tail utility provides the –f option, which I use all of the time when troubleshooting. When you use the –f option, tail will display the last lines of a log file as per normal. However, it doesn't exit after it initially displays the text on the screen. Instead, it monitors the file being displayed and displays new lines as they are added to the log file. For example, you could use the tail –f /var/log/messages command to monitor your system log file for error messages as you troubleshoot a system.

The tail command monitors the /var/log/messages file waiting for new lines to be added. If something happens on the system that generates messages, such as stopping and then restarting a network interface, the results are instantly displayed on the screen without having to run tail again. You can quit monitoring the file by pressing CTRL-C.

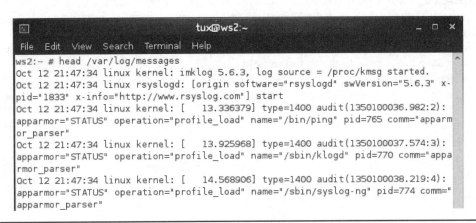

Figure 11-18 Using head to view a log file

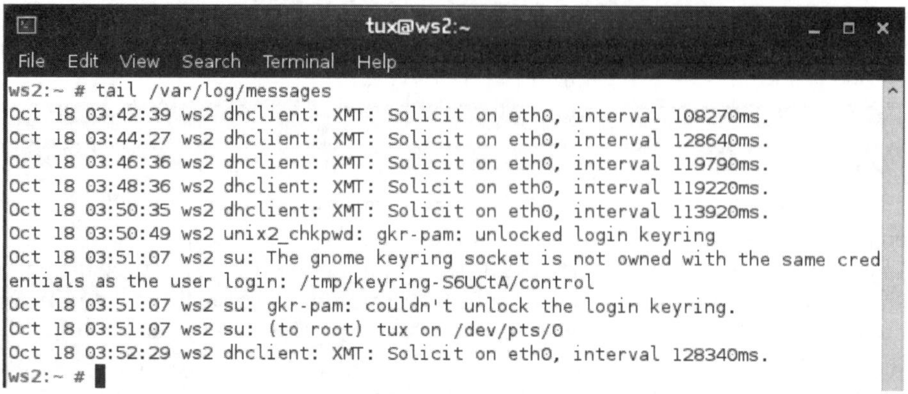

```
┌─────────────────────────────────────────────────────────────────────┐
│ ▣                           tux@ws2:~                      _ □ ✕     │
│  File   Edit   View   Search   Terminal   Help                       │
│ ws2:~ # tail /var/log/messages                                     ▲ │
│ Oct 18 03:42:39 ws2 dhclient: XMT: Solicit on eth0, interval 108270ms.│
│ Oct 18 03:44:27 ws2 dhclient: XMT: Solicit on eth0, interval 128640ms.│
│ Oct 18 03:46:36 ws2 dhclient: XMT: Solicit on eth0, interval 119790ms.│
│ Oct 18 03:48:36 ws2 dhclient: XMT: Solicit on eth0, interval 119220ms.│
│ Oct 18 03:50:35 ws2 dhclient: XMT: Solicit on eth0, interval 113920ms.│
│ Oct 18 03:50:49 ws2 unix2_chkpwd: gkr-pam: unlocked login keyring     │
│ Oct 18 03:51:07 ws2 su: The gnome keyring socket is not owned with the same cred│
│ entials as the user login: /tmp/keyring-S6UCtA/control               │
│ Oct 18 03:51:07 ws2 su: gkr-pam: couldn't unlock the login keyring.  │
│ Oct 18 03:51:07 ws2 su: (to root) tux on /dev/pts/0                  │
│ Oct 18 03:52:29 ws2 dhclient: XMT: Solicit on eth0, interval 128340ms.│
│ ws2:~ # ▊                                                             │
└─────────────────────────────────────────────────────────────────────┘
```

Figure 11-19   Using tail to view a log file

You can check one of the system log files listed previously in Table 11-2 to trouble-shoot problems. However, the files in Table 11-2 are the default log files used with SUSE Linux. On other distributions, such as Fedora, you may need to look at other log files, including

- **cron**   Contains entries from the cron daemon.
- **dmesg**   Contains hardware detection information.
- **maillog**   Contains entries generated by the sendmail daemon.
- **secure**   Contains information about access to network daemons.
- **rpmpkgs**   Contains a list of installed rpm packages.

To troubleshoot problems associated with an application or service, you may need to check for a log file maintained specifically for that service. For example, you would check the mail, mail.err, mail.info, or mail.warn files on a SUSE Linux system or the maillog file on Fedora system to troubleshoot problems with the postfix or sendmail daemons. If you were having trouble with the mysqld daemon, you would look in the mysqld.log file within the /var/log/mysql directory. To troubleshoot problems with the Apache web server, you would investigate the various log files within the /var/log/apache2 directory.

Chapter Review

In this chapter, you learned how to manage Linux processes. We began by reviewing what a process is. We established that whenever you run a command from the shell prompt or when a daemon is run by init, a process is created on the system as the associated program's code is loaded into RAM and the code is executed by the CPU.

I pointed out that Linux is a multitasking operating system. Even though the CPU can only run one process at a time, Linux continually switches CPU time among many processes loaded into RAM, making it appear that the CPU is processing many processes concurrently.

I also pointed out that when the init process loads a daemon using an init script, a system process is created. When an end user enters a command at the shell prompt, a user process is created. User processes are associated with a shell session; system processes are not.

We then discussed the heredity of Linux processes and how Linux processes can spawn other Linux processes. The process that spawned another process is called the parent. The new process that was created by the first process is called the child. Every Linux process has a parent process. All Linux processes can trace their heredity back to the init process, which is the first process loaded by the kernel on system boot.

Every Linux process is assigned a process ID (PID) that uniquely identifies the process on the system. Processes are also assigned a PPID, which is the PID of the process's parent process. Whenever you run a command from the shell prompt, a new shell (called a subshell) is created and the command is run within it. When the process is complete, the subshell is destroyed and control is returned to the original shell.

We then turned our attention to managing Linux processes. We first discussed how you go about creating processes. User processes are created by entering commands at the shell prompt. System processes are created by running a daemon startup script from your system's init directory. Some distributions use System V init scripts, which are stored in /etc/rc.d/init.d. Other distributions use BSD init scripts, which are stored in /etc/init.d.

We next discussed how to view running processes. The first utility we looked at was the top utility. You load top by entering **top** at the shell prompt. You can press the H key while top is running to view a help screen that will show you how to sort by a specific column or even add columns of data to the display.

You can also use the ps command to view running processes. By default, the ps command only displays running processes associated with the current shell session. To view all running processes, use the –e option with the ps command. You can also use the –f and –l options with ps to view extended process information.

Next, we discussed how to prioritize processes on your system. A process's overall priority is heavily influenced by its nice value. Nice values can range from –20 to +19, and the lower the nice value, the higher the priority of the process. To adjust the nice value of a process when it's loaded, you can use the nice command. The syntax is nice –n *nice_value command*. You can't use a nice value lower than 0 unless you are logged in as root. You can also adjust the nice value of a running process without unloading it by using the renice command. The syntax is renice *nice_value PID*.

Then we discussed how to run processes in the foreground and the background. By default, processes you launch from the shell prompt run in the foreground. In this situation, the shell prompt is locked until the process is complete. You can also run a process in the background. In this situation, the program runs, but it does so in the background and control is returned to the shell prompt, allowing you to run additional commands. To run a process in the background, you append an & character to the end of the command, and the background process will be assigned a job ID number.

You can move a process that is running in the background to the foreground by entering **fg** *job_ID* at the shell prompt. You can also move a foreground process into the background. To do this, first press CTRL-Z to stop the process. The process will then be assigned a job ID number. Then enter **bg** *job_ID* to move the process to the background.

Finally, we discussed how to kill a running process from the shell prompt. You can use the kill command or the killall command to do this. Both of these commands use a variety of kill signals. Some of the most useful signals include

- SIGHUP (1)
- SIGINT (2)
- SIGKILL (9)
- SIGTERM (15)

The syntax for kill is kill *–signal PID*. The syntax for killall is killall *–signal process_name*. When working with a hung process, you should try less aggressive kill signals, such as SIGINT and SIGTERM, before using more aggressive kill signals such as SIGKILL.

You can use your Linux system's log files to troubleshoot problems with the system. Your system log files are stored in /var/log. Some of the more important log files in this directory include

- boot.log
- boot.msg
- faillog
- firewall
- lastlog
- mail
- messages
- warn
- wtmp
- xinetd.log
- cron
- dmesg
- maillog
- secure
- rpmpkgs

Not all distributions use the same log files. Logging is handled by the syslogd daemon on a Linux system. The way syslogd manages log files can be customized using the /etc/syslog.conf file. Most Linux distributions are configured to automatically rotate your log files periodically, preventing them from growing too large. The cron daemon periodically runs the logrotate utility to do this. How logrotate rotates specific log files is configured using the /etc/logrotate.conf file and the configuration files for individual services located in /etc/logrotate.d/.

Accelerated Review

- Whenever you run a command from the shell prompt, a process is created on the system.
- When a process loads, the program's code is loaded into RAM and is executed by the CPU.
- Linux is a multitasking operating system.
- Most CPUs can only run one process at a time.
- Linux continually switches CPU time among the many processes loaded into RAM, making it appear that the CPU is processing many processes concurrently.
- When the init process loads a daemon from an init script, a system process is created.
- When an end user enters a command at the shell prompt, a user process is created.
- User processes are associated with a shell session; system processes are not.
- Linux processes can spawn other Linux processes.
- The process that spawns another process is called the parent.
- The new process that is created by the first process is called the child.
- Every Linux process has a parent process.
- All Linux processes can trace their heredity back to the init process, which is the first process loaded by the kernel on system boot.
- Every Linux process is assigned a process ID (PID) that uniquely identifies the process on the system.
- Processes are assigned a PPID value, which is the PID of the process's parent process.
- Whenever you run a command from the shell prompt, a subshell is created and the command is run within it.
- When the process is complete, the subshell is destroyed and control is returned to the original shell.
- User processes are created when you enter commands at the shell prompt.
- System processes are created when you run a daemon startup script from your system's init directory.
- Some distributions use System V init scripts, which are stored in /etc/rc.d/init.d.
- Some distributions use BSD init scripts, which are stored in /etc/init.d.

- You can use the top utility to view system processes. You load top by entering **top** at the shell prompt.
- You can press the H key while top is running to view a help screen that will show you how to configure the data displayed by top.
- You can use the ps command to view running processes.
- By default, the ps command only displays running processes associated with the current shell session.
- You can use the –e option with the ps command to view all running processes.
- You can use the –f and –l options with ps to view extended process information.
- Linux allows you to prioritize processes running on your system.
- A process's overall priority is heavily influenced by its nice value.
- Nice values can range from –20 to +19.
- The lower the nice value, the higher the priority of the process.
- You can use the nice command to adjust the nice value of a process as it's loaded.
- To use nice, enter **nice –n** *nice_value command*.
- You can't assign a nice value lower than 0 unless you are logged in as root.
- You can adjust the nice value of a running process without unloading it using the renice command.
- The syntax for using renice is renice *nice_value PID*.
- By default, processes you launch from the shell prompt run in the foreground.
- Foreground processes lock the shell prompt until the process is complete.
- You can run Linux processes in the background.
- Background processes return control to the shell prompt.
- You can run a process in the background by appending an & character to the end of the command.
- When you load a process into the background, the process is assigned a job ID number.
- You can move a process that is running in the background to the foreground by entering **fg** *job_ID* at the shell prompt.
- You can move a foreground process into the background by pressing CTRL-Z to stop the process and then entering **bg** *job_ID* to move the process to the background.
- You can use the kill or the killall commands to kill a running process.
- There are many kill signals that can be sent using kill or killall; some of the most useful include:
  - SIGHUP (1)
  - SIGINT (2)

- SIGKILL (9)
- SIGTERM (15)
- To kill a process with kill, enter **kill** *–signal PID* at the shell prompt.
- To kill a process with killall, enter **killall** *–signal process_name*.
- You should use less aggressive kill signals, such as SIGINT and SIGTERM, before attempting to use more forceful kill signals such as SIGKILL.
- You can use your system log files (stored in /var/log) to troubleshoot problems with your system.
- Some of the more important log files in this directory include boot.log, boot.msg, faillog, firewall, lastlog, mail, messages, warn, wtmp, xinetd.log, cron, dmesg, maillog, secure, and rpmpkgs.
- Not all distributions use the same log files.
- Logging is handled by the syslogd daemon, which can be customized using the /etc/syslog.conf file.
- Most Linux distributions are configured to automatically rotate your log files periodically, preventing them from growing too large.
- The cron daemon periodically runs the logrotate utility to rotate log files.
- How logrotate rotates specific log files is configured using the /etc/logrotate.conf file and the configuration files for individual services located in /etc/logrotate.d/.
- You can configure syslogd to send all logging events to a syslogd daemon running on a different Linux system.

Questions

1. Which of the following best describes a multitasking operating system?

    A. An operating system that can run multiple tasks concurrently on multiple CPUs

    B. An operating system that can run a single task concurrently across multiple CPUs

    C. An operating system that runs multiple tasks concurrently on a single CPU

    D. An operating system that constantly switches CPU time between loaded processes

2. You just entered **vi** at the shell prompt. What type of process was created on your Linux system?

    A. User

    B. System

    C. Daemon

    D. System V

3. Your current shell session has a PID of 3456. You run the su command to change to the root user account. The su process has a PID of 3457. You then run vi from the shell prompt as root. The vi process has a PID of 3458. What is the PPID of the vi process?

   A. 3456

   B. 3457

   C. 3458

   D. 3459

4. Which process is the grandparent of all processes running on your Linux system?

   A. bash

   B. init

   C. sh

   D. ps

5. You're running a Fedora Linux system that uses System V init scripts. Where are these scripts stored in your file system?

   A. /etc/init.d

   B. /etc/rc.d/init.d

   C. /etc/sysv/init.d

   D. /etc/init.d/rc.d

6. You want to use ps to display extended information about only the processes associated with your current terminal session. Which command will do this?

   A. ps

   B. ps –e

   C. ps –f

   D. ps –ef

7. What is a zombied process?

   A. A process that has finished executing but whose parent process hasn't released the child process's PID

   B. A process that has stopped executing while waiting for user input

   C. A process that is being traced by another process

   D. A process that has gone to sleep and can't be interrupted

8. Which ps option displays all currently running processes?

   A. –a

   B. –e

   C. –f

   D. –l

9. The myapp process has a nice value of 1. Which of the following nice values would increase the priority of the myapp process? (Choose two.)

   A. –15

   B. 5

   C. 19

   D. 0

   E. 2

10. Which of the following shell commands will load the myapp program with a nice value of –5?

    A. myapp –n –5

    B. nice –5 myapp

    C. renice –5 myapp

    D. nice –n –5 myapp

11. The myapp process (PID 2345) is currently running on your system. Which of the following commands will reset its nice value to –5 without unloading the process?

    A. myapp –n –5 –p 2345

    B. renice –n –5 2345

    C. renice –5 2345

    D. nice –n –5 2345

12. You want to load the myapp program from the shell prompt and run it in the background. Which command will do this?

    A. myapp –b

    B. myapp &

    C. myapp –bg

    D. load myapp into background

13. Which kill signal sends a CTRL-C key sequence to a running process?

    A. SIGHUP

    B. SIGINT

    C. SIGKILL

    D. SIGTERM

14. You need to kill a hung process. You know its process name, but you don't know its PID. Which utility can you use?

    A. killall

    B. kill

    C. hangup

    D. SIGKILL

15. You're configuring the /etc/logrotate.d/ntp file to customize logging from the Network Time Protocol daemon on your system. You want old, archived logs to be saved using the current date in the file name extension. Which directive in the ntp file will do this?

   A. notifempty

   B. dateext

   C. rotate

   D. create

16. Which log file contains messages from all services running on the system?

   A. /var/log/faillog

   B. /var/log/messages

   C. /var/log/wtmp

   D. /var/log/services

17. You need to view the first few lines of the /var/log/boot.msg file. Which of the following commands will do this? (Choose two.)

   A. head /var/log/ boot.msg

   B. tail /var/log/ boot.msg

   C. grep –l 10 /var/log/boot.msg

   D. less /var/log/boot.msg

   E. cat /var/log/boot.msg

Answers

1. **D.** A multitasking operating system constantly switches CPU time between loaded processes, creating the impression that the CPU is executing processes concurrently.

2. **A.** Because the command was entered from the shell prompt, a user process was created.

3. **A.** Because the command was entered from the shell prompt, its parent process is the bash process, which has a PID of 3456.

4. **B.** The init process is the grandparent of all other Linux processes on the system. All other processes can trace their heredity to init.

5. **B.** The init scripts for distributions that use System V init scripts are stored in /etc/rc.d/init.d.

6. **C.** The ps –f command will display extended information about processes associated with the current shell session.

7. **A.** A zombied process is one where the process has finished executing, but the parent process wasn't notified and therefore hasn't released the child process's PID.

8. **B.** The **ps –e** command displays a list of all running processes on the system.

9. **A, D.** The lower the nice value, the higher the priority of the process. Therefore, nice values of 0 and –15 will increase the priority of the myapp process.

10. **D.** The nice –n –5 myapp command will load myapp with a nice value of –5.

11. **C.** The renice –5 2345 command will reset the nice value of the myapp process while it's running.

12. **B.** The myapp & command will cause myapp to run in the background.

13. **B.** The SIGINT kill signal sends a CTRL-C key sequence to the specified process.

14. **A.** The killall utility uses the process name in the command line and kills the process in this scenario.

15. **B.** The dateext directive will cause old, archived log files to be saved using the current date in the filename extension.

16. **B.** The /var/log/messages log file contains messages from all services running on the system.

17. **A, D.** The head /var/log/boot.msg and less /var/log/boot.msg commands will display the first few lines of the file on screen.

Creating Scripts

In this chapter, you will learn about
- Working with shell scripts
- Creating a basic scripts
- Using control structures in scripts
- Processing text streams

One of the cool things about Linux is the fact that it allows you to create your own powerful *shell scripts* that you can run right from your shell prompt. A shell script is a text file that contains a series of commands that are executed by the shell. Shell scripts can be used to run a series of Linux programs with a single command. They can also be used to read input from the end user or from shell commands and make decisions based on the input.

Working with Shell Scripts

To understand how shell scripts work, you need to know the following:

- The components of a shell script
- How shell scripts are executed

The Components of a Shell Script

As I mentioned, a shell script is a simple text file that contains a series of commands that are executed from top to bottom. Here is a sample shell script named runme:

```
#!/bin/bash
#A simple script that displays the current date and time
echo "The current date and time is:"
date
exit 0
```

Notice that this script contains several parts:

- **#!/bin/bash**   The first line of any shell script must specify which shell the script is written to run under. In this case, the /bin/bash shell is specified. When a script is run, a subshell will be created using the shell specified here and the script contents will be processed within it.

- **#A simple script that**...   This part of the script is a comment that describes what the script does. Notice that this part of the script begins with a # character to indicate that the text that comes after it is a comment. Because it is a comment, this part of the script is not displayed on the screen when the script is run. Comments are optional; the script will run just fine without them. However, it's considered good form to include a comment at the beginning of your scripts right after the shell declaration that describes what the script does and, optionally, who wrote it.

- **echo, date**   These elements in the script are simple commands that are typically used at the shell prompt. The echo command is used to display text on the screen. The date command is used to display the current date and time on the screen.

- **exit 0**   This part of the script is its end. It tells the shell what to do after it is done running the commands in the script. In this case, it tells the shell to exit the script.

When we run this script, the output shown in Figure 12-1 is displayed on the screen.

Notice that this script first displayed the text specified by the echo command. Then the next command was processed, which directed the shell to run the date command. When the script was done, the shell exited the script and returned you to the command prompt.

How Shell Scripts Are Executed

Notice in Figure 12-1 that, to run the script, I had to call the shell (/bin/bash) and then tell it what script to execute (./runme). This is one option for running a script.

However, there's a second option (and a better one in my opinion) for running shell scripts. Remember in Chapter 9 when we talked about permissions? Recall that one of the file permissions you could assign to a file is named *execute*. With the execute permission assigned, any file, including a text file, can be allowed to execute from the shell prompt. This is a great option for making scripts easy for end users to run.

To do this, simply enable the execute attribute for Owner, Group, and/or Others. As you learned earlier, this is done using the chmod command. For example, I can configure the runme file to be executed by the file Owner by entering **chmod u+x runme** at

Figure 12-1   Running a simple shell script

the shell prompt. Then I can run the runme script by simply entering its name at the shell prompt, just as I would with any other system command, as shown next:

```
tux@ws2:~> chmod u+x runme
tux@ws2:~> ls -l runme
-rwxr--r-- 1 tux users 118 2012-011-07 15:29 runme
tux@ws2:~> ./runme
The current date and time is:
Thu Nov  7 15:36:02 MDT 2012
tux@ws2:~>
```

If necessary, I could have also given the execute permission to Group and/or Others as well.

There is one other issue you need to be aware of when working with scripts, and that is the issue of paths. Notice in the preceding example that I had to enter **./runme** at the shell prompt. Even though the file resided in the current directory (in this case, /home/tux), this directory is not in my PATH environment variable.

If you're creating scripts for yourself, then this probably doesn't pose a problem. By now, you should be familiar enough with Linux to understand why you have to specify the path to the file at the shell prompt and know how to do it. However, if you're creating a script for your end users to run, this may present a problem. To save yourself frustration, you should consider putting the script in a directory that is part of the PATH or adding the directory to your existing PATH.

One option you can use is the ~/bin directory in each user's home directory. Most Linux distributions automatically create a directory named /bin for each user. Then, one of the bash configuration files, discussed in Chapter 5, is used to automatically add ~/bin to the PATH environment variable when a shell is started, as shown in Figure 12-2.

Figure 12-2   Putting scripts in ~/bin

Because it's in the PATH, any files you put in ~/bin can be run from the shell prompt without specifying the full path to the file. You could also, of course, create your own directory and manually edit your bash configuration files to add it to your user's PATH environment variable as well.

With this background in mind, let's spend some time discussing how to create a basic shell script.

Creating a Basic Script

To create basic shell scripts, you'll need to learn how to do the following:

- Display text on the screen.
- Add commands to a script.
- Read input from the user.

Displaying Text on the Screen

Displaying text on the screen is pretty easy. As you saw in the earlier examples, you can display text on the screen in a shell script using the echo command. The syntax for using echo is to enter **echo "***text_to_be_displayed***"** in the script file.

In the simple script example we looked at earlier, I entered **echo "The current date and time is:"** to display the associated text on the screen. Because the shell script simply calls and runs the echo command, you can use all of the options you would use if you were to run echo at the shell prompt. Check out the man page for echo to see what's available.

Adding Commands to a Script

To run a shell command from within a script, enter the appropriate command in the script with all of the options you want to include with it. In the simple script example we looked at earlier, I used the date command to display the current date and time. You can include just about any command you want in your shell scripts, but remember to put each command on a separate line, unless you are using pipes to move data between commands.

When you run a command from within a shell script, there may be situations when you need to know whether the command ran and exited correctly or whether it ran into an error and exited incorrectly. All Linux commands return an exit status when they are done running, regardless of whether they terminate normally or abnormally. You can check the exit status of a command in a shell script and use the results to determine what the script should do next, such as continue processing or display an error message. For example, you could create a file system backup script using the tar command and check the exit status of the tar command to see if it exited correctly or not. If it didn't, you could include code in your script to display an error on screen so you would know that there was a problem with your backup.

The exit status of a Linux command is indicated using a number. The actual numbers used will vary from command to command. However, an exit status of 0 always means the command exited successfully without any errors. An exit status of any number other than 0 indicates an error of some type occurred and that the command exited abnormally. Check the man page of the command in question to see a listing of error codes and what they mean.

You can use the "?" shell variable to get the exit status of the previously executed command. As with any other variable, you can use the echo command to display the value of ? on the screen. An example is shown next:

```
tux@ws2:~> cat ./runme
#!/bin/bash
# A simple script that displays the current date and time
echo "The current date and time is:"
date
echo "Exit status is" $?
exit 0
tux@ws2:~> ./runme
The current date and time is:
Tue Nov 20 07:14:01 MST 2012
Exit status is 0
tux@ws2:~>
```

As you can see in the preceding example, using echo with the ? variable ($?) prints the exit status of the preceding command (date) on the screen. We know the command ran and exited correctly because the exit status is 0.

Let's look at another example where a command exits with an error. In the script that follows, we are running the ls command to view a file that doesn't exist in the file system:

```
tux@ws2:~> cat runme2
#!/bin/bash
# A simple script that displays the current date and time
echo "Searching for a file named bob.txt"
ls bob.txt
echo "Exit status is" $?
exit 0
tux@ws2:~> ./runme2
Searching for a file named bob.txt
ls: cannot access bob.txt: No such file or directory
Exit status is 2
tux@ws2:~>
```

In this example, the ls command couldn't find the file specified in the script (bob.txt). As a result, it exited with an error (2). Checking the ls command's man page, you see that an exit status of 2 indicates an error where the command can't find a specified file or directory.

By reading the exit status, you can then branch the script and make it do different things based upon what the exit status value is. This can be done using control operators or control structures. We'll discuss control structures a little later in this chapter, but let's look at control operators now.

There are two control operators that you can use in a shell script:

&& (AND)
|| (OR)

The syntax for && is *command_1 && command_2*. Using &&, the second command (command_2) is executed only if the first command (command_1) runs and exits correctly; in other words, only if command_1 returns an exit status of 0.

The syntax for || is *command_1 || command_2*. Using ||, the second command (command_2) is executed only if the first command (command_1) runs and exits abnormally with a nonzero exit status.

You can use both control operators together in the same line. This allows you to account for the successful or unsuccessful running of the first command. The syntax is *command_1 && command_2 || command_3*.

If the first command (command_1) runs successfully, then the second command (command_2) will run. If the first command doesn't run correctly, then the third command (command_3) is run. For example, if you wanted to add a line to a script that deleted a file, you could use && and || to determine what command to run, depending upon whether the deletion was successful or not. The syntax would be as follows:

```
rm file_name && echo "File deleted" || echo "File not deleted"
```

If the file is deleted successfully with an exit status of zero, then the first echo command is executed. If not, the second echo command is executed.

In the bash shell, you can use *command substitution*, which allows you to run a command and have its output pasted back on the command line as an argument for another command. Essentially, command substitution allows you to perform multiple tasks at once.

Command substitution works by creating a child process that runs the first command. The stdout from this command is then piped back to the bash shell. The shell parses the output from the first command into words separated by white space. After the pipe from the first command closes (indicating the first command is done running), the shell starts another child process to run the second command using the stdout from the first command as arguments.

For example, suppose you need to use the tail command in a script to grab the last few lines of all the files in /etc that contain the text "ws2". You could use the following command substitution as a line in the script:

```
tail $(fgrep -l ws2 /etc/*)
```

First the fgrep –l command runs to search through all of the files in the /etc directory for the text string "ws2". Using the –l option with fgrep causes the command to return a list of filenames only, not the actual matching text. This list of files is then piped to the tail command, which then displays the last few lines of each file it receives.

You can use the xargs command to accomplish a similar task. For example, it's possible for command substitution to fail if the first command pipes too many results back to the second command. In this situation, you end up with a too many arguments error as shown here:

```
Argument list too long
```

Due to a limit imposed by the Linux kernel, the maximum length of a bash command line is 128KB. If you are bumping up against this limit, you can use xargs instead of command substitution. The xargs command breaks down a long command line into 128KB chunks and passes each chunk as an argument to the command listed within the xargs command line. For example, suppose you wanted to delete all of the temporary files, which usually end with a ~ character, created by your word processing application from your home directory. You could use the following command in a script:

```
find ~/ -name "*~" | xargs rm
```

The find command first generates a list of matching files and then pipes it to the input of the xargs command, which then processes the text stream 128KB at a time and sends it to the stdin of the rm command.

Let's make things a little more interesting by discussing how to solicit and capture input from the end user in a script.

Reading Input from the User

Up to this point, our scripts have been noninteractive, meaning that the user simply types the command at the shell prompt and the script does whatever it's been written to do.

However, you can make your scripts more flexible by making them interactive, meaning that you can have your scripts ask the user a question and then capture their input for processing. This is done using the echo command discussed previously in conjunction with the read *variable* command. The echo command is used to present the user with a question. The read *variable* command pauses the script, presents a prompt on the screen, and reads the information the user supplies into a variable you define. Consider this example:

```
#!/bin/bash
#A script for adding a directory to the PATH environment variable
echo "What directory do you want to add to the PATH?"
read MYNEWPATH
echo "You want to add " $MYNEWPATH
exit 0
```

In this script, the user is prompted for the name of the directory he or she wants to add to the PATH environment variable. The read command provides the user with a prompt to enter the directory name. When the user presses the ENTER key, the value he or she typed is assigned to the variable named MYNEWPATH.

Once the variable is stored in memory, the echo command is used a second time to display the value of MYNEWPATH on the screen. Now, in the preceding script we didn't actually modify the PATH variable. To do this, we need to add some more commands to the shell script. The best way to approach this is to ask yourself: "If I were doing this from the shell prompt, what commands would I need?" Then enter the commands in the script and try it out.

In this next example, we need to add the directory specified by the user to PATH and then export PATH. This could be done using the commands shown here:

```
#!/bin/bash
#A script for adding a directory to the PATH environment variable
echo "What directory do you want to add to the PATH?"
read MYNEWPATH
echo "Adding the " $MYNEWPATH " directory to PATH."
PATH=$PATH:$MYNEWPATH
export PATH
echo "Your PATH environment variable is now:"
echo $PATH
exit 0
```

If you've done any programming, you probably noticed that we didn't have to declare the MYNEWPATH variable anywhere in the script. With many scripting and programming languages, you have to first declare a variable, set its size, and specify what type of information (text string, real number, integer, Boolean value, and so on) it will contain. The bash shell is a little more forgiving: it will create the variable in memory dynamically for you from the read command and assign the user's input as its value.

Of course, bash does let you declare and type the variable if you want to. This is done using the declare command in the script. This can be useful if you want to have the user enter numbers in a read command. The issue here is that the bash shell interprets anything entered at the read command as *text*, even if the user enters a number. Consider this script:

```
#!/bin/bash
#A script that adds variables together.
echo "Enter a number:"
read NUM1
echo "Enter a second number:"
read NUM2
TOT=$NUM1+$NUM2
echo "The sum of these numbers is " $TOT
exit 0
```

When run, this script asks the user for two numbers, adds them together and assigns the result to a variable named TOT, and echoes the value of TOT on the screen. Notice what happens when the script is run in Figure 12-3.

Figure 12-3 The results of not declaring variables

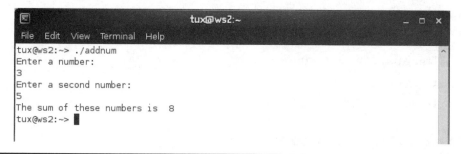

Figure 12-4   Adding declared variables to a script

Because we didn't declare the NUM1, NUM2, or TOT variables, bash treated them all as simple text. No arithmetic took place; the text values of each variable were concatenated together into a single text string. However, if we declare these variables and type them as integers, something very different will happen. Consider a revised version of this script, shown here:

```
#!/bin/bash
#A script that adds variables together.
declare -i NUM1
declare -i NUM2
declare -i TOT
echo "Enter a number:"
read NUM1
echo "Enter a second number:"
read NUM2
TOT=$NUM1+$NUM2
echo "The sum of these numbers is " $TOT
exit 0
```

Notice that NUM1, NUM2, and TOT are declared at the beginning of the script using the –i (integer) option. Now the bash shell will interpret the user's input as a whole number, not as text. When we use the + operator on the variables in the script, the numbers are actually added, not just concatenated, as shown in Figure 12-4.

You're doing great! We've gone from relatively simple scripts to ones that are a little more complex. Let's ratchet things up a notch and add some control structures to our scripts.

Using Control Structures in Scripts

In addition to the interactivity provided by control operators, it can also be very beneficial to add control structures to your shell scripts. Our scripts, to this point, have executed straight through from beginning to end. This works fine, but what if we need the script to make some decisions? You may want the script to determine a course of action based on user input or output from a command. You can do this by implementing control structures in the script; we'll discuss the following types of control structures:

- Using if/then/else structures
- Using case structures
- Using looping structures

Using if/then Structures

Using an if/then/else structure within your shell script gives your script the ability to execute different commands based on whether or not a particular condition is true or false. The structure appears as follows:

```
if condition then
       commands
else
       commands
fi
```

The if part of the structure tells the shell to determine whether the specified condition evaluates to *true* or *false*. If it is true, then the commands under the then part of the structure are run. If the condition evaluates to false, then the commands under the else part of the structure are run.

For example, in the script we've been working with so far in this chapter, we've asked the user to enter the name of a directory he or she wants to add to the PATH environment variable. When we add the directory to PATH, the shell doesn't check to see if the directory the user entered actually exists. It would be beneficial to run a quick test and verify that the specified directory exists. If it does, we should go ahead and add it to the PATH variable. If not, we should post an error message on the screen telling the user what happened. The script shown in this next example does this very thing:

```
#!/bin/bash
#A script for adding a directory to the PATH environment variable
echo "What directory do you want to add to the PATH?"
read MYNEWPATH
if [ -e "$MYNEWPATH" ]; then
        echo "The " $MYNEWPATH " directory exists."
        echo "Adding the " $MYNEWPATH " directory to PATH."
        PATH=$PATH:$MYNEWPATH
        export PATH
        echo "Your PATH environment variable is now:"
        echo $PATH
else
        echo $MYNEWPATH " doesn't exist."
fi
exit 0
```

In this example, the "[–e "$MYNEWPATH"]" condition calls a utility called test and directs it to check and see if the directory contained in the MYNEWPATH variable exists (as specified by the –e option). If test returns a value of TRUE, then the steps immediately under the if statement are executed. However, if the test program returns a value of FALSE, then the statements under the else portion of the structure are executed. In this case, an error message will be displayed indicating that the directory doesn't exist. When we run this script and supply a valid directory, the output in Figure 12-5 is displayed.

In addition to using the –e option in the if/then/else structure to test a condition, you can also use the test command itself. You can use the following options with test:

- **–d** Checks to see if the specified directory exists.
- **–e** Checks to see if the specified file exists.
- **–f** Checks to see if the specified file exists and if it is a regular file.
- **–G** Checks to see if the specified file exists and is owned by a specified group.
- **–h or –L** Checks to see if the specified file exists and if it is a symbolic link.
- **–O** Checks to see if the specified file exists and if it is owned by the specified user ID.
- **–r** Checks to see if the specified file exists and if the read permission is granted.
- **–w** Checks to see if the specified file exists and if the write permission is granted.
- **–x** Checks to see if the specified file exists and if the execute permission is granted.

For example, the following structure tests to see if a file named myfile in the /home/ rtracy directory exists:

```
if test -f /home/rtracy/myfile; then
      echo "myfile exists"
else
      echo "myfile does not exist"
fi
```

You can do more than test whether files exist with the test command. Some sample conditions you can evaluate with test are shown next.

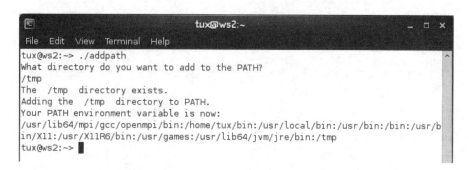

Figure 12-5   Using an if/then/else structure

True if the text is the same:

```
test "text1" = "text2"
```

True if strings are not equal:

```
test "text1" != "text2"
```

True if both numbers are the same:

```
test num1 -eq num2
```

True if num1 is less than num2:

```
test num1 -lt num2
```

True if num1 is greater than num1:

```
test num1 -gt num2
```

You can also use regular expressions when working with the test command. Regular expressions are strings consisting of metacharacters, regular characters, and numerals. Metacharacters are characters that do not represent themselves but instead represent other characters. They can also be used to specify a character's location within a text string. Some regular expressions you can use with the test command are listed in Table 12-1.

Metacharacter	Function	Example
*	Matches any number of any characters.	**Myfile*** would match Myfile1, Myfile2, Myfiles, Myfiles23, etc.
.	Matches a single character	**Myfile.** would match Myfile1, Myfile2, and Myfiles, but would not match Myfiles23.
^	Matches an expression if it appears at the beginning of a line.	**^server** would match any instance of "server" as long as it appears at the beginning of a line.
$	Matches an expression if it appears at the end of a line.	**server$** would match any instance of "server" as long as it appears at the end of a line.
|	Matches the expressions on either side of the pipe character.	**Server|server** would match either "Server" or "server".
[nnn]	Matches any one character between the braces.	**[xyz]** would match any one of "x", "y", or "z".
[^nnn]	Matches an expression that does *not* contain any one of the characters specified.	**[^aei]** would *not* match the characters "a", "e", or "i".
[n-n]	Matches any single character in the range.	**[1-5]** would match any number between 1 and 5.

Table 12-1 Regular Expressions

Using case Structures

The case statement is really just a glorified if/then statement. The if/then statement works perfectly if we have a condition that can be evaluated in one of two ways. In the preceding examples, the condition could be evaluated as true or false. However, what do you do if you have a condition that could be evaluated in many different ways, but you still want your script to take certain actions based on how it evaluates?

You could use a whole series of if/then statements instead of a case statement. However, it can get really messy and is considered poor form. If you have a condition that can be evaluated to return more than two responses, you should use a case statement instead. The syntax for using a case structure is as follows:

```
case variable in
     response_1 ) commands
               ;;
     response_2 ) commands
               ;;
     response_3 ) commands
               ;;
esac
```

Essentially, the case statement compares the value of the variable listed to the list of responses within the case statement. If a match is found, then the commands associated with that response are run. Commands for all other list items are ignored.

For example, you could write a script that asks users what month they were born in. Based on the response they give, you could cause the script to provide a customized response using a case statement. Here is a sample script that does this:

```
#!/bin/bash
#A simple script to demonstrate the case structure.
echo "What month were you born in?"
read MYMONTH
case $MYMONTH in
     December | January | February ) echo "Being born in" $MYMONTH", you
were born during the winter in the Northern Hemisphere."
     ;;
     March | April | May ) echo "Being born in" $MYMONTH", you were born
during the spring in the Northern Hemisphere."
     ;;
     June | July | August ) echo "Being born in" $MYMONTH", you were born
during the summer in the Northern Hemisphere."
     ;;
     September | October | November ) echo "Being born in" $MYMONTH", you
were born during the fall in the Northern Hemisphere."
     ;;
     * ) echo "Sorry, I'm not familiar with that month!"
     ;;
esac
exit 0
```

This script asks users what month they were born in and then determines the season of their birth using a case structure. Five options are provided:

- December, January, or February
- March, April, or May

- June, July, or August

- September, October, or November

- *

Notice that the different terms on the same line are separated with a pipe character (|). This means "or." If the user's response matches one of the terms, then the command associated with its line is executed. In Figure 12-6, the script has been run and the user has responded with a birth month of June.

Because the value of the MYMONTH variable matched the line in the case statement for *June*, the echo command for June, July, or August response was run. Notice that we added one extra response at the end of the case statement using an asterisk (*). This option allows us to provide users with feedback in the event that their response doesn't match any of the other items listed in the case statement.

Using Looping Structures

The if/then/else and case structures are called *branching structures*. Depending on how a condition evaluates, the script branches in one direction or another. You can also use *looping* control structures within a shell script. Looping structures come in three varieties: the *while loop*, the *until loop*, and the *for loop*. A while loop executes over and over until a specified condition is no longer true. The structure of a while loop is

```
while condition
do
      script commands
done
```

A while loop will keep processing over and over and over until the condition evaluates to false.

An *until* loop works in the opposite manner: it runs over and over as long as the condition is false. As soon as the condition is true, it stops. The structure for an until loop is as follows:

```
until condition
do
      script commands
done
```

```
tux@ws2:~> ./casetest
What month were you born in?
June
Being born in June, you were born during the summer in the Northern Hemisphere.
tux@ws2:~>
```

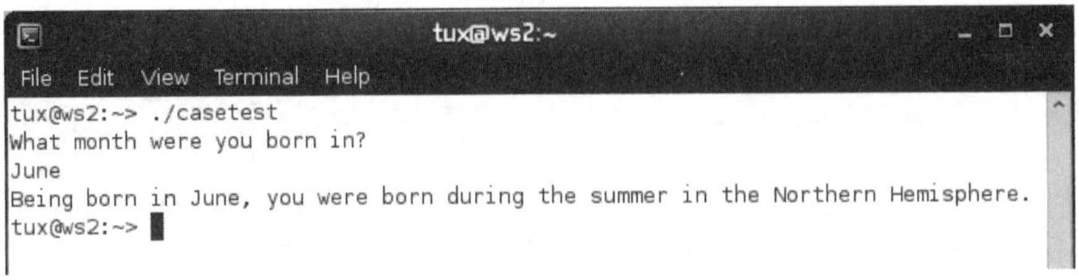

Figure 12-6   Running a script that uses a case statement

You can also use a for loop, which operates in a different manner than until or while loops. The until and while loops keep looping indefinitely until the specified condition is met. A for loop, on the other hand, loops a specific number of times.

It is very common to use the seq command within a for loop to create the sequence of numbers to determine how many times it will loop. There are three options for creating a number sequence with seq:

- If you specify a single value, the sequence starts at one, increments by one, and ends at the specified value.

- If you specify two values, the sequence starts at the first value, increments by one, and ends at the second value.

- If you specify three values, the sequence starts at the first value, increments by the second value, and ends at the third value.

Consider the following example:

```
seq 5 15
```

This command creates a sequence of numbers that starts at 5, increments by 1, and ends at 15. Here is an example of using seq in a for loop:

```
for i in 'seq 15'
    do
            echo "The current number in the sequence is $i."
    done
exit 0
```

The biggest danger with looping structures is that it is possible to get stuck in an infinite loop. This happens when the condition never changes to a value that will break the loop. In this situation, the script gets "hung" because it keeps running the same loop structure over and over and over and will continue to do so until you manually break out of it using the CTRL-C key.

Let's practice working with basic shell scripts in the following exercise.

Exercise 12-1: Creating a Basic Shell Script   In this exercise, you will practice creating a basic shell script. This script will ask the user for a series of three numbers. It will then ask the user if he or she wants to sum the three numbers or average them. You will also add the execute permission to the file to allow the file owner to run it. Complete the following:

1. If necessary, boot your Linux system and log in as a standard user.

2. Change to the ~/bin directory.

3. At the shell prompt enter **vi domath**.

4. Enter the following script:
   ```
   #!/bin/bash
   #A script to do some simple math.
   clear
   ```

```
declare -i A
declare -i B
declare -i C
declare -i ANSWER
echo "Enter the first number:"
read A
echo "Enter the second number:"
read B
echo "Enter the third number:"
read C
echo "What would you like to do with these numbers?"
echo "P: Add them up!"
echo "V: Average them!"
echo "Enter your choice:"
read CHOICE
case $CHOICE in
        p | P ) ANSWER=A+B+C
        ;;
        v | V ) ANSWER=A+B+C
                ANSWER=$ANSWER/3
        ;;
esac
echo "Your answer is" $ANSWER "."
exit 0
```

5. Save your changes to the script and exit vi.

6. Make the script executable by the file owner by entering **chmod u+x domath** at the shell prompt.

7. Test the script by entering **domath** at the shell prompt.

8. Test the script and verify that it works.

Processing Text Streams

When processing text streams within a script or when piping output at the shell prompt, there may be times when you need to filter the output of one command such that only certain portions of the text stream are actually passed along to the stdin of the next command. There are a variety of tools you can use to do this. In the last part of this chapter, we'll look at using the following commands:

- cut
- sort
- wc

cut

The cut command is used to print columns or fields that you specify from a file to the standard output. By default, the Tab character is used as a delimiter. The following options can be used with cut:

- **–b***list*   Select only these bytes.
- **–c***list*   Select only these characters.
- **–d***delim*   Use the specified character instead of Tab for field delimiter.
- **–f***list*   Select only the specified fields. Print any line that contains no delimiter character, unless the –s option is specified.
- **–s**   Do not print lines that do not contain delimiters.

For example, you could use the cut command to display all group names from the /etc/group file. Remember, the name of each group is contained in the first field of each line of the file. However, the group file uses colons as a delimiter between fields, so you must specify a colon instead of a Tab as the delimiter. The command to do this is **cut –d: –f1 /etc/group**. An example is shown in Figure 12-7.

sort

The sort command sorts the lines of a text file alphabetically. The output is written to the standard output. Some commonly used options for the sort command include the following:

- **–f**   Fold lowercase characters to uppercase characters.
- **–M**   Sort by month.
- **–n**   Sort numerically.
- **–r**   Reverse the sort order.

For example, the **sort –n –r firstnames** command sorts the lines in the firstnames file numerically in reverse order, as shown in Figure 12-8.

Figure 12-7   Using the cut command to extract a field from /etc/group

Figure 12-8   Sorting lines in a file

The sort command can be used to sort the output of other commands by piping the standard output of the first command to the standard input of the sort command.

wc

The wc command prints the number of newlines, words, and bytes in a file. The syntax is **wc** *options files*. You can use the following options with the wc command:

- **–c**   Print the byte counts.
- **–m**   Print the character counts.
- **–l**   Print the newline counts.
- **–L**   Print the length of the longest line.
- **–w**   Print the word counts.

For example, to print all counts and totals for the firstnames file, you would use the **wc firstnames** command, as shown in this example:

```
tux@ws2:~> wc firstnames
  3 6 21 firstnames
tux@ws2:~>
```

You are now an experienced bash shell user!

Chapter Review

In this chapter, you learned how to create basic shell scripts on a Linux system. A shell script is a text file that is interpreted and run by the bash shell. A shell script contains a series of commands that automate tasks and process information for you, and it is composed of the following parts:

- #!/bin/bash
- #Comments
- *shell commands*
- exit 0

Shell scripts can be edited with any text editor. They can be executed in one of two ways:

- Entering **/bin/bash** *script_filename*.
- Adding the execute permission to the script file using the chmod utility and entering the filename of the script at the shell prompt.

In addition, you can also add the path to the script file to your PATH environment variable so users won't have to remember the full path to the file to use it. Alternatively, you can move the script file to a directory that is already in the user's PATH environment variable, such as ~/bin.

Any command you run from the shell prompt can also be run from within a script. You can check the exit status of a command in script to determine whether it ran correctly or not. An exit status of 0 always means the command exited successfully without any errors. An exit status of any number other than 0 indicates an error of some type occurred and that the command exited abnormally. You can use the "?" shell variable to get the exit status of the previously executed command.

You can branch a script and make it do different things based upon what the exit status value is. This can be done using control operators or control structures. There are two control operators that you can use in a shell script: && (AND) and || (OR).

By inserting && between two commands on the same line of a script, the second command is executed only if the first command returns an exit status of 0. By inserting || between two commands on the same line of a script, the second command is executed only if the first command exits abnormally with a nonzero exit status.

The bash shell allows you to use command substitution, which allows you to run a command and have its output pasted back on the command line as an argument for another command. Due to a limit imposed by the Linux kernel, the maximum length of a bash command line is 128KB. If you are bumping up against this limit using command substitution, you can use xargs instead of command substitution. The xargs command breaks down a long command line into 128KB chunks and passes each chunk as an argument to the command listed within the xargs command line.

In addition to running commands from a script, you can also read input from the user and assign it to a variable using the **read** *variable_name* command in a script. Script variables don't need to be declared if you are going to read text into them. However, if you want to read numbers into a variable that will be actually treated as numbers (so that you can perform arithmetic functions, for example), then you need to declare them first using the **declare –i** *variable_name* command in the script.

You can also use control structures in your scripts. Control structures allow you to configure your scripts such that they branch or loop based on conditions that you supply. To make a script that branches in two directions, you can use an if/then/else structure in your script. If the condition you specify in the structure is true, the set of commands under then is executed. If the condition is false, the commands under the else portion of the structure are executed. The syntax for using if/then/else structures in a script is as follows:

```
if condition then
     commands
else
     commands
fi
```

You can use the test command in an if/then/else structure to test a condition. You can use the following options with test:

- **–d** Checks to see if the specified directory exists.
- **–e** Checks to see if the specified file exists.
- **–f** Checks to see if the specified file exists and if it is a regular file.
- **–G** Checks to see if the specified file exists and is owned by a specified group.
- **–h or –L** Checks to see if the specified file exists and if it is a symbolic link.
- **–O** Checks to see if the specified file exists and if it is owned by the specified user ID.
- **–r** Checks to see if the specified file exists and if the read permission is granted.
- **–w** Checks to see if the specified file exists and if the write permission is granted.
- **–x** Checks to see if the specified file exists and if the execute permission is granted.

You can also use regular expressions with the test command.

If you want more than two branches in your script, you can use the case structure. The case structure is an advanced if/then/else statement that allows you to evaluate multiple conditions and execute a series of commands according to which condition is true. The case structure is a handy way to replace multiple if/then/else statements in a script. The syntax for using the case structure is as follows:

```
case variable in
     condition_1 ) commands
     ;;
     condition_2 ) commands
     ;;
     condition_3 ) commands
     ;;
esac
```

You can also use looping control structures within a shell script. Looping structures come in three varieties: the *while* loop, the *until* loop, and the *for* loop.

A while loop executes over and over until a specified condition is no longer true. The structure of a while loop is

```
while condition
do
     script commands
done
```

A while loop will keep processing until the condition evaluates to false.

You can also use an until loop in your script. An until loop runs over and over as long as the condition is false. As soon as the condition is true, it stops. The structure for an until loop is as follows:

```
until condition
do
      script commands
done
```

You can also use a for loop, which loops a specific number of times. It is very common to use the seq command within a for loop to create the sequence of numbers to determine how many times it will loop. There are three options for creating a number sequence with seq:

- If you specify a single value, the sequence starts at one, increments by one, and ends at the specified value.

- If you specify two values, the sequence starts at the first value, increments by one, and ends at the second value.

- If you specify three values, the sequence starts at the first value, increments by the second value, and ends at the third value.

We then discussed how to process text streams to manipulate and modify text within a script or within a pipe. We looked at the following utilities:

- **cut**   The cut command is used to print columns or fields that you specify from a file to the standard output. By default, the Tab character is used as a delimiter.

- **sort**   The sort command sorts the lines of a text file alphabetically.

- **wc**   The wc command prints the number of newlines, words, and bytes in a file.

Accelerated Review

- Shell scripts are text files that contain a variety of commands that can be used to automate tasks and process information.

- All shell scripts begin with #!/bin/bash to specify that the bash shell should be used to run the script.

- You should include a comment at the beginning of each script that describes what it does.

- Your shell scripts should end with exit 0 to tell the script to exit.

- You can run shell scripts by running /**bin/bash** *script_filename* or by adding the execute permission to the script file.

- You can check the exit status of a command in script to determine whether it ran correctly.

- An exit status of 0 always means the command exited successfully without any errors.

- An exit status of any number other than 0 indicates the command exited abnormally.

- You can view the value of the "?" shell variable to get the exit status of the previously executed command.

- By inserting && between two commands on the same line of a script, the second command is executed only if the first command returns an exit status of 0.

- By inserting || between two commands on the same line of a script, the second command is executed only if the first command exits abnormally with a non-zero exit status.

- Command substitution allows you to run a command and have its output pasted back on the command line as an argument for another command.

- The xargs command breaks down a long command line into 128KB chunks and passes each chunk as an argument to the command listed within the xargs command line.

- You can read user input in a script using read *variable_name* in a script.

- To make your scripts more powerful, you can add branching structures in a script.

- Control structures allow you to configure your scripts such that they branch or loop according to conditions that you supply.

- To make a script that branches in two directions, you can use an if/then/else structure in your script.

- If the condition you specify in the structure is true, then one set of commands (under then) is executed.

- If the condition is false, then the commands under the else portion of the structure are executed.

- You can use the test command in an if/then/else structure to test a condition.

- If you want more than two branches in your script, you can use the case structure.

- With a case structure, you can evaluate multiple conditions and execute a series of commands that are executed according to which condition is true.

- You can also use looping control structures within a shell script.

- Looping structures come in three varieties: the while loop, the until loop, and the for loop.

- A while loop executes over and over until a specified condition is no longer true.

- An until loop runs over and over as long as the condition is false. As soon as the condition is true, it stops.

- You can also use a for loop, which loops a specific number of times.

- It is very common to use the seq command within a for loop to create the sequence of numbers to determine how many times it will loop.

- There are three options for creating a number sequence with seq:

  - If you specify a single value, the sequence starts at one, increments by one, and ends at the specified value.

  - If you specify two values, the sequence starts at the first value, increments by one, and ends at the second value.

  - If you specify three values, the sequence starts at the first value, increments by the second value, and ends at the third value.

- You can process text streams to manipulate and modify text within a script or within a pipe.

- You can use the following utilities to process a text stream:

  - cut

  - sort

  - wc

Questions

1. Which of the following elements must be included at the beginning of every shell script?

   A. #Comment

   B. #!/bin/bash

   C. exit 0

   D. #begin script

2. You've created a shell script in your home directory named myscript. How can you execute it? (Choose two.)

   A. Enter **/bin/bash** ~/**myscript** at the shell prompt.

   B. Enter **myscript** at the shell prompt.

   C. Select Computer | Run in the graphical desktop; then enter ~/**myscript** and select Run.

   D. Enter **run** ~/**myscript** at the shell prompt.

   E. Enter **chmod u+x** ~/**myscript**; then enter ~/**myscript** at the shell prompt.

3. Which command will create a new variable named TOTAL and set its type to be "integer"?

   A. variable –i TOTAL

   B. declare –i TOTAL

   C. declare TOTAL –t integer

   D. TOTAL=integer

4. You need to display the text "Hello world" on the screen from within a shell script. Which command will do this?

    A. echo "Hello world"

    B. read Hello world

    C. writeln "Hello world"

    D. print "Hello world"

5. From within a shell script, you need to prompt users to enter their phone number. You need to assign the value they enter into a variable named $PHONE. Which command will do this?

    A. read "What is your phone number?" $PHONE

    B. read $PHONE

    C. read PHONE

    D. ? "What is your phone number?" PHONE

6. Which command can be used from within an if/then/else structure to evaluate whether or not a specified condition is true?

    A. eval

    B. ==

    C. test

    D. <>

7. Which command will evaluate to True within an if/then/else structure in a shell script if the variable num1 is less than the variable num2?

    A. eval num1 < num2

    B. test num1 < num2

    C. test num1 –lt num2

    D. test "num1" != "num2"

    E. eval "num1" != "num2"

8. In a shell script, you need to prompt the user to select from one of seven different options presented with the echo command. Which control structure would best evaluate the user's input and run the appropriate set of commands?

    A. while loop

    B. for loop

    C. until loop

    D. if/then/else

    E. case

9. Which control structure will keep processing over and over until a specified condition evaluates to false?

   A. while loop

   B. for loop

   C. until loop

   D. if/then/else

   E. case

10. Which control structures are considered to be branching structures? (Choose two.)

    A. while loop

    B. for loop

    C. until loop

    D. if/then/else

    E. case

11. Which control structure will keep processing over and over as long as the specified condition evaluates to false?

    A. while loop

    B. for loop

    C. until loop

    D. if/then/else

    E. case

12. Which control structure will process a specified number of times?

    A. while loop

    B. for loop

    C. until loop

    D. if/then/else

    E. case

13. Consider the following use of the seq command: "seq 3 9." What sequence of numbers will this command generate?

    A. 3, 4, 5, 6, 7, 8, 9

    B. 3, 6, 9

    C. 1, 4, 7, 10, 13, 16, 19, 22, 25

    D. 9, 18, 27

Answers

1. **B.** The **#!/bin/bash** element must be included at the beginning of every bash shell script.

2. **A, E.** You can enter **/bin/bash ~/myscript** or **chmod u+x ~/myscript** to make the script execute.

3. **B.** The **declare –i TOTAL** command will create the TOTAL variable and type it as integer.

4. **A.** The **echo "Hello world"** command will display the text "Hello world" on the screen from within a shell script.

5. **C.** The **read PHONE** command in a shell script will assign the value entered by the user into a variable named $PHONE.

6. **C.** The test command can be used from within an if/then/else structure to evaluate whether or not a specified condition is true.

7. **C.** The **test num1 –lt num2** command will evaluate to True within an if/then/else structure if the variable num1 is less than the variable num2.

8. **E.** The case structure is the best option presented to evaluate the user's choice of multiple selections and run the appropriate set of commands as a result.

9. **A.** A while loop will keep processing over and over until the specified condition evaluates to false.

10. **D, E.** The if/then/else and case structures are considered to be branching structures because they branch the script in one of several directions based on how a specified condition evaluates.

11. **C.** The until loop control structure will keep processing over and over as long as the specified condition evaluates to false.

12. **B.** The for loop control structure will process a specified number of times.

13. **A.** The **seq 3 9** command will generate the following sequence of numbers: 3, 4, 5, 6, 7, 8, 9. The first number specifies the starting number, while the second number specifies the ending number in the sequence. Because an increment is not specified, the sequence increments by 1.

## CHAPTER 13

Connecting Linux to a Network

In this chapter, you will learn about:

- Understanding IP networks
- Configuring network addressing parameters
- Troubleshooting network problems
- Encrypting remote access with OpenSSH

Up to this point, we've focused on configuring and using Linux as a stand-alone computer system. However, Linux functions extremely well in a networked environment. You can take just about any distribution and configure it to fill a wide variety of roles on your network, all for little or no cost. For example, you can configure a Linux system as any of the following:

- A networked client workstation
- A file and print server
- A domain controller
- A database server
- A DHCP server
- A DNS server
- A Web server
- An e-mail server
- A router
- A packet-filtering, stateful, or application-level firewall
- A proxy server
- A content filter

Linux is awesome! With other operating systems, you have to pay a lot of money to get this kind of functionality. With Linux, you've got just about everything you need to set up a very complex network, all at little or no cost. In this chapter, we'll focus on enabling basic networking on your Linux system so that it can talk to other computers.

Let's begin this chapter by reviewing how the IP protocol can enable communications between networked systems.

Understanding IP Networks

Before you can configure your Linux system to participate on a computer network, you have to first install a network interface, physically connect it to your network medium, and then configure it to communicate with the other computers on your particular network. Back in the early days of networking, you could choose from a variety of network interfaces and network protocols. Today, most of the networks you will work with will be Ethernet networks using the IP protocol.

Therefore, you need to know what an IP address is, what a subnet mask is, and how to configure the protocol such that a system can communicate with other systems on the network. To make sure you have the information you need, we'll briefly review IP addressing in this part of this chapter. We'll cover the following topics:

- What is a protocol?
- How IP addresses work
- How the subnet mask works
- Specifying the DNS server and default gateway router addresses

What Is a Protocol?

Strictly speaking, a protocol is a set of rules, and in the context of networking, a protocol is the set of rules that govern communication between two systems. A good analogy for a protocol is a human language. Before two people can communicate, they must speak the same language; otherwise, no information can be transferred between them. For example, suppose you were to call someone on the phone who doesn't speak your language. Even though they establish a connection by answering the call and they are listening to the information that you are sending, communication doesn't occur because they can't understand what you are saying. Why? Because the two of you don't share a common language.

The same holds true with computer systems. Before they can share information, they must be configured to use the same protocol. The protocol specifies how the information is encoded and sent on the network so that the receiving system can interpret it and reconstruct the data that was originally sent.

While there are many different protocols you can use on a computer network, you will probably spend most of your time working with the IP protocol, which is the networking protocol used on the Internet. IP works in conjunction with other protocols, such as the Transmission Control Protocol (TCP) or the User Datagram Protocol (UDP), to divide information being transmitted on the network into chunks.

To understand how this process works, you need to have a solid understanding of the OSI Reference Model. The OSI Reference Model was designed by delegates from major computer and telecom companies back in 1983. The goal was to design a network communications model that was modular in nature, allowing products from different vendors to interoperate. Prior to this, networking solutions tended to be proprietary, forcing implementers to purchase all of their components from the same vendor. By defining the OSI Reference Model, the industry created a standard that allows you to pick and choose components from a variety of vendors.

The OSI Reference Model divides the communication process between two hosts into layers. This is shown in Figure 13-1.

These layers break down the overall communication process into specific tasks. Information flows down through the layers on the sending system and is transmitted on the network medium. The information then flows up the layers on the receiving side.

The OSI Reference Model has seven layers:

1. **Physical** Transmits electrical signals between hosts.

2. **Data Link** Defines the rules and procedures for accessing the physical layer. It defines how hosts are identified on the network and how the network medium is accessed. It also specifies how to verify that the data received from the physical layer doesn't have any errors. Information received from upper layers is organized into *datagrams*.

3. **Network** Enables the routing of the data. It specifies how to recognize the address of neighboring nodes and routers. It also specifies how to determine the next network point to which a packet should be forwarded toward its destination. The *Internet Protocol (IP)* operates at this layer, as does the *Internet Control Message Protocol (ICMP)*.

Figure 13-1
The OSI
Reference Model

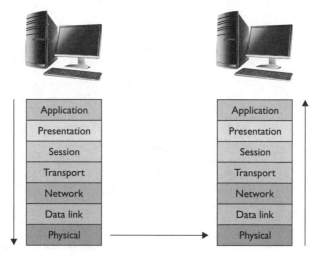

4. **Transport** On the sending host, the Transport layer receives information from the upper layers of the OSI model and divides it into small, transmittable chunks called *packets.* On the receiving host, the Transport layer reassembles packets from datagrams received from lower layers of the OSI model. The Transport layer provides error-checking mechanisms to ensure that data arrives at the destination host intact. The Transmission Control Protocol (TCP) and *User Datagram Protocol (UDP)* operate at this layer.

5. **Session** Responsible for establishing and maintaining connections between source and destination network hosts. These connections are called *sessions.*

6. **Presentation** Responsible for ensuring that information passing through the OSI layers is formatted correctly for the application on the destination system.

7. **Application** Responsible for providing applications with a way to access the network.

The IP protocol itself is used to only make sure each packet arrives at the destination system. The TCP or UDP protocol is used with IP to fragment the data from the sending host and then reassemble and resequence it when it arrives at the destination system, as shown in Figure 13-2.

The Internet Protocol (IP) is the protocol used on the Internet. It is a connectionless protocol designed to ensure data arrives at its destination host. The IP protocol relies upon information being broken down into transmittable chunks (packets) by the TPC or UDP protocol. Each packet is treated by IP as an independent data unit, separate from other data units. IP isn't concerned with fragmentation or resequencing; it's concerned only with making sure each packet arrives at the destination.

The job of keeping track of individual packets belongs to the Transmission Control Protocol (TCP). TCP is one of the two original components of the IP protocol suite.

Figure 13-2
Transferring
data with the IP
protocol

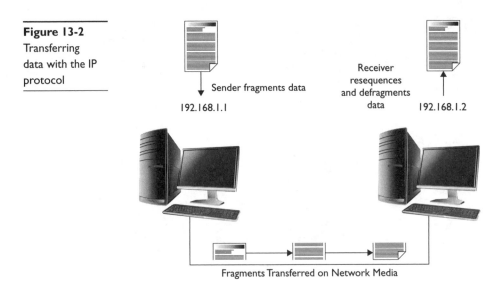

Sender fragments data

192.168.1.1

Receiver
resequences
and defragments
data

192.168.1.2

Fragments Transferred on Network Media

Frequently, the entire suite is commonly referred to as TCP/IP, but that isn't technically correct because UDP may be used with IP as well.

The TCP protocol ensures data is exchanged reliably directly between two network hosts. It does this by requiring acknowledgment of each packet sent from the sender to the receiver. Because of the way the IP protocol works, packets can be lost, duplicated, or delivered out of sequence. TCP detects these problems, requests retransmission of lost packets, and resequences packets received out of order. Essentially, TCP ensures the final reassembled data on the receiving system is a perfect copy of the data originally transmitted.

Using TCP with IP is kind of like using signature confirmation with a shipping company. When you send a package, the shipper requires the receiver to sign for the package, allowing the sender to verify that the package was received correctly. TCP/IP works in much the same manner. The TCP protocol is used by upper-layer applications that require a high degree of data integrity, including

- Web servers

- E-mail servers

- FTP servers

However, the data fidelity offered by TCP comes at a cost, primarily in the form of latency; in other words, it's kind of pokey. TCP requires a fair amount of network and processing overhead. Not all network applications require the high degree of data fidelity provided by TCP. Some upper-layer applications require less latency and can tolerate less reliability. These applications use the User Datagram Protocol (UDP) protocol instead of TCP.

UDP functions in a manner similar to TCP; however, it is a *connectionless* protocol. With UDP, IP packets are sent unacknowledged. It is usually implemented with applications that send very small amounts of data at a time or with applications that aren't affected if some of the data is lost and doesn't make it to the destination. UDP assumes that error checking and correction is either not necessary or will be performed somehow by the application, avoiding the processing overhead.

In this respect, UDP is similar to sending someone a postcard through the mail. A postcard doesn't contain much data, and the receiver doesn't have to sign for it. Essentially, the sender assumes that the mail carrier is reasonably reliable and that the information on the postcard isn't important enough to require the receiver to sign for it. UDP works in much the same way. Some upper-layer applications that make use of UDP include

- Streaming audio and video

- VoIP

These applications need very low latency and can tolerate the loss of some data, as long as it isn't excessive. If you think about it, losing a chunk of an e-mail message because some of the packets got lost would be unacceptable. You would have no way to reconstruct the missing information. With a video stream, however, a small amount of lost data may not even be noticeable. The video keeps playing with new data from the data stream.

In addition to IP, TCP, and UDP, you also need to be familiar with the Internet Control Message Protocol (ICMP) protocol. ICMP is another core protocol in the IP protocol suite. It differs in purpose from TCP and UDP, which are transport protocols. The primary role of ICMP is to test and verify network communications between hosts.

For example, to test network connectivity, the ping utility will send ICMP Echo Request packets to a remote host. If the host receives them, it will respond with an ICMP Echo Response packet to the sender. If the ICMP Echo Response packet is received, the sender knows that a viable network connection exists between the sender and receiver and that the receiver is responding to network requests. If an ICMP Echo Response packet is not received, the sender knows something is wrong and can begin trouble-shooting communications.

You also need to understand the concept of IP *ports.* Ports are provided by both the TCP and UDP protocols at the Transport layer. In essence, a port is a logical connection provided by TCP and UDP for upper-layer protocols. Ports allow a single host with a single IP address assigned to provide multiple network services. Each service uses the same IP address but operates using a different TCP or UDP port number.

For example, suppose you have a network server with an IP address of 192.168.1.1 assigned to it. You could configure both a web server and an FTP server to run at the same time on this server. Each service will listen for requests on the interface assigned an IP address of 192.168.1.1. However, the web server runs on port 80, while the FTP server runs on ports 20 and 21. Requests sent to port 80 are handled by the web service, while information sent to ports 20 and 21 is handled by the FTP service.

 NOTE The FTP service is somewhat unique in that it uses two ports: one for the control connection (port 21), and the other (port 20) for transferring data. Most services only use a single port.

You should become familiar with the various categories used to organize IP ports. Port numbers can range from 0 up to 65536 for each IP address. The way these ports are used is regulated by the Internet Corporation for Assigned Names and Numbers (ICANN). There are three different categories that IP ports are lumped into:

- **Well-known ports**   Reserved for specific services, well-known ports are those numbered from 0 to 1023. For example,
  - Ports 20 and 21: FTP
  - Port 23: Telnet
  - Port 25: SMTP
  - Port 80: HTTP
  - Port 110: POP3
  - Port 119: NNTP (news)

- Ports 137, 138, 139: NetBIOS

- Port 443: HTTPS

- **Registered ports**   ICANN has reserved ports 1024 through 49151 for special implementations. Organizations can program their own network service and then apply for a registered port number to be assigned to it.

- **Dynamic ports**   Dynamic ports are also called *private ports*. Ports 49152 through 65535 are designated as dynamic ports and are available for use by any network service. They are frequently used by network services that need to establish a temporary connection. For example, a service may negotiate a dynamic port with the client. It will then use that port just during the current session. When the session is complete, the port is closed and no longer used. The next time a connection is made, the service will negotiate a new dynamic port with the client.

How IP Addresses Work

Every host on an IP-based network must have a unique IP address assigned to it. An IP address is a Network layer (3) address that is *logically* assigned to a network host. Because the IP address is a logical address, it's not permanent. It can be changed at any time.

The IP address is different than the MAC address. The MAC address is a Data Link layer (2) hardware address that is burned into a ROM chip on every network board sold in the world. The MAC address is hard-coded on the board and can't be changed.

 NOTE   The ARP protocol maps logical IP addresses assigned to systems to their hard-coded MAC addresses.

An IP address consists of four numbers, separated by periods. Examples of valid IP addresses include

- 12.34.181.78

- 192.168.1.1

- 246.270.3.8

In decimal notation, each number must be between 0 and 255. For example, 192.168.1.1 is a valid IP address. Examples of *invalid* IP addresses include the following:

- **256.78.1.3**   Can't use a value greater than 255.

- **10.3.4**   Must use four values.

A decimal number in an IP address can't be greater than 255 because each number in the address is an eight-bit binary number, called an *octet*. Because each octet is a binary number, it can be represented as 0's and 1's. For example, the address 192.168.1.1 can be represented in binary form as

```
11000000.10101000.00000001.00000001
```

There are several simple ways to convert between the eight-bit binary address and the three-digit decimal version of an IP address. One option is to use the calculator software that comes with most Linux distributions (and even Windows) in Scientific or Programmer mode. To convert a decimal IP address number to binary, enter the decimal version and then click the Bin option.

You can also go the other direction by entering a binary number in Bin mode and then switching to Dec mode, which will convert the binary number to its decimal equivalent.

If you're the mathematical type, you can also perform the conversion manually. Use the following to determine the value of each bit in a binary number:

- Bit 1 = 128
- Bit 2 = 64
- Bit 3 = 32
- Bit 4 = 16
- Bit 5 = 8
- Bit 6 = 4
- Bit 7 = 2
- Bit 8 = 1

For example, 11000000 = 128 + 64 = 192. If all eight bits in an octet are set to a value of 1 (such as 11111111), then the decimal value of the octet is 128 + 64 + 32 + 16 + 8 + 4 + 2 + 1 = 255. That's why no decimal value of an octet can exceed 255: we used up all the available binary 1's!

Some IP addresses are reserved and can't be assigned to a host. For example, the last octet in a host IP address can't be a 0. This is reserved for the address of the network segment itself that the host resides on. For example, the network address for the host assigned an IP address of 192.168.1.1 is 192.168.1.0.

In addition, the last octet of an IP address assigned to a host can't be 255. This is reserved for sending a broadcast to all hosts on the segment. In the preceding example, the broadcast address for a host with an IP address of 192.168.1.1 would be 192.168.1.255.

It's critical that you understand that every host on an IP-based network must have a *unique* IP address assigned to it. No two hosts on the same IP network can have the same IP address assigned. If the host resides on a public network, such as the Internet, it must use a *globally* unique IP address. You can apply to the Internet Assigned Numbers Authority (IANA) for a block of registered IP addresses. Once assigned, no one else in the world can use those IP addresses on a public network.

This introduces an important problem with IP version 4. The 32-bit addressing scheme used by IPv4 allows for a maximum of four billion possible unique addresses. This seemed like a lot of addresses back when IPv4 was originally defined. However, today this finite amount of available addresses is quickly running out. In fact, at the time this was written, there are very few registered IP addresses available.

To address this issue, a new version of IP has been proposed called IP version 6 (IPv6), which is expected to replace IPv4 over the next decade. Instead of 32 bits, IPv6 defines 128-bit IP addresses. This allows for a maximum of 3.4×10^{38} total unique IP addresses! (We can only hope this will be enough!)

IPv6 addresses are composed of eight four-character hexadecimal numbers, separated by colons instead of periods. For example, a sample valid IPv6 address could be 35BC:FA77:4898:DAFC:200C:FBBC:A007:8973. Most Linux distributions support both IPv4 and IPv6.

The uptake of IPv6 has been slower than originally anticipated. Back in the early 1990s, IPv6 was known as IP Next Generation (IPNG) and was predicted to replace IPv4 in a very short time frame. Obviously, this didn't happen. One of the key reasons is that a rather elegant interim solution was arrived at while everyone was working on IPv6: using private networks with Network Address Translation (NAT).

Using Network Address Translation, you can use a NAT router to present a single registered IP address to a *public* network while using *private* IP addresses on the network behind it. This is shown in Figure 13-3.

NAT routers have many advantages. Primary among these is that you can hide a huge private network behind a very limited number of public interfaces. This allows a large organization to implement their network and only need a relatively small number of globally unique public IP addresses.

Within each class of IP address are blocks of addresses called *private* or *reserved* IP addresses. These addresses are unallocated and can be used by anyone who wants to use them. This allows you to use private addresses on your local network and still be able to connect to public networks, such as the Internet. All traffic from your private network appears to be originating from the one registered IP address configured on the public side of the NAT router. The private IP address ranges are

- 10.0.0.0–10.255.255.255 (Class A)
- 172.16.0.0–172.31.255.255 (Class B)
- 192.168.0.0–192.168.255.255 (Class C)

These are nonroutable addresses, meaning that if you try to use them on a public network, such as the Internet, IP routers won't forward data to or from them. These addresses

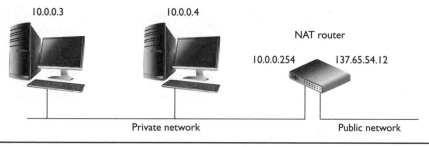

Figure 13-3 Using a NAT router to separate public and private networks

are translated via network address translation to a public IP address by a NAT router, which allows anyone in the world to use these private IP address ranges without worrying about conflicts even if multiple instances are used. NAT makes this all possible!

How the Subnet Mask Works

If you've ever configured a system with an IP address, you probably noticed that you also had to assign a *subnet mask*. To understand how a subnet mask works, you first need to understand that IP addresses are divided into two parts:

- Network address
- Node address

Part of an IPv4 address identifies the network the host resides on. The rest uniquely identifies a particular host (node) on the network. The main thing to remember is that every system on the same network segment must have exactly the same numbers in the network portion of the address. However, they each must have a unique node portion. This is shown in Figure 13-4.

How much of the address is used for the network and how much is used for the node is defined by the subnet mask. Default subnet masks include the following:

```
255.0.0.0
255.255.0.0
255.255.255.0
```

Any subnet mask octet with a 255 in it identifies a portion of the IP address that is used for the network address. Remember that the operating system sees IP addresses in binary notation. It also sees subnet masks in binary notation. If you have an IP address of 192.168.1.1 and a subnet mask of 255.255.255.0, the subnet mask specifies that the first three octets of the address are network and the last octet is node. This is shown in Figure 13-5.

IP addresses are divided into five different classes. Each address class has its own default subnet mask. For our purposes here, we only need to be concerned with the first three address classes:

- **Class A** The decimal value of the first octet must be between 1 and 126. In a Class A address, the first octet is the network address and the last three octets are the node address. Therefore, the default subnet mask is 255.0.0.0. Class A allows 126 total possible networks (that's not a lot), but they do offer 16.7 million possible node addresses per network (that is a lot!).

Figure 13-4
Network vs. node
in an IP address

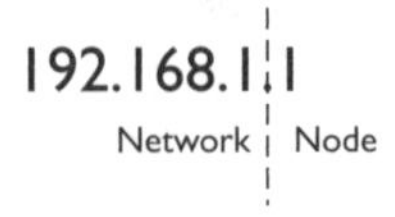

192.168.1.1

Network | Node

Figure 13-5

Using the subnet mask to define the network and node portions of an IP address

11000000.10101000.00000001:00000001 (192.168.1.1)
11111111.11111111.11111111:00000000 (255.255.255.0)

Network ⋮ Node

- **Class B** The decimal value of the first octet must be between 128 and 191. In a Class B address, the first two octets are the network address and the last two octets are the node address. Therefore, the default subnet mask is 255.255.0.0. Using Class B addressing allows 16,384 possible networks with 65,534 million possible nodes each.

- **Class C** The decimal value of the first octet must be between 192 and 223. In a Class C address, the first three octets are the network address while the last octet is the node address. Therefore, the default subnet mask is 255.255.255.0. Because so much of the address is used for the network address, a huge number of Class C networks are available (2,097,152 possible networks). However, only a limited number of hosts (254 maximum) can exist on any given Class C network.

Subnet masks are sometimes noted using a type of shorthand. This is done by adding a slash (/) and the number of bits used in the mask after the IP address; for example, 192.168.1.1/24. The /24 parameter indicates 24 bits are used for the subnet mask, which would be written out in longhand as 255.255.255.0.

You don't have to use these default subnet masks. You could define a subnet mask of 255.255.0.0 for a Class A address, for example. You can also use only part of an octet for the network address. This is called *partial subnetting*. For example, you could define a subnet mask of 255.255.252.0 for a Class B address. In addition to the first and second octets, this mask would also include the first six of the eight bits in the third octet to be used for the network portion of the address. In essence, bits are "stolen" from the available node addresses to be used for network address, adding additional subnets. This allows you to create additional networks, but reduces the number of host addresses available on each.

The important thing to remember is that for two hosts on the same network segment to communicate, they need to have exactly the same network address, which means they must have exactly the same subnet mask. For example, suppose you have three systems as shown in Figure 13-6.

Host 1 and Host 2 both have the exact same network address and subnet mask. These two hosts can communicate on the IP network segment. However, Host 3 uses a subnet mask of 255.255.252.0 instead of 255.255.255.0. Therefore, Host 3 has a different network address than Host 1 and Host 2 and won't be able to communicate with them without the use of a network router.

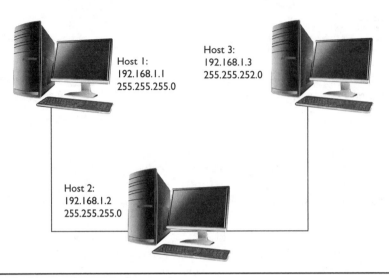

Figure 13-6   Hosts with wrong subnet masks

Specifying the DNS Server and Default Gateway Router Addresses

So far, we've discussed the IP address and subnet mask parameters that you need to specify when configuring the IP stack on a Linux system. However, you should also specify the DNS server address and the default gateway router address.

If you've used the Internet, you know that you can use domain names, such as www .google.com, to navigate to particular hosts on the Web. However, your system can't work with alphanumeric domain names. It has no idea where www.google.com is or what it has to offer.

To make this work, your local system needs to resolve domain names into IP addresses. One of the ways this can be done is to submit the domain name to a DNS server. When a DNS server receives a name resolution request, it matches the domain name submitted with an IP address and returns it to the requesting system. Then your system can contact the specified host using its IP address. For example, in Figure 13-7, the domain name www.google.com has been resolved to an IP address of 74.126.224.81 by the DNS server.

To make this system work, you need to provide your system with the IP address of the DNS server you want it to use. We'll spend more time working with DNS later in this chapter.

In addition, you also need to specify the IP address of your network's default gateway router. The IP protocol was designed from the ground up with internetworking in mind. In an internetwork, multiple network segments are connected together using routers. If a system on one segment tries to send data to a host that doesn't reside on the same network, the IP protocol will redirect the packets to the default gateway router for its segment. The router will then use a variety of routing protocols to determine where the packets should be sent to get them to their destination, as shown in Figure 13-8.

```
                        tux@ws2:~/Desktop                    _  □  ×
  File  Edit  View  Terminal  Help
ws2:/ # dig www.google.com

; <<>> DiG 9.7.1 <<>> www.google.com
;; global options: +cmd
;; Got answer:
;; ->>HEADER<<- opcode: QUERY, status: NOERROR, id: 50615
;; flags: qr rd ra; QUERY: 1, ANSWER: 6, AUTHORITY: 4, ADDITIONAL: 0

;; QUESTION SECTION:
;www.google.com.                        IN      A

;; ANSWER SECTION:
www.google.com.         604782  IN      CNAME   www.l.google.com.
www.l.google.com.       284     IN      A       74.125.224.81
www.l.google.com.       284     IN      A       74.125.224.82
www.l.google.com.       284     IN      A       74.125.224.83
www.l.google.com.       284     IN      A       74.125.224.84
www.l.google.com.       284     IN      A       74.125.224.80

;; AUTHORITY SECTION:
google.com.             172780  IN      NS      ns2.google.com.
google.com.             172780  IN      NS      ns3.google.com.
google.com.             172780  IN      NS      ns1.google.com.
google.com.             172780  IN      NS      ns4.google.com.
```

Figure 13-7   Resolving a domain name into an IP address

In Figure 13-8, the sending system 192.168.1.1 is sending data to 10.0.0.1. However, 10.0.0.1 resides on the 10.0.0.0 network segment, not the 192.168.1.0 network segment. Therefore, the IP stack on the sending system redirects the data to the router connecting the two segments together. The routing software on the router knows where the 10.0.0.0 network segment resides and forwards the packets on to that network, where they are delivered to the receiving system.

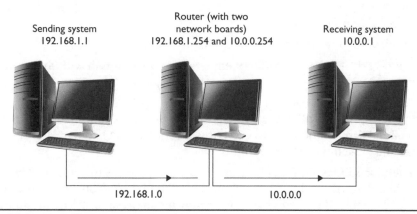

Figure 13-8   Using IP in a routed network

This system is very powerful. It's what allows you to connect to the Internet and pull down web pages from a server somewhere else in the world. However, for it to work, your local system needs to know the IP address of the router to which it should forward packets if they are addressed to a system that doesn't reside on the local network segment. You need to configure this parameter whenever you configure network settings on a Linux system. If you don't, the system will be able to communicate only with systems on the same local network segment.

Configuring Network Addressing Parameters

Probably the most common network interface you will work with in a Linux system is an Ethernet interface. Under Linux, when we refer to a "network interface," we are referring to:

- The physical network interface card (NIC) hardware installed in the system
- The kernel modules (drivers) loaded to support the physical NIC
- The IP networking configuration parameters assigned to the interface

Most newer computers already have an Ethernet interface integrated in the motherboard. However, if you need to install an Ethernet network interface in your system, complete the following tasks:

- Install the Ethernet board.
- Configure IP parameters.
- Configure routing parameters.
- Configure name resolver settings.

Installing the Ethernet Board

Obviously, the first thing you need to do when configuring an Ethernet interface is to install the NIC hardware in the system. To do this, follow these steps:

1. Power your system off.
2. Install your Ethernet board in an available expansion slot.
3. Connect the Ethernet board to your network switch or hub with the appropriate drop cable.
4. Power your system back on. If you installed a PCI Ethernet board, your Linux operating system will probably detect it as it boots and automatically load the required kernel modules. However, this will not always happen. Here are some general guidelines to keep in mind:
   - **Plug-and-Play Ethernet boards** If Linux recognizes the Plug-and-Play board, it will load the appropriate kernel module for you automatically if it is available. If not, you may have to download the appropriate module from the board manufacturer's web site and load it manually.

- **ISA Ethernet boards** Linux probably won't automatically detect older ISA boards. You'll most likely need to manually load the appropriate kernel module using modprobe. You'll also need to specify the IRQ and the I/O port used by the board when you load the kernel module. Better yet, just go get a Plug-and-Play NIC and use it instead.

5. After the system has booted, you should check your module configuration file and verify that the appropriate kernel module has been loaded and that an alias has been created for the new board. Ethernet adapters in your Linux system use the following aliases:

- **eth0** The first Ethernet adapter in your system

- **eth1** The second Ethernet adapter in your system

- **eth2** The third Ethernet adapter in your system, and so on . . .

The file to check depends on your distribution. Some distributions use the /etc/modprobe .conf or /etc/modules.conf file, while others use a configuration file in /etc/modprobe.d. For example, my OpenSUSE system (which is installed in a VMware virtual machine) uses the /etc/modprobe.d/50-vmnics.conf file, as shown in Figure 13-9.

At this point, your network interface is loaded and active. However, before you can use it, you have to configure it with the IP protocol.

Configuring IP Parameters

Remember, you need to configure your network interface with four parameters in order for the system to participate on an IP-based computer network:

- IP address
- Subnet mask
- Default gateway router address
- DNS server address

There are two different ways to do this, as outlined in Table 13-1.

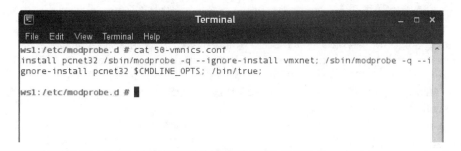

Figure 13-9 A kernel module configuration file for an Ethernet board

Option	Description	Advantages	Disadvantages
Static address assignment	You manually configure a network host with IP address parameters.	The address used by a particular host never changes. This option is usually used by servers in the network.	The host consumes the address regardless of whether the system is powered on or off. This strategy also requires a lot of legwork on the part of the system administrator. He or she has to visit each computer in the network and manually specify IP parameters.
Dynamic address assignment	A network host contacts a Dynamic Host Configuration Protocol (DHCP) server when it boots. The DHCP server dynamically assigns an IP address to the host for a specified period of time called a *lease*.	This option makes configuring IP parameters for a large number of network hosts very easy. Just power the system on and it gets its IP address information. It also conserves IP address usage. Addresses used by systems that are powered off can be reassigned to other network hosts.	You must have a DHCP server installed and configured before you can use this option. In addition, the address assigned to a particular host can change frequently, making it an unsuitable option for network infrastructure systems such as servers. Because of this, this option is usually used for workstations.

Table 13-1   IP Address Assignment Options

If you want to statically assign IP address parameters to a Linux system, you can use the ifconfig command. If **ifconfig** is entered without any options, it displays the current status of all network interfaces in the system, as shown in Figure 13-10.

Notice in Figure 13-10 that two network interfaces are displayed, eth0 and lo. The eth0 interface is the Ethernet network interface installed in the system. The lo interface is the local loopback virtual network interface. The lo interface is required for many Linux services to run properly, so don't tinker with it. Notice in Figure 13-10 that ifconfig also displays extensive information about each network interface. Some of the more important parameters include those shown in Table 13-2.

In addition to displaying information about a particular network interface, ifconfig can also configure it with the IP address parameters discussed earlier. The syntax for using ifconfig is ifconfig *interface ip_address* netmask *subnet_mask* broadcast *broadcast_address*. For example, suppose I wanted to assign the eth0 interface an IP address of 192.168.1.1, a subnet mask of 255.255.255.0, and a broadcast address of 192.168.1.255. I would enter **ifconfig eth0 192.168.1.1 netmask 255.255.255.0 broadcast 192.168.1.255** at the shell prompt.

It's important to remember that this IP address assignment isn't persistent. If you reboot the system, it will be lost. To make it persistent, you need to configure a special file in the /etc/sysconfig/network directory. For example, the file used to configure the

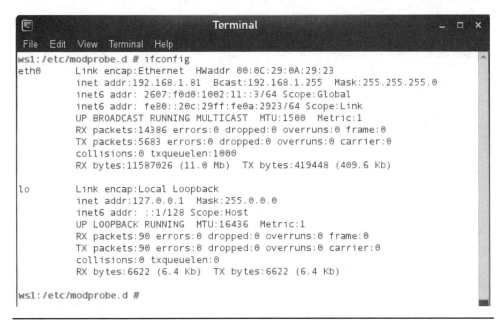

```
ws1:/etc/modprobe.d # ifconfig
eth0      Link encap:Ethernet  HWaddr 00:0C:29:0A:29:23
          inet addr:192.168.1.81  Bcast:192.168.1.255  Mask:255.255.255.0
          inet6 addr: 2607:f0d0:1002:11::3/64 Scope:Global
          inet6 addr: fe80::20c:29ff:fe0a:2923/64 Scope:Link
          UP BROADCAST RUNNING MULTICAST  MTU:1500  Metric:1
          RX packets:14386 errors:0 dropped:0 overruns:0 frame:0
          TX packets:5683 errors:0 dropped:0 overruns:0 carrier:0
          collisions:0 txqueuelen:1000
          RX bytes:11587026 (11.0 Mb)  TX bytes:419448 (409.6 Kb)

lo        Link encap:Local Loopback
          inet addr:127.0.0.1  Mask:255.0.0.0
          inet6 addr: ::1/128 Scope:Host
          UP LOOPBACK RUNNING  MTU:16436  Metric:1
          RX packets:90 errors:0 dropped:0 overruns:0 frame:0
          TX packets:90 errors:0 dropped:0 overruns:0 carrier:0
          collisions:0 txqueuelen:0
          RX bytes:6622 (6.4 Kb)  TX bytes:6622 (6.4 Kb)

ws1:/etc/modprobe.d #
```

Figure 13-10   Using ifconfig to view network interface information

first Ethernet interface on some distributions is named ifcfg-eth0. On other distributions, this file will be named using the MAC address of the NIC; for example, ifcfg-eth-id-00:0c:29:d1:52:d4 would be the configuration file for the Ethernet interface in the system with a MAC address of 00:0C:29:D1:52:D4, which would also be your eth0 interface if there was only one NIC installed. Others distributions will name this file using the alias assigned to the interface, such as eth0.

ifconfig Parameter	Description
HWaddr	The MAC address of the network board
inet addr	The IP address assigned to the interface
Bcast	The broadcast address of the network segment
Mask	The subnet mask assigned to the interface
RX packets	Statistics for received packets
TX packets	Statistics for transmitted packets
Collisions	The number of Ethernet collisions detected
RX bytes	The number of bytes of data received by the interface since it was brought up
TX bytes	The number of bytes of data transmitted by the interface since it was brought up

Table 13-2   ifconfig Output

Whatever it happens to be named in your particular distribution, this file configures the interface when the system is powered on. Sample parameters for this interface are shown here:

```
ws1:/etc/sysconfig/network # cat ifcfg-eth0
BOOTPROTO='static'
BROADCAST=''
ETHTOOL_OPTIONS=''
IPADDR='192.168.1.81/24'
MTU=''
NAME='82545EM Gigabit Ethernet Controller (Copper)'
NETMASK=''
NETWORK=''
REMOTE_IPADDR=''
STARTMODE='auto'
USERCONTROL='no'
LABEL_0='0'
IPADDR_0='2607:f0d0:1002:0011:0000:0000:0000:0003'
PREFIXLEN_0='64'
```

Some of the configuration options you can use in this configuration file are listed in Table 13-3.

The lines for IPADDR, NETMASK, NETWORK, and BROADCAST are not required if BOOTPROTO is set to dhcp.

After making any changes to these files, you will need to restart your network interface to apply the changes. To do this, enter **ifdown** *interface* followed by **ifup** *interface*, where *interface* is the alias of the interface, such as eth0.

This is all well and good if you want to use a static address assignment, but what if you want to get an address dynamically from a DHCP server? You can configure your network interface to do this using the dhclient command at the shell prompt. The syntax for using this command is dhclient *interface*. For example, you could enter **dhclient eth0** to specify that your eth0 interface get its IP address information dynamically from a DHCP server. This is shown in Figure 13-11.

Notice in Figure 13-11 that the dhclient utility broadcasted a DHCPREQUEST packet on the eth0 interface. In response, the DHCP server with an IP address of 192.168.1.1 sent a DHCPACK packet back with an IP address of 192.168.1.131 that was assigned to the eth0 interface.

In addition to the command-line utilities discussed here, most Linux distributions provide some kind of graphical interface you can use to configure your network interfaces. For example, on SUSE Linux, you can use the Network Settings YaST module to configure your network board as well as the IP address information assigned to it. This module is shown in Figure 13-12.

Other distributions usually have similar graphical utilities that you can use to manage IP addressing information.

Let's practice working with the ifconfig command in the following exercise.

Option	Description	Other Possible Values
BOOTPROTO="static"	This option specifies that the interface use a static IP address assignment.	Set to dhcp to dynamically assign an address.
STARTMODE="auto"	This option specifies that the interface be brought online when the system is booted.	Set to manual to manually start the interface. Some distributions use onboot instead of auto.
IPADDR="192.168.1.81/24"	Assigns an IP address of 192.168.1.10 to the interface with a subnet mask of 255.255.255.0 (a 24-bit mask).	
NETMASK="subnet_mask"	If the netmask isn't assigned with a prefix in the IPADDR parameter, you can use NETMASK= to assign a subnet mask to the interface.	
NETWORK="192.168.1.0"	Specifies the network address of the segment that the interface is connected to.	
BROADCAST="192.168.1.255"	Specifies the broadcast address of the segment the interface is connected to.	
MTU=	Specifies the size of the Maximum Transmission Unit (which is 1500 by default on an Ethernet network).	If your network uses jumbo frames, you can set this parameter to 9000.
LABEL_0='0' IPADDR_0='2607: f0d0:1002:0011:0000:0000:0000:0003' PREFIXLEN_0='64'	These parameters are used to assign an IPv6 address to the eth0 interface.	

Table 13-3   Configuring Persistent Parameters for a Network Interface

Exercise 13-1: Working with Network Interfaces   In this exercise, you will practice using the ifconfig command to manage your network interface. This exercise assumes that you have an Ethernet network board installed in your Linux system. Follow these steps:

1. Boot your Linux system and log in as a standard user.

2. Open a terminal session.

3. Switch to your root user account by entering **su –**, followed by your root user's password.

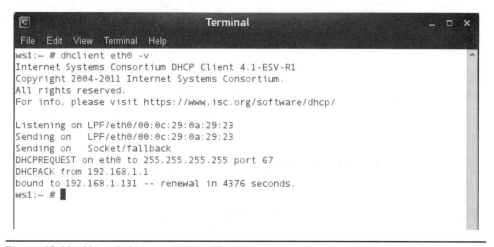

Figure 13-11   Using dhclient to obtain an IP address lease

4. At the shell prompt, enter **ifconfig**. Record the following information about your Ethernet interface:

- MAC address
- IP address
- Broadcast address
- Subnet mask

5. At the shell prompt, enter the **cd** command to change to the /etc/sysconfig/ network directory.

6. Enter the **ls** command to identify the configuration file for your network board.

7. Enter the **cat** command to view the contents of the configuration file for your Ethernet network interface board.

8. Bring your interface down by entering **ifdown eth0** at the shell prompt.

9. Bring your interface back up by entering **ifup eth0** at the shell prompt.

10. Change the IP address assigned to your Ethernet network interface to 192.168.1.100 by entering **ifconfig eth0 192.168.1.100 netmask 255.255.255.0 broadcast 192.168.1.255** at the shell prompt.

11. Enter **ifconfig** again and verify that the change was applied.

12. Enter **ifconfig** again to change your IP configuration parameters back to their original values.

13. If you have a DHCP server on your network segment, modify your network interface configuration to use DHCP and then dynamically assign an IP address to your Ethernet board by entering **dhclient eth0** at the shell prompt.

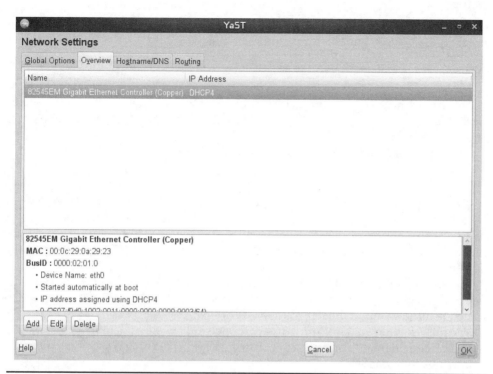

Figure 13-12   Using the YaST Network Settings module

Configuring Routing Parameters

You may have noticed that we didn't configure two important IP parameters in the preceding topics in this chapter: the default gateway router address and the DNS server address.

Using the IP protocol, routers do just what their name implies: they route data across multiple networks to deliver information to a destination host. Routers operate at the Network layer and connect various networks together.

Routers are usually implemented in conjunction with a gateway. The router hardware itself may be as simple as a computer system with two NICs installed, or it may be a specialized hardware appliance dedicated to routing.

One of the primary jobs performed by routers is to determine the best way to get information to the right destination host. To do this, a router maintains a routing table of available routes. Routers use an algorithm that evaluates distance, cost, and network status to determine the best route to the destination host. Even if it isn't configured as a router, every Linux system maintains a routing table in RAM that it uses to determine where to send data on a network.

When configuring networking parameters on a Linux system, one of the most important tasks you need to perform is configuring the default router address. The default router is the default location that packets are sent to if they are addressed to a host that doesn't reside on the local network segment. Your default gateway router address is stored in the /etc/sysconfig/network/routes file, shown here:

```
ws1:~ # cat /etc/sysconfig/network/routes
default 192.168.1.1 - -
```

The syntax for specifying the default route in this file is default *router_IP_address*. Notice in the preceding example that the default gateway router address is set to 192.168.1.1.

The syntax for adding a route to the routes file is shown next:

```
DESTINATION          GATEWAY NETMASK   INTERFACE    [TYPE]
```

The first column contains the route's destination. It may contain the IP address or DNS hostname of a network or host. I recommend you use IP addresses, not DNS names, in this file. If your DNS server were to go down or become unreachable, routing would cease to function. Entering **default** in this column indicates the route is the default gateway.

The second column contains the default gateway or a gateway through which a host or a network can be accessed. In this column, specify the IP address of a router that can route the information to the remote network or host.

The third column contains the netmask for networks or hosts behind a gateway. The fourth column applies the route to a specific interface. If nothing is specified, the route applies to all interfaces.

 NOTE If you need to leave a column in this file blank, be sure to enter a dash (-).

The fifth column is optional and is used to specify the route type. You can enter one of the following:

- **unicast** The route specifies a real path to the destination route.
- **local** The destination is the localhost. Packets sent to this route are looped back and delivered to the local machine.
- **broadcast** The destination is a broadcast address. Packets sent to this route are sent as link broadcasts.
- **multicast** Used for multicast routing. This type of route is not typically used with most routing tables.
- **unreachable** Configures the route destination as unreachable. Packets sent to this route are silently dropped.

This is a sample entry in a routes file:

```
207.68.156.51      207.68.145.45      255.255.255.255      eth1
```

After making any changes to the routes file, you will need to restart your network interface by entering **ifdown** *interface* followed by **ifup** *interface*.

You should also be familiar with how to manage routes with the route command at the shell prompt. You use the route command to display or modify the routing table on the Linux host. If you enter route without options, it displays the current routing table, as shown in this example:

```
ws1:~ # route
Kernel IP routing table
Destination     Gateway         Genmask         Flags Metric Ref    Use Iface
192.168.1.0     *               255.255.255.0   U     0      0        0 eth0
link-local      *               255.255.0.0     U     0      0        0 eth0
loopback        *               255.0.0.0       U     0      0        0 lo
default         192.168.1.1     0.0.0.0         UG    0      0        0 eth0
```

You can add routes to the host's route table by entering **route add –net** *network_address* **netmask** *netmask* **gw** *router_address*. For example, suppose you needed to add a route to the 192.168.2.0/24 network through the router with an IP address of 192.168.1.254. You could do this by entering **route add –net 192.168.2.0 netmask 255.255.255.0 gw 192.168.1.254** at the shell prompt.

You can also remove existing routes from the routing table on a Linux host using the route command. This is done by entering **route del –net** *network_address* **netmask** *netmask* **gw** *router_address* at the shell prompt. For example, suppose you wanted to remove the route just added in the preceding paragraph. You could do this by entering **route del –net 192.168.2.0 netmask 255.255.255.0 gw 192.168.1.254** at the shell prompt.

You can also use route to set the default route by entering **route add default gw** *router_address* at the shell prompt. For example, if you wanted to add 192.168.1.254 as your default gateway router, you would enter **route add default gw 192.168.1.254** at the shell prompt.

Be aware that any changes you make with the route command are not persistent. If you were to reboot your system, the changes would be gone. If you want the route changes to be persistent across reboots, you need to add them to your /etc/sysconfig/network/routes file.

Configuring Name Resolver Settings

When configuring IP settings for a network interface, you also need to specify the system's hostname and the IP address of your DNS server. Because you are most likely a savvy Internet user, you know that you can use domain names to navigate to particular hosts on the Web. However, your Linux system (or any other operating system, for that matter) can't work with the alphanumeric domain names that we are used to.

For example, when you open a browser window and enter **http://www.google.com** in the URL field, your browser, IP protocol, and operating system have no clue where to go to get the requested information. To make this work, your local system needs to first resolve these domain names into IP addresses.

In the old days, basic hostname-to-IP address resolution was performed by the /etc/hosts file, which contains IP address-to-host name mappings. The hosts file contains one line per host record. The syntax is

```
IP_address host_name alias
```

For example, consider the following hosts file entry:

```
192.168.1.1 mylinux.mydom.com mylinux
```

This record resolves either the fully qualified DNS name of mylinux.mydom.com or the alias (CNAME) of mylinux to an IP address of 192.168.1.1. Usually this file only contains the IP address and host name of the local system. But you can add other entries too.

 NOTE The /etc/hosts file still exists on Linux systems. In fact it is the first name resolver used by default by most distributions. Only if a record for the requested domain name doesn't exist in the hosts file will the operating system then try to resolve the host name using DNS. Because of this, you have to manage your hosts file very carefully. Many network hacks exploit this function of the operating system. A malicious web site or malware may try to rewrite your hosts file with name mappings to fake web sites that look like your favorite auction or banking site but instead are elaborate phishing web sites designed to steal your personal information.

Using the hosts file to resolve hostnames works just fine; however, it really isn't feasible as the sole means of name resolution. The file would have to be enormously huge in order to resolve all of the domain names used by hosts on the Internet. In addition, you would have to manually add, remove, and modify hostname mappings in the file whenever a domain name changed on the Internet. What a nightmare! Can you imagine trying to manage this type of hosts file for an entire network of users?

A better option is to submit the domain name to a DNS server. When a DNS server receives a name resolution request, it matches the domain name submitted with an IP address and returns it to the requesting system. Your system can then contact the specified host using its IP address. Here's how it works:

1. The system needing to resolve a hostname sends a request to the DNS server it's been configured to use on IP port 53. If the DNS server is authoritative for the zone where the requested hostname resides, it responds with the appropriate IP address. If not, the process continues on to Step 2.

 NOTE A DNS server is considered to be authoritative if it has a record for the domain name being requested in its database of name mappings.

---

2. The DNS server sends a request to a root-level DNS server. There are 13 root-level DNS servers on the Internet. Every DNS server is automatically configured with the IP addresses of these servers. These root-level DNS servers are configured with records that resolve to authoritative DNS servers for each top-level domain (.com, .gov, .edu, .au, .de, .uk, and so on).

3. The root-level DNS server responds to your DNS server with the IP address of a DNS server that is authoritative for the top-level domain of the domain name you are trying to resolve.

4. Your DNS server sends the name resolution query to the DNS server that is authoritative for the hostname's top-level domain (such as .com).

5. The top-level domain DNS server responds to your DNS server with the IP address of a DNS server that's authoritative for the DNS zone of the hostname you need to resolve.

6. Your DNS server sends a name resolution request to the DNS server that's authoritative for the zone where the hostname you are trying to resolve resides.

7. The authoritative DNS server responds to your DNS server with the IP address for the hostname.

8. Your DNS server responds to your system with the IP address mapped to the hostname, and the respective system is contacted using this IP address.

 NOTE After this process happens once for a particular name mapping, most DNS servers will cache the mapping for a period of time. That way, if a resolution request for the same hostname is received again, it can respond directly to the client without going through this whole process.

Therefore, to make this system work, you must provide your system with the IP address of the DNS server you want it to use. This is configured in the /etc/resolv.conf file. This file defines the search prefix and the nameservers to use. Here is sample content from my system's resolv.conf file:

```
search mydom.com
nameserver 192.168.1.1
nameserver 192.168.1.2
```

As you can see in this example, the file contains two types of entries:

- **search**   Specifies the domain name that should be used to fill out incomplete hostnames. For example, if you were to try to resolve a host name of WS1, the name would be automatically converted to the fully qualified domain name of WS1.mydom.com. The syntax is search *domain*.

- **nameserver**   Specifies the IP address of the DNS server you want to use for name resolution. You can configure up to three DNS servers. If the first server fails or is otherwise unreachable, the next DNS server is used. The syntax is nameserver *DNS_server_IP_address*.

You can use the /etc/nsswitch.conf (name service switch) file to define the order in which services will be used for name resolution. These are the two lines of the file you need to be concerned with:

```
hosts:        files dns
networks:     files dns
```

These two entries specify that the /etc/hosts file (files) is consulted first for name resolution. If there is no applicable entry, the query is then sent to the DNS server (dns) specified in the resolv.conf file.

Troubleshooting Network Problems

Getting your network interface installed is only half the battle. To enable communications, you need to use a variety of testing and monitoring tools to make sure the network itself is working properly. We'll discuss how to do this in this part of the chapter and cover the following topics:

- Using ping
- Using netstat
- Using traceroute
- Using name resolution tools

Using ping

The ping utility is my best friend. It is one of the handiest tools in my networking virtual toolbox. I use ping all the time to test connectivity between hosts through the network. Ping works by sending an ICMP echo request packet from the source system to the destination system. The destination system then responds with an ICMP echo response packet. This process is shown in Figure 13-13.

If the ICMP echo response packet is received by the sending system, you know three things:

- Your network interface is working correctly.
- The destination system is up and working correctly.
- The network hardware between your system and the destination system is working correctly.

This is valuable information to know! Be warned, however, that many host-based firewalls used by many operating systems are configured by default to not respond to ICMP echo request packets. This is done to prevent a variety of denial of service (DoS) attacks that utilize a flood of ping requests. This configuration can give the false impression that the destination system is down. It's actually up and running just fine; it's just that the firewall on the host is stopping the ping packets from reaching the operating system.

Figure 13-13
Using ping

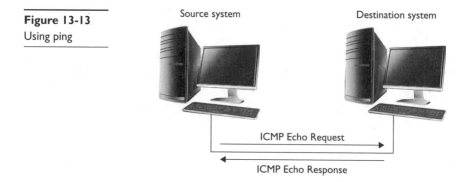

The basic syntax for using ping is ping *destination_IP_address*. This causes ICMP echo request packets to be sent to the specified host. For example, you could enter **ping 192.168.1.1** to ping a host with this address. This is shown in Figure 13-14.

Notice in Figure 13-14 that the results of each ping sent are shown on a single line. Each line displays the size of the echo response packet (64 bytes), who it came from (192.168.1.1), its time to live value (127), and the round-trip time (0.162 ms to 0.769 ms).

NOTE The time to live (TTL) value specifies the number of routers the packet is allowed to cross before being thrown away.

By default, the ping utility will continue sending ping requests to the specified host until you press CTRL-C to stop it. You can use the –c option with the ping command to specify a number of times to ping. For example, you can enter **ping –c 10 192.168.1.1** to ping ten times and then exit.

You can also ping by hostname instead of IP address. As long as you've configured your system with a valid DNS server address, ping will resolve the hostname into an IP address and send ping requests to it. This is shown in Figure 13-15.

Pinging with a host name can be a valuable troubleshooting tool. It lets you know if there is a problem with the DNS server. For example, if pinging by IP address works but pinging by host name does not work, you know that your basic network configuration and connectivity is working properly but there is a problem with the DNS server.

Using netstat

The netstat utility is another powerful tool in your virtual toolbox that can do the following:

- List network connections.
- Display your routing table.
- Display information about your network interface.

```
                          Terminal                        _ □ ✕
  File  Edit  View  Terminal  Help
ws1:/ # ping 192.168.1.1
PING 192.168.1.1 (192.168.1.1) 56(84) bytes of data.
64 bytes from 192.168.1.1: icmp_seq=1 ttl=127 time=0.162 ms
64 bytes from 192.168.1.1: icmp_seq=2 ttl=127 time=0.728 ms
64 bytes from 192.168.1.1: icmp_seq=3 ttl=127 time=0.769 ms
64 bytes from 192.168.1.1: icmp_seq=4 ttl=127 time=0.680 ms
64 bytes from 192.168.1.1: icmp_seq=5 ttl=127 time=0.764 ms
^C
--- 192.168.1.1 ping statistics ---
5 packets transmitted, 5 received, 0% packet loss, time 4003ms
rtt min/avg/max/mdev = 0.162/0.620/0.769/0.233 ms
ws1:/ # ▊
```

Figure 13-14   Pinging a host by IP address

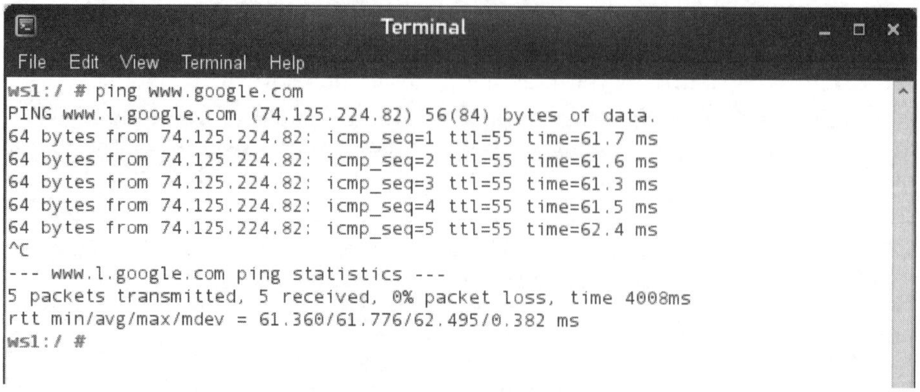

```
┌─────────────────────────────────────────────────────────────────┐
│ ▣                            Terminal                   _  □  ✕  │
│  File  Edit  View  Terminal  Help                                 │
│ ws1:/ # ping www.google.com                                       │
│ PING www.l.google.com (74.125.224.82) 56(84) bytes of data.       │
│ 64 bytes from 74.125.224.82: icmp_seq=1 ttl=55 time=61.7 ms       │
│ 64 bytes from 74.125.224.82: icmp_seq=2 ttl=55 time=61.6 ms       │
│ 64 bytes from 74.125.224.82: icmp_seq=3 ttl=55 time=61.3 ms       │
│ 64 bytes from 74.125.224.82: icmp_seq=4 ttl=55 time=61.5 ms       │
│ 64 bytes from 74.125.224.82: icmp_seq=5 ttl=55 time=62.4 ms       │
│ ^C                                                                │
│ --- www.l.google.com ping statistics ---                          │
│ 5 packets transmitted, 5 received, 0% packet loss, time 4008ms    │
│ rtt min/avg/max/mdev = 61.360/61.776/62.495/0.382 ms              │
│ ws1:/ #                                                           │
└─────────────────────────────────────────────────────────────────┘
```

Figure 13-15   Pinging by hostname

The syntax for using netstat is to enter **netstat** *option* at the shell prompt. You can use the options listed in Table 13-4.

Using traceroute

The traceroute utility is really cool. Remember, if you try to send information to an IP host that doesn't reside on your local network segment, the packets will be sent to your default gateway router. This router will then use a variety of routing protocols to figure out how to get the packets to the destination system. In the process, the packets may have to be transferred from router to router to router to get them there. This is shown in Figure 13-16.

This is one of the beauties of an IP-based network. You can connect multiple networks together using routers and transfer data between them. It's this functionality that allows the Internet to exist. You can use a Web browser to send HTTP request packets to a Web server located somewhere in the world and have it respond with the Web page you want to view. The routing protocols used by routers dynamically determine the best route for packets to take based on calculations made by various routing protocols that factor in proximity, cost, and router loads. The route taken can change as network conditions change.

netstat Option	Description
–a	Lists all listening and nonlistening sockets.
–i	Displays statistics for your network interfaces.
–l	Lists listening sockets.
–s	Displays summary information for each protocol.
–r	Displays your routing table.

Table 13-4   netstat Options

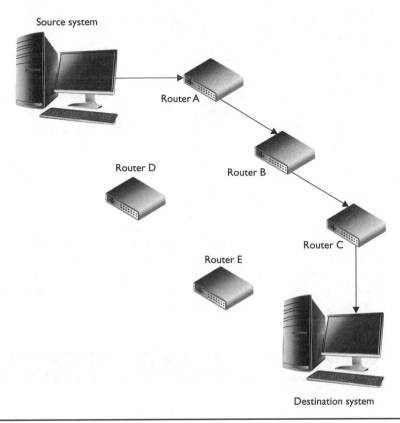

Figure 13-16 Routing in an IP network

The traceroute utility traces the route a packet must traverse through these routers to arrive at its destination. It does this using the same ICMP echo request and ICMP echo response packets used by the ping utility. An ICMP echo response packet is sent back to the source system each time packets cross a router, providing you with a list that comprises the route between the source and destination systems.

This utility can be a very useful tool if you're experiencing communication problems between networks. The traceroute utility can help you track down which router in the route isn't working correctly. The syntax for using this utility is traceroute *destination_hostname_or_IP_address*. When you run it, traceroute creates one line for each router your packets cross as they make their way to the destination system. This is shown in Figure 13-17.

```
                                Terminal                            _ □ x
 File  Edit  View  Terminal  Help
ws1:/ # traceroute www.google.com
traceroute to www.google.com (74.125.93.99), 30 hops max, 40 byte packets using UDP
 1  192.168.1.1 (192.168.1.1)  0.748 ms   0.375 ms   0.178 ms
 2  192.168.0.1 (192.168.0.1)  1.678 ms   1.375 ms   1.478 ms
```

Figure 13-17 Using traceroute

As you can see in Figure 13-17, the IP address of the router is displayed along with round-trip time statistics.

Using Name Resolution Tools

Using DNS for name resolution works great—unless it doesn't work correctly, that is. Then it can be a royal inconvenience for you, as your end users won't be able to check Facebook. Fortunately, there are a couple of tools you can use to troubleshoot name resolution on your network:

- dig
- host

dig

You can use the Domain Information Groper (dig) utility to perform a DNS lookup on your DNS server and display detailed information about the hostname being resolved and about the DNS server itself. If you don't specify a particular DNS server with the dig command, the DNS servers configured in the resolv.conf file will be used. The syntax is dig @*dns_server hostname*. An example is shown in Figure 13-18.

```
                                   Terminal                                _ □ ×
 File   Edit   View   Terminal   Help
ws1:/ # dig www.google.com

; <<>> DiG 9.7.3 <<>> www.google.com
;; global options: +cmd
;; Got answer:
;; ->>HEADER<<- opcode: QUERY, status: NOERROR, id: 27684
;; flags: qr rd ra; QUERY: 1, ANSWER: 7, AUTHORITY: 4, ADDITIONAL: 4

;; QUESTION SECTION:
;www.google.com.                        IN      A

;; ANSWER SECTION:
www.google.com.         572152  IN      CNAME   www.l.google.com.
www.l.google.com.       83      IN      A       74.125.93.106
www.l.google.com.       83      IN      A       74.125.93.147
www.l.google.com.       83      IN      A       74.125.93.99
www.l.google.com.       83      IN      A       74.125.93.103
www.l.google.com.       83      IN      A       74.125.93.104
www.l.google.com.       83      IN      A       74.125.93.105

;; AUTHORITY SECTION:
google.com.             315342  IN      NS      ns1.google.com.
google.com.             315342  IN      NS      ns2.google.com.
google.com.             315342  IN      NS      ns3.google.com.
google.com.             315342  IN      NS      ns4.google.com.

;; ADDITIONAL SECTION:
ns1.google.com.         313027  IN      A       216.239.32.10
ns2.google.com.         313206  IN      A       216.239.34.10
ns3.google.com.         313213  IN      A       216.239.36.10
ns4.google.com.         313035  IN      A       216.239.38.10
```

Figure 13-18   Using dig to resolve a hostname

The output from dig is considerably more extensive than that displayed by other DNS troubleshooting tools such as nslookup or host. The dig command returns the IP address associated with the host name in the ANSWER SECTION. It also lists the authoritative name server for the hostname and zone in the AUTHORITY SECTION. You can use the following options with dig:

- **a** Resolve a record information.
- **ptr** Resolve a ptr record.
- **cname** Resolve cname record information.
- **in** Resolve Internet record information.
- **mx** Resolve mx record information.
- **soa** Resolve start of authority information.

host

You can also use the host command to resolve hostnames. Whereas the dig command provides extensive name resolution information, host provides simple, quick information. The syntax is similar to that used with dig. You enter **host** *hostname DNS_server* at the shell prompt. Again, if you don't specify a DNS server, the default DNS server specified in /etc/resolv.conf will be used. An example of using host is shown in Figure 13-19.

Let's practice working with network commands in the following exercise.

Exercise 13-2: Working with Network Commands In this exercise, you will practice using network commands to manage and troubleshoot your network interface. This exercise assumes that you have an Ethernet network board installed in your Linux system and that it is connected to the Internet. Complete the following:

1. Boot your Linux system and log in as a standard user.
2. Open a terminal session.
3. Switch to your root user account by entering **su** – followed by your root user's password.

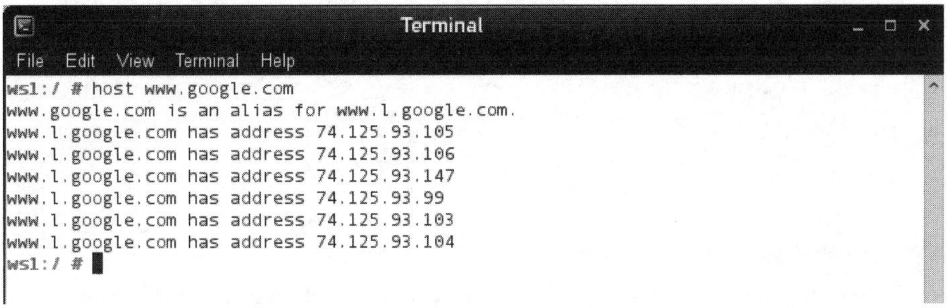

```
wsl:/ # host www.google.com
www.google.com is an alias for www.l.google.com.
www.l.google.com has address 74.125.93.105
www.l.google.com has address 74.125.93.106
www.l.google.com has address 74.125.93.147
www.l.google.com has address 74.125.93.99
www.l.google.com has address 74.125.93.103
www.l.google.com has address 74.125.93.104
wsl:/ #
```

Figure 13-19 Using host to resolve a hostname

4. Test connectivity by entering **ping www.google.com** at the shell prompt. Your system should resolve the host name into an IP address and send ICMP echo request packets to it. (If your system isn't connected to the Internet, this step won't work.)

5. Display summary information about your network interface by entering **netstat –s | more** at the shell prompt. Review the information displayed.

6. Trace the route to www.google.com by entering **traceroute www.google.com** at the shell prompt. Note the various routers crossed as your packets traverse the Internet to www.google.com.

7. Generate extended name resolution about www.google.com by entering **dig www.google.com** at the shell prompt.

Encrypting Remote Access with OpenSSH

In the early days of UNIX/Linux, we used a variety of tools to establish network connections between systems. You could access the shell prompt of a remote system using Telnet, rlogin, or rshell. You could copy files back and forth between systems using rcp and FTP. However, these utilities all had one glaring weakness: they transmit data as clear text. Anyone running a sniffer could easily capture usernames and passwords along with the contents of the transmissions.

For example, suppose I remotely access my Linux system from another system somewhere else on the network using Telnet. After authenticating to the remote system, I decide that I need to switch to root using the su command to complete several tasks. If someone were sniffing the network wire while I was doing this, they could easily grab the following information:

- My username and password
- The root user password

This is not a good thing! The attacker now has everything he needs to gain unfettered access to my Linux system.

To prevent this from happening, you can use the OpenSSH software to accomplish these same management tasks using encryption. In this part of the chapter, you'll learn how to use OpenSSH. The following topics are addressed:

- How encryption works
- How OpenSSH works
- How to configure OpenSSH

How Encryption Works

In today's security-conscious world, the need to encrypt the contents of network communications is paramount. Using freely available network monitoring tools, it is quite easy for a malicious individual to capture (sniff) network transmissions off the network medium and read them. If they contain sensitive information, such as usernames, passwords, financial data, credit card numbers, or personal information, we could have a real problem on our hands.

To protect this information, we need to encrypt critical network communications. Unlike the simple codes you may have used in elementary school, network cryptography today uses very sophisticated encoding mechanisms. There are two general approaches to encrypting network data:

- Symmetric encryption
- Asymmetric encryption

Symmetric Encryption

For *symmetric encryption* systems, the sender and the receiver must have exactly the same key to both encrypt and decrypt messages, as shown in Figure 13-20. For this reason, symmetric encryption is sometimes also called secret key encryption. Using the wrong key on either the sending or receiving end results in gibberish.

Symmetric encryption works very well. One of its key advantages is speed. It is much faster than asymmetric encryption (discussed later). However, one of the difficulties associated with symmetric encryption is determining a way to securely distribute the key to all the parties that need to communicate with each other without malicious individuals also getting a copy. Examples of cryptographic standards that use symmetric encryption include the following:

- **Triple Data Encryption Standard (3DES)** Commonly used by many Linux services, 3DES encrypts data in three stages and uses either a 112-bit or a 168-bit key.
- **Advanced Encryption Standard (AES)** An improved version of 3DES that supports 128-bit, 192-bit, and 256-bit keys.
- **Blowfish** Uses variable key lengths up to 448 bits.

An important factor to keep in mind when selecting any encryption scheme is the number of bits used to encode the data. Older encryption schemes used only 40 or

Figure 13-20
Symmetric
encryption

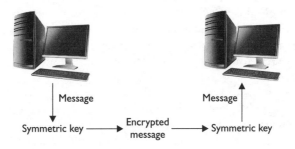

56 bits to encode data. In today's computing world, this isn't strong enough. A fast PC from your local discount retail store can crack 40-bit encryption in a relatively short amount of time. When selecting an encryption scheme, you should pick one that supports a minimum of 128 bits. The longer the key, the more secure the data is.

Symmetric encryption is used to encrypt the contents of network communications as well as to generate digital signatures. In a digital signature, the contents of a message aren't encrypted. Instead, the private key is used by the sender to create an encrypted hash of the message. This hash is sent along with the message to the recipient. The recipient generates its own hash of the message. Then it uses the public key to decrypt the hash sent with the message. If the hashes are the same, the recipient can be assured that the message arrived without being altered en route.

Asymmetric Encryption

Symmetric encryption has a weakness. If both the sender and the receiver must have the same key to encrypt and decrypt data, how do you securely transfer the common key to both parties without someone else getting a hold of it? Because of the difficulties associated with key distribution, another encryption mechanism is commonly used today called *asymmetric encryption.*

Unlike symmetric encryption, asymmetric encryption uses two keys instead of one: the public key and the private key. Data that has been encoded with the public key can be decoded only with the private key. Data that has been encoded with the private key can only be decoded with the public key. For this reason, asymmetric encryption is frequently referred to as public key cryptography. Rivest Shamir Adleman (RSA) and the Digital Signature Algorithm (DSA) are examples of cryptographic standards that use asymmetric encryption. Private/public key pairs should be much longer than those used for symmetric encryption: 1024 bits or longer.

Because of its flexibility, public key cryptography is a widely used method for encrypting data. It allows you to easily scramble and send sensitive information over a public network, especially the Internet. If you've ever bought anything online from an e-commerce web site, you've used public key cryptography. When you send your credit card number, the retailer's web site should encrypt your data and send it using HTTPS so that prying eyes will be unable to read it.

One of the main disadvantages of asymmetric encryption is its slower speed; symmetric encryption is much faster. Hence, you will frequently see implementations that use a hybrid of both mechanisms. Asymmetric encryption is used for an initial key exchange to securely copy a secret key to both parties in a session. Once that is done, both parties have the same key and can switch to symmetric encryption for the remainder of the session.

Another problem associated with public key cryptography is the issue of how to verify that the public key is legitimate. To do that, we use a *certificate authority (CA)*. The CA is a network service responsible for issuing and managing encryption keys. When a key pair is requested from a CA, it generates a public key and a private key simultaneously, using a specified encryption scheme, such as RSA or DSA.

The private key in the pair is given only to the requesting entity. It is not shared with anyone else. The public key in the pair, on the other hand, can be made available to anyone who needs it. The primary role of the CA is to verify that parties involved in an encrypted exchange are who they say they are. A CA accomplishes this by issuing *public key certificates.* A public key certificate is a digital message signed with the private key that provides a cryptographic binding between the public key and the organization that owns the private key. A certificate contains the following information:

- The name of the organization
- The public key of the organization
- The expiration date of the certificate
- The certificate's serial number
- The name of the CA that signed the certificate
- A digital signature from the CA

There are two types of CAs that you need to be familiar with:

- **Internal CA**   An internal CA is one that is maintained by an organization for internal use. On most Linux distributions, the OpenSSL package is installed automatically and creates a CA on your system. This CA is used to create keys and issue certificates for services running on the server. However, this CA is not a *trusted* CA. If other systems connect to a service on your system via a secure connection, users on the remote system will be issued a warning in their client software. This message will indicate that the certificate it received was valid, but it didn't come from a trusted CA. That's because the certificate came from the CA on your own system. For internal communications, this doesn't represent a serious issue. We trust ourselves. If you're going to be dealing with external parties, however, an internal CA won't suffice.

- **External CA**   External parties need assurance from a trusted, objective third party that the certificates they are receiving are legitimate and that you are who you say you are. This is done by using an external CA, such as VeriSign or GTECyberTrust. These organizations perform the same functions as an internal CA. However, they are globally trusted. For example, suppose you were to access a secure web site on the Internet using the Firefox web browser. If the site is using an external CA, you won't be presented with the warning that you see when using your internal CA. That's because your browser has been preconfigured with a list of trusted CAs, as shown in Figure 13-21.

Let's look at an example to see how public key cryptography works. Suppose you're using a web browser to visit www.mydomain.com and you've found some product that you just can't live without. You've put it in your shopping cart and are in the process of

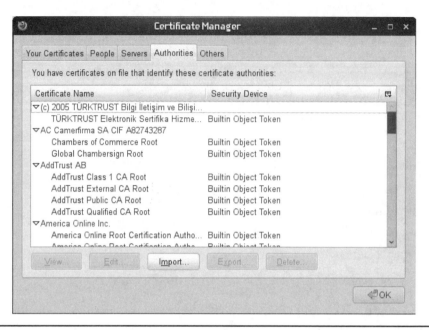

Figure 13-21 Trusted CAs

checking out from the online store. The process shown in Figure 13-22 occurs as you submit your credit card information to the e-commerce web server.

1. Your browser requests the public key for www.mydomain.com from the external CA.

2. The CA returns the public key to the browser, which then uses that key to encrypt the message.

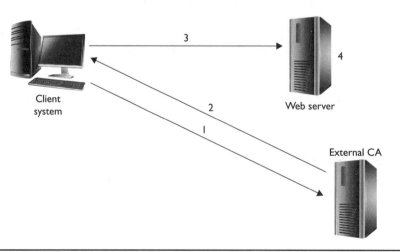

Figure 13-22 How public key encryption works

3. The browser sends the encrypted message to www.mydomain.com.

4. The web server at the other end then uses its private key to decrypt the transmission.

The whole reason this process works is because only the private key can decrypt a message encoded by the public key. For example, a hacker could easily intercept the public key used in the transaction in Figure 13-22. But that's not a problem because it can't be used to decrypt information encrypted with the same public key (in this case, the credit card submission). That can only be done by the private key, which is kept safe on the web server and is never transmitted openly.

Because your Linux system installed its own CA when you initially installed the system, you can use it to mint your own certificates and use them to encrypt both network transmissions and files in the file system.

How OpenSSH Works

OpenSSH provides the functionality of Telnet, rlogin, rsh, rcp, and FTP, but it does so using encryption. To do this, OpenSSH provides the following encryption-enabled components:

- **sshd** The ssh daemon that allows remote access to the shell prompt.
- **ssh** The ssh client used to connect to the sshd daemon on another system.
- **scp** A utility that securely copies files between systems.
- **sftp** A utility that securely transfers files between systems.
- **slogin** A utility that accesses the shell prompt remotely.

To establish a secure connection, OpenSSH uses both private/public key encryption along with secret key encryption. First, the SSH client first creates a connection with the system where the SSH server is running on IP port 22. The SSH server then sends its public keys to the SSH client. The SSH server uses the host key pair to store its private and public keys, which identify the host where the SSH server is running. The keys are stored in the following files:

- **Private key** /etc/ssh/ssh_host_key
- **Public key** /etc/ssh/ssh_host_key.pub

The client system receives the public key from the SSH server and checks to see if it already has a copy of that key. The SSH client stores keys from other systems in the following files:

- /etc/ssh/ssh_known_hosts
- ~/.ssh/known_hosts

By default, if it doesn't have the server's public key in either of these files it will ask the user to add it. When it does, the client trusts the server system and generates a 256-bit secret key. It then uses the server's public key to encrypt the new secret key and sends it to the server. Because it was encrypted with the public key, the server can decrypt it using its private key. Once this is done, both systems have the same secret key and can use symmetric encryption during the duration of the SSH session. The user is presented with a login prompt and can authenticate securely because everything he or she types is sent in encrypted format.

After this secure channel has been negotiated and the user has been authenticated through the SSH server, data can be securely transferred between both systems.

In SSH version 2, several things work a little differently. First of all, the host key files used on the server are different. The /etc/ssh/ssh_host_rsa_key and /etc/ssh/ssh_host_dsa_key files are used (along with their associated public keys) instead of /etc/ssh/ssh_host_key. The key pair used depends on which encryption mechanism (RSA or DSA) the client and server have been configured to use. In addition, the secret key is not transmitted from the client to the server system. A Diffie-Hellman key agreement is used instead to negotiate a secret key to be used for the session without sending it over the network medium. The Diffie-Hellman key agreement method allows two systems to jointly establish a shared secret key over an insecure communications channel.

Configuring OpenSSH

To use ssh, you must first install the openssh package on your system from your distribution media. This package includes both the sshd daemon and the ssh client. OpenSSH is usually installed by default on most Linux distributions. You can use the package management utility of your choice to verify that it has been installed on your system.

The process of configuring OpenSSH involves configuring both the SSH server and the SSH client. You configure the sshd daemon using the /etc/ssh/sshd_config file. The ssh client, on the other hand, is configured using the /etc/ssh/ssh_config file or the ~/.ssh/ssh_config file.

Let's look at configuring the SSH server (sshd) first. There are many directives within the /etc/ssh/sshd_config file. The good news is that after installing the openssh package the default parameters work very well in most circumstances. To get sshd up and running, you shouldn't have to make many changes to the sshd_config file. Some of the more useful parameters in this file include those shown in Table 13-5.

The ssh client on a Linux system is configured using the /etc/ssh/ssh_config file. The /etc/ssh/ssh_config file is used to specify default parameters for all users running ssh on the system. A user can override these defaults using the ~/.ssh/ssh_config file in his or her home directory. The precedence for ssh client configuration settings are as follows:

1. Any command-line options included with the ssh command at the shell prompt

2. Settings in the ~/.ssh/ssh_config file

3. Settings in the /etc/ssh/ssh_config file

As with the sshd daemon, the default parameters used in the ssh_config file usually work without a lot of customization. However, some of the more useful parameters that you can use to customize the way the ssh client works are listed in Table 13-6.

Option	Description
AllowUsers	Restricts logins to the SSH server to only the users listed. Specify a list of users separated by spaces.
DenyUsers	Prevents the users listed from logging in through the SSH server. Specify a list of users separated by spaces.
HostKey	Specifies which private host key file should be used by SSH. As discussed previously, the default private key file for SSH version 1 is /etc/ssh/ssh_host_key, while SSH version 2 can use the /etc/ssh/ssh_host_rsa_key and /etc/ssh/ssh_host_dsa_key files. You can configure sshd to use multiple host key files. Be aware that if a key file has read or write permissions assigned to Group or Others, sshd will refuse to use it.
ListenAddress	If the host where sshd is running has multiple IP addresses assigned, you can restrict sshd to only listening on specific addresses using this parameter. The syntax is ListenAddress *IP_address:port*.
PermitRootLogin	Specifies whether you can authenticate through the SSH server as root.
Port	Specifies the port on which the sshd daemon will listen for SSH requests. The default is port 22.
Protocol	Specifies which version of SSH to use. Specify one of the following: 1 Configures SSH version 1. 2 Configures SSH version 2. 2,1 Configures sshd to support both SSH versions, but preference is given to version 2.

Table 13-5   Options in the sshd_config File

Option	Description
Port	Specifies the port number to connect to on the SSH server system to initiate an SSH request.
Protocol	Specifies which version of SSH to use. Specify one of the following: 1 Configures SSH version 1. 2 Configures SSH version 2. 2,1 Configures the ssh client to support both SSH versions, but preference is given to version 2.
StrictHostKeyChecking	The SSH server sends the SSH client its public key when you initiate an SSH connection. By default, the first time you connect to a given SSH server, you are prompted on the client end to accept the server's public key. However, you can change this behavior using the StrictHostKeyChecking parameter in the ssh_config file. If you set it to a value of yes, then the client can establish connections only to SSH servers whose public key has already been added to either the ~/.ssh/known_hosts or the /etc/ssh/ssh_known_hosts file. Be aware that if you do this and then want to connect to a new SSH server, you must manually add that server's key to one of the aforementioned files.
User	Specifies the user to log in to the SSH server as.

Table 13-6   Options in the ssh_config File

Of course, before you can connect to an SSH server, you must open up port 22 in the host-based firewall of the system where sshd is running. For example, in Figure 13-23 the YaST firewall module has been loaded on a SUSE Linux Enterprise Server 10 system and configured to allow SSH traffic through.

After configuring your firewall, you can load the ssh client on your local computer and connect to the sshd daemon on the remote Linux system by entering **ssh –l** *user_ name ip_address*. Don't forget the –l parameter. If you don't include it, the SSH client will attempt to authenticate you to the remote system using the same credentials you used to authenticate to the local system. If the credentials are the same on both the client and server systems, you'll still be able to authenticate. But if they aren't, you won't be able to authenticate.

For example, if I wanted to connect to a remote Linux system with a hostname of WS3 (which has an IP address of 192.168.1.125) as the user rtracy using the ssh client on a local computer system, I would enter **ssh –l rtracy WS3** at the shell prompt. This is shown in Figure 13-24.

Notice in Figure 13-24 that I was prompted to accept the public key from WS3 because this was the first time I connected to this particular SSH server. Once I connected, I was authenticated to the remote system as the rtracy user (notice the change in the shell prompt). At this point, I had full access to the shell prompt on WS3 and I could complete any task as if I were sitting right at the console of the remote system. To close the connection, just enter **exit** at the shell prompt.

 TIP Windows workstations don't provide an ssh client. You can download the PuTTY.exe ssh client from the Internet and use it to connect to a Linux SSH server from a Windows workstation.

Let's practice working with SSH in the following exercise.

Exercise 13-3: Working with SSH In this exercise, you set up the sshd daemon on your Linux system and then connect to it using the SSH client on another Linux system.

Figure 13-23 Configuring the firewall to allow ssh traffic

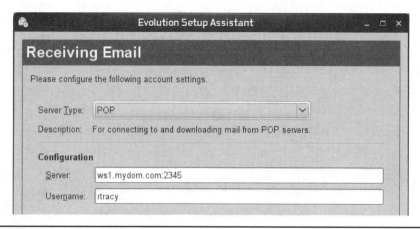

Figure 13-24   Connecting remotely via SSH

Obviously, you'll need at least two Linux systems for this and the remaining exercises in this chapter. Complete the following:

1. Configure the SSH server system by doing the following:

   a. Boot the Linux system that you want to function as an SSH server and log in as a standard user.

   b. Open a terminal session.

   c. Switch to your root user account by entering **su** – followed by your root user's password.

   d. At the shell prompt, use the package management utility of your choice to ensure the openssh package has been installed.

   e. At the shell prompt, enter **vi /etc/ssh/sshd_config**.

   f. Locate the PermitRootLogin setting.

   g. Press INS; then set PermitRootLogin to a value of no.

   h. Press ESC; then enter **:exit** to save your changes and exit the editor.

   i. At the shell prompt, enter **service sshd restart** to restart the SSH service and apply the change.

   j. If necessary, open port 22 in the host firewall of the system where the SSH server is running. The steps for doing this will depend upon your particular distribution.

2. Create an SSH connection from a client system by doing the following:

   a. Start your second system that will function as an SSH client and log in as a standard user.

   b. Open a terminal session.

   c. Open an SSH session with the first Linux system by entering **ssh –l** *user_name IP_address_of_SSH_server* at the shell prompt. For example, to connect to a system with an IP address of 192.168.1.125 as the rtracy user on that system, I would enter **ssh –l rtracy 192.168.1.125** at the shell prompt.

   d. If prompted, enter **yes** to accept the public key from the SSH server.

   e. Enter the password for the user you specified on the SSH server system.

   f. Enter **exit** at the shell prompt to log off from the remote system.

3. Practice working with SSH utilities from your client system by doing the following:

   a. Run the ifconfig command on the remote system using SSH by entering **ssh –l** *user_name IP_address_of_SSH_server* **/sbin/ifconfig** at the shell prompt.

   b. Enter the password of the remote user when prompted. You should see the networking configuration assigned to the various interfaces on the remote system. Notice that the connection automatically closed once the command finished running.

   c. Copy a file using a secure SSH connection by doing the following:

     i. Create a new file in your user's home directory by entering **echo "This is my new file."** > **~/mytestfile.txt** at the shell prompt.

     ii. Copy this new file to the home directory for your remote user account on your SSH server system by entering **scp ~/mytestfile.txt** *user_name@IP_address_of_SSH_server:* at the shell prompt.

     iii. Enter the remote user's password when prompted. You should see that the file was copied.

     iv. Use the ssh command to establish an SSH connection again with your SSH server system using the same username you entered previously to copy the file.

     v. Verify that the file exists in the remote user's home directory.

     vi. Enter **exit** to close the connection.

   a. Use the sftp command to copy the mytestfile.txt file down from the SSH server system to the local /tmp directory by doing the following:

     i. At the shell prompt of your workstation system, enter **sftp** *user_name@IP_address_of_SSH_server*.

     ii. Enter the remote user's password when prompted.

     iii. At the sftp> prompt, enter **get mytestfile.txt /tmp/**.

     iv. At the sftp> prompt, enter **exit**.

     vi. At the shell prompt, enter **ls /tmp**. You should see the mytestfile.txt file that was copied down from the SSH server system.

Chapter Review

In this chapter, you learned how to set up networking on your Linux system. I first pointed out that you will most likely work with Ethernet network boards and the IP protocol in most modern organizations. I also pointed out that a protocol is a common networking "language" that must be configured for two hosts to communicate.

We discussed the way the Internet Protocol (IP) works in conjunction with the Transmission Control Protocol (TCP) or the User Datagram Protocol (UDP) to fragment, transmit, defragment, and resequence network data to enable communications between hosts. We also looked at the Internet Control Message Protocol (ICMP), another core protocol in the IP protocol suite. ICMP differs in purpose from TCP and UDP, which are transport protocols. The primary role of ICMP is to test and verify network communications between hosts.

We reviewed the role and function of the OSI Reference Model and that the OSI model layers break down the overall communication process into specific tasks. Information flows down through the layers on the sending system and is then transmitted on the network medium. The information then flows up the layers on the receiving side. The OSI Reference Model has seven layers:

1. Physical

2. Data Link

3. Network

4. Transport

5. Session

6. Presentation

7. Application

We then discussed the concept of IP ports. Ports are provided by both the TCP and UDP protocols at the Transport layer. In essence, a port is a logical connection provided by TCP and UDP for upper-layer protocols. Ports allow a single host with a single IP address to provide multiple network services. Each service uses the same IP address but operates using its own different TCP or UDP port number. Port numbers can range from 0 up to 65536. The way these ports are used is regulated by the Internet Corporation for Assigned Names and Numbers (ICANN). There are three different categories that IP ports are lumped into

- Well-known ports

- Registered ports

- Dynamic ports

For this process to work, each host on the network must have a correctly configured, unique IP address assigned to it. It must also have the correct subnet mask assigned. The subnet mask defines how much of a given host's IP address is the network address and how much is the IP address. When viewed in binary form, any bit in the subnet mask that has a 1 in it represents a network address bit in the IP address. Any bit with a 0 in it represents a host address. IP addresses are categorized into several classes. The first three classes each have a default subnet mask assigned:

- **Class A** 255.0.0.0
- **Class B** 255.255.0.0
- **Class C** 255.255.255.0

Hosts on the same network segment must have the same network address for them to communicate. Therefore, the same subnet mask must be assigned to each host.

To resolve domain names into IP addresses, your Linux system must also be configured with the IP address of your organization's DNS server. You must also configure it with the IP address of your network segment's default gateway router for it to communicate with hosts on other network segments.

We also looked at IPv6. Valid IPv6 addresses are composed of eight four-character hexadecimal numbers, separated by colons instead of periods; for example, 35BC:FA77:4898:DAFC:200C:FBBC:A007:8973. Most Linux distributions support both IPv4 and IPv6.

We also looked at the concept of public and private IP addressing. Public networks use globally unique, registered IP addresses. Private networks use nonroutable, nonregistered, nonunique IP addresses. You can use a NAT router to hide a private network behind one or more public interfaces. This allows you to implement their network using only a relatively small number of globally unique public IP addresses. Within each class of IP address are blocks of addresses called private or reserved IP addresses. These addresses are unallocated and can be used by anyone who wants to use them. The private IP address ranges are

- 10.0.0.0–10.255.255.255 (Class A)
- 172.16.0.0 –172.31.255.255 (Class B)
- 192.168.0.0–192.168.255.255 (Class C)

We then shifted gears and discussed how to configure an Ethernet network interface in a Linux system. The first task is to install the network board in the system and connect it to your network. Then you need to load the appropriate kernel modules for the board. For newer boards, this happens automatically. For older or uncommon network boards, you may have to do this manually. Once installed, the network board should have an alias created for it named eth0. Subsequent network boards should have aliases of eth1, eth2, eth3, and so on created for them.

After the board is installed, you need to use the ifconfig command or dhclient command to configure the network interface with the appropriate IP configuration parameters. When you enter **ifconfig** at the shell prompt without any parameters, the details of your installed network interfaces are displayed. To assign IP information, enter **ifconfig** *interface ip_address* **netmask** *subnet_mask* **broadcast** *broadcast_address* at the shell prompt. To make the assignment persistent, you need to enter your IP configuration parameters in the appropriate file located within /etc/sysconfig/network directory.

However, you can't use ifconfig to assign the DNS server address or the default gateway router address. To do this, you need to edit several configuration files:

- **DNS server address**   /etc/resolv.conf
- **Default gateway router address**   /etc/sysconfig/network/routes

To bring a network interface down, you can enter **ifdown** at the shell prompt. To bring it up, enter **ifup**. To use a DHCP server to dynamically assign IP address information to a Linux host, enter **dhclient** *interface* at the shell prompt.

Next we looked at several command-line utilities you can use to test and monitor the network. You can use the ping command to test connectivity between systems. The syntax is ping *destination_host*. You can use the netstat command to view a variety of network interface information using the –a, –i, –l, –s, and –r options. You can also use the traceroute utility to trace the route your packets must follow to reach a remote system. The syntax for using traceroute is traceroute *destination_host*. We also looked at tools you can use to test name resolution, including dig and host.

Next, you learned how to use encryption to secure data transmissions. We first reviewed how encryption works. The first type of encryption we looked at was symmetric encryption, where the key used to encrypt a message is the same key used to decrypt the message. That means the sender and the receiver must both have the exact same key. One of the key advantages of using symmetric encryption is speed: it processes much faster than asymmetric encryption. One of the difficulties associated with symmetric encryption is how to securely distribute the key to all the parties that need to communicate with each other. Examples of cryptographic standards that use symmetric encryption include

- 3DES
- AES
- Blowfish

When selecting an encryption scheme, you should pick one that supports a minimum of 128 bits. The longer the key, the more secure the data is.

We then turned our attention to asymmetric encryption, which uses two keys instead of one: the public key and the private key. Data that has been encoded with the public key can be decoded only with the private key. Data that has been encoded with the private key can only be decoded with the public key. Asymmetric encryption is frequently referred to as public key cryptography. Commonly used asymmetric encryption mechanisms include

- RSA
- DSA

Private/public key pairs should be much longer than those used for symmetric encryption: 1024 bits or longer.

You will frequently see implementations that use a hybrid of both symmetric and asymmetric encryption. In these cases, asymmetric encryption is used for an initial key exchange to securely copy a secret key to both parties in a session. Once both parties have the same key, they can switch to symmetric encryption for the remainder of the session.

A certificate authority (CA) is responsible for issuing and managing encryption keys. When a key pair is requested from a CA, it generates a public key and a private key simultaneously, using a specified encryption scheme, such as RSA or DSA. The private key in the pair is given only to the key owner. The public key, on the other hand, can be made available to anyone who needs it. The primary role of the CA is to verify that parties involved in an encrypted exchange are who they say they are. There are two types of CAs that you need to be familiar with:

- Internal CA
- External CA

Because your Linux system installed its own internal CA when you installed the operating system, you can use it to mint your own certificates and use them to encrypt both network transmissions and files in the file system.

We then discussed how you can use OpenSSH to encrypt remote access sessions between Linux systems. Early Linux network services such as Telnet, rlogin, rcp, rshell, and FTP transmit data as clear text, which exposes usernames, passwords, and other sensitive data to sniffers. OpenSSH, on the other hand, provides a suite of utilities that you can use to encrypt these data transfers:

- sshd
- ssh
- scp
- sft
- slogin

OpenSSH uses both private/public key encryption along with secret key encryption. First, the SSH client creates a connection with the system where the SSH server is running on IP port 22. The SSH server then sends its public key to the SSH client. The client system receives the public key from the SSH server and checks to see if it already has a copy of that key. By default, if it doesn't have the server's public key in either of these files it will ask the user to add it. The client then trusts the server system and generates a 256-bit secret key. Next, it uses the server's public key to encrypt the new secret key and sends it to the server. The server decrypts it using its private key. Once these steps are complete, both systems can now use symmetric encryption for the session. In SSH version 2, the secret key is not transmitted from the client to the server system; a Diffie-Hellman key agreement is used instead to negotiate a secret key to be used for the session without sending it over the network.

The process of configuring OpenSSH involves configuring both the SSH server and the SSH client. You configure the sshd daemon using the /etc/ssh/sshd_config file. The ssh client is configured using the /etc/ssh/ssh_config file or the ~/.ssh/ssh_config file. Before you can connect to an SSH server, you must open up port 22 in the host-based firewall of the system where sshd is running.

You can load the ssh client on your local computer and connect to the sshd daemon on the remote Linux system by entering **ssh –l** *user_name ip_address*.

Accelerated Review

- You will most likely work with Ethernet network boards and the IP protocol when managing Linux systems.

- A protocol is a common networking language that must be configured for network hosts to communicate.

- The Internet Protocol (IP) works in conjunction with the TCP or the UDP to fragment, transmit, defragment, and resequence network data.

- The Internet Control Message Protocol (ICMP) is used to test and verify network communications between hosts.

- The OSI Reference Model is composed of layers that break down the overall communication process into specific tasks:
  - Physical
  - Data Link
  - Network
  - Transport
  - Session
  - Presentation
  - Application

- Ports are provided by both the TCP and UDP protocols at the Transport layer.

- A port is a logical connection provided by TCP and UDP for upper-layer protocols.

- Ports allow a single host with a single IP address to provide multiple network services.

- There are three different categories that IP ports are lumped into
  - Well-known ports
  - Registered ports
  - Dynamic ports

- Each host on the network must have a unique IP address assigned as well as the correct subnet mask.

- The subnet mask defines how much of a given host's IP address is the network address and how much is the IP address.
- IP addresses are categorized into several classes, each of which has a default subnet mask assigned:
  - **Class A** 255.0.0.0
  - **Class B** 255.255.0.0
  - **Class C** 255.255.255.0
- Hosts on the same network segment must have the same subnet mask and must be assigned to each host.
- A network host must be configured with the IP address of a DNS server to resolve domain names into IP addresses.
- A network host must be configured with the IP address of the segment's default gateway router for it to communicate with hosts on other network segments.
- IPv6 addresses are composed of eight four-character hexadecimal numbers, separated by colons instead of periods.
- Public networks use globally unique, registered IP addresses.
- Private networks use nonroutable, nonregistered, nonunique IP addresses.
- Within each class of IP address are blocks of addresses called private or reserved IP addresses:
  - 10.0.0.0–10.255.255.255 (Class A)
  - 172.16.0.0–172.31.255.255 (Class B)
  - 192.168.0.0–192.168.255.255 (Class C)
- You can use a NAT router to hide a private network behind one or more public interfaces.
- To install an Ethernet interface in a Linux system, you first need to install the network board in the system and connect it to the network medium.
- Next, you need to load the appropriate kernel modules for the board.
- The network board should have an alias created for it named eth0.
- Additional boards will have aliases of eth1, eth2, and so on assigned.
- You can enter **ifconfig** at the shell prompt to view the details of your installed network interfaces.
- To assign an IP address to a network interface, enter **ifconfig** *interface ip_address* **netmask** *subnet_mask* **broadcast** *broadcast_address* at the shell prompt.
- To make IP address assignments persistent, enter them in the appropriate file within the /etc/sysconfig/network directory.
- Enter your organization's DNS server address in the /etc/resolv.conf file.

- Enter your segment's default gateway router address in the /etc/sysconfig/network/routes file.

- Enter **ifdown** at the shell prompt to bring a network interface down.

- Enter **ifup** to bring a network interface back up.

- To dynamically assign an IP address to a Linux host, enter **dhclient** *interface* at the shell prompt.

- Linux includes a variety of command-line utilities you can use to test and monitor the network.

- Use ping to test connectivity between systems. The syntax is ping *destination_host*.

- Use the netstat command to view a variety of network interface information using the –a, –i, –l, –s, and –r options.

- Use the traceroute utility to trace the route your packets follow to reach a remote system. The syntax is traceroute *destination_host*.

- Use the route command or the **netstat –r** command to view your system's route table.

- Use the route command to add or remove routes from the route table.

- You can use the dig and host commands to test DNS name resolution.

- With symmetric encryption, the key used to encrypt a message is the same key used to decrypt the message.

- In symmetric encryption, the sender and the receiver must both have the exact same key.

- Symmetric encryption processes much faster than asymmetric encryption.

- One of the difficulties associated with symmetric encryption is how to securely distribute the key to all the parties that need to communicate with each other.

- Symmetric encryption standards include

  - 3DES

  - AES

  - Blowfish

- In encryption, the longer the key, the more secure the data is.

- Asymmetric encryption uses two keys instead of one: the public key and the private key.

- In asymmetric encryption, data that has been encoded with the public key can be decoded only with the private key.

- In asymmetric encryption, data that has been encoded with the private key can only be decoded with the public key.

- Asymmetric encryption is frequently referred to as public key cryptography.

- Commonly used asymmetric encryption mechanisms include
  - RSA
  - DSA
- Private/public key pairs should be at least 1024 bits or longer in length.
- You will frequently see implementations that use a hybrid of both symmetric and asymmetric encryption.
  - Asymmetric encryption is used for an initial key exchange to securely copy a secret key to both parties in a session.
  - Once done, both parties have the same key and can switch to symmetric encryption for the remainder of the session.
- A certificate authority (CA) is responsible for issuing and managing encryption keys.
- When a key pair is requested from a CA, it generates a public key and a private key simultaneously, using a specified encryption scheme, such as RSA or DSA.
- The private key is given only to the key owner.
- The public key can be made available to anyone who needs it.
- The primary role of the CA is to verify that parties involved in an encrypted exchange are who they say they are.
- Early Linux network services such as Telnet, rlogin, rcp, rshell, and FTP transmit data as clear text, which exposes usernames, passwords, and other sensitive data to sniffers.
- OpenSSH provides a suite of utilities that you can use to encrypt these data transfers:
  - sshd
  - ssh
  - scp
  - sft
  - slogin
- OpenSSH uses both private/public key encryption, along with secret key encryption.
  - The SSH client first creates a connection with the system where the SSH server is running on IP port 22.
  - The SSH server then sends its public key to the SSH client.
  - The client system receives the public key from the SSH server and checks to see if it already has a copy of that key.

- If it doesn't have the server's public key in either of these files, it will ask the user to add it.

- The client generates a 256-bit secret key, uses the server's public key to encrypt it, and sends it to the server.

- The server decrypts it using the private key.

- After all these steps have been completed, both systems will be able to use symmetric encryption for the session.

- You can load the ssh client on your local computer and connect to the sshd daemon on the remote Linux system by entering **ssh –l** *user_name ip_address* at the shell prompt.

Questions

1. Which of the following are true of the MAC address? (Choose two.)

   A. It's hard-coded in the network board.

   B. It's logically assigned by the operating system.

   C. They are globally unique.

   D. The network administrator can configure its value.

   E. It is used by the DNS server to resolve domain names.

2. Which transport protocol is used by network applications that need very low latency and can tolerate a certain degree of unreliability?

   A. User Datagram Protocol

   B. Transmission Control Protocol

   C. Internet Protocol

   D. Internet Control Message Protocol

3. You've just set up an e-mail server on your Linux system and enabled the SMTP and POP3 daemons to allow users to send and receive mail. Which ports must be opened in your system's host firewall to allow this? (Choose two.)

   A. 20

   B. 21

   C. 25

   D. 110

   E. 119

   F. 80

4. Which of the following are valid IP addresses that can be assigned to a network host? (Choose two.)

   A. 192.168.254.1

   B. 11.0.0.0

   C. 257.0.0.1

   D. 192.345.2.1

   E. 10.200.0.200

5. Which of the following is the default subnet mask for a class B network?

   A. 255.255.0.0

   B. 255.0.0.0

   C. 255.255.255.0

   D. 255.255.255.252

6. You've configured three hosts on your network with the following IP addresses and subnet masks:

   • **Host A**   IP = 23.0.0.1, Mask = 255.0.0.0

   • **Host B**   IP = 23.0.0.3, Mask = 255.255.0.0

   • **Host C**   IP = 23.0.0.4, Mask =255.255.0.0

   Is this network configured properly?

   A. Yes, this network is configured properly.

   B. No, the 23.0.0.1 IP address used by Host A is a reserved IP address.

   C. No, Host A uses the wrong subnet mask.

   D. No, Host B and Host C must use the default Class A subnet mask.

7. Your network interface has been assigned an IP address of 10.0.0.1. What is the binary equivalent of this decimal address?

   A. 10001010.00000000.00000000.00000001

   B. 00001010.00000001.00000001.00000001

   C. 10100000.00000000.00000000.00000001

   D. 00001010.00000000.00000000.00000001

8. You just installed a second Ethernet board in your Linux system. What alias is assigned to this interface by default?

   A. eth0

   B. eth1

   C. eth2

   D. eth3

9. You need to use ifconfig to assign an IP address of 176.23.0.12 and a subnet mask of 255.255.0.0 to your eth0 interface. Which of the following commands will do this?

    A. ifconfig eth0 176.23.0.12 netmask 255.255.0.0

    B. ifconfig 176.23.0.12 netmask 255.255.0.0

    C. ifconfig eth0 176.23.0.12 mask 255.255.0.0

    D. ifconfig dev=eth0 ipaddr=176.23.0.12 subnetmask=255.255.0.0

10. Which option in your eth0 network interface configuration file should you use to configure the NIC to get its IP address information dynamically from a DHCP server?

    A. STARTMODE

    B. BOOTPROTO

    C. IPADDR

    D. DHCP

11. You've opened your /etc/sysconfig/network/routes file in the vi editor. You want to specify a default gateway router address of 10.200.200.254. Which of the following directives would you enter in this file to do this?

    A. default 10.200.200.254

    B. gw_addr 10.200.200.254

    C. gateway 10.200.200.254

    D. router 10.200.200.254

12. You've opened your /etc/sysconfig/network/resolv.conf file in the vi editor. You want to specify a DNS server address of 10.200.200.1. Which of the following directives would you enter in this file to do this?

    A. host 10.200.200.1

    B. resolver 10.200.200.1

    C. dnsserver 10.200.200.1

    D. nameserver 10.200.200.1

13. You want to use your organization's DHCP server to dynamically assign an IP address to your eth0 network interface. Which of the following commands would you enter at the shell prompt to do this?

    A. dhcp eth0

    B. dhclient eth0

    C. get address dynamic eth0

    D. ip address=dhcp dev=eth0

14. You want to temporarily disable the second interface in your Linux system. Which of the following commands would you enter at the shell prompt to do this?

    A. ifdown eth1

    B. ifdown eth0

    C. ifdown eth2

    D. ifconfig disable dev eth1

15. You need to verify that a remote host with a host name of fs1.mycorp.com is up and running. Which of the following commands would you enter at the shell prompt to do this?

    A. finger fs1.mycorp.com

    B. ping fs1.mycorp.com

    C. netstat –s fs1.mycorp.com

    D. verify fs1.mycorp.com

16. Your users can't access your organization's e-mail server, which is hosted by a third-party vendor. You suspect that a router may be down somewhere within your organization. Given that the host name of the e-mail server is pop.mymail .com, which of the following commands would you enter at the shell prompt to test this? (Choose two.)

    A. traceroute pop.mymail.com

    B. netstat –r pop.mymail.com

    C. finger pop.mymail.com

    D. verify pop.mymail.com

    E. tracepath pop.mymail.com

17. Which of the following commands will add a default gateway router address of 10.200.200.254 to your route table?

    A. route 10.200.200.254

    B. route add default gw 10.200.200.254

    C. netstat –a default 10.200.200.254

    D. gateway 10.200.200.254

18. Which of the following is true of asymmetric encryption? (Choose two.)

    A. The private key is sent to the recipient.

    B. The public key is sent to the recipient.

    C. Information encrypted with the public key can only be decrypted with the private key.

    D. Information encrypted with the public key can be decrypted with the public key.

    E. Information encrypted with the private key can be decrypted with the private key.

19. Which port does the sshd daemon listen on by default for incoming SSH connections?

    A. 20

    B. 22

    C. 389

    D. 631

    E. 80

    F. 443

20. Which of the following shell commands will load the ssh client and connect as the ksanders user to an SSH server with an IP address of 10.0.0.254?

    A. sshd –l ksanders 10.0.0.254

    B. ssh –u ksanders 10.0.0.254

    C. ssh –l ksanders 10.0.0.254

    D. ssh user=ksanders 10.0.0.254

Answers

1. **A, C.** MAC addresses are hard-coded into the firmware of every Ethernet network board. Theoretically, no two network boards in the world should have the same MAC address. There are a few types of network boards that do allow you to manually configure the MAC address.

2. **A.** The User Datagram Protocol is an unacknowledged, connectionless protocol that sends packets without requesting a confirmation of receipt. This makes it ideal for network applications that need very low latency but can tolerate a certain degree of unreliability, such as streaming video.

3. **C, D.** The SMTP daemon uses port 25 by default, while the POP3 daemon uses port 110 by default.

4. **A, E.** 192.168.254.1 and 10.200.0.200 are both valid IP addresses that can be assigned to network hosts.

5. **A.** 255.255.0.0 is the default subnet mask for a Class B network.

6. **C.** The network isn't configured properly because Host A uses the wrong subnet mask.

7. **D.** The binary equivalent of the first octet (10) is 00001010. The binary equivalent of the second and third octets (0) is 00000000 each. The binary equivalent of the fourth octet (1) is 00000001.

8. **B.** The second Ethernet board in your Linux system is assigned an alias of eth1 by default.

9. **A.** The ifconfig eth0 176.23.0.12 netmask 255.255.0.0 command will assign the IP address and subnet mask to the eth0 interface.

10. **B.** The BOOTPROTO option is used to specify whether the interface uses a static or dynamic IP address assignment.

11. **A.** The default 10.200.200.254 directive specifies a default gateway router address of 10.200.200.254.

12. **D.** The nameserver 10.200.200.1 directive specifies a DNS server with an IP address of 10.200.200.1.

13. **B.** The dhclient eth0 command will configure the eth0 interface with IP address information from a DHCP server.

14. **A.** The ifdown eth1 command will disable the second Ethernet interface in the system.

15. **B.** The ping fs1.mycorp.com command will test communications between your system and the specified host.

16. **A, E.** The traceroute pop.mymail.com and the traceroute pop.mymail.com commands will list all of the routers between the source and destination hosts, allowing you to identify a router that isn't working correctly.

17. **B.** The route add default gw 10.200.200.254 command will add the specified IP address as the default gateway router.

18. **B, C.** With asymmetric encryption, the public key is sent to the recipient. Information encrypted with the public key can only be decrypted with the private key.

19. **B.** The sshd daemon listens on port 22 by default for incoming SSH connections.

20. **C.** The ssh –l ksanders 10.0.0.254 command will load the ssh client and connect as the ksanders user to an SSH server with an IP address of 10.0.0.254.

About the CD-ROM

The CD-ROM included with this book comes complete with MasterExam and the electronic book in PDF format. The software is easy to install on any Windows XP/Vista/7 computer and must be installed to access the MasterExam feature. To register for the bonus MasterExam, simply click the Bonus MasterExam link on the main launch page and follow the directions to the free online registration.

System Requirements

Software requires Windows XP or higher and Internet Explorer 8 or above and 200 MB of hard disk space for full installation. The electronic book requires Adobe Acrobat Reader.

Installing and Running MasterExam

If your computer CD-ROM drive is configured to auto run, the CD-ROM will automatically start up upon inserting the disk. From the opening screen you may install MasterExam by clicking the MasterExam link. This will begin the installation process and create a program group named LearnKey. To run MasterExam, select Start | All Programs | LearnKey | MasterExam. If the auto run feature does not launch your CD, browse to the CD and click the LaunchTraining.exe icon.

MasterExam

MasterExam provides you with a simulation of the actual exam. The number of questions, the type of questions, and the time allowed are intended to be an accurate representation of the exam environment. You have the option to take an open book exam, including hints, references, and answers; a closed book exam; or the timed MasterExam simulation.

When you launch MasterExam, a digital clock display will appear in the bottom right-hand corner of your screen. The clock will continue to count down to zero unless you choose to end the exam before the time expires.

Help

A help file is provided through the Help button on the main page in the lower left hand corner. An individual help feature is also available through MasterExam.

Removing Installation(s)

MasterExam is installed to your hard drive. For best results removing programs, select Start | All Programs | LearnKey| Uninstall to remove MasterExam.

Electronic Book

The entire contents of the book are provided in PDF format on the CD. This file is viewable on your computer and many portable devices. Adobe's Acrobat Reader is required to view the file on your PC and has been included on the CD. You may also use Adobe Digital Editions to access your electronic book.

For more information on Adobe Reader and to check for the most recent version of the software, visit Adobe's website at www.adobe.com and search for the free Adobe Reader or look for Adobe Reader on the product page. Adobe Digital Editions can also be downloaded from the Adobe web site.

To view the electronic book on a portable device, copy the PDF file to your computer from the CD and then copy the file to your portable device using a USB or other connection. Adobe does offer a mobile version of Adobe Reader, the Adobe Reader mobile app, which currently supports iOS and Android. Customers using Adobe Digital Editions and the iPad may have to download and install a separate reader program on your device. The Adobe web site has a list of recommended applications, and McGraw-Hill Education recommends the Bluefire Reader.

Technical Support

Technical Support information is provided next by feature.

LearnKey Technical Support

For technical problems with the software (installation, operation, removing installations), please visit www.learnkey.com, e-mail techsupport@learnkey.com, or call toll free at 1-800-482-8244.

McGraw-Hill Technical Support and Customer Service

For questions regarding the electronic book, e-mail techsolutions@mhedu.com or visit http://mhp.softwareassist.com.

For questions regarding book content, please e-mail customer.service@mcgraw-hill .com. For customers outside the United States, e-mail international_cs@mcgraw-hill.com.

absolute path The full path to a file or directory in the Linux file system starting from the root directory. For example, to refer to a file named myfile.txt in the tmp directory, you would use an absolute path of /tmp/myfile.txt.

Accelerated Graphics Port (AGP) A special type of expansion bus used only for video expansion boards in many PC systems.

Advanced Configuration and Power Interface (ACPI) A power management standard used in modern PC systems. Using ACPI, system devices can be managed to reduce power consumption. ACPI divides power management tasks between BIOS and the operating system.

Advanced Power Management (APM) APM is an older power management implementation that is being phased out. APM uses software within the BIOS to manage power consumption within the system. To do this APM uses device activity timeout periods to determine when to transition devices in to lower power states

AGP See *Accelerated Graphics Port*.

alias An alias is a shortcut to a different file or command on a Linux system. Many aliases are automatically defined when the Linux system is booted. For example, the **md** alias actually runs the **mkdir –p** command. You can also define your own custom aliases.

APM See *Advanced Power Management*.

application Computer software designed to perform a specific function. Applications are usually designed to be used by end users. Commonly used applications include word processors, database programs, graphics/drawing programs, web browsers, or e-mail programs. Application is also the process of choice, demonstration, performing a procedure, solving, plotting, calculation, changing, interpretation, and operation.

asymmetric encryption A process that uses two keys, a public key and a private key. Data encrypted with the private key can only be decrypted with the public key. Data encrypted with the public key can only be decrypted with the private key.

authentication Occurs when a user supplies credentials, usually a username and password, that match those stored in the Linux username and password store, allowing the user access to the system.

background   When a command is launched in the background, the program will run normally. However, control will be returned immediately to the shell. You can use the shell to launch other programs or perform other shell tasks.

backup   The process of creating a copy of the data in a Linux file system on a secondary storage device. You can create three different types of backups with most Linux backup utilities:

- **Full**   All specified files are backed up, regardless of whether or not they've been modified since the last backup. After being backed up, each file is flagged as having been backed up.

- **Incremental**   Only the files that have been modified since the last backup (full or incremental) are backed up. After being backed up, each file is flagged as having been backed up.

- **Differential**   Only the files that have been modified since the last full backup are backed up. Even though they have been backed up during a differential backup, the files involved are not flagged as having been backed up.

baseline   A snapshot of a system's performance. To create a system baseline, you can monitor and document a variety of system parameters, including:

- Processor utilization
- Memory utilization
- Swap partition utilization
- Free disk space
- Disk write performance
- Disk read performance
- Network throughput

bash   The Bourne-Again Shell (*bash*). An improved version of the sh shell and one of the most popular shells today. It's the default shell used by most Linux distributions.

basic input/output system (BIOS)   A ROM chip integrated in the motherboard that contains a series of very small programs and drivers that allow the CPU to communicate with basic system devices, such as the keyboard, I/O ports, the system speaker, system RAM, floppy disk drives, and hard drives.

Bazaar Model   A software development model that relies on extensive collaboration from software developers around the world.

Berkeley Software Distribution (BSD)   A cousin of Linux. BSD is an operating system derived from UNIX that was developed at the University of California, Berkeley. Original versions shared source code with UNIX, and as such, were proprietary in nature and not considered open source software. However, just like Linux, BSD eventually inspired several open source versions of the operating system, most notably FreeBSD and NetBSD.

BIOS See *basic input/output system*.

boot The process of loading the Linux operating system kernel into RAM.

boot sector On a hard disk drive, the sector that contains the master boot record (MBR).

bootloader Software the BIOS can load from the MBR of the hard drive that allows the CPU to load the Linux kernel into RAM. To do this, the bootloader is configured with the location of the operating system files on the hard disk drive. The bootloader software itself may or may not actually be in the MBR. You can install some bootloaders within the MBR, or you can install them within a partition somewhere else on the hard drive and place a pointer in the MBR. Other bootloaders install components in both places. The LILO and GRUB bootloaders are commonly used with most Linux distributions.

cache Static RAM implemented within the CPU itself to store frequently accessed data.

Cathedral Model A very organized software development model. Software development is restricted to a group of specific programmers for a particular open source software project. The source code is released to the public when the project is complete.

central processing unit (CPU) The component in a PC that interprets computer program instructions and processes data.

change log A type of log maintained by the Linux system administrator that contains an entry each time a change is made to the system, such as an operating system upgrade or a hard drive replacement.

CMOS See *Complimentary Metal Oxide Semiconductor*.

checksum A value generated by calculating the contents of a file using a Message Digest 5 (MD5) algorithm. You can run a checksum on a downloaded file and compare the results with the checksum value of the original file on the download source site. Identical values indicate that the file arrived intact. Differing values indicate corruption occurred during transfer.

command line interface (CLI) An interface that uses keyboard commands to send input to the operating system.

command substitution A method of entering commands that allows you to run a command and have its output pasted back on the command line as an argument for another command. Command substitution allows you perform multiple tasks at once.

Complimentary Metal Oxide Semiconductor (CMOS) A rewritable chip on a PC motherboard that works in conjunction with the BIOS to store system parameters such as the type of floppy drive installed in the system, the type of hard drive(s) installed in the system, power management features of the motherboard, and the order of boot devices in the system.

control structures   Decision-making routines that can be added to shell scripts. Samples of control structures include if/then/else, case, while loops, and until loop structures.

Common UNIX Printing System (CUPS)   A Linux printing system. The CUPS service is provided by the cupsd daemon, which automatically announces the availability of its print queues on the local network. CUPS client systems listen to these announcements, allowing the user to select the printer he or she wants with little networking knowledge. In addition, CUPS supports network printing over the Internet Printing Protocol (IPP) on port 631.

CPU   See *central processing unit.*

Creative Commons   An organization founded in the early 2000s by Lawrence Lessig, Eric Eldred, and Hal Abelson. The goal of this organization is to create a new option for sharing copyrighted works. Creative Commons introduced the Creative Commons License, which uses a "some rights reserved" copyright model. Under this license, the copyright owners specify specific rights they reserve for themselves and other rights they do not, which are granted to public to freely use.

CUPS   See *Common UNIX Printing System.*

daemon   Software that runs in the background on a Linux system and usually don't provide any kind of user interface. Also called a *system process.* Examples of common Linux daemons include named, httpd, and dhcpd.

default gateway   An IP router. If a system on one segment tries to send data to a host that doesn't reside on the same network, the IP protocol redirects the packets to the default gateway router for its segment. The router will then use a variety of routing protocols to determine where the packets should be sent to get them to their destination.

dependency   The state when a Linux software package is dependent upon another package being installed on the system before it can work properly.

DHCP   See *Dynamic Host Configuration Protocol.*

Direct Memory Access (DMA)   A chip on the motherboard that transfers data between the system RAM and a device in the system without the intervention of the CPU.

distribution   A customized version of Linux. Currently hundreds of Linux distributions are available.

DMA   *See* Direct Memory Access.

Domain Name System (DNS)   A system on an IP network that resolves alphanumeric domain names into IP addresses. DNS is a client-server system. DNS clients send resolution requests to DNS servers. DNS servers resolve domain names into IP addresses and return the results to the DNS client.

driver   Software that the CPU needs to communicate with hardware devices installed in the system. As the system boots, the operating system loads driver software from the hard disk into RAM. Once this is done, the CPU has the instructions it needs to communicate with the associated hardware. On Linux, drivers are implemented using kernel modules.

Dynamic Host Configuration Protocol (DHCP)   A protocol used to automatically assign IP address, subnet masks, router addresses, and DNS server addresses to network hosts. DHCP is a client-server protocol. When a DHCP client is booted, it sends out a DHCPDISCOVER broadcast. The DHCP server receives the broadcast and selects an IP address from its range of available addresses that it can assign to the DHCP client.

The server sends a proposed IP address assignment back to the host in a DHCP OFFER message. The DHCP client reviews the offers it has received and then selects the offer it wants to accept. The DHCP client then sends a DHCPREQUEST broadcast. This broadcast informs the DHCP server that it has accepted the addressing offer. The DHCP server responds to the client with a DHCPACK message, which contains the IP address assignment.

Emacs   A commonly used Linux text editor that uses a menu-driven user interface.

environment variable   Variables that are created, named, and populated by the operating system. Environment variables are used to configure the system's computing environment. Common environment variables used on a Linux system include MANPATH, HOST, SHELL, and DISPLAY.

ext2   Second Extended File System (*ext2*). A file system that stores data in the standard hierarchical fashion used by most other file systems. Data is stored in files; files are stored in directories. A directory can contain either files or other directories called subdirectories. File names can be up to 255 characters long. The ext2 file system supports Linux file system users, groups, and permissions (called POSIX permissions). It also supports file compression.

ext3   Third Extended File System (*ext3*). An updated version of ext2. The ext3 file system offers journaling. Before committing a transaction to the hard disk drive, the ext3 file system records the transaction to a journal and marks it as incomplete. After the disk transaction is complete, the ext3 file system marks the transaction as complete in the journal. By doing this, the ext3 file system can keep a log of the most recent file transactions and whether or not they were actually completed.

ext4   Fourth Extended File System (*ext4*). An update to ext3, released in late 2008. The ext4 file system supports very large volumes and files and allows a maximum of four billion files in the file system; it uses checksums to verify the integrity of the journal file, which helps improve the overall reliability of the system.

FHS   See *Filesystem Hierarchy Standard*.

FIFO   See *First In First Out*.

file descriptors   There are three file descriptors that are available for every command entered at a Linux shell prompt:

- **stdin**   Standard input. The input provided to a particular command to process. The stdin for a command is represented by the number 0.

- **stdout**   Standard output. The output from a particular command. The stdout for a command is represented by the number 1.

- **stderr**   Standard error. The error code generated, if any, by a command. The stderr for a command is represented by the number 2.

file system   When conducting disk I/O operations, the operating system needs to know where data is stored, how to access it, and where it is safe to write new information. The role of the file system is to reliably store data on the hard drive and organize it in such a way that it is easily accessible.

Filesystem Hierarchy Standard (FHS)   A method of defining the directories that must exist under the root directory on a Linux system.

firewall   A combination of hardware and software that acts like a gatekeeper between your network and another network. A firewall monitors traffic that flows between the networks, both inbound and outbound. You configure the firewall with rules that define the type of traffic is allowed through. Any traffic that violates the rules is not allowed.

FireWire   Also known as IEEE 1394 and i.Link. FireWire devices are PnP compatible and hot swappable. FireWire is frequently used for external hard drives, external CD and DVD drives, digital cameras, and digital video cameras and can transfer data at 400 Mbps. Firewire connects devices in a true bus fashion by running a cable from device to device, forming a chain. A maximum of 63 devices can be connected together in this manner.

First In First Out (FIFO)   A type of file that moves data from one running process on the system to another. A FIFO file is a queue where the first piece of data added to the queue is the first piece of data removed from the queue. Data can only move in one direction through a FIFO.

flash storage   Instead of using magnetically encoded platters or optical discs to store data, flash drives use a memory chip called flash memory. Flash memory can be electronically erased and reprogrammed. Flash memory is also persistent. Once written, it retains its contents even if the electrical current is turned off. Essentially, a flash drive is little more than a printed circuit board with a flash memory chip installed that is connected to a USB or SATA interface.

FLOSS   See *Free Libre Open Source Software*.

floppy diskette drive   Older storage devices in PCs. Floppy diskettes use an oxide-coated Mylar disk to store data. Floppy diskette drives are slowly being phased out.

foreground   When a command is entered at the Linux shell prompt, a subshell is created and the process is run within it. As soon as the process exits, the subshell is destroyed. During the time that the process is running, the shell prompt of the parent shell disappears.

forking   A process of creating a new subshell and running the command process within it.

forward lookup   In a forward-lookup, a DNS client system sends a request to the DNS server asking it to resolve a host name into an IP address.

Free and Open Source Software (FOSS)   A term that refers to both free software and open source software designed to overcome the division that exists between the OSI and FSF by not labeling software as "open source" or "free software." The goal is for everyone to refer to both types of software generically as FOSS.

Free Libre Open Source Software (FLOSS)   A term designed to overcome the division between OSI and FSF by not labeling software as "open source" or "free software." The goal is for everyone to refer to both types of software generically as FLOSS.

Free Software Foundation (FSF)   An organization founded by Richard Stallman, who is responsible for launching the GNU Project and the GPL in the early 1980s. The mission of this foundation is to promote the creation and proliferation of free software.

GNU Project   A free software project launched by Richard Stallman in 1983. The goal of the project was to develop a body of freely available software.

GNU General Public License (GPL)   A free software license used by the GNU project. The source code for software governed by the GPL is freely distributable and modifiable.

graphical user interface (GUI)   An interface that displays information on the computer screen graphically. The user interacts with the system using a pointing device, such as a mouse, as well as keyboard input. A graphical user interface usually includes pull-down menus, dialog boxes, buttons, graphics, and icons.

GRUB   GRand Unified Bootloader (*GRUB*). A bootloader that can be used to boot a Linux kernel from your system's hard drive. Recently, there has been a steady shift away from LILO toward GRUB on the part of most distributions and many Linux administrators

GUI   See *graphical user interface*.

hard disk drive   The primary type of persistent storage used in PC systems. Hard disk drives read and write magnetic information to and from spinning aluminum disks called platters.

Hardware Compatibility List (HCL) A list of hardware that is supported by the software in the distribution. Most Linux distributions publish an HCL.

HyperText Transfer Protocol (HTTP) A request/response protocol used by a web browser to get information from a web server. The browser initiates the request by establishing a TCP/IP communication session between the client system and the web server, which runs on IP port 80 by default. The web server then listens for the browser to tell it what information it wants. The browser does this by sending a GET message to the web server, which responds with the requested files.

hypervisor A hypervisor is used in virtualization to manage access to physical hardware resources consumed by virtual machines running on the hypervisor host.

ICMP See *Internet Control Message Protocol*.

IDE See *Integrated Drive Electronics*.

IMAP See *Internet Message Access Protocol*.

Industry Standard Architecture (ISA) The earliest type of expansion bus used in the PC. The earliest version of the ISA bus was eight bits wide. A 16-bit version of the ISA bus was introduced in the mid-1980s with the Intel 80286 CPU that ran at a clock speed of 8.33 MHz and used a 98-pin expansion slot.

info A utility that allows you to view documentation for commands, utilities, services, and files on your Linux system. Most info nodes contain the same information as a man page. However, info nodes are usually more verbose and can teach you how to use a particular Linux tool.

initrd image The initrd image contains a basic file system that can be used to complete a variety of startup tasks. The kernel can't mount some Linux file systems, such as RAID, Samba, and NFS, until special software is loaded. To make the system boot correctly, the bootloader creates a small, virtual hard drive in memory called a ramdisk and transfers a temporary root file system from the initrd image to it. The Linux kernel can then use this temporary file system to load the software and complete the tasks required for it to mount the file systems on these types of devices.

Integrated Drive Electronics (IDE) A standard for connecting storage devices to a PC system. IDE drives implement the hard disk drive controller hardware on the drive itself instead of a separate expansion board. A single controller on one drive can control a total of two different IDE devices. Each device is connected using a 40-pin, 80-wire ribbon cable. Today, IDE devices are referred to as Parallel ATA (PATA) devices.

Internet Control Message Protocol (ICMP) A commonly used IP protocol that provides data transfers between systems for diagnostic purposes. The PING command is an example of a utility that uses the ICMP protocol.

Internet Message Access Protocol (IMAP) A protocol used by MUAs to download messages from an MDA. IMAP uses port 143. IMAP allows you to determine the messages to be downloaded; you can download the entire message from the MDA or only pull down the message headers. IMAP also allows you to retain a copy of downloaded messages on the MDA. IMAP also allows you to create your own folders on the MDA for organizing messages.

interrupt request (IRQ)   An electrical signal that a device in the system sends to the computer's CPU requesting the processor's attention.

input/output (I/O) port   I/O addresses allow communications between the devices in the PC and the operating system. They serve as mailboxes for the devices installed in the system. Data can be left for a device in its I/O address. Data from the device can be left in the I/O address for the operating system to pick up.

IP address   An address that is logically assigned to a network host. In IP version 4 (IPv4), an IP address consists of four numbers, separated by periods. In decimal notation, each number must be between 0 and 255. For example, 192.168.1.1 is a typical IP address. Each number in the address is actually an 8-bit binary number called an *octet*. To address the shortage of available registered IPv4 addresses, a new version of IP has been proposed called IP version 6 (IPv6). Instead of 32 bits, IPv6 defines 128-bit IP addresses, allowing for a maximum of 3.4×1038 total unique IP addresses. IPv6 addresses are composed of eight 4-character hexadecimal numbers, separated by colons instead of periods. For example, a sample valid IPv6 address could be 35BC:FA77: 4898:DAFC:200C:FBBC:A007:8973.

IRQ   See *interrupt request*.

ISA   See *Industry Standard Architecture*.

ISO Image   A disk image of an optical disc, such as a CD or DVD. All data files, folders, and file system metadata is contained within a single file.

kernel   The central software component of the Linux operating system.

kernel module   A file that contains code to extend the running kernel. Kernel modules are typically used to add support for new hardware to the kernel.

life cycle   The phases of Linux distribution. A Linux distribution goes through the following software development life cycle:

- Design
- Develop
- Deploy
- Manage
- Retire

LILO   LInux LOader (LILO). A flexible bootloader that can be used to launch just about any operating system from your computer's hard drive, including Linux, Windows, or DOS. LILO used to be the default bootloader used by most Linux distributions. However, it has been replaced by GRUB as the bootloader of choice.

link   A type of file in the Linux file system that is a pointer that points to another file. You can create two different types of link files:

- **Hard**   A file that points directly to the inode of another file. An inode stores basic information about a file in the Linux file system; including its size, device, owner, and permissions. Because the two files use the same inode, you can't tell which file is the pointer and which is the pointee after the hard link is created.

- **Symbolic**   A file that also points to another file in the file system. However, a file that is a symbolic link has its own inode. Because the pointer file has its own inode, the pointer and the pointee in the file system can be easily identified.

login shell   A login shell is in use if your Linux system boots to a text-based login screen in runlevel 3 and you use it to log in to the system.

MAC address   A hardware address that is burned into a ROM chip on every network board sold in the world. The MAC address is written using hexadecimal notation. For example, 00-08-74-4C-7F-1D. The MAC address is hard-coded into the network board and can't be changed.

Mail Transfer Agent (MTA)   A software agent that transfers e-mail messages from one computer system to another. The postfix and sendmail daemons commonly used on Linux systems are examples of MTAs.

maintenance log   A log maintained by the Linux system administrator that contains events for each maintenance action taken.

man pages   One of the primary means used by the Linux operating system to maintain system documentation. These manual (man) pages contain documentation about the operating system itself as well as any applications installed on the system. These man pages are viewed using the man utility.

Master Boot Record (MBR)   The MBR resides in the boot sector of your system's hard disk drive. It plays a key role in the process of booting your Linux system. The MBR tells the system where a bootloader resides.

MTA   See *Mail Transfer Agent*.

multiplier   The multiplier allows the CPU to perform multiple cycles during a single cycle of the front side bus.

multitasking   A method that Linux uses that allows the system to quickly switch between the various processes running on the CPU, making it appear as if that the CPU is working on multiple processes concurrently. However, the CPU actually only executes a single process at a time. All other currently running processes wait in the background for their turn. The operating system maintains a schedule that determines when each process is allowed access to the CPU.

NAT   See *Network Address Translation*.

needs assessment   The process of determining why the Linux deployment is being undertaken and what outcomes are expected when it is complete.

network   Two or more computers connected together by cable or wireless media for the purpose of sharing data, hardware peripherals, and other resources.

Network Address Translation (NAT)   Network Address Translation allows a router to translate private, nonroutable IP addresses into public, registered IP addresses.

network interface card (NIC)   An expansion board installed a computer system that connects the system to the network medium, allowing data to be sent and received on the network.

open source software   Software created under an open source license. This software must make its source code freely available so that other developers can work collaboratively on the application and, hopefully, make it better.

Open Source Initiative (OSI)   An organization that promotes the creation and proliferation of open source software, founded in the late 1990s by Bruce Perens and Eric S. Raymond. The focus of this organization is to make open source software a viable alternative for mainstream business use.

operating system (OS)   A set of programs that manage a computer's hardware and software resources.

OSI Reference Model   A model designed by delegates from major computer and telecom companies in 1983. The goal was to design a network communications model that was modular in nature, allowing products from different vendors to interoperate. The OSI Reference Model divides the communication process between two hosts into layers that break down the overall communication process into specific tasks:

- Physical
- Data Link
- Network
- Transport
- Session
- Presentation
- Application

owner   The Linux user and group account that created a process or file.

Packet Inter-Network Groper (PING)   Ping is a very useful utility that can be used to test communications between two network hosts. Ping works by sending ICMP echo requests to a remote host. The remote host responds with an ICMP echo response message.

package A bundle of one or more files that are necessary for the installation and execution of a service or application on a Linux system.

Parallel ATA (PATA) See Integrated Drive Electronics (IDE).

parent process ID number (PPID) The PID of a process' parent process.

partition A logical division of your hard disk drive. Using the read-write heads inside the hard disk drive, an operating system can create magnetic divisions on the drive platters to divide it into separate sections. A hard drive can have a single partition that encompasses the entire hard drive or it can have many partitions.

password aging The process of specifying a finite lifetime for user passwords. After passwords reach the specified age, they expire and must be changed.

Peripheral Component Interconnect (PCI) A common expansion bus used in most PC systems today. The PCI bus is 32 bits wide and runs at 33 MHz, allowing it to transfer data at a rate around 66MB/sec.

Peripheral Component Interconnect Express (PCIe) An updated version of the PCI bus that can transfer data much quickly than the original PCI bus. Most modern motherboards include both PCI and PCIe buses. PCIe is frequently used for high-throughput devices such as video boards. PCIe devices each have dedicated communication channels called transport lanes for data transmission and reception. The speed of each transport lane depends upon the PCIe version:

- PCIe version 1   250MB/sec
- PCIe version 2   500MB/sec
- PCIe version 3   1GB/sec
- PCIe version 4   2GB/sec

permissions Permissions specify exactly what a particular user may do with files and directories in the file system. Each file or directory in your Linux file system stores the specific permissions assigned to it, called the mode of the file. Any file or directory can have the following permissions in its mode:

- Read
- Write
- Execute

These permissions are assigned to each of three different entities for each file and directory in the file system:

- Owner
- Group
- Others

PID   See *process ID number*.

piping   The process of chaining the output of one Linux command to the input of another Linux command. For example, you can pipe the output of the ls command to the grep command by entering **ls | grep** *search_term* at the shell prompt.

Plug and Play (PnP)   The Plug-n-Play (PnP) standard was introduced in the late 1990s. It is designed to automatically configure the system resources used by your expansion boards for you every time you boot the system. A PnP system requires three components to be present in your system:

- A PnP-compatible BIOS
- A PnP-compatible device
- A PnP-compatible operating system

When the system is powered on, the PnP BIOS negotiates with the PnP expansion board to determine what interrupt, I/O addresses, and DMA channels it will use. If necessary, the operating system can also add its input as to what resources it thinks should be assigned.

POP3   See *Post Office Protocol version 3*.

port   A logical connection provided by TCP and UDP at the Transport layer of the OSI Model for upper-layer protocols. Ports allow a single host with a single IP address assigned to provide multiple network services.

Post Office Protocol version 3 (POP3)   An IP protocol that operates on port 110. POP3 is used by MUAs to download e-mail messages from an MDA.

Power On Self Test (POST)   A test that happens when the BIOS tests the various system components and makes sure they are working properly when the system is first powered. If POST encounters a problem with system devices, it will either display an error message on the screen or sound a series of beeps in code.

power supply   The power supply in a PC system converts 110-volt AC current from the wall outlet into 12-volt, 5-volt, and 3.3-volt DC current.

PPID   See *parent process ID number*.

process   A program that has been loaded from a long-term storage device, usually a hard disk drive, into system RAM and is currently being processed by the CPU on the motherboard.

process heredity   The relationship between parent and child processes. Any process running on a Linux system can launch additional processes. The process that launched the new process is called a *parent process*. The new process that was created is called the *child process*. This parent/child relationship constitutes the heredity of processes.

process ID number (PID)   A number assigned to each process that uniquely identifies it on the system.

protocol   A set of rules that computers use to communicate with one another.

quota   Quotas establish disk space limitations for users on a Linux system.

Random Access Memory (RAM)   Random Access Memory is used to store data in PC systems. RAM uses memory chips that allow any storage cell to be accessed at random, regardless of its physical location and whether or not it is related to the previous storage location.

regular expressions   Strings consisting of metacharacters, regular characters, and numerals that make it easy to search for patterns of text within a file or within a text stream. For example, Myfile*, ^server, or [xyz].

Reiser   A file system that is an alternative to the ext3 file system. Like ext3, ReiserFS utilizes journaling to make crash recovery very fast. However, ReiserFS is a completely different file system from ext2 and ext3, using a dramatically different internal structure. This allows the Reiser file system to support a larger maximum file size of 8TB and maximum volume size of 16TB. In addition, the different structure of ReiserFS allows it to perform much faster than ext2 or ext3.

relative path   A path used in a Linux command that is relative to some other point in the file system.

reverse lookup   A process where the DNS server resolves an IP address into a host name.

root   A type of user account. The root user account is the super-user account on a Linux system.

root directory   The top-most directory in the Linux file system hierarchy, denoted as the / directory.

routing   The process of connecting multiple network segments together using special network devices called routers. Routing forwards IP packets from the source network to a destination network. This may involve forwarding the packets through intermediary networks. Routers use routing tables to determine the best routes to remote networks.

runlevel   A representation of one of seven different modes that a Linux system can run in.

Samba   A Linux service that can be used to configure a Linux system to communicate over the network using the Server Message Block (SMB/CIFS) protocol. Effectively, this allows the system to emulate a Windows server or a Windows client.

SATA   See *Serial ATA*.

script A text file that contains a series of commands and control structures that are executed by the shell. Shell scripts can be used to run multiple commands at once. They can also be used to read input from the end user or from shell commands and make decisions based on the input.

SCSI See *Small Computer System Interface.*

Secure Shell (ssh) A service that works in almost the same manner as Telnet. ssh allows you to access the shell prompt on a remote Linux system. ssh is a client-server system. The sshd daemon runs on the Linux system you want to connect to. You run an ssh client on the remote client system. ssh uses encryption to scramble that data being transmitted between the ssh client and the sshd daemon.

Serial ATA (SATA) The default storage device interface using in most desktop PC systems. SATA drives are much faster than the fastest PATA drives and are designed to replace PATA technology. SATA uses a serial bus architecture that implements two channels. The first serial channel is used to transmit data serially, bit by bit. The second serial channel is used to return receipt acknowledgments to the transmitter, ensuring the data was received correctly.

Set Group ID (SGID) A permission that can be applied to binary executable files (not shell scripts). When a user runs an executable file with SGID set, the user temporarily becomes a member of the file's owning group. When a user creates a file in a directory that has SGID set, the file's owner is set to the user's account (as per normal). However, the owning group assigned to the new file is set to the owning group of the parent directory.

Set User ID (SUID) A permission that can be applied only to binary executable files (not shell scripts). When an executable file with the SUID set is run, the user who ran the file temporarily becomes the file's owner.

sh The Bourne Shell (*sh*). The earliest shell, developed for UNIX in the late 1970s. While not widely used on Linux systems, it is still very widely used on UNIX systems.

shell Software that provides a command-line user interface on a Linux system.

Simple Mail Transfer Protocol (SMTP) An IP protocol that operates on port 25 used to transfer e-mail messages from MUAs to MTAs and between MTAs.

Small Computer System Interface (SCSI) A general-purpose interface that can be used to connect a variety of different types of devices to a PC system, including:

- Hard disk drives
- CD/DVD drives
- Tape drives
- Scanners
- RAID arrays
- Printers

SMTP See *Simple Mail Transfer Protocol*.

socket A type of file similar to FIFO files in the Linux file system. They are used to transfer information bi-directionally between sockets.

ssh See *Secure Shell*.

sticky bit When the sticky bit is assigned to a directory, users can only delete files within the directory for which they are the owner of the file or the directory itself. This negates the effect of having the write permission to a directory, which could allow a user to delete files in a directory that he or she doesn't own.

strong password A password with eight or more characters that is not found in the dictionary, uses numbers and/or symbols as well as letters, and uses upper- and lowercase characters.

subnet mask The subnet mask associated with an IP address determines how much of the address is used for the network address and how much is used for the node address.

SUID See *Set User ID*.

symmetric encryption A system of using a single encryption key to encrypt and decrypt data.

tape drive A drive that uses magnetic tape, much like the tape used in an 8mm video camera, to store data. Tape drives can store a lot of data and are relatively inexpensive. They are commonly used to back up data on a Linux system.

Telnet A protocol that, with its utilities, is used on a Linux system to access the shell prompt on a remote Linux system. Telnet does not encrypt transmissions, making it insecure. The ssh protocol and utility is usually used in place of Telnet today to access the shell prompt of a remote system.

tarball An archive file containing one or more files created with the tar utility. The archive file may or may not be compressed with the gzip utility.

UID Unique ID (*UID*). A unique number assigned to every Linux user account when it is created. No two user accounts on a Linux system can have the same UID.

UNC See *universal naming convention*.

Uniform Resource Locator (URL) A path used by your browser that specifies the exact information you need from the web server as well as how it is to be retrieved. The syntax for a URL is protocol://domain_name or IP_address:port/filename.

Universal Serial Bus (USB) A high-speed removable hardware interface. Most PC systems today include an integrated USB interface in the motherboard. USB can be used to connect a wide variety of external devices, including external hard drives, external CD and DVD drives, printers, scanners, digital cameras, mice, keyboards, and flash drives. A single USB bus can support up to 127 external devices. USB devices are self-configuring, self-identifying, and hot swappable. USB has been implemented in three different versions:

- **USB 1.1**   The oldest USB version. It transfers data at a rate of 12 Mbps.
- **USB 2.0**   A newer version of USB. It can transfer data at 480 Mbps.
- **USB 3.0**   The latest version of USB. It can transfer data at 5 Gbps.

universal naming convention (UNC)   A standard for addressing systems on an SMB network. The syntax for using UNC names is: \\server_name\share_name.

URL   See *Uniform Resource Locator*.

USB   See *Universal Serial Bus*.

user account   The information that defines a particular user on a network, which includes the username, password, group memberships, and rights and permissions assigned to the user.

user process   A process created by the end user when he or she executes a command from the shell prompt or though the X Windows graphical interface.

vi/vim   A common text editor used by most Linux distributions.

Virtualization   A way of pooling multiple operating system instances onto the same physical hardware that allows them to run concurrently, using a mediator called a hypervisor to manage access to system resources. Each operating system instance is installed into a virtual machine instead of onto physical hardware. Each virtual machine appears and functions just like a physical host.

web server   A server that sends web pages, graphics, and other files to web clients requesting them. A web server can transfer just about any type of computer file between the server and the client. However, the most common type of file used with a web server is a web page, which is simply a text document written using a special mark-up coding system (called Hyper-Text Markup Language, or HTML) that instructs the web browser how the information should be formatted and displayed.

window manager   The window manager's job is to customize how the windows in the Linux GUI appear and behave. It works in conjunction with the X Server. A wide variety of window managers are currently available for Linux.

X Server   The heart of the Linux GUI. The X Server draws windows graphically on the display screen. It's also responsible for managing the mouse and the keyboard.

Zombie   A zombied process is one where the process has finished executing and exited, but the process' parent didn't get notified that it was finished and hasn't released the child process' PID.

LICENSE AGREEMENT